The Israeli–Palestinian Peace Process

Yair Hirschfeld

The Israeli–Palestinian Peace Process

A Personal Insider's Account

With Jackson al Khoury de Concini

Yair Hirschfeld
Ramat Yishai, Israel

ISBN 978-3-031-43284-2   ISBN 978-3-031-43285-9 (eBook)
https://doi.org/10.1007/978-3-031-43285-9

© The Editor(s) (if applicable) and The Author(s), under exclusive license to Springer Nature Switzerland AG 2024

This work is subject to copyright. All rights are solely and exclusively licensed by the Publisher, whether the whole or part of the material is concerned, specifically the rights of translation, reprinting, reuse of illustrations, recitation, broadcasting, reproduction on microfilms or in any other physical way, and transmission or information storage and retrieval, electronic adaptation, computer software, or by similar or dissimilar methodology now known or hereafter developed.

The use of general descriptive names, registered names, trademarks, service marks, etc. in this publication does not imply, even in the absence of a specific statement, that such names are exempt from the relevant protective laws and regulations and therefore free for general use.

The publisher, the authors, and the editors are safe to assume that the advice and information in this book are believed to be true and accurate at the date of publication. Neither the publisher nor the authors or the editors give a warranty, expressed or implied, with respect to the material contained herein or for any errors or omissions that may have been made. The publisher remains neutral with regard to jurisdictional claims in published maps and institutional affiliations.

This Springer imprint is published by the registered company Springer Nature Switzerland AG
The registered company address is: Gewerbestrasse 11, 6330 Cham, Switzerland

Paper in this product is recyclable.

It is up to us to turn hatred into understanding. No matter how hopelessly entrenched two parties seem, their feud can be solved through an act of human will.

Sari Nusseibeh

Foreword

I   Arrival

I landed at Ben Gurion on the morning of October 9. At passport check, I usually have to wait in the "time out" corner for at least an hour. That's if they don't pull me into a separate room for additional questioning. This time it was just a matter of minutes. It was clear that security priorities were. The airport security officer started, quite confused, at my passport. "You know we are at war?" he asked from behind the glass.

The office did not need to remind me. As I walked into the arrival hall of Terminal 3, the sirens started. Frightened travelers dropped their luggage and rushed to the airport's bomb shelter. The chaos quickly devolved into a stampede. So many people were pushing to get into the shelter that I, standing in the hallway outside, was pushed up against the wall, unable to move. I watched a father try to calm his crying children, as they too were stuck in the hallway. "We just have to go to the room downstairs. Daddy's going to keep us safe." The fear on his face was evident. I watched him jump as the explosions sounded overhead. The rockets had been intercepted by the Iron Dome.

Six months earlier, Dr. Hirshfeld and I were taking the train from Haifa to East Jerusalem to meet with an ambassador to the State of Palestine. A friend of his, who had an appointment in West Jerusalem, joined us on the ride down. The friend, a retired Israeli rocket scientist, was one of the architects behind the Iron Dome. During the train ride, he explained to me, in very general lay terms, the physics behind why the Iron Dome had been so successful since its inception. Although I understood very little of the mathematics, I did understand one thing: the Iron Dome's counter-rockets provide exponentially greater protection to people than running toward a bomb shelter does. That said, I couldn't blame anyone for taking the precaution.

It only took a few days of staying with family in Tel Aviv Jaffa for me to become less confident in that position. One morning, as I ran through the Florentine, I passed a friend's apartment where I had often spent the night. The street directly ahead of me was blocked by traffic barriers and construction vehicles. As I looked beyond, I saw the rumble of an entire apartment building strewn across the street. ZAKA volunteers were filing out of the building next door. A news crew was parked on the street corner, catching every moment. I didn't need to ask them what had happened.

A year before, when the rocket sirens had sounded in August, my roommates and I had brought drinks and a speaker into the hallway we called our bomb shelter. This time, although their apartment was now equipped with a proper shelter, there wasn't that same sense of ease. The next Friday, my roommates invited me to Shabbat. Always a lively time, this one was particularly eventful. I sat next to a man who volunteered for the Tel Aviv Jaffa police and a woman who coordinated monetary and supply donations to the IDF. Both were clearly overworked but proud of their contribution to the national defense. After they traded stories about how busy the last two weeks had been for them, the conversation shifted to stories about those who survived the massacre on October 7.

The stories they told of those who had hidden under dead bodies and in closets were nearly identical to the stories I had heard about those who had hidden under floorboards and in attics 80 years earlier. At one point, the military donation coordinator said "I just know that every Palestinian who watches those videos from October 7th wishes they could have been there too." I, a little surprised by the totality of the claim asked, quite genuinely, "well, do you really think every Palestinian feels that way?" She turned to me and said, gently but firmly: "That is just what I know from my own experience."

She then shared a story about a family friend who used to live in Hatzor. Every day for many years, the friend and her siblings had been driven to school by the family's driver. One day, after dropping the youngest sibling off at school, the driver entered the school with a rifle and killed every child in the building. The table then began to share stories of people they knew who had not survived terror shootings or bus explosions over the years.

Before the conversation continued, another rocket siren went off. In the shelter downstairs, we celebrated the birthday of another friend. While they were scrambling to get down into the basement, my roommate, of course, had remembered to grab the cake. After "Happy Birthday" was sung in Hebrew, English, Spanish, and Portuguese, he asked if anyone knew the song in another language. I remained silent.

II   Delusional Diplomacy

In my sophomore year of college, I took a course on Israel and Palestine. The core reading of the course was Alan Dowty's book on the subject, creatively titled *Israel/Palestine*. Despite over 400 pages of history, this is his only mention of what actually happened *during* the Oslo negotiations in 1993:

> After months of secret negotiations in discreet Norwegian venues, an agreement on mutual recognition and a framework for a comprehensive peace treaty was achieved and dropped like a bombshell on the international scene. For the first time, the two core actors in the Arab–Israel drama would sit at the same table, negotiating directly and openly through their recognized representatives.[1]

Dowty accurately describes the general understanding of these negotiations. Like most descriptions of what happened in Oslo, however, there is no mention of who first sat down at that table long before any of those "recognized representatives." The omissions in this passage underscore both why those negotiations failed to achieve peace and why the actors have not returned to "the same table" since.

Two years after that course, I was sitting on a couch across from Dr. Yair Hirschfeld on the porch of his home in Ramat Yishai. I eventually mustered up the courage to ask him a question I had been wondering since that sophomore year course: "Do you think Oslo was a success?" Coming from a 22-year-old American college student, it surely carried an undertone of arrogance. He paused for a few moments. Suddenly, I worried I would not have

---

[1] Alan Dowty, *Israel/Palestine*, Polity Press, 2019 (fourth edition), pp. 183. The course was taught by Dr. Ezzedine Fishere, a former Egyptian diplomat who had worked on Egyptian-Israeli relations, and designed with Dr. Bernard Avashai, who usually co-taught the course. Despite what I am about to say, Alan Dowty's *Israel/Palestine* contains the most extensive, thorough analysis of the history of the Israel/Palestine conflict. It is possibly the most insightful book on the conflict, of course, only after the book you are currently reading.

a job that summer. Then, he chuckled and said "the short answer is no. But, for the long answer, I need to tell you a joke about the French Revolution."[2]

I clearly did not lose my summer job. Instead, I spent the greater part of a year working as Dr. Hirschfeld's assistant. From dinners at foreign embassies to pool days with his grandchildren, I have gained a rich insight into the life of a career track-two negotiator. The past year has taught me more about the innerworkings of unofficial diplomacy than any of the government colleges' courses that I took on the subject.[3]

This work is not for the faint of heart, especially in times like these. Just suggesting the possibility of cooperation between actors in Palestinian and Israeli civil societies will start arguments with many people I know. Expressing the belief that these actors could bridge the divides that their own leaderships have unequivocally failed to close will get you branded as a terrorist-sympathizer, a Zionist collaborator, or, worst of all, a delusional American.

Yet it was that exact, delusional belief that convinced Dr. Hirschfeld to first meet with Abu Ala' in 1992. Three decades later, I have watched him express that same belief at every opportunity. From diplomatic dinners to conversations on the train, there appears to be no setting where he will not engage in these controversial conversations. When we speak in public, I find myself looking over my shoulder, just to see if anyone else is as surprised as I often am.

You would be forgiven for thinking that this belief was, in fact, nothing more than academic fantasy. That is, after all, exactly how every channel begins. After that, outlines for cooperation between actors in Israeli and Palestinian societies are meticulously drafted, redesigned, and eventually agreed upon. Even then, it is still a daunting process to actually bring these actors from very different factions into the same room. Then, finally, cooperation begins to produce meaningful results. But then cooperation stops. It

---

[2] The eventual punchline of the joke is more impactful after we have delved into the historical events that have followed the Accords. Fortunately, I included it at the end of Chapter 10, just before the final chapter on the work still ahead.

[3] For example, although the Dutch embassy serves a delicious truffle ravioli for dinner meetings, no pasta is tastier than Ruth Hirshfeld (Dr. Hirschfeld's wife) tomato crème Fusilli. As a sophomore, my university's diplomacy course was taught by Jake Sullivan who, nine months later, became the National Security Advisor to the White House. Lacking that foresight, I switched into a course on Jewish humor instead. Although I regret that decision, I now have a series of Jewish jokes that I can tell myself whenever I need to lighten the mood.

eventually starts again, but then it stops again. Each time we start back up, it can be easy to think we never left the fantasy.[4]

Despite all of these challenges, Dr. Hirschfeld has kept back channels between Israelis and Palestinians open ever since his first meeting in London. [footnote about Oslo starting in London] That work has required an unflinching, decades-long persistence just to keep these channels alive. He is steadfast in his commitment to preserve an unofficial channel, in any form, until two very different parties are ready to come back to the table.

When envisioning that future point in time, however, one question seems unavoidable. Given the 30 years of conflict that succeeded Oslo, what could possibly happen differently when these "recognized representatives" eventually return? I asked Dr. Hirschfeld the question at the end of that first summer. I flew out of Ben Gurion Airport very unsatisfied with his answer. Six months later, Dr. Hirschfeld emailed me the link to his Zoom meeting room.[5]

III   Comfortable Monologues

At the beginning of July 2023, marking six months of the anti-judicial reform protests, a 10,000-person large demonstration was planned at Ben Gurion Airport. After a meeting that ran very late in East Jerusalem, I took the train from Jerusalem-Quds to the Airport. I was worried I would miss it altogether. The protests are usually quite loud, with drums and *tzaftefhs*[6] creating a thundering energy throughout the crowd.

However, toward the end of many demonstrations, there was a brief moment of silence when the energy quieted. Then, the protestors sang *haTiqva*. As I rode the escalator up from the train station, I mistook the quiet for confirmation that I had indeed missed the protests. But, by

---

[4] This reminds me of another joke from Dr. Hirschfeld. In an attempt to save the Oslo process, he told it to Abu Ala' in 1993. You can find it in Footnote 28 of Chapter 3, although my transcription of the joke will never do justice to Dr. Hirschfeld's very animated rendition.

[5] I was working in Lebanon at the time. There, it is still illegal (and technically punishable by death) to communicate with any Israeli citizens. Illegal communication with the enemy, however, is exactly how the 1993 negotiations started. So, I closed my door and used a VPN to tunnel me through an internet server bank in Norway. Part of me seriously wondered if Dr. Hirshfeld was planning on telling me that, given the current Israeli government, peace was hopeless and so he has finally decided to retire. Instead, he told me to turn on Channel 4 of the Israeli news. Then, remembering I was in Lebanon, he chuckled.

[6] This is one of the colloquial terms for the little plastic trumpets that the protestors use to create a lot of noise (in Hebrew: הפצפצ). Mostly, however, the protestors just called them "beepers."

the time I had walked out of the station and into the courtyard in front of Terminal 3, the protestors had just begun to sing. At this moment, the determination of these protestors to fight for the future of their democracy was palpable.

Every time I hear *haTiqva*, I am reminded of the Jewish education in my childhood. While I went to a secular school, it had a large presence of Jewish students. *Hanukkah* was always celebrated in elementary school as a day when students would play *dreidel* and parents came to fry *latkes*.[7]

Friends from school often invited my family to *Shabbat* dinners. The mother of one of my best friends taught me how to set the *Seder* table and the debate over what belonged on the *ke'ara*. In my childhood room, there is a drawer full of colorful *kippot* inscribed with many of my classmates' names.

However, I am more grateful for the education I received in primary and secondary school concerning the historical and contemporary danger of Anti-Semitism. From reading "Maus" in seventh grade to "The Merchant of Venice" in twelfth grade, Anti-Semitism, and the continued importance of combating it, was consistently addressed in the school curriculum. I remember multiple field trips to the Holocaust exhibit at the Simon Wiesenthal Museum of Tolerance. In the summer before college, I even served on a youth jury there. The case concerned a student accused of committing anti-Semitic hate crimes against a teacher. We found him guilty.

While my school was diligent in educating us about Anti-Semitism, curriculum discussions about Israel-Palestine were largely avoided. The theme of my seventh-grade Global Studies course was a Ms. Fritzl-styled airplane that flew our classroom around the globe. However, the shift in my teacher's tone when we "landed" on the topic of Israel and Palestine was palpable. Her usual jovial attitude was replaced by a somber seriousness. This is a sensitive subject that tended to cause "turbulence" among students, she cautioned.

When I shared that my maternal grandmother was an Israeli citizen, a classmate turned to me and remarked that she never knew I was Jewish. When I said that I was not, she disagreed. If my grandmother was Jewish, then that meant both my mother and I were Jewish too. When I said that neither my mother nor my grandmother was Jewish, she became visibly confused. It was a brief interaction without any malicious intent. Yet, it had a

---

[7] Olga Nevin, our universally beloved music teacher, made sure that the holiday performances included songs from Jewish culture. If you ask my mother nicely, she may even pull out the DVD recording of my classmates and me singing "If I Were a Rich Man" on stage.

profound impact on an impressionable seventh-grade student. For the rest of the Israel-Palestine unit, I was silent.

IV   Conflict Management

My educational gaps in this region extend well beyond the political leaders of Israel. There was a glaring absence of Arab history, culture, and traditions in my primary and secondary education. This definitely influenced my decision to study the Middle East in college, but that answer never seems to satisfy Ben Gurion Airport security when they ask about why I'm majoring in the field. Nevertheless, even with all my coursework in the major, Palestinian subjects were rarely, if ever, addressed. In the joint Israeli-Palestinian workshops where I have joined Dr. Hirschfeld, I inevitably feel I am the least knowledgeable person in the room.

As I was riding the train back home, I learned that "אמבאלה / Imbala / مبل,"[8] a Jerusalem-Quds-based co-resistance organization had hosted a protest that same evening at Sheik Jarrah against the impending eviction orders of Palestinian Nora Gaith and Mustafa Sub Laban.[9] It was an issue that was not addressed at the Ben Gurion Airport protest, as was the case with the vast majority of democratic inequalities that Palestinians living in the occupied territories. Although groups such as "מסתכלים לכיבוש בעיניים / Looking the Occupation in the Eye / النظر إلى المهنة في العين" and "לוחמים לשלום / Combatants for Peace / مقاتلون من أجل السلام" were present at many of these protests, they were rarely central to the largely conversation.

This was made evidently clear to me during the one protest that I witnessed in Tel Aviv Jaffa at the end of July 2023. I wanted to get Ruth, Dr. Hirshfeld's wife, a book as a thank you gift for all the lovely meals and conversations that we had shared that summer. The only Steimatzky that had the latest Isabelle Allende book was the one right by Rabin Square. As I was leaving the store, book in hand, I was swept into the wave of people heading for Azreali Mall.

As I passed Rabin Square, I noticed a group of activists congregating with Palestinian flags and anti-occupation signs. Then, they began to march

---

[8] After five years of operations, Imbala closed at the end of 2023. It was through Imbala, under the leadership of Yoni, that I was exposed to the anti-occupation civil protest movement within Jerusalem, as well as many volunteering opportunities. I am confident that the generation of activists they mentored will continue their legacy long after their café stops serving coffee. Their manifesto is available here: https://imbala.community/en/manifesto/.

[9] https://www.ohchr.org/sites/default/files/documents/countries/palestine/A_78_554_AUV.docx.

toward Azreali under a banner that said something along the lines of "פלסטינים נהרגים בשירות ההתנחלויות / Palestinians are killed in the service of the settlements / الفلسطينيون يُقتلون في خدمة الاستيطان." As I read the sign, I was shocked by the boldness. It was the first protest I had witnessed live in Tel Aviv, and already it was distinctly different from the ones I had witnessed in Haifa.[10]

As the anti-occupation protestors marched forward, their chants were met with visible disapproval by many of the onlookers. When they got to the outskirts of the Azreali demonstration, the nearby anti-reform protestors began to become more agitated. One became physical with the protestors and was literally held back by other onlookers. As I watched from the sidelines, I started a conversation with some onlookers who were visibly uncomfortable by the anti-occupation presentation. Although they left the protest shortly after, two messages were very clear from our discussion: First, this is not the time to discuss these issues. Second, they risked distracting from and dividing the momentum toward the wider issues of the protests.

Given the ongoing war in Gaza, I wonder when there will be a convenient time to discuss these issues. I understand the resistance from many Israelis to engage in this discussion, especially now. Moreover, in my own experience, those who are willing to have these discussions are contained within a small circle inside the anti-reform movement. I wonder how productive those conversations can be at bringing Palestinians and Israel peacemakers back "to the table."

"yishrali lo dyktatuvrha" (*trans*: Israel is not a dictatorship)

Months after the last anti-reform protest, this chant rings in my head when I think about the future of peace work in the region. I believe it epitomizes the barriers that divide the next generation of Palestinian and Israeli peacemakers. Ironically, it is one thing that pro-reform and anti-reform largely agree on: Israel is not currently a dictatorship. One only needs to look at our neighbors, such as Iran, to see how real dictators act in the face of public resistance. The Israeli government does not use wonton violence to suppress people who disagree with their policies.

---

[10] At all protests, the Israeli flag, and infinite variations, was visible everywhere. But it is never the only flag present. I saw Traditional and Transgender Pride flags at every protest I have been to. In Haifa, as well as Acre, the Druze star and flag are popular as well. The flag is often hung beside the Israeli flag on the speaker stages. The one flag that is rarely seen is the Palestinian one. Earlier in 2023, the Israeli National Security Ministry ordered police to remove any Palestinian flag seen in public, because the display demonstrates an identification with terrorism. Last year, police in Jerusalem-Quds were recorded beating people carrying the flag at the funeral of Shireen Abu Akleh. Several activists declined to speak at the protests because they asked not to bring the Palestinian flag nor speak about the military occupation. However, I do not think these were the primary reasons for the general absence of the Palestinian flag at many of the protests.

However, for the millions of Palestinians who are surviving under a military invasion and occupation, that dichotomy is not as clear. When the IDF launched an aerial drone strike into the Jenin refugee camp earlier this year, I was living in Jerusalem-Quds. No Palestinian I spoke with after would have been convinced that they were not, in fact, living under a dictatorship. Now, when I speak with Palestinians who have evacuated from Gaza, they use much stronger words than dictatorship to describe the horrors they have endured since the beginning of the 2023 Gaza war. Given the security situation in Israel, the indefinite halt of the physical protests is understandable. However, should those protests eventually resume, I do not sense a willingness to include the anti-democratic existence of the territories at the core of the anti-reform movement. Given the current mentality of the larger Israeli public, the protest movement may not be the most effective place to include these issues at all.

V Diapraxis

When Dr. Hirshfeld had called me back to work at the beginning of 2023, I had been living in the north of Lebanon at the "Peace Centre" run by the non-governmental organization Relief & Reconciliation. Akkar, the northernmost and poorest governorate of Lebanon, is also one of the most religiously diverse areas of the Levant. The region hosts sizable Sunni and Maronite populations, along with Orthodox, Alawite, and Shia minorities. The ideology behind Relief & Reconciliation for Syria, the branch dedicated to the exodus of refugees after the Syrian Civil War, is premised on inter-religious dialogue through youth programming. Their programming is built around faith-based praxis through dialogue. This concept, first proposed by Dr. Lissi Rasmussen in 1988, is known as "diapraxis."

> While dialogue indicates a relationship in which talking together is central, diapraxis indicates a relationship in which common praxis is essential. Thus, by diapraxis I do not mean the actual application of dialogue but rather dialogue as action. We need a more anthropological contextual approach to dialogue where we see diapraxis as a meeting between people who try to reveal and transform the reality they share.[11]

---

[11] Lissi Rasmussen, "From Diapraxis to Dialogue. Chris- tian-Muslim Relations," in Lars Thunberg and ally (eds.), Dialogue in Action, New Delhi: Prajna Publications 1988), pp. 282.

Diapraxis guides inter-religious dialogue not as the precursor to, but rather the very medium of cooperation. Cooperation does not require changing the views of the other camp (a term I will use both literally and figuratively). Rather, participation often starts from a place of serious ideological divide. Acknowledging these differences, and seeking cooperation despite them, is critical to building the trust that is necessary to preserve the dialogue beyond individual conversations. As cooperation transforms into joint activities, groups learn to solve problems together. This joint struggle creates shared experiences that challenge accepted stereotypes and reaffirm the mutual confidence groups have toward each other.

In Akkar, I witnessed how joint programming on youth education can develop intra-camp confidence that then builds the foundation for increased areas of social cooperation. During four days of the week, my colleagues and I would drive to different communities and camps within Akkar to teach courses to the youth. On Fridays, our students would in turn come to the Peace Center to play games and to socialize with each other. The Friday programming was led by the youth leaders of each community. Although my colleagues and I would sometimes join in on the fun, the most enjoyable experience for me was to sit back and watch my students transcend these barriers of religion, ethnicity, and nationality and interact with each other as children.

The Peace Center was also pivotal in my own cross-camp education. Relief & Reconciliation was founded and modeled after the peace work of Father Paolo Dall'Oglio, an Italian priest who reconstructed the monastery in Dier Musa in southern Syria. Father Paolo had reformed the monastery to be a home for interfaith dialogue. When he was kidnapped by the Islamic State in 2013, his movement shifted its focus to aiding Syrian refugees who had fled to Lebanon. The secretary general of the organization, "Fritz," now continues Father Paolo's work from the Peace Center in Akkar.

Every Friday morning, before the children would come to the Peace Center, the instructors would engage in our own form of inter-religious dialogue. At 8:00 am sharp, Fritz would ring a bell, sometimes incessantly, until all the instructors had filed out of bed and into the "Abrahamic Corner" of the classroom downstairs. Then, we would light the candles while singing an assortment of Christian and Islamic hymns. Mohammed, the organization's treasurer and self-termed "funcle," would play his oud while we sang. Once, my roommate Masaki played his kanoon as well. After the framing hymns, the instructors would read passages from Father Paolo and share other writings.[12]

This work is replicated with our students as well. Every summer, Relief & Reconciliation hosts a summer camp in the wilderness of Akkar. At the end of each session, they erect the "Abrahamic Tent" under which the youth leaders read different texts from their respective religions. Then, students of different faiths discuss the philosophies within the writings, highlighting both similarities and differences they notice. In the end, the instructors led them in the hymns we had since memorized from our own Friday prayers. The work of Relief & Reconciliation does not exist in a vacuum. It builds both off of decades of research into the transformative nature of diapraxis and also contemporary research, much of which is coming out of the region, on how interfaith exposure in education increases trust and cooperation between groups.[13]

When differing camps can trust each other enough to allow their children to interact with each other, specifically through religious dialogue, you begin to build serious momentum for cooperation at the level of local, faith-based leadership. Relief & Reconciliation hosts conferences where Akkari imams and priests discuss the issues their communities face and how interfaith cooperation could address these issues for all parties. The actual scope of these projects is never the focus. Rather, the existence of these projects alone indicates that interfaith dialogue, starting through youth education, naturally develops a framework for larger trust and confidence-building initiatives.

VI   Difficult Dialogues

The true failure of the Oslo Accords was that the agreement was developed by governments before either population was prepared to translate the political formula into social reality. Neither Palestinian nor Israeli civil society had fostered a commitment to a mutual understanding of their opposition. Consequently, there was no political will to compel governments to

---

[12] Guangmiao, one of my fellow instructors, once read the Biblical dialogue where Jesus reveals himself as the son of G-d to the Samaritan woman. It led to a fascinating discussion that includes parallels between Abrahamic religious texts on the role of women as builders of trust between communities. When Rev. Catherine-Amy (the only other American I found in Akkar) shared her poetry on the Syrians and Turks who had been killed in the earthquake in early 2023, the group debated the importance of faith in developing one's capacity for sympathy.

[13] https://docs.iza.org/dp15206.pdf.

implement the compromises promised by Oslo. Instead, the Israeli government exploited a much weaker Palestinian Authority, expanded its population into the West Bank, and maintained military control over millions of Palestinians.

Therefore, while the Oslo Accords were an honest attempt at cooperation between governments, it never truly had a chance to succeed. Without the societal determination to cooperate with opposing camps, there is no deal so sweet that it would not fail as well. Building mutual understanding and empathy between Palestinians and Israelis through extensive cross-border dialogue is crucial for establishing a solid foundation that can support any future agreement. Without a genuine commitment to understanding the grievances, fears, and aspirations of the opposing camp, any agreement risks being hollow and unsustainable.

Neven Shalom-Wahat al-Salam is an archetype for what is possible when cross-camp education develops into serious cross-border coexistence, but it is by far the exception. There are countless non-governmental organizations (NGOs) that have worked tirelessly to promote Palestinian and Israeli dialogue through youth education. I have had the privilege to learn from similar initiatives that EcoPeace Middle East has led under Gidon Bromberg, that Si'ah Shalom has led under Dr. Alik Isacs, and that Seeds for Peace has led under Fr. Josh Thomas. Larger umbrella organizations, like the Alliance for Middle Eastern Peace (ALLMEP), have also played a vital role in empowering these individual NGOs to maximize their impact.

This work, however, does not necessitate the weight or financial backing of any NGO. My roommates at the Kerem House originally started working together through Model United Nations (MUN) youth programming between Palestinian and Jewish students. One night, after a long day of compiling research on environmental peace-building for EcoPeace, I walked into my Tel Aviv apartment to find an MUN event filled primarily with students from East Jerusalem. These experiences taught me the value of taking a small group of students out of their traditional bubbles. By exposing them to neighboring, yet foreign communities through educational programming, I witnessed these children naturally step out of their individual cultural identities and engage in dialogue through their common identity as students.

Jean Monnet, one of the framers behind the European Union, is often misquoted in his memoirs as saying "if I were to do it again from scratch, I would start with culture." What he actually did say, when in 1962 he feared France would oppose the notion of a supranatural union with other

European states was "perhaps we had neglected the task of education, against which were mustered all the resources of counter-education."[14] After the 2023 Gaza war, these education projects must not only deepen their efforts, but also be supported by both the global and national protest movements.

We need more local steering bodies, with the support of religious authorities, to support education-focused diapraxis as a form of trust-building between communities. The strategy is not to prescribe any specific larger political action from these initiatives, but rather to allow them to guide what local trust and confidence-building looks like. They will need to emphasize the value of respecting others in their differences. The focus must also be on allowing the youth of each group exposure to the other. We must allow them to discover dialogue of their own creation.

Nevertheless, we cannot pretend that either camp is approaching dialogue from an equal footing. The power dynamics between Palestinians and Israelis on the ground are massively imbalanced. So, we seek to find a domain of incorporation that has an opportunity for more equal engagement. Education is an imperfect domain. However, because of the nature of youth actors, power dynamics are less pronounced and those that exist can be more easily mitigated than in economic, political, or security domains.

Ultimately, we will need to maximize domains of cooperation. We are nowhere near a genuine security union, but that is a requirement for serious conflict transformation. The thought of having a Palestinian police force patrolling Tel Aviv is far from reality, but so too were the security guarantees within the development of the EU. Trust and confidence in security cooperation will take time, but it is conceivable. An eventual union between several disparate entities, where each redefines its own concept of sovereignty in the name of a larger political project, maybe a possible conclusion of these trust and confidence-building measures. Ultimately, we will need to maximize domains of potential collaboration from the bottom up.[15]

---

[14] https://ia800208.us.archive.org/34/items/MonnetJeanMemoirs/Monnet,%20Jean%20-%20Memoirs.pdf at page 44.1.

[15] While civil society is establishing the framework, the international community would like to attempt to establish top-down control in response to the 2023 Gaza war. They will push for an international peacekeeping force to re-enter the occupied territories, the International Criminal Court will investigate both sides for war crimes, and the process for a two-state solution will resume. I don't know if these measures will ultimately succeed. They must be careful not to interfere with the leadership of local communities in trust and confidence-building measures. This conflict may very well be the original sin of the United Nations, so the international community must be careful not to infringe on these people-to-people activities.

For new definitions of sovereignty to develop naturally, international actors should first acknowledge their role as supporters from the outside. Nevertheless, they should continue to support local diapraxis initiatives. For example, the UN Strategic Learning Exchanges in 2010 emulate the exact projects that international actors should augment and expand within the region.[16] Redefining sovereignty is an amorphous concept by design and should be heavily influenced by local, youth-focused, and religiously-involved steering committees. It is a process that must be adopted genuinely by both sides, with the trust and confidence that the other side is participating genuinely as well.

The 2023 Gaza war calls for a serious rethinking of the nation-state as an exclusive project centered on a monolithic identity. The idea of a Jewish nation may need to be rethought as a nation that protects the Jewish people, just as the Christian identity of Lebanon was rethought in terms of an Arab nation that protects the Christian people. The ideology of the commonwealth may be reframed as a movement for Abrahamic hospitality. This would not ask us to simply make room for the Other but rather to work with the Other in the management of the Commonwealth.

VII Conflict Transformation

I left Ben Gurion Airport on October 18. In response to the 2023 war in Gaza, I reached out to an organization that I had come across when I was working on the Turkish-Syria earthquake response from northern Lebanon. The organization had sent one of the first medical teams into Syria and was now planning to do the same for Gaza. They needed logistical support from someone familiar with the region and could coordinate closely with relevant stakeholders and authorities. Largely because of the work I had done with Dr. Hirschfeld, I found myself quickly packing my bags for Cairo.

After LAX and JFK, TLV is the most common airport I fly through. I rarely enjoy airports, but my experiences at Ben Gurion are uniquely unpleasant. Only the names from my father's side of the family are written on my passport. The pre-check-in airport security guards, dressed in their black suits, always follow the same script: "Why did you choose to study the Middle East?" "For how long have you been learning Arabic?" "Do you have family that live in the country?" It is about halfway through the next question when the security officer's demeanor changes. "And what are their

---

[16] https://sur.conectas.org/en/from-dialogue-to-diapraxis-in-international-development/.

names?" The names Michael and Elias usually slip by without suspicion. When I get to Fayrouz and Samir, however, I watch the security guard's uncomfortable realization that they now must ask me several more questions. That is usually when they call the supervisor.

"Where do they live in Israel?" I never knew how to order the answer to the question. In the end, however, it does not matter in which order I list Jaffa, Haifa, Nazareth, or Ramallah. They always put the white sticker on the back of my passport, which tells the security officers at the post-check-in security to send me to the "Arab line." There, airport security takes every item out of my checked bags, including every pen, every cord, and every receipt. My items are wiped down incessantly for traces of explosive materials while I am subject to another round of questioning.

I have since memorized the order in which I will be asked for the names of each of my great-grandparents born in Palestine, the names of each person I have stayed with while in Israel, and, of course, the names of any and everyone I know in the West Bank. Only sometimes, however, does the security officer tell me to write down the addresses of my family's homes and the phone numbers of friends and colleagues.

This time, however, the questioning took a much more unpleasant turn. While flipping through my passport, a (now fourth) airport security officer began asking about all the places I had been to in the last three years: "Why were you in Lebanon?" "I was working with Syrian refugees." "Only *Syrian* refugees?" "No, I was also working with local host communities." "What did you do while in Israel?" "I volunteered at Hangar 11 in Tel Aviv and then at the YMCA in Jerusalem-Quds." "And what was the nature of this volunteering?" "I packed boxes of care packages with supplies" "And who were these boxes for?" "The families that were displaced in the south." "What kind of families?" "Jewish families." At this point the officer paused and looked up from my passport, "and why would you care about them?"

I completely froze. Although I thought I had memorized every question I did not know how to answer the question. I had never really asked it to myself. I had volunteered because there were people who needed support and I was capable of providing that support. It had not occurred to me that the Ben Gurion Airport security would ask me why I cared about the Jewish and Bedouin families that had been displaced by the attack on October 7. It was then, as I was fumbling to come up with an answer, that I saw something distinct in the security officer's face: worry.

The psychology around security has plagued this conflict since its inception. Now, more than ever in my lifetime, all camps have understandable reasons to be afraid. The 2023 Gaza war will leave deep psychological scars for millions of people. That trauma is the biggest impediment to any trust and confidence-building measure between these groups. The resistance to cooperation, or even dialogue, with the other side will likely persist for decades. However, this emphasizes exactly why cross-camp youth dialogue is critical now more than ever. The window of opportunity to demonstrate the humanity of the other side is growing smaller every day.

Around a year ago, while on the train from Haifa to Ramat Yishai, I was speaking on the phone with a Jordanian friend. The train car I was in was fairly empty, and I was probably talking louder than I had expected. After the call finished, I got up to go use the restroom. As I was returning to my seat, I saw the face of the woman who was sitting in the row in front of me. She was extremely relieved. I could not understand why until, as I was passing her, she looked at me with relief in her eyes. She put her hand over her chest and said "you came back." Then, I looked at the backpack that I had left on my seat. It suddenly became deeply clear to me the visceral trauma that exists within these communities.

In my conversations with Gazans who have been evacuated to Egypt, I have witnessed only a small impact of that trauma. I have watched whole rooms of people brought to tears from the harrowing stories that evacuees will tell my colleagues and me. Every time, these testimonies harden my determination to continue coordinating humanitarian aid into Gaza. However, they also leave me with a deep worry about the divides that will have to be crossed once the bombing stops. Dr. Hirschfeld knows far too well the threat terror attacks pose to any diplomatic process, but especially the informal, trust-based channels.

My grandmother tells me to thank G-d every time I make it through Israeli border security.[17] It is a privilege that not everyone in my family, even those returning home to Ramallah, has been afforded. She always worries for me when I tell her I am flying through Ben Gurion. As a child, she was only allowed to cross into the West Bank to visit her family in Ramallah for Christmas. Now at 89, crossing between into and out of the West Bank is still a difficult experience in which she gets hassled for a Palestinian identification document that she was never issued.

My grandmother, Jeannette Khoury, was born in Palestine. Her father was born in Gaza. Under British rule, he oversaw the customs office at the Haifa port. In 1947, anticipating the coming war, he took my grandmother

---

[17] The spelling here is something I credit my seventh-grade English teacher, Leonard Magier, was the first to demonstrate to me. Although he never asked us to follow his example, it is a gesture that I have tried to emulate ever since.

and her three younger siblings to live with his sister in Beirut. He returned to Haifa shortly after, afraid he would lose their family home if he did not return. Ultimately, that decision made little difference. When my grandmother eventually returned, it was clear that she was now in a very different country. Eventually, she and her siblings all would leave for the USA. Even though we still have family in Jaffa, Nazareth, and Ramallah, traveling back to their homeland is a difficult experience for all of them.

My Palestinian heritage was something that I only ever shared with a few of my high school peers. In elementary school, we would have a yearly "grandparents and special friends' day" in which relatives were invited to come to school for a celebration of heritage and culture. The year that my grandmother came, my mother told me to say that she was Middle Eastern. If someone asked where in the Middle East, I was told to just say "the Holy Land." It was only when I was in college that, after my grandmother and I attended a family friend's bat mitzvah, some of my high school peers learned that she could read Torah passages, respectfully, a lot better than they could.

My academic and professional journey is intrinsically linked to my identity as a member of the Palestinian diaspora. However, it was something that Dr. Hirschfeld himself was unaware of until I asked for a few days off to go visit my aunt in Ramallah. "What is she doing in Ramallah?" he asked. "Well, she lives there."

The morning I was flying to Cairo, I rode the Tel Aviv Jaffa 12 bus to HaShalom station. As the bus crossed the overpass at Azreali Mall, I was reminded of the tens of thousands of people I had seen protesting there just four months ago. The protests, which typically occurred every Saturday, had since been halted as a safety measure because of the rockets launched at Tel Aviv. Now, in the early morning, the streets were largely empty. Instead of thousands of Israeli flags, only two large white banners hung over the overpass. I could not read the one written in Hebrew, and there wasn't one written in Arabic this time. But, I felt a deep sense of dread when I read the one written in English: "It's now or never. It's time to wipe Gaza off the map."

After the 2023 Gaza war, cross-camp dialogue through youth education programming will seem impossible. Yet, it is exactly then that both camps must find the courage to allow their children to interact with each other. If the youth protestors I spoke with were serious about creating a democracy in which no one lives under dictatorship, then they need to engage in genuine dialogue with the children currently living under military invasion and occupation. To paraphrase what Dr. Hirschfeld has often told me: conflict management requires convincing those you generally agree with to work together to achieve what is possible. Conflict transformation requires convincing those you generally disagree with to work together to achieve what is impossible.

My work in Lebanon proved to me that diapraxis is not an ideology that is easily implemented in communities that deeply distrust each other. However, when I witnessed Sunni, Alawite, Maronite, and Orthodox Christian children speaking with each other after learning and playing together, I understood the real potential that this ideology holds. It is easy to forget that Israelis and Palestinians are not the only populations in the region to experience invasion, occupation, terror, or genocide. Upon returning to Ramat Yishai, Dr. Hirschfeld gave me a brief history lesson from his own peace work in Lebanon during the first Israeli-Lebanon war. Having witnessed firsthand the bloodshed that these religious sects had inflicted on each other, it was not lost on him the real significance of witnessing their grandchildren sleep next to each other at the same summer camps.

The Oslo process did not succeed when the accords were signed on the White House lawn on September 17, 1993. Rather, Oslo succeeded much sooner, possibly as early as 1992. An Israeli economics professor speaking freely with an economic advisor within the PLO was as transformative as it was illegal. In his memoir, Abu Ala' writes: "I overcame my initial antipathy to the idea of talking to the enemy. I agreed at once, when he suggested that we meet again."[18] Ultimately, it is that process rather than the content that brought both of them back to the table later that evening.

Where Oslo failed was in the view that their back room, top-down negotiations would gain the support of the Israeli and Palestinian civil society. Effective democracy requires the public to constantly hold their government accountable for their commitments toward their constituencies. But how can any public hold their governments accountable for a commitment that they had no part in writing? When framed this way, it seems as though Oslo was destined to fail. By the time Israeli and Palestinian societies found out that negotiations were even happening, the deal had already been finalized. In a democracy, the resolve for true, lasting peace must first and foremost be a commitment of the people.

Ultimately, Prime Minister Barak was right to be skeptical of the back-channel negotiations in the "woods of Norway." Dr. Hirschfeld has assured me that there will not be an Oslo III. I firmly believe that conflict transformation is only possible if dialogue starts, and continues, between the youth within the populations themselves. Democratic projects that attempt

---

[18] Ahmed Qurei (Abu Ala'), From Oslo to Jerusalem – the Palestinian Story of the Secret Negotiations, Tauris, London 2006, pp. 43.

to prevail despite serious ethnic and religious divides are difficult by definition. Disagreement in these projects is inevitable. However, it is likely necessary before parties can build a trust that is strong enough to transform stalemates into breakthroughs.

As I reflect on both my Palestinian heritage and Jewish education, I am reminded of the immense, complicated divides that millions of Israelis and Palestinians younger than me have no choice but to inherit, largely from those who actively worked to grow those divides. Nevertheless, from Ramat Yishai to Ramallah, I have confidence in the growing political activism among this next generation. By integrating the importance of cross-border discourse into the broader struggle for justice and democratic values, there is a real opportunity to bridge the gap between communities and bring new actors in to work toward a more equitable, peaceful, and secure future for all.

Rafah, Gaza   Jackson al Khoury de Concini

Acknowledgements

This book could not have been written without the joint many decades long work of the entire ECF team. Yossi Beilin's political leadership, Nimrod Novik's intellectual brilliance, and Boaz Karni's moral strictness were all essential for turning our theoretical work into practical action, during the ten years, before ECF was founded at the end of 1990. From then onward, a determined younger generation, Gidi Grinstein, Avivit Hai, Gary Sussman, Ron Shatzberg, Celine Touboul, Yael Banaji, Eilon Javetz, Yoni Eshpar, Xiomara Hurni-Cranston, Ronit Porat, and Anat Kaufmann, by their dedication and willingness to follow in our footsteps and challenge us, turned ECF into a power house of ideas, action, and peace-seeking regional and international network building.

The work of the in-house group of activists was most forcefully upgraded by the support we received from the out-of-house experts. General Baruch Spiegel's work was and still is invaluable. His friendship and cooperation with General Mansur Abu Rashed laid the foundation for Israeli-Jordanian cooperation that has reached far beyond the activities of ECF and has become an essential safety network, helping to overcome crisis situations between Israel and Jordan. General Spiegel's commitment to improve relations with the Palestinian people on a daily basis, and his influence upon the work of Israel's security authorities addressing civil affairs in the West Bank and Gaza, has been invaluable. David Brodet, who as Director General of the Israeli Ministry of Finance, negotiated the Paris Agreement, has added wisdom and influence to our work. General Dov Sedaka's influence and connections within the Israeli security structure and his intimate relations and friendship with Palestinian leaders have opened possibilities of action that otherwise would not have been available.

Our work described in all the chapters of this book would not have been possible without the cooperation and friendship of our Palestinian counterparts. To name only a few: Faisal el-Husseini's leadership, Hussen Agha's, Ahmed Samih Khalidi's, Hanan Ashrawi's, and Sari Nusseibeh's intellectual brilliance, Samih el-Abed's, Samir Hileleh's, and Maher el-Kurd's great professionalism, Zuheir Menasreh's great courage to save lives under most difficult circumstances, and the commitment of them all to find a way forward to peace have made the narrative told here, possible, while providing also hope for the future.

I also received great support from senior diplomats. Sir Tom Phillips friendship and advice was of great importance at the time of the Oslo negotiations as well as later, and his help and suggestions were also essential in writing an earlier version of this book. Robert Serry's diplomatic initiatives, way back at the end of the 1980s, and later during the first two decades of this century are part of the narrative told. Jon-Hanssen Bauer's commitment helped to rethink the peace process under Norwegian auspices. Eberhard Rhein, Jean-Paul Jesse, Lieselotte Kjaersgad Plesner, Emiel de Bont, and Suzanne Wasum-Rainer were all instrumental in brainstorming and obtaining political and other support from the EU, Denmark, the Netherlands, and Germany.

My particular gratitude is to the Friedrich Ebert Foundations and its many heads of the Israel office. The Ebert Foundation was responsible for getting me in touch with Yossi Beilin, for allowing me to attend the Madrid Conference behind the scenes, to found ECF and finance its first projects, to allow Pundak and me to attend the signing ceremony at the White House of the first Oslo Accord. Thereafter, the Ebert Foundation initiated and funded our cross-border cooperation activities; the unfolding of People-to-People activities and its re-evaluation after the outbreak of the Second Intifada; our study visit to Macedonia and Kosovo; and workshops on various hoped for forms of international intervention, how to upgrade economic growth in the Palestinian territories, and how to test different possible strategies, essential for seeking an Israel-Palestine peace agreement. Similar gratitude is due to US-AID and its heads of the Israel-Palestine office.

Ambassador Ed Djerejian assisted all the way. I am grateful for his friendship, advice, as well as his many initiatives in organizing meetings and workshops. Secretary of State James A. Baker III advice, at specific junctions and his kind words for me, is well remembered.

The book in this present form could not have been written, without the criticism and advice of Jackson al Khoury de Concini. His commitment to seek a bottom-up Israeli-Palestinian understanding and his determination to seek new ways provide me with hope for the future, particularly as his commitment is being matched on the Israeli side, by Ofer Zalzberg, Gidon Bromberg, Alick Isaacs, Ro'i Ravitzky, Nimrod Goren, and many others.

I am grateful to Prof. Nicole Deitelhoff and Simone Wisotzki of the Peace Research Institute Frankfurt for assisting in getting this book published. Particular gratitude is due to the team of the Springer International Publishing House. Johannes Glaeser offered most important critical remarks on the manuscript and helped to improve it, while accompanying Jackson al Khoury de Concini and me through the process essential to get the book published. Sudhany Karthick's help and advice to review the manuscript was of essential assistance. Saranyaa Vasuki Balasubramanian helped to guide us through the various legal and technical issues that had to be taken care off.

Most of all Ruthi, my wife's support was not merely in assisting to write this book, but far more by accompanying me all the way of the long journey described. At times her advice was critical, while she carried the burden. Her capability to read people's mind and sense the emotional inputs essential to bridge gaps offered most essential guidance all along. But I owe much more to her.

The book is dedicated to all my grandchildren, Naama, Hillel, Stav, Tomer, Amitai, Elad, Shira, Rona, Ben, and Emma.

Introductory Note

Way back, at the end of the 1970s I discussed with Bernt Carlsson, then Secretary General of the Socialist International, ideas on how to reach an Israeli-Palestinian understanding. He then remarked: "Yair, the Israeli-Palestinian conflict is the most difficult and complex to solve, can't you choose another conflict area to become active?" My answer was simple: What is at stake is the life of my generation, my children and grandchildren, and the dreams of our fathers and fore-fathers. Whatever it might take we need to leave no stone unturned, whatever the costs might be. This simple truth has kept me involved ever since. The horror of the events of October 7, 2023 and the presently still ongoing war, have not changed our determination to find ways and means to end the vicious circle of violence and achieve stability, security, prosperity and peace for all.

Since that conversation forty-four years of peace activism achieved important victories and many defeats along the way, allowing for a continuous learning process from trial and error. Conceptually, I played a leading role in formulating the principles and approach for what became the Oslo process. Yet, I never had political power. Instead, I knew how to listen to former enemies, while always having the interests of my country, Israel, in mind. Early on, I was given full access to Israel's decision-makers, and over the years, I built a trusting relationship with a wide network of Palestinian, Jordanian, and Egyptian counterparts, in addition to many American and European diplomats as well.

Some months ago, Ginzach Hamedina (the Israeli State Archive) asked for all my documents. Forty-two years of activism filled a full truckload of documents. The historian of the State Archive, Dr. Louise Fischer, then copied also computerized documents that accumulated over the last twenty years. When I saw the truck leaving for Jerusalem, I knew time had come for the younger generation, to lead the struggle for a better future, while continuing to build on the learning curve I had experienced.

By profession, I am a historian. Very few people had the privilege that I had to witness the historical unfolding of the Israeli-Palestinian peace process from within, as well as an observer from outside. On some decisive details, in the early phase of negotiations in Norway between December 1992 and the end of May 1993, I am possibly the only source to tell. Ron Pundak, who was my pupil, assistant, and colleague, has told some of the events but he did not have the full picture. Several meetings and discussions were held on a four eyes basis between me and my Palestinian counterpart, Abu Ala'. In addition, many others who have written or spoken publicly about this process have often invented distorted accounts.

Writing history, or the art of historiography, is based on two premises. Leopold von Ranke, possibly the West's greatest historiographer, defines the practice both as "to tell the story as it unfolded" ("*wie es gewesen war*") and also reviewing events of the past with the knowledge and understanding of the present. In this book, I tried to do both. Undoubtedly my personal convictions, hopes, and fears have clearly colored my account. Moreover, even though I participated in many policy discussions with the most senior decision-makers, at the time, much of their thinking remained unknown to me. In writing this account, I have tried to fill that void based on interviews and published documents. Reviewing and studying documents written (often by myself) at the time taught me that often my memory was mistaken. The material written at the time helped to correct this.

This book is a reflection on over forty years of the Israeli-Palestinian peacemaking effort, hoping to understand successes, crises, and setbacks. Yet, I also hope to overcome the prevailing despair by documenting that there is, in fact, a way forward. I do not believe in the determinism of history, but rather in the power of human thinking and action. Today, the younger generation of strategists, politicians, and peace activists are achieving important headway where we failed. The obstacles are still tremendous, and the reality we face today has become complex, almost beyond absurdity. Never have we been so close to a viable path toward regional cooperation and understandings and hereby also to an Israel-Palestine two-state agreement, and never so far.

I am convinced that the need to create win-win-win-win solutions and understand the pitfalls of unintended consequences can—after repeated failures—play a decisive role in forging a better future for us Israelis, our neighbors the Palestinians, and the people of the Middle East at large. This book aims to provide insights and tools to help achieve this, knowing perfectly well, win-win solutions cannot stand alone. On certain issues, win-lose will be unavoidable. There a fair balance will have to be achieved.

Chapter 1 discusses the October 7, 2023 event. The horror, the causes, the impact and the way forward are being described from the vantage point of my personal experiences and activities.

Chapter 2 refers to my formative years in Vienna, when I gained historical and political awareness from a relatively very early age. The tragedies my family and people had experienced had a very decisive impact on my upbringing. Growing up in the Shomer Hatzair, (the left-wing Zionist Youth Movement), had a decisive influence on forming my Weltanschauung and a sense of responsibility, many years later, when I was asked to advise decision-makers.

Chapter 3 describes from both a personal and a general vantage points, the unfolding of the peace process after the Six-Day War of June 1967, until the start of Israeli-Palestinian negotiations at the Madrid Conference, on November 3, 1991. It tells the story, how from 1979 onward, some of my analytical ideas turned with the help of Dr. Kreisky into policies. It became a protracted exercise in building trust against all odds and creating multiple networks with relevant stakeholders in Israel, the Palestinian territories, Egypt, Jordan, different European states, and the USA. I also describe the emerging regional and international rules of engagement that made the Oslo process possible as well as its shortcomings.

Chapter 4 describes the story of the Oslo negotiations, until the signing of the Declaration of Principles on the White House Lawn, on September 13, 1993. I tell the story of how I planned for the negotiations; what obstacles and dilemmas I recognized before the negotiations started; and how I intended to overcome them. The historical review emphasizes strategic considerations and techniques of negotiations, which have not lost their relevance.

Chapter 5 describes the dilemmas we faced, while taking the Oslo process forward: How—behind the scenes—a complex track-two dialogue assisted to sustain the Oslo process, against all odds; how we negotiated the first blueprint for a Permanent Status Agreement causing President Clinton's comment, "let us change the title and sign it" and how I learned to understand the need of achieving progress step by step and not in one go. While recognizing achievements, I describe and explain the three decisive battles we lost: not being able to prevent the vicious circle of terror and violence; experiencing the rise of Jewish radical militancy, which eventually caused the murder of Yizchak Rabin; and causes leading to the ongoing failure of Palestinian State-building.

Chapter 6 offers a critical review of Prime Minister Barak's counter-productive negotiating effort, based on the "everything or nothing" approach, irrespective of understanding Palestinian policies. In contrast, I describe how my team of ECF and I studied Arafat's strategic thinking and political behavior and built on it a strategy, allowing for gradual progress, which Barak eventually dismissed. The chapter provides a map of the potential "mines" to be avoided, an evaluation of successful negotiating methods, as well as a description of the disastrous negotiating tactics of Barak. For political scientists and students of negotiations, the chapter offers important insights, for the research of "alternative history," as well as lessons to be learned for future engagements.

Chapter 7 refers to the dramatic changes caused by the Second Intifada, Nine/Eleven, the US wars in Afghanistan and Iraq, and the need to rethink the peace-seeking process. In this context, I describe efforts made to apply the theoretical findings of Robert Putnam's "Double-Game Theory," of John Paul Lederach's study on protracted conflicts and of Jan Hofmeyr's and Butch Rice's South-African based study on conversion theory. We hoped to learn also from study visits to Northern Ireland, Macedonia, and Kosovo and three visits to South Africa. Applying lessons learned, the chapter describes the growing strategic divide between my search of how to obtain a "sufficient majority" for peace and against the (eventually destructive) effort to create a new blueprint for agreement, dividing hereby the Israeli peace camp. I describe the emerging friendship and strategic alliance between me and Othniel Schneller, former Secretary General of the Settler Movement.

Chapter 8 is dedicated to developments in the peace process under the governments of Ariel Sharon (2001–2006) and Ehud Olmert (2006–2009). I describe the emerging learning curve and the emerging understanding of the need to reach the "Take-Off Point," not knowing yet, what it might entail. In order to support Prime Minister Sharon's Unilateral Disengagement we coordinated policies with Palestinian counterparts and with the international community to allow for security coordination—which succeeded, and an orderly transfer of assets left behind, worth US $ 4 billion, which failed. The critical review of events illustrates the potential advantages of coordinated unilateral action. Under Prime Minister Olmert's government, I describe the backchannel exercise, David Brodet and I were undertaking in cooperation with Palestinian counterparts appointed by Abu Mazen. Analyzing the causes of failure became an important step forward in the learning curve described.

Chapter 9 offers a critical review of the Obama years (2009–2017). I describe how we failed to prevent the Obama administration from ending successful policies introduced by the George W. Bush presidency; how Obama's policy toward Turkey and Egypt radicalized rather than moderated the reality in the Middle East, causing two Israeli-Gazan wars, allowing eventually ECF members, Novik, Spiegel, and myself to play a decisive role, in helping to negotiate the ceasefire agreement of 2012. I discuss the opportunities and risks, in seeking a religiously pursued peace, as well as emerging understandings with Palestinian partners, how to get to the Take-Off Point, stressing important conceptual headway achieved by the official secret negotiators, Yizchak Molcho on behalf of Netanyahu, and Hussein Agha on behalf of Abbas.

Chapter 10 is entitled "Seeking a Way Forward: Brainstorming in Norway, and the Conclusion of the Abraham Accords." It tells the story of a Norwegian-led track-two policy planning exercise that started in the late autumn of 2015 and ended in June 2020 and produced two important documents, which may help to prepare a future peace process. It refers also to the conclusion of the Abraham Accords and argues that this development opens important options for present and future action, adding to the learning curve.

In Chap. 11, I discuss Netanyahu's Uphill and Downhill Road to Disaster.

In Chap. 12, answering questions of young activists, I describe the learning curve gained during over forty years, the impact of the October 7, 2023 aggression and the presently still continuing war and suggest conclusions for future peace work either to accept, to adapt to changing circumstances, or possibly also to change and seek new ways and means, but never give up.

Contents

**1   October 7, 2023: The Horror, Causes, Impact,
    and Working on the Way Forward**   1
   The Horror   1
   The Causes of the War   3
   The Impact of the War   5
   The Need for Humanitarian Relief as Against the Logic
   of Conflict and War   8
   The Emerging Global Reality   9
   The Emerging Regional Reality   10
   Working on the Way Forward   11
      Preparing for the Political Struggle in Israel
      on the Day After   14
      The Religiously Legitimized Peace Approach   14
      Promoting Reconstruction, Economic Growth,
      Interdependence, and Cooperation   16
      The Security-Based Approach   18
      The Need to Define Milestones Starting with the
      Conclusion of a Long-Term Ceasefire   19

2   Growing up in Vienna (1949–1967)   23
   First Experiences in Vienna   23
   Stories from My Grandparents   25
   Growing Up with the "Forces of Light" in Vienna   27
   My Emerging Convictions   30

3	**Experiencing the Unfolding of the Peace Process (1967–1990)**	35
	My Experiences During and Shortly After the Six-Day War	36
	Making Aliya and Studying in Israel	37
	A Complicated Chess Game After the Six-Day War	38
	The Yom Kippur War: A Decisive Formative Experience	41
	The Foundations of Peace in the Camp David Accords	42
	Iran and the Beginning of a Complex Relationship with Chancellor Kreisky	45
	First Experiences in Egypt	47
	The Middle East Policy of the Socialist International	49
	Kreisky Pursues My Policy Suggestion	51
	The Suggested Socialist International Peace-Building Initiative	53
	Joining Yossi Beilin's Group "Mashov"	54
	Peres' Early Proposals Are Rejected	55
	The Americans Reshuffle the Cards	56
	Close Bonds with Faisal el-Husseini and Hanan Ashrawi	58
	The Madrid Conference	60
4	**From the Madrid Conference to the Conclusion of Oslo**	67
	The Importance of Earned Trust	67
	Rabin Becomes Israel's Prime Minister	72
	Track-Two Negotiations Start in Norway	75
	Hoping for a US Shuttle Diplomacy	80
	Rabin Takes Control of the Renewal of Negotiations in Washington and Oslo	86
	The Official Back-Channel Negotiations Get Underway	90
	Each Player Had Their Role	94
5	**The Oslo Process of Trial and Error Unfolds**	99
	An Awkward Beginning to the Tough Ride Ahead	99
	The Continuing Riddle of Arafat	100
	The Challenges Ahead	103
	The Battle Against Terror is Lost	103
	The Increasing Threat of Jewish Militant Radicalism	106
	The Failure of Palestinian State-Building Efforts	108
	Learning to Navigate Uncharted Territory	111
	Finalizing a Blueprint for a Permanent Status Agreement	111
	Netanyahu Continues the Oslo Process with Our Support	114

	Preparing an Agreement on Jerusalem, Refugees, and Security	116
	Initiating a Wide Range of People-to-People Activities	118
	Warning Signs	119
	The Danger of Ambiguity	119
	Security Warnings	119
6	**From Hope Under Netanyahu to Disaster Under Ehud Barak**	125
	Adapting the Israeli Approach to Arafat's Strategic Behavior	125
	Preparing a Code of Conduct	126
	Supporting Palestinian Economic Growth	127
	Preparing Trilateral Security Understandings	128
	Preparing People-To-People (P2P) and Government-To-Government (G2G) Cooperation	129
	ECF Influence in Barak's Peace Administration Proved Futile	131
	Ehud Barak's Initial Policy Approach	132
	The Several Delusions of Barak's Approach to Negotiating	133
	The Delusion of an Unprepared Summit	134
	The Delusion of Negotiating like in the Persian Bazar	134
	The Delusion of Rejecting "Backward Negotiations"	135
	The Delusion of Playing in Domestic Palestinian Politics	135
	The Delusion that the Substance of the Offer of "All or Nothing" Could NOT be Rejected and There Would be No Need for "Plan B"	136
	My Ignored Warnings	136
	Efforts to Prevent Disaster	138
	The Salvage Attempt	141
	The Need and Weakness of Track-Two Policy Planning	144
7	**The Need to Rethink Possible Action**	147
	The Three Most Important Building Blocks for a Peace Policy Fall Apart	147
	The Breakdown of the Shared Israeli-Palestinian Narrative for Peace-Seeking	148
	The US Understanding of and Support for Israeli-Peace Making Falters	148
	The Rethinking Process Got Underway	151
	Seeking Ways and Means to Break the Vicious Circle of Crises in a Protracted Conflict	152

	Putnam's Double Game Theory	156
	Beilin and I Pursue Different Approaches	157
8	**Maintaining the Struggle for a Two-State Solution Under Sharon and Olmert (2001–2009)**	**163**
	Rebuilding Jewish–Arab Relations at Home to Foster Close Working Relationship with Sharon's Government	163
	Violence Replaces Diplomacy	164
	Testing the Option of Internationalizing Security	165
	Seeking Economic Relief and Development for the Palestinian Territories	168
	Hoping to Recreate a Political Horizon	169
	Emerging Threats from the Region	170
	The Second Phase: Sharon's Unilateral Disengagement Policy	171
	Attempting to Coordinate Israeli-Palestinian National Interests	172
	The Economy	172
	Security	173
	Creating a Political Horizon—Getting Back to Roadmap Implementation	174
	The Mistakes that Strengthened the Most Radical Elements in the Settlement Community	175
	Postscript: Lessons Learned Show the Value of Multilateral-Coordinated Unilateral Move	176
	Olmert's Government, 2006–2009	176
	The Rise and Fall of the Agha-Khalidi-Brodet-Hirschfeld Negotiating Channel	179
	PM Olmert's Peace Proposal is Rejected	184
	Understanding What Would Be Needed to "Get Israeli-Palestinian Negotiations to the 'Take Off-Point'"	186
	The Emerging Concept	186
	Supportive Action Gets Underway	186
	The Lasting Legacy of Bush and Olmert: Understanding the Importance of the Phased Roadmap Approach	188
9	**The Netanyahu-Obama Years: 2009–2017**	**193**
	The Growing Gap of Perceptions	193
	A Challenging Start: Olmert's Failed Peace Effort, Gaza, and Iran	194

First Disappointments	196
Iran—My Concerns Turn into Substantial Worries	198
Turkey	200
Egypt and Gaza: Spreading Destabilization	202
Seeking to Understand and Overcome the Gap of Interests and Perceptions	204
Our Cautious Recommendations Ignored	208
Hoping for a Religious-Led Peace: Opportunities and Threats	210
The Opportunity: Negotiating Non-Negotiable God-Ordained Commands	210
The Threat: Inflaming Religious Militant Fanaticism Through Political Rhetoric	213
Addressing Joshua A. Cohen's "Misconclusion"	213

10 Seeking a Way Forward: Brainstorming in Norway, and the Abraham Accords (2017–2021)   217

The Ten Point (Non)-Paper	218
The Very Real Reactions to the Non-paper	219
Assembling a New Israeli Working Group	221
"Joint Declaration on Mutual Recognition and Agreed Arrangements for a Return to Negotiations	222
"Letter to the Quartet	224
From Working Group to Workshops	224
Various Leadership Shows Interest in an "Academic Exercise"	226
Specific Reactions from the Israeli and Palestinian Leadership	227
The Nine-Point Paper	230
Abu Ala' Takes Over	231
The Abraham Accords Are Signed: Abu Dhabi, Bahrain, and Casablanca Begin the Waltz	233

11 Netanyahu's Uphill and Downhill Road to Disaster   237

The Folly and the Seeming Success of Netanyahu's Conflict Management Strategy	237
Hoping for a US-Saudi Arabia-Israel-(Palestinian) Peace Initiative	240
Netanyahu's Strategy	240
The Strategy of the EU Peace Envoy	241
Netanyahu's March of Downhill Folly	243
Taking the Path to Disaster	244

12	**My Suggested Conclusions for Future Peace Work**	247
	My Take on the Iran-Hamas-Hisbollah-Jihadist-Houti— Genocidal Challenge Against Israel and the Jewish People	247
	Addressing Past and Future Conceptual Issues	251
	My Take on Palestinian Rejectionism	253
	My Take on Israel's Strategy and Policies Towards Regional Powers	256
	My Take on the Role of the USA, European Powers and Russia	258
	My Take on Forthcoming Security Challenges	260
	My Take on People-To-People Activities	265
	My Take on What Happens if All This Does not Succeed	266

Timeline of the Israeli-Palestinian Conflict and Peace-Seeking Process	269
Glossary	275
Index	287

1

October 7, 2023: The Horror, Causes, Impact, and Working on the Way Forward

The Horror

Saturday-Shabat October 7, Hamas terrorists turned our villages and towns close to the Gaza Strip into a slaughter house. Men and women were decapitated; children were tortured in front of their parents and afterward shot; babies burnt to death and over 240 Israelis and foreigners taken as hostages and brought to Gaza. My first love, Vera, who grew up with me in Vienna, her husband Amos, and our friends from Vienna and Switzerland, all of whom live in Kibbutz Magen survived miraculously. Their security guards fought heroically for three hours, without help from the IDF. They drove the terrorists away. One of the security guards died, a second was seriously wounded, and a third, the son of Yoram who grew up with us in Vienna, was also wounded. Hamas murdered 1400 Israelis as well as foreign citizens. They did so, copying the tactics of ISIS. These massacres were preceded and followed by a barrage of Hamas rockets directed at civilian targets over most of Israel, as well as attacks from Hezbollah in the North. In the following days, 180,000 Israelis had to be evacuated from their homes. They still live in temporary shelters.

It was the beginning of the horror that continued in the days and weeks that followed. Iran, Russia, Turkey, Qatar, and all too many in the Arab world, portrayed Hamas murderers as heroes. Iran's decades-old genocidal call of "Death to Israel" echoed far and wide. And the scenario of a new Holocaust emerged as a still unlikely, but nevertheless possible future course. Hamas speaker Ghazi Hamad declared that Hamas would fight Israel again and again, that it believed all genocidal means legitimate, and that it intended to act until Israel is wiped off the map.[1] If there were any doubts, a cease-fire, while Hamas still in control, would only render a later war unavoidable. Meanwhile, demonstrations in the Arab and Muslim world as well as in the US and Europe are supporting and/or demanding the killing of Jews. These calls for murder were and are being followed by attacks on Jewish targets, individual persons, schools, synagogues, and cemeteries.

Hamas' terror has also led to horror for the Palestinian people. So far, 30,000 Palestinians—many of them civilians—have been killed by Israeli attacks; over 1,000,000 Palestinians had to leave their homes and taken refuge in the South of the Gaza Strip. Their conditions for survival are extremely difficult. Hamas fighters are hiding under hospitals, schools, and mosques, using the civilian population as human shields against Israeli attacks, while shooting or publicly executing Palestinians who oppose Hamas. The Palestinian trauma of *Naqba* has been revived. In the West Bank, Israeli militant settlers are attacking innocent Palestinians. In Israel, Israeli-Palestinians have lost their jobs and Arab-owned businesses their customers while the overheated atmosphere of hate and revenge is creating a sense of insecurity with possibly devastating effects.

The next dreaded phase of the war might come from the North. Hezbollah might attack Israel's towns, villages, ports, airports, and industries with over one hundred thousand rockets, hereby unleashing a regional war. This would come close to what has been feared for many years: "MAD," mutually assured destruction.

The ongoing catastrophe may be better understood if one visualizes its numerical dimensions. A comparison with the tragedies of the 9/11 ISIS attack on the United States may illustrate this. Israel with its close to 10 million inhabitants is about 1/30 of the 330,000,000 Americans. This means that 1400 murdered victims of October 7 would be equivalent to over 40,000 victims in America. Another 8000 heavily injured would amount to 240,000 wounded Americans; and over 180,000 Israelis evacuated would be equal to 5400.000 Americans having to leave their homes. Over 20,000 rockets aimed at civilian Israeli targets add to this nightmare scenario.

---

[1] See the New York Post, November 2, 2023, reporting but not fully quoting Ghaza Hamad.

The Causes of the War

Hamas launched a war not only against Israel but also against peace. In the last chapters of this book, I have described some of the unfolding peace efforts. Three complementary efforts were underway: President Biden worked with the Saudi Crown Prince, Muhammad Ben Salman (MBS), and with Prime Minister Netanyahu on a US-Saudi-Israeli peace plan. Parallel hereto, the Europeans developed a European dialogue with Saudi Arabia, the United Arab Emirates, the Arab League Secretariat, Egypt, and Jordan on expanding the peace effort to the entire Middle East, certain to include Israel and Palestine.

This initiative was launched on September 18, 2023 (three weeks before the war), at the United Nations in New York, establishing working groups with Israeli and Palestinian participation. A team I coordinated on the Israeli side, and the Middle East Nonviolence and Democracy team on the Palestinian side, worked on the details of Palestinian State-Building, addressing the territorial dimension, as an opening to renewed trust and a renewed Israeli-Palestinian negotiating process within a wider regional framework. What we hoped to achieve was peace and stability in the entire region. We planned to include Malaysia and Indonesia in the peace agreement with Israel. As their economies are very strong, these countries have a partial competitive advantage over Israeli business branches. As a mark of the ongoing initial progress, the Israeli Ministry of Finance was already planning how to protect Israeli business interests from the expected competition with Indonesian and Malaysian imports.

On the global level, this Peace Plan was a threat to Russia, to China, and to Iran and its proxies. Such a development would have strengthened a United States global coalition, which would reach from Washington to London, Brussels, Paris, and Berlin, to Israel, the Sunni Arab world, and then via Malaysia and Indonesia, extend to South Korea, Japan, Australia, and New Zealand. Indeed, it would weaken Chinese global aspirations, but even more so Russia. If successful, this plan would turn Iran into an isolated island, under a regime in an ongoing struggle against its own population, using torture and executions to remain in power. At the regional level, such an arrangement would have undermined President Bashar Assad's regime and presented Erdogan's Turkey with complex policy dilemmas. Locally, Hamas rule had been seriously jeopardized on earlier occasions. Qatar had stopped or largely decreased funding for Hamas civil servants in Gaza. In local elections to the Bar Association and at Universities, Hamas had obtained only 25% of the votes, in spite of its oppressive and totalitarian rule. The murderous attack changed all of this. The US-Saudi peace plan seems an unachievable utopia, and Hamas has become the celebrated hero in all too many places.

A major cause for the war was the repeated failure of the many peace efforts undertaken on earlier occasions. Israeli peace efforts offering the establishment of a Palestinian state, at first in 97% of the originally occupied territories, and later under Olmert offering 100% of the territory based on territorial swaps, were rejected. Later, under the premiership of Netanyahu and the leadership of President Obama and Secretary of State Kerry, a framework agreement was concluded. It was accepted by Premier Netanyahu but rejected by President Abbas. Unfortunately, the climate was worsened when international community was too quick to forget that it was the Palestinian side which rejected the peace offers. Israel was forever accused of maintaining the occupation.

The Netanyahu government which followed the 2014 rejection is to blame for the policy adopted since then. It was the strategy of "conflict management" otherwise also known as "mow the lawn" regularly. This meant sustaining the Israeli occupation of Palestinian land and deny hope by invoking a policy of divide and rule. Prime Minister Netanyahu adopted this policy of weakening the Palestinian Authority by sustaining Hamas, its main adversary. Out of five major Hamas funding channels, Israel controls four. Israel permitted Hamas to receive over $ 2 billion annually, allowing them to divert a massive part of these monies to finance their military units and their armament.[2] It was arrogance on Netanyahu's part to believe that Hamas would not be able to challenge the Israel military. This was nurtured in part by Netanyahu's assumption that Hamas cared for the economic well-being of its Palestinian population once they were duly "deterred" from a military confrontation.

Strengthening Hamas and weakening the Palestinian Authority radicalized the thinking of the Palestinian public. In a detailed opinion poll done by the Palestinian Center for Policy and Survey Research in June 2023, 71% of the interviewed supported the formation of armed groups (79% in the Gaza Strip and 66% in the West Bank; 82% in the refugee camps of Gaza; and 72% in the refugee camps in the West Bank) and 52% of the interviewees believed that armed conflict was the only way to end the occupation.[3]

Another cause for the war, allowing Hamas to obtain the most substantial support from all over the Muslim world was continuing Israeli rightwing provocations on Haram ash-Sharif/the Temple Mount. Al-Jazeera, the QATAR-based TV station added further incitement. Three days before the

---

[2] Annex A, to Report 231026 Thinking of the Endgame, October 26, 2023.
[3] Palestine Center for Policy and Survey Research, Ramallah; June 2023 Poll.

attack, on October 4, 2023, Israeli right-wing extremists entered the outside area of the Haram ash-Sharif. The Al-Jazeera's report created the impression that the Israelis had entered the al-Aqsa mosque.[4]

Israel has been accused of turning Gaza into a big prison. This accusation reverses the cause and its effect. When Israel withdrew from the Gaza Strip and evacuated all settlements from there, and five settlements from the Northern West Bank, the Israeli government planned to hand over all non-movable assets—a value of over US $ 4 billion—to the Palestinian Authority. This was expected to jumpstart a massive process of economic growth and investment (see Chapters 6, 7 below). However, Minister Dahlan and the International Community opposed the peaceful handover of these assets. They argued that according to international law, the economic assets created on Occupied Territory were illegal and had to be destroyed. And the Israeli government was obliged to sign an agreement to destroy these assets. This created the opportunity for images of destruction rather than growth and development. Then, after Hamas took control of the Gaza Strip, Israel tried to prevent the delivery of weapons, rockets and missiles to Hamas. I would argue that Hamas turned Gaza into a self-imposed prison. It is true nonetheless that Israel could have taken a variety of measures to change this, and it did not.

The deeper causes of the war arise from the multiple failures of the many earlier peace efforts. Every party, Israel, the Palestinians, but also many third parties, all too often contributed to the failures. The coming chapters describe them. We should finally learn many of the lessons gained. I have argued repeatedly that a failure to advance peace initiatives offers opportunities for sabotage and retrogression. Insincere actors or actors who can benefit from the halt in progress then worsen the terms and poison the atmosphere.

The Impact of the War

The first impact was personal. On the first day of the war, my son Yehonathan was conscripted. He is a paramedic in a fighting unit. He asked his wife Vicky and our two grandchildren Ben and Emma to go to Hungary and stay with their family there, in order to be safe. Rockets hit a building and killed two people several hundred meters away from the flat of my son David, his wife Meirav, and two granddaughters Shira and Rona. Living in Rishon leZion rockets continue to be launched at their neighborhood.

---

[4] Al-Jazeera October 4, 2023; "Israeli settlers storm Al-Aqsa Mosque Compound …."

My two grandchildren Naama and Tomer mourn the death of their friends murdered in Re'im on the Gaza border, while attending a music festival. Hillel, Naama's brother who serves in the Israeli Air Force mourns the death of seven soldiers of his unit.

The first reaction was anger, and then determination to fight and defeat these villains. The second emotional reaction was to care for our Palestinian friends and colleagues. We phoned, and we asked if there was anything we could do to help. Miriam, my sister, who worked for the WHO and serves on the board of the Physicians for Human Rights, Israel, phoned many of her Palestinian friends and colleagues. A head nurse in a West Bank Palestinian hospital, one of Miriam's friends, lost her parents and extended family in an Israeli bombing attack on Gaza. We share the grief.

War is cruel. **A doomsday scenario unfolded**: The Israeli-Palestinian conflict is existential for both sides. Hamas declares its goal to wipe out the Jewish people. As Ghazi Hamed, the spokesperson of Hamas, stated, Hamas will attack again and again. Holocaust images returned. Our worst fears were no longer irrational. Hamas, Hezbollah, Iran, and Turkey were turning the entire Arab and Muslim world against the Jewish people, and most people in Europe and the United States, sooner or later, would opt to appease the Arab and Muslim world on Israel's account. Many (not all) UN organizations would continue to act as a propaganda instrument for Hamas, ignore or deny Hamas's murderous deeds, and accuse Israel. Our Palestinian friends might privately speak to us and comfort but would not dare to speak up publicly.[5]

For the Palestinian people, the war is also existential. Hamas was and is hiding behind civilian human shields with military facilities under schools, hospitals, and mosques. Israel's military superiority and Hamas' lack of concern ascertains that the number of Palestinian civilian deaths is substantially higher than Israeli losses. Being asked by the IDF to move toward the South into secure zones, over one million Palestinians are displaced, leaving their homes and reliving the *Naqba* of 1948.

Planning for the Day After: We need to develop not merely a scenario but an **action plan as how to restore hope** and plan for the **Day After. Based on the understanding** that the cause of the war had been the common US-European-Arab–Israeli search for a peace, security, and stability in the Middle East, the outcome of the war has to achieve exactly this: peace, security, and stability. We must now define milestones on how to get there. In seeking to develop such a plan there was much good news, as well as much bad news.

---

[5] The INSS – Tel Aviv is preparing a hereto related comprehensive documentation.

The good news: President Biden took the necessary action. He made it evident that the United States stood by Israel in our struggle for survival. More so, he filled the political void created in Israel by a failing and non-functioning government. Since the beginning of the war, he is often speaking twice a day with Prime Minister Netanyahu, influencing Israeli decision-making. Generals Gantz' and Eisenkot's condition for joining an Israeli emergency government and a war cabinet was to define the exit strategy and the endgame of the war. To do so, the IDF created dozens of brainstorming groups to address the many different issues that had to be planned for the end of the war. Paradoxically, the Israeli, American, and Palestinian leadership reached an almost identical conclusion: The Gaza Strip could not be ruled either by Israel, nor straightaway by the Palestinian Authority, but law and order, security and reconstruction had to be administered by an international (temporary) government body.

My friends and I believe that the only way this would become possible is by starting to change the minds of the people and reach a religious commitment for peace and non-violence, endorsed by both, Jewish and Muslim religious authorities.[6] We see this as a precondition to paving the way to acceptance of the Saudi Peace Plan, offering Israel peace with most if not all of the Sunni Muslim and Arab world and offering the Palestinian people, a state of their own; allowing both Israel and Palestine to contribute to peace and stability in the entire area.

In Israel, there was some other good news, the protest movement against the judicial reforms, turned over night into a civil society governing structure, filling in the void of a not functioning government; preparing also to replace the government rather sooner than later, when elections would be held. Civil society activities helped to reach out to many former supporters of Israel's right-wing parties. Polls predicted at large swing to Israel's opposition parties on the center and left of the Israeli political spectrum. In Palestine, President Abbas engaged in a close dialogue with the Saudi leadership and reportedly planned to replace his serving Prime Minister, by the present head of the Palestine Investment Fund, Dr. Muhammad Mustafa, a brilliant economist, planning to put him in charge, of a comprehensive reconstruction process.

The bad news: Hate and misinformation are politically powerful and poison every rational effort. Worse, politicians on both sides, fighting for their survival are dangerous and powerful agents. On the Israeli side, Ministers

---

[6] This will be discussed more in detail in Chaps. 9 and 11 (?).

Smotrich and Ben Gvir, having been excluded from the internal decision-making circle of the war cabinet, are instigating dangerous provocations and attacks against Palestinian civilians on the West Bank. Violence creates fertile ground for more violence, which is all too easy to unleash and all too difficult to control and contain.

The Need for Humanitarian Relief as Against the Logic of Conflict and War

An unnamed member of one of the IDF think tanks asked me to corroborate the following proposal to Ambassador David Satterfield, President Biden's nomination to address humanitarian relief. The suggestion was to announce a time-limited ceasefire and assist the entire Palestinian civilian population in Northern Gaza to leave in buses through a secure corridor to the South, near Dahaniya airport, where their safety could be assured. It would save human lives, prevent the Palestinian civilians from becoming human shields protecting Hamas, diminish danger to Israeli soldiers, and it would allow to upgrade humanitarian relief action in the South. The proposal included assuring all displaced persons the return to their former places of residence, as an integral part of reconstruction. Ambassador Satterfield's answer was not encouraging. He did not spell it out, but it was clear that the situation on the ground, when Hamas was shooting at Palestinians trying to leave, did not, yet, make this plan possible.[7]

Following, the IDF introduced short pauses in fighting to allow Gazan residents from the North to move toward the South. This created tremendous pressure on relief activities carried out in the Gaza Strip mainly by UNRWA facilities.[8] As a next step, the Dutch Prime Minister with US support flew to Qatar and for one and half hours to Israel to propose a four-component deal: Hamas would release 100 hostages, all women, children, and elderly; Israel would release also women, youth, and elderly security prisoners; a three to four days humanitarian pause would allow substantial relief to enter Gaza from Israel; and all foreign passport-holders staying in Gaza would be allowed to leave Gaza via the Gazan-Egyptian border. It took almost another month to make this happen. Strong Israeli public pressure convinced the Israeli government to go along; Israeli military pressure on the ground helped to obtain Hamas' agreement, and American pressure on Qatar helped so far to

---

[7] David Satterfield to Yair Hirschfeld, October 26, 2023, 4.58 p.m.
[8] Hostilities in the Gaza Strip and Israel = Flash Update #33, November 8, 2023.

free seventy women and children, albeit, without their fathers and their older brothers.[9]

Hoping to prevent a human disaster, a group of Israeli NGOs submitted to the Israeli government detailed suggestions as how Israel could offer the most needed support.[10] It is likely that some of these suggestions will be followed up, but we do not know, if what will be done, will not be far too late, and far too little. In a world of hate and violence, human compassion and the understanding of the suffering of others is missing. The following anecdote illustrates this: A group of holocaust survivors are telling each other holocaust jokes. God wants to join them. Yet, they tell God, "You won't understand, you were not there." Humans understand even less.

The Emerging Global Reality

The world has changed on October 7, 2023. "The axis of evil," Iran and its proxies, Russia, and China were now successfully defeating not only Israel, but the entire free world. Incitement and hate distance the Arab and Muslim world from the West. The War in Ukraine had split the world into two blocks and now the Free World is caught in a seemingly unsolvable dilemma: Strong military action directed at Hamas causes immense human suffering of Palestinian civilians and increases Arab and Muslim hate against Israel, and the United States and thus fortifies the anti-Western bloc. An immediate ceasefire, allowing Hamas and its supporters to announce victory spells disaster and can only increase the support and prestige of Hamas and its murderous actions.

To overcome the dilemma and create a wide as possible regional and global coalition the United States has announced five principles: No Displacement (of Palestinians from Gaza); No (Israeli) Reoccupation of Gaza; No Return of Hamas to Gaza; Need for Humanitarian Assistance; the PA/PLO is the responsible partner for Gaza and the West Bank.

---

[9] When in 2014 Qatar prevented an Egyptian mediated ceasefire and prolonged the war for several days, American pressure against Qatar's support for terror groups was asked for. Yet, no such American action was taken. This time it appears that the US government is willing and determined to call Qatar to order. And Qatari support for the release of hostages is being highly appreciated.

[10] Five activities were suggested: To offer direct Israeli support to ongoing efforts of Egypt to send Humanitarian Relief from El Arish via Israel to overcrowded secure areas; to develop close cooperation with HERC (Humanitarian Emergency Relief Coalition) and assist them to get aid into Gaza, both via Egypt, and also via Israel. Encourage Jordanian Relief Activities, possibly also financed by the UAE, to bring in more field hospitals and other emergency aid; in areas controlled by the IDF allow for direct Israeli assistance to Palestinian civilians, and support with the help of the Israeli Arab Economic Forum formed by Israeli Arab business magnates, to revive small businesses in the areas of Gaza controlled by the IDF.

In effect, this means to revive the international commitment for an Israel-Palestine two-state solution and embed it in a wider regional peace-making effort. As there is the need to split the Iran-Hezbollah-Jihadist-Houti-Hamas-Russian-Chines axis, it hopefully will open the opportunity to revive US-European-Chinese and parallel US-European-Russian diplomatic consultations, on how to plan for the Day After. China and Russia will have to be made to understand that the destruction of Hamas' military capacities is also in their interest. Russia and China have legitimate trade interests in the Mediterranean and elsewhere that can only be guarded by effective multilateral security understandings. One could start with a dialogue on the promotion of multilateral actions of Rescue and Safety in the Eastern Mediterranean; protecting the maritime environment, and most important guaranteeing safe trade routes.

Other diplomatic and political action is asked for to break the unity of "the axis of evil," allowing the United States and Europe to rebuild stability together with China and Russia, while continuing the support for Ukraine in its war against Russia. This is obviously a complex challenge.

The Emerging Regional Reality

The war against Hamas cannot and should not be won only on the military field. While it is important to destroy their military capacities, the decisive victory has to be won in the region. Here, at first Qatar, and later Saudi Arabia, as well as the United Arab Emirates have a major role to play. Today, Qatar's many decades-long support of Hamas is an important asset. The Qataris are assisting in freeing hostages; they have an important role to play in allowing for humanitarian relief in areas where Hamas will still be able to interfere. Qatari participation will most probably be needed in a multilateral working group, on how to establish a Comprehensive Humanitarian Relief Program for Gazan temporarily displaced persons (including financing, operation, and management, etc.); in tandem with a decision to rebuild the destroyed parts of the Israeli villages and towns East of the Gaza Strip, and speedy return of all displaced persons to rebuilt homes in their pre-war communities.

Qatar has not only an important role to play to end the war with an agreed or non-agreed de facto ceasefire. Qatar's decisive role is in building peace and security, ending the Qatari former support for policies of hate, incitement and violent action. This means that all the Hamas leaders residing in Qatar will have to be expelled; the delivery of arms and monies to terrorist organizations will have to stop and the TV outlet Al-Jazeera could learn to play a constructive role presenting the fears and hopes of each side fairly. Compliance will allow Qatar to play an important role in building a more secure, peaceful, and stable Middle East. Qatar's contribution then would honestly deserve the Nobel Peace Prize.[11]

Saudi Arabia and the United Arab Emirates have a vested security, political, economic, diplomatic, and prestige interest to build a secure and peaceful Middle East and reassure Israel and the Palestinian people that we all can live together. It will need US leadership and European support to achieve this. In doing so, they will also deserve the Nobel Peace Prize. The United Arab Emirates commitment to pursue a peace-seeking religious interfaith dialogue should lead the way in obtaining the necessary support from the most influential Jewish and Muslim religious authorities.

Working on the Way Forward

Preparing a Concept for the Day After

After the October 7 shock, Israeli civil society got rapidly organized to care for the needs of the bereaved families, of the family members of the 240 hostages taken, and of 180,000 inhabitants of the border areas, evacuated. A foreign diplomat suggested I should write a paper on the Endgame, and how to get there. He, Yizchak Gal, and I in a kind of ping-pong process rewrote the paper. It was clear to us, that the planned US-Saudi-Israeli Peace Initiative had to be the Endgame and that Hamas had to be toppled in a four-legged struggle: by delegitimizing Hamas in the eyes of the world and the region; by cutting off the financing lifeline of Hamas, by military action, and by caring, (as much as possible), for the well-being of the Palestinian citizens. We discussed the need for internationally agreed and supported arrangements, fully coordinated with Israel, for the administration of Gaza when the war ends. We learned that there was paradoxically common ground

---

[11] In 2014, Qatar prevented Egypt to mediate a ceasefire in the war between Israel and Hamas (see Chapter 9, below). Instead of allowing Qatar to continue to support the Hamas regime with the silent endorsement of Prime Minister Netanyahu and the Americans, I then wrote a piece for the James Baker III Institute in Houston, demanding that the United States would end Qatar's multiple support for Hamas. The United States had then, as well as today, all the power in the world, to "convince" the Qatari leadership to put an end to their double game of supporting terror by all possible means available. However, money had a devastating effect. The piece I wrote was never published and I lost my fellowship, as Qatar was funding the James Baker III Institute.

between the Israeli government and the PLO/PA of the need for a Transitional Government Body for Gaza. Israel would not trust the PLO/PA and the PLO/PA would not want to move into Gaza behind the Israeli tanks. The Transitional Government Body will have to provide security for all, in full cooperation with the IDF and Israel's other security authorities. It will have to plan and implement a Comprehensive Humanitarian Relief Program for Gazan temporarily displaced persons (including financing, operation, and management, etc.); in tandem with a decision to rebuild the destroyed parts of the Gaza Strip, and speedy return of all displaced persons, Israelis and Palestinians, to rebuilt homes in their pre-war communities. The revival of the Gazan economy and of the Israeli villages and towns that had been vandalized will have to be embedded in a comprehensive regional economic structure. Our plan lays out detailed projects on how to integrate Gaza in the regional economy, offering massive investments also in the Egyptian, Jordanian, and West Bank economies in full cooperation with Saudi Arabia, the United Arab Emirates, and Israel.[12] After having eliminated Hamas' military capacities, having recreated hope, the Transitional Government Body would have to prepare the necessary supportive conditions, agreed by all parties, for the PLO/PA to take over governmental responsibilities for Gaza. Alas, a necessary precondition is a reformed PLO/PA, enjoying a clear mandate of the people to create a stable, secure, and prosperous Palestinian society, without repeated return to violence, leading to end of conflict.

We spoke of the need to address the Israeli and Jewish fear of a repeated Holocaust and the Palestinian fear of a repeated Naqba, addressing the narratives of both sides.[13] Already, a joint Israeli-Palestinian NGO, Combatants for Peace started to work on such an understanding, still isolated in both societies.[14] The document had a very detailed Annex B, discussing in some detail the Economic Reconstruction Plan.[15]

We disseminated the document to a wide range of potential actors and decision-makers. The response we received was that many different actors had prepared similar papers; our paper was the most detailed one and hence

---

[12] See Annex B The Day After quoted above in footnote 2.

[13] We suggested to look at the text of Arafat's speech in Stockholm, December 1998, celebrating the 10th anniversary of the successful Swedish mediation preparing the USA-PLO dialogue on December 14, 1988. See chapter 6,

[14] Zoom recordings: "Staying Together, Holding on to Hope—A Conversation with Palestinians and Israelis" American Friends of Combatants for Peace; October 19, 2023; "Humanity and Hope" American Friends of Combatants for Peace; October 21, 2023; and "Solidarity—A Path to Liberation"; American Friends of Combatants for Peace; October 30, 2023.

[15] Document in Annex B, on the Endgame, quoted above in footnote 1.

would be coopted. What was needed was to prepare several more specific papers.

Being aware that over 1,000,000 Palestinians had fled to the South of Gaza, the most immediate issue to deal with remains how best to take care of their basic needs when the arms will rest. The Jerusalem Strategic Tribune published an initial checklist of ten points:

1. Restore sewer, water, electricity, and trash removal.
2. Prevent looting and Hamas control and terror.
3. Create a detention center for prisoners.
4. Identify the Gazan businesses needed for ordinary life and provide them with the ability to re-open quickly. Be ready to help with rebuilding inventories of necessities. This will likely require purchasing supplies in Israel or elsewhere for delivery into the parts of Gaza where the shooting has stopped.
5. Bring in field hospitals to let Palestinian doctors and staff treat patients.
6. Seize Hamas's cash while not interfering with local Gazans.
7. Survey damage in order to plan for reconstruction.
8. Set up a trusted cell phone network.
9. Seek possible ways and means to fight corruption.
10. Set up efficient capabilities to inspect people and goods moving in and out of areas where fighting has ended.[16]

Several planning teams of the IDF are studying possible related action. Civil society can do little, but still important work. On medical relief, the Physicians for Human Rights (PHRI) work with dedicated Palestinian and Jewish Israeli medical experts. They are pursuing several action programs to provide emergency aid for evacuated Israeli citizens; offer assistance to displaced Thai and other foreign workers, provide humanitarian aid deliveries to Gaza, keep existing mobile clinic activities in the West Bank, and possibly check whether such activity could be possible in Gaza, too.[17] We are trying to connect and combine the PHRI activities where my sister is on the board of governors, with the ongoing activities of the Humanitarian Emergency Response Coalition (HERC), formed by different aid organizations, where Jackson Khouri DeConcini is working out of Cairo, seeking cooperation with experts from the UAE, Saudi Arabia, Jordan, Egypt, and elsewhere.

---

[16] Tom Warrick "Postwar Gaza Planning: An Initial Checklist" in Jerusalem Strategic Tribune, October 30, 2023.
[17] See PHRI Response to Israel-Gaza War, 30.10.2023 pdf.

The Israeli Arab Economic Forum headed by Dr. Sami Miaari is leading action aimed at reviving the Gaza Business sector. The organization is composed of leading Israeli-Palestinian companies. They are well connected to Palestinian counterparts, UAE, and Saudi enterprises, as well as to the World Bank. Together with (Jewish) Israeli economist and business people, they are presently preparing a detailed action program.

Preparing for the Political Struggle in Israel on the Day After

I anticipate an inner Israeli political struggle among three different approaches. An updated version of "business as usual" putting the emphasis on security arrangements, while still opposing an Israel-Palestine two-state solution of any kind; an aggressive radical militant approach perceiving every Palestinian as a potential threat to Israel, aiming to turn Israel into a fully armed and fortified island; and a third option, hoping to renew a global and regional peace process, allowing for the creation of an Israel-Palestine two-state solution, embedded in a more comprehensive regional peace-, prosperity-, stability- and security-building strategy.

The case for the third approach is overwhelming, while at the same time politically problematic: the great majority of Israelis—living still under the trauma of October 7—fear that a Palestinian State would sooner or later renew terror and armed action with more devastating means than ever before. Speaking to as many political thinkers as possible, I encountered three different in essence complementary strategy concepts:

The Religiously Legitimized Peace Approach

The most important lesson learned when reviewing the ups and downs of peace efforts during the last fifty years is to understand the need of creating and disseminating a religious command-based Jewish and Muslim commitment to peace. Hence, most intense political and civil society work has been carried out to achieve this goal. (see Chap. 9). Today, after October 7, hope for success is based on four different assumptions.

(1) Most important is the understanding that both religions, Islam and Judaism commit in their Holy Scriptures and legal rulings to moral and ethical principles, obliging the commitment of believers to peace, tolerance and the need for coexistence. The Quran obliges the Muslim

community to recognize that God has allowed the emergence of different tribes and nations as part of his creation; and the Quran teaches compassion for all. The Bible and Jewish prayers are full of quotations of God's commitment to peace. If this is accepted, it does create the obligation to translate the commitment for peace into practical action.

(2) Assumption two, postulates that without religious and moral commitment, political and diplomatic understandings and signed agreements can be (and have been) broken at any given time. As an example, the fact is quoted, that the US government concluded about 370 agreements with Native Americans, but none of them was kept. When power relations change, or in case they are too asymmetric, the one or the other side to an agreement is all too often tempted to disregard former obligations.

(3) Most important, the renewed trauma experience of the Jewish fear of a new Holocaust, or of repeating pogroms, parallel to the Palestinian fear of another Naqba, creates the basic human and political need to avoid the renewal of these tragedies. The challenge is to translate this understanding into a majority-winning political reality. On the Israeli Arab side, the teachings of Sheikh Nimr Darvish, who founded the Southern Islamic movement, have laid the basic theological and political foundations.[18] Dr. Mansour Abbas, continuing the work of Sheikh Nimr Darvish, has engaged in an intense political dialogue not only with Israel's center-left leadership, but also with pragmatic religious-nationalist leaders, as Naftali Bennet, in a common search to find a way forward. Should Dr. Mansour Abbas obtain sufficient electoral support in the coming elections, it would offer him and his Arab and Jewish dialogue partners, important clout for action. Parallel there is already Jewish religious activism initiated by the "Talking Peace" and "Rabbis for Peace groups and others.

(4) The local Israeli-Palestinian, the regional Middle Eastern and the global political, cultural need for a religious-based Muslim-Jewish doctrine of peace is overwhelming. In the Middle East, the United Arab Emirates is leading a religious-based effort, obtaining passive support from Saudi Arabia and Jordan, as well as—differently—from Egypt. Similarly, for Europe's future socio-cultural stability, the defeat and rejection of jihadist

---

[18] *Lieber, Dov (May 14, 2017). "Founder of Israel's Islamic Movement Dies at 69." The Times of Israel;* Rubin Lawrence (April 2014). "Islamic Political Activism in Israel" (PDF). The Saban Center for Middle East Policy at Brookings (32) "The Islamic Movement in Israel." Jaffe Center for Strategic Studies: Strategic Assessment. Tel-Aviv University. February 2000. Archived from the original on October 24, 2007. Retrieved 2008-04-29.Kingsley, Patrick (2021-07-04). "As Secular Peace Effort Stutters in Israel, Religious Mediators Hope to Step In." The New York Times. ISSN 0362–4331. Retrieved 2021-07-04. "The Pursuit of Religious Peace in the Israeli-Palestinian Conflict." blogs.timesofisrael.com. Retrieved 2021-07-04.

ideas, and a commitment to non-violent religious ethics is of immense importance.

There are many political forces who have a vested interest to kill this effort, before it becomes too powerful. Thus, while action has to be immediate, other peace-building elements are essential to protect this island of decency and sanity in an all too stormy emotional and political reality.

Promoting Reconstruction, Economic Growth, Interdependence, and Cooperation

Already before October 7, we worked on an ambitious plan: A Gaza Reconstruction Program (GRP); the enhancement of trade and other economic ties between Gaza and the West Bank and a set of game-changing infrastructure projects as major generators of employment and economic growth.

While the 2023 Gaza War is still on, it is clear that its magnitude of destruction and the derived scale and costs of required immediate reconstruction are vast. The war may end with a million-plus displaced persons and probably 200,000–250,000 housing units destroyed or damaged to a level requiring complete rebuilding.

Thus, a preliminary guestimate of the requirements of the 2023 immediate crisis-support and reconstruction plan amounts to:

(1) Food support and other social requirements, education, health, etc.: USD 1.5–2 billion.
(2) Housing and shelter: USD 3–4 billion.
(3) Infrastructure and non-residential buildings: USD 1.5 billion.
(4) Rehabilitation of industrial, agricultural, trade, and other business-sector facilities, as well as immediate support to revitalization of economic activity: USD 2–3 billion.
(5) Reconstruction and reactivation of government services, other governance-related support: USD 0.5–1 billion.[19]

The immediate crisis-support and reconstruction plan should be designed and executed with an eye on the wider, longer-term "Economic Leap Plan," which will be based on integrating Gaza with key regional projects and regional economic cooperation at large and will demand investments of over $70 billion, which will have to be business-wise viable.

---

[19] These are estimates based on the experience gained after the Gaza war of 2014.

- **The India—Middle East—Europe Economic Corridor (IMEC).** IMEC is probably the most transformative initiative for the coming two decades, especially for Jordan, but for other countries of the region as well. **The integration of Gaza and the West Bank into this initiative** would be a major game-changer for their trade and economic development.
- **A network of large-scale solar power plants that will be built in desert areas of Jordan and Egypt.** These solar power plants could generate great amounts of electricity at low cost, for export to neighboring countries. In essence, it will be an expansion of the Emirati and Saudi successful model, using the expertise gained in the UAE and Saudi Arabia of such large solar power plants.
- **If the electricity interconnector linking Israel and Europe through Cyprus advances, a second interconnector can be considered linking Gaza and Europe as well.** This needs to implement plans for the Renewable Middle East project designed to export renewable energy from the Middle East to meet potentially a third of Europe's electricity needs.
- **Large-scale clusters of seawater desalination and wastewater treatment plants**, which would provide water for domestic use and for agriculture throughout the region. As with solar power plants, here too, the initiative will be an expansion of the Emirati and Saudi model of such large desalination plants, in tandem with the Israeli successful model in wastewater treatment for re-use in agriculture. Gaza will be part of this regional network, as a provider of desalinated water, while the West Bank and Jordan will be on the receiving end.
- **Natural gas**: Expansion and advancement of the already developing Israeli–Egyptian–Jordanian cooperation in this field. **The Gaza Marine gas field** will be integrated into this initiative.
- **Development of the North Red Sea Area.** The Saudi emphasis on the development of the north Red Sea area, at the heart of which is the **NEOM flagship project,** opens unprecedented opportunities for the development of surrounding areas as well: Sinai in Egypt and the southern parts of Jordan and Israel. The Gaza "Economic Leap" plan will connect to this powerful engine of regional economic development.[20]

Given the tremendous investments of Saudi Arabia and the United Arab Emirates, the promotion of already planned regional projects provides the

---

[20] Google search on expected long-term Saudi investment in the area of Neon and beyond states that presently, an annual investment of $103 billion is planned, intending to increase annual investments by 2030 to $ 453 billion. The United Arab Emirates present Foreign Trade volume amounts to $ 599 billion.

necessary means to finance most of the needed capital for the reconstruction of Gaza and the upgrading of the Palestinian economy at large, allowing to achieve most of it by public and private investment. This is of course only achievable if the threat of renewed violence can be eliminated.

The Security-Based Approach

All the above-described developments are only achievable, if Israel together with the international coalition will be able to create an effective and sustainable security structure. The political direction of Israel will be largely determined by the activism of the community of over 180,000 evacuated Israelis and civil society organizations which supported them all along. Determined to return to their homes and rebuild their wounded communities, the overriding demand is: security; security and again security.

We can realistically assume that isolated Hamas military strongholds will remain in the Gaza Strip, when a long-term ceasefire will be concluded. This will necessitate to combine Israeli security oversight and capability to act, with the formation of a tight security structure formed by a combination of NATO, Egyptian, Moroccan, and other forces. A variety of imaginative diplomatic solutions to achieve this will have to be found. An important component will have to be to adapt the Mandate of an international-regional security structure. The language of UN Security Council Resolution 1368 of September 12, 2001,[21] might now read:

> Unequivocally condemns in the strongest terms the horrifying terrorist attacks which took place on October 7, 2023, in Southern Israel, and condemns Hamas' action to hide behind the Palestinian civilian population to protect their military action and equipment; regards such acts, like any act of international terrorism, as a threat to international peace and security; expresses its deepest sympathy and condolences to all victims and their families, Israelis and Palestinians; calls on all States to work together urgently to bring to justice the perpetrators, organizers and sponsors of these terrorist attack and stresses that those responsible for aiding, supporting or harboring the perpetrators, organizers and sponsors of these acts will be held accountable."

Such a regional and international commitment is also in the interest of the Palestinian Authority. In a first meeting between President Abbas and a European head of state, the Dutch Prime Minister, Mark Rutte, on October

---

[21] UN SCR 1368, September 12, 2001.

23, Abbas remarked that 35 leaders of Hamas were staying in Qatar, and it would make sense to expel them.[22]

The Need to Define Milestones Starting with the Conclusion of a Long-Term Ceasefire

Milestone One will be to agree on the formation, the structure and the mandate of a regional-international security structure for Gaza;

Milestone Two will be to organize massive humanitarian aid to temporarily replaced Palestinians, within the compounds with an effective Egyptian-Moroccan-Qatari security control to prevent Hamas or other criminal agitation; and outside the compounds under Israeli security control;

Milestone Three: Developing a Plan for the Reconstruction of Gaza and the Reconstruction of Israel's destroyed border area in tandem; planning should be carried out on an expert level, as well as on a diplomatic level, re-creating the three working groups which were formed on September 18, 2023, at the UN, by the EU-Saudi-UAE-Arab League Secretariat-Egyptian-Jordanian Initiative.

A **Political and Security Working Group**, focusing on developing an outline of potential post-peace regional, political, and security cooperation mechanisms; an **Economic and Environmental Working Group**, focusing on developing proposals for economic cooperation, including in the areas of trade, investment, innovation, transport infrastructure, natural resources, as well as climate change and the environment; and a **Human Dimension Working Group**, focusing on developing proposals for cooperation in humanitarian, inter-cultural, and human security issues as stipulated by UNGA Resolution 66/290.[23]

The expert group will have to be formed by Israeli, Palestinian, Jordanian, Egyptian, Saudi, UAE, and other experts supported by their governments and prepare Action Plans for all three working groups. On the diplomatic level, an International-Regional Donor Conference will have to be prepared, to create the necessary political, financial, and technical support.

---

[22] Meeting with foreign diplomat October 24, 2023.
[23] For a detailed description see Chapter 11 and "MEPP: The European Union, Saudi Arabia, the Arab League in cooperation with Egypt and Jordan launch the Peace Day Effort for the Middle East and invite the world to join"; September 18, 2023, New York; eeas.europe.eu/eea/mepp-european-union-saudi-arabia-arab-league-cooperation-egypt-and-jordan-launch-peace-day effort/en.

Milestone Four: Has to allow for a first phase of repatriation of temporarily displaced persons either to their former or to their newly built homes and for the normalization of the post-war situation.

Milestone Five: Has to focus on the human dimension of the conflict and allow Israel and the Palestinians to work on an agreement "How to move from the Logic of War to the Logic of Peace."[24] This will have to include work on strengthening religious-based commitment to peace.

Milestone Six: The "Wider Economic Leap Plan" including the major regional development projects, (see above) the reconnection between the Gaza and West Bank economies and upgrading regional economic cooperation.

Milestone Seven: Elections in Israel, and Palestine.

Milestone Eight: Confidential negotiations to prepare the substance of a US-Saudi-UAE-Egypt-Jordanian-Israeli-Palestinian Peace Plan.

Milestone Nine: President Biden, Crown Prince MBS, King Abdallah of Jordan, President MBZ of the UAE, and President as-Sisi from Egypt will submit the Peace Plan to the Israeli Knesset and to the most suitable Palestinian body at that time (either a revived Palestinian Legislative Council if possible or the PLO National Council or the PLO Central Council).

Milestone Ten: The Israeli Knesset and the Palestinian body will ratify the Peace Plan.

Addressing Palestinian and Israeli Fears and Hopes

Two Palestinian scholars of high standing, Yezid Sayigh and Khalil Shikaki, discussed at the Crown Center, Brandeis University, possible outcomes of the War. They argued rather convincingly that to enable the success of the envisaged Endgame basic dynamics of Israeli and Palestinian policies adopted during the last decade (or even longer) had to change: Will Israel cease to prefer a deal with Hamas, rather than with the Palestinian Authority? Will Israel stop to oppose a unification of the West Bank and Gaza? Will Israel insist that the Palestinian Authority will remain weak? And will Israel really be willing to revive the two-state solution as part of a wider Roadmap? And will Israeli policies of further settlement expansion under the protection of the IDF continue or stop? And on the Palestinian side, will Fatah rejuvenate and be able to create a workable strategy and assure Israel that the way forward is

---

[24] The idea of this concept was originally developed in 1998, see below chapter four.

a way to peace and good neighborly relations, even if not all issues of conflict are being solved at once? And last but not least will the United States and the international community be willing to invest the necessary political, security, and economic capital to allow the suggested Endgame to unfold?[25]

Most of these questions address the internal political development in Israel. Some of these questions address the need for internal Palestinian reform.

Israeli fears relate to the danger of Palestinian, wider Arab and Muslim hate-mongering and incitement, threatening the Jewish people in Israel and the Diaspora, while the international community will forgive or ignore the crimes of Hamas, present them as freedom fighters, and accuse Israel for defending itself.

These Palestinian and Israeli fears—which are by no means unsubstantiated—reinforce old political behavioral patterns and militant messianic beliefs on both sides, which all too easily can destroy the hope for peace.

We do not know what will be. But we do know what we have to fight for.

---

[25] Crown Center for Middle East Studies "After the Israel-Hamas War—Likely Scenarios and Outcomes for Israelis and Palestinians" November 4, 2023.

2

Growing up in Vienna (1949–1967)

First Experiences in Vienna

When I arrived in Vienna, I hardly saw a house, or really any building, that was not destroyed. My family and I had arrived from London, where I had first seen the terrible destruction of the war. When my sister wanted to buy candies for her and me, we were told they were rationed and we would need the necessary stamps. Vienna was much darker.

I was only five years old when, on November 19, 1949, I arrived in Vienna. Still, I understood that Vienna had been liberated by the Russian troops, as well as by the other allied forces. My mother told me that "the forces of light and decency had won, and the forces of evil had been defeated." I did not, yet, know, what it meant. I would learn very soon.

Traveling on Vienna's *Ringstraße* (the "Ring-Road") in a street car, strangers frequently asked me, in German, what my name was ("*wie heisst Du?*"). I answered: "my name is Peter Naftuli Hirschfeld" and added, "my parents left Vienna some years ago and now they have come back." The most common response was staggering: complete and utter silence. They immediately understood; I was a little Jewish kid.

The other response was even worse. The grown-ups who had asked my name would start to explain to me, the little boy, that they had known nothing about Hitler's crimes and that they had had no part in it. Sometimes they added that their best friends had been Jews. I soon tried to avoid these unwanted discussions, although they would follow me for many more years, like a shadow that I just could not get rid of.

Lola, my mother, had told my sister and me that the forces of light had won. Nevertheless, we got strict orders not to play with children named Dieter, Horst, or Isolde or children who wore white socks and leather trousers. It was very clear that not all Austrians belonged to the "forces of light." Rather, we were to avoid children whose parents most probably had been Nazis.

My mother had attended a socialist-led vocational school to become a kindergarten teacher. It was *das rote Wien* (the red Vienna) that she admired and to which she felt a sense of belonging. Her heroes were Viktor Adler, Julius Tandler, Hugo Breitner, and Otto Bauer. Viktor Adler was a physician in poverty-stricken districts of Vienna. He understood the need for political action and founded Austria's Socialist Party. Professor Julius Tandler created the Viennese healthcare system and the city's kindergartens to serve its poor population. Hugo Breitner, serving in the municipality of Vienna, financed and built affordable housing for the poor. Otto Bauer, the founder of Austro-Marxism, allowed my mother to dream of a better world.[1]

They all were Jewish. My mother explained that they had always taken the side of the weak against the strong. She emphasized that my sister and I, both as children and later as grown-ups, should take this same side. This was—she taught us—the essence of Judaism. In her political views, my mother was a cosmopolitan and conceptually did not identify with Zionism, which she would remind us of repeatedly.

Over a decade earlier, on March 11, 1938, the Nazis marched into Austria. My sister Ruth, almost three years old, was in hospital. My mother would come to see her every day. Toward the end of the first week, my mother was told Ruth had been healed and she could go home. When my mother came to take her home, she was dead. We never knew what really happened. The death of little Ruthi strengthened my mother in the following months, yet it would remain a dark shadow of longing for the rest of her life.

Jews not in prison, such as my mother, were forced to clean the streets and pavements. When my mother was told she could go home, she refused and would stay until the others were allowed to go home (this is not a story I got from my mother). Normally, such behavior caused disastrous repercussions, yet my mother got away with it. My mother's grief somehow created respect. She acted exactly how she meant when she had told us "to always take the side of the week."

---

[1] Joachim Riedl (ed.), *Wien, Stadt der Juden—Die Welt der Tante Jolesch;* Zsolnay, Wien 2004, pp. 388–397 (look at 270 biographies to understand the political, social, economic, and cultural influence of Jews in Vienna).

My parents succeeded in coming to Palestine. In Tel Aviv, my mother took care of a little boy about the age of Ruthi. Walking on Allenby Street, the boy ran onto the street in front of a car, yet the driver stopped at the last moment. My mother, in shock, apologized thousand times. Yet the driver responded in Yiddish: "you do not honestly believe I will cause harm to a Jewish child." Back in Vienna, my mother told my sister and me this story many times and would always cry by the end of it. For us, the message was simple: Austria signified death, yet Israel signified life.

Stories from My Grandparents

My grandfather, Milan Hammer was born in Tarnopol (which is in Western Ukraine today). His father would sell soda water during the day and would reportedly study Torah all evening and night. There was very little to eat at home. My grandmother came from a little village outside Tarnopol, Chimalov, which today has become part of the city. Her mother died when she was eight years old and, from then on, Grandma Rachel (Rosa) had to earn a living for herself and her little sister. At the turn of the century, my grandparents married and came to Vienna to make a living. Grandma never learned proper German, but she helped Grandfather build a successful tailor shop that mainly severed the very poor.

The Kishinev pogrom of 1903 caused many Jews to leave and seek refuge in Vienna. The mayor of the city, Karl Lueger, led a political party that had an Anti-Semitic platform and refused to permit the Jews to enter Vienna. In protest, Austrian Emperor Franz Joseph opened *Schoenbrunn*—his summer residence. He gave the order to put up tents in the park, allowing them to stay, and remarked that "they are all my subjects" (*sie sind ja alle meine Untertanen*).[2]

At that time, and many years later, the small flat in the Schoenbrunner Strasse became the first safe haven for relatives. It was a small immigrant community, allowing little Lola to grow up safely and protected. Yet it was not so for grandma Rachel. Feeling insecure and threatened all her life, she made a tremendous effort to please her non-Jewish neighbors. It turned out her fears were not completely unsubstantiated. On November 9, 1938, the evening of Crystal Night, Nazis came to throw her out of her flat. The neighbors came and took her side, arguing: "Frau Hammer has always helped us, she is a good women."

---

[2] Zvi Yavetz, *Erinnerungen an Czernowitz—wo Menschen und Buecher lebten;* C.H. Beck, Muenchen 2007, pp. 13–14.

The Nazis went away but returned several days later. This time, the protective support had come to an end, and the comment had changed: "She is only a Jewess", and therefore they had no qualms about throwing her out of her flat that night. A sense of complete insecurity would haunt her all her life. When I was a child, I noticed how it would affect her reaction to any development. Even when an Austrian skier won all gold medals, she would ask me: "Tell me is this good for the Jews, or bad for the Jews?" She did not say, but it sounded like she was asking: "Will they find another reason to go against us?"

Grandfather Milan Hammer was different. He slowly enlarged his little tailor business. In order to save the money to pay for public transport, he would walk from one side of Vienna to the other (from Meidling to Simmering) and eventually buy a house with several flats with his savings. He would read the *Arbeiter-Zeitung* (the newspaper of the Socialist Party) and theoretical socialist literature. He and my mother would dream together of a better world. Still, he insisted that I would get circumcised in an orthodox religious ceremony and not merely in hospital, as my mother would have wanted. He passed away in December 1944. I was six months old. I was told that he had dreamed his son would study at the Hebrew University in Jerusalem. Although I was late by one generation, I would make this dream become true.

My father came from a different social background. His parents were factory owners. Grandmother Keile (Kala) was born in Brody. During the 1770s, then Empress Maria Theresa's son, Crown Prince Joseph, visited the town, located on the border between the Austro-Hungarian and Russian Empires. Being impressed by the emerging trade, he turned the city into a free-trade zone and hereby allowed Brody to flourish and become a center of international trade. At the same time, the emerging movement of Jewish Enlightenment (led in Germany by Moses Mendelsohn) achieved an important foothold in the city. The family of my grandmother (Schwarz and Barach) grew up in the atmosphere of the rising Jewish bourgeoisie.

Keile, at 16 years old, was married off to Jakob Hirschfeld. He was six years older and lived in Balarssat-Jarmat, a little town in Hungary that borders Slovakia. He managed a land estate for a gentile aristocrat and had learned the profession of coppersmith. Keile and Jakob had 16 children, yet five died at birth. Of the eleven children who grew up, the youngest four, my father among them, were born in Vienna.

One of the stories my father told me of his father was that he was given the advice never to go hunting. I asked why. My father did not know, but he told me the demand had been expressed in so strong terms to him that he wanted me to promise that I would never go hunting too. I did promise. Years later, I visited the Jewish museum in Eisenstadt, (Eastern Austria, close to the area where my grandfather came from). The exhibition showed pictures and stories of the practice of hunting of the local aristocrats. As a "warm-up," before hunting deer or rabbits, they would hunt a Jew on the way. Sometimes, the Jew would get killed; sometimes they would let him run away.

Six of the eight Hirschfeld boys would serve in World War I (my father, born 1903, and his brother Sigi, born 1901, were too young). Max reached the rank of Major. He disobeyed an order and launched an attack under his command and won that battle. For such bravery the Austro-Hungarian army offered two responses: As the attack failed, the sentence would be death; as the attack had succeeded, it was rewarded with the Highest Honor, the Maria Theresien-Order. However, Max was Jewish, and the highest honor was denied to him. Instead, he was offered the second-best but he refused. The message was clear, all the bravery and excellence, would not open the door for acceptance. Eventually, all the Hirschfeld-Boys became Zionists.

I was also told that Martin Buber, the Jewish philosopher, had been—when in Vienna—guest in the home of my grandparents. Buber, teaching at Hebrew University in Jerusalem, was during the 1930s a leading member of Brit Shalom (the Alliance for Peace). I do not know, whether there is any connection at all, but all my cousins, who live in Israel, and are children and grandchildren of my father's brothers, politically identify today with the peace camp.

Growing Up with the "Forces of Light" in Vienna

From 7 years old, my sister and I were allowed to sit with guests during the evenings. We would have to be bathed, be dressed in our pajamas, and would listen until the guests would leave. Mother would buy very delicious "bestrichene Broetchen" from Trjesnewski; a shop of a Polish Jewish immigrant to Vienna, which had become the meeting place of the Viennese bourgeoisie. The cakes came from Gerstner, the second most expensive cafe in Vienna. We would help to serve our guests and then would sit and listen quietly, in order not to miss one word.

We loved Felix Hubalek. At the time he headed the department on culture and art at the *Arbeiter-Zeitung* the newspaper that belonged to the Socialist Party. He also edited two other socialist periodicals. He was not Jewish. In 1934 he joined the clandestine struggle against Austria's fascist regime. Under Hitler, he went to the Netherlands and was active in the underground. He was caught and then kept most of the time in the cellars of the Gestapo. We adored him. He would tell us jokes in Yiddish and would carefully listen to my grandmother to learn some other idiomatic expressions. He would speak about the past, as well as about Vienna's cultural life. We would read his poems. I owe him my early understanding of the Holocaust, reading his words:

> Der Mond der dort am Himmel steht, ist bleich wie mein Gesicht,
>   Und wie mein Mund der zitternd fleht, dass diese Nacht zu Ende geht;
>   Doch diese Naechte enden nicht, mit eines Tags Beginn;
>   Ihr Schatten dunkelt jedes Licht und ihre Duesternis zerbricht des Daseins wahrgeglaubten Sinn.[3]

(The Moon standing on the sky is pale like my face, and like my mouth, begging for this night to end; yet such nights do not end with the beginning of the day, their shadow darkens all the light, and their darkness breaks the belief in the meaning of our being.)

Another poem of Hubalek was written one year after the Hungarian revolt was brutally put down by the Soviet army. The decisive lines read:

> Ein Jahr ist lang, und ein Jahr ist es her,
>   Um Ungarn ist es laengst geschehen,
>   Die freie Welt laesst schwarze Fahnen wehen.

(A year is long and a year has gone by; Hungary has been left alone, the Free World has raised black flags.)

The message was clear, whenever you can, you have to stand up against injustice and fight for freedom. He died in November 1958, from the after-effects of Gestapo tortures. Other guests at our home were the head of the foreign policy section of the *Arbeiter-Zeitung*, Friedrich Scheu and his wife, Herta; the head of the finance and economic section, Karl Ausch, the head of the cinema section Harry Walden, and a communist judge Herr Herbert and sometimes also his son, who later also became a judge.

Thus, my parents somehow belonged (and also did not belong) to the Viennese Socialist elite. So did my sister Miriam. In school, two friends were the daughters of the Viennese Police President Josef Holaubek, and Austria's Minister of Justice, Christian Broda. Later, Miriam would meet Liesl Pittermann, the daughter of Austria's Vice-Chancellor. Her mother was Jewish and

---

[3] "Verzweiflung" in Felix Hubalek, *Vom Tag zum Morgen-Gedichte*; Danubia Verlag, Wien 1955, pp. 30.

had attended religious lessons as a child together with my mother. I admired particularly, Joseph Holaubek. He had served as the commander of the fire brigade in Austria's 21st district, Floridsdorf. There the main square was the Viktor Adler Platz. The Nazis wanted to change the name. Holaubek mobilized sufficient public support to prevent this. The Nazis came to his home and asked him to join the party, and he showed them the door. Evidently, this was the reason why the Allied Forces appointed him as head of police in 1945.

We spent the winter holidays in Hof Gastein together with the families of Vienna's socialist elite. The daughter of the head of Vienna's social housing agency, Liesl Salinger, would tell us ghost stories. Many years later, when my father had lost all his money, Liesl's father would help my parents to get a flat to rent at extremely low cost, a move that saved them from poverty.

For medical reasons, I had to go leave Hof Gastein earlier than the others. On the train ride, I was babysat by the son of Giacomo Matteotti, the Italian socialist leader who was murdered in 1924 by Mussolini. I was of course impressed by the bravery of Matteotti, who stood up against the fascist leader, aiming to protect his people, from the intended misuse of power. Matteotti's son was kind to me and we spoke all the way to Vienna much about politics. He told me, I would become a politician when I grew up. My questions and knowledge seemed to have impressed him.

My father was creative and a great communicator. Arriving penniless to New Zealand, in only four years he became a successful businessman. After the end of World War II he received a contract from the New Zealand Labor government that made him a rich man. At the next election campaign in 1948, the conservative newspaper *Truth* asked, "why a Jew" was given this privilege from the labor government and they added many invented accusations against my father. He would organize strikes and undermine New Zealand's economy. My father stood up, and together with us, left New Zealand. My mother would comment: "if there is Anti-Semitism at least let us be at home."

The office of my father was situated in a building that belonged to Baron Reitzes, a Jewish banking family, who had financed the Viennese streetcar network in the nineteenth century. Spending holidays in the same hotel, Baron Reitzes and his wife stayed in, I admired their big white puddle. Several months later, the Reitzes couple committed suicide. They had mismanaged funds of Austrians and feared it would cause a new wave of Anti-Semitism. I was told the white poodle refused to eat and actually committed suicide with them. Years later, my father was in a similar situation. He had built summer houses and sold them. Being in financial trouble, he refused to announce bankruptcy, which would have caused the people who had purchased houses from him, to lose all their money. Instead he sold everything he had and remained almost completely penniless for the rest of his life. Yet, he never gave up, and he would continue to work until 90. I admired my father for doing so. Miriam and I took from him two traits: Anything you hoped for and believed in, was achievable; and not less important; never give up.

My Emerging Convictions

Being young and hoping to build a better world it is hard to decide whether the universal good has priority over the national good, or vice versa. We tested this in the *Hashomer Hatzair* youth movement in Austria. At summer camps, we tended to stage "trials" in order to sharpen our minds. Following the events in South Africa at the end of the 1950s, we invented a story, which—we learned later—happened in reality: The young leadership of the Hashomer Hatzair in Johannesburg worked clandestinely together with the local activists of the ANC (African National Congress). South African secret police discovered these activities and threatened to close down the youth movement. Repeated warnings were disregarded and caused eventually the end of all activities and the arrest of the young leaders. We imagined an internal trial of the youth movement, against the young leaders who disrespected the warnings and caused the ending of important Zionist activity. In our game I, age 16, became the accusing attorney and my sister Miriam, the lawyer for the defense.

Miriam argued that the Apartheid regime had supported Nazi Germany, and their policy was racist and fascist. They disregarded basic human rights, they murdered and tortured opponents, and they fought an innocent mostly unarmed civil population. We Jews had the duty to fight for universal human rights, also, but not only, as there are also black Jews. We should admire the young *Shomer* leaders, take their example, and not put them on trial.

While impressed by Miriam's argumentation, I advocated a very different approach. I argued that being Zionists we were engaged in a national liberation struggle, as others. The Jewish people were still threatened in Israel by surrounding Arab nations, who spoke of their intention to drive us into the sea. In the Jewish Diaspora, where we lived, virulent Anti-Semitism had been revived. As leaders of the youth movement we had prime responsibility for our community, for the children who had joined us and for their families. It might be ok to leave the youth movement and join as individuals the struggle of the ANC, and this was a legitimate personal choice. However, as a collective move, it was wrong and dangerous to implicate our movement and the Jewish community at large.

Not without emotional wounds, I won, (not because I argued better, but because the head of the movement sent from Israel, decided in my favor) and we decided to expel the young Johannesburg leadership from the movement. With just 16, I was not aware that we were engaged in defining the dividing lines among the Jewish Left within Israel and the Diaspora. In many ways, the discussion then has placed me irretrievably in the national Zionist camp, as against the more cosmopolitan approach, my mother would have argued for and Miriam still does.

Emotionally, the need for collective self-defense and security was apparent to me from a very young age. For my father, Zionism was not merely a national liberation movement of the Jewish people, and the essence was, to stand up and fight—even with the "broken sword" as he would sing—against any assault. One of the stories we children heard repeatedly was that, after he had been beaten by a group of Anti-Semitic youth, his older brothers came and beat them up, so they would never attack again; "the Hirschfeld boys" were the strongest in the district.

As a child my big heroes were Winston Churchill and Mordekhai Anilewicz, the commander of the Warsaw Ghetto uprising. About ten years old, I read John Hersey's *The Wall*, which was a collection of diaries from the Warsaw Ghetto, describing life in the Ghetto and the heroic Warsaw Ghetto uprising. I read more than one biography of Churchill and until today I am not ready to hear any criticism, even if justified, against either one of them.

In spite of my need for self-defense against any verbal or physical attack, I was never embroiled in a physical fight. The only time, when twelve years old, a boy of my class, who had been a friend, called me "Sau-Jud" (Jewish Swine). I smacked his face four times, although he was far bigger and stronger than I. What happened seemed miraculous. The entire class separated us one from the other. He had received his punishment, and I was protected from his rage. I never spoke to him again. Alas, I started to appreciate "third party support."

In many discussions with my uncle Sigi (my father's brother) we discussed the Maccabean Revolt, (169 B.C.) as well as the Bar Kochba Revolt (132–125 A.D.) Uncle Sigi convinced me how irresponsible the Bar Kochba Revolt had been. It caused the death of hundreds of thousands, the destruction of over one thousand Jewish villages in Eretz Yisrael, the renaming of Judea and Israel into Palestine, and 2000 years of painful exile for the majority of the Jewish people. It made sense to launch a war of liberation against a declining power like the Seleucids. It did not make sense to start a war against the all-powerful Roman Empire, at the height of its strength.

Thus, my youthful admiration and commitment for a heroic military struggle went together with a healthy intellectual curiosity to find out, when military action had a chance to succeed, and when not; and what alternatives might be available. Although I might have dreamt of becoming a big hero, my natural tendency—already as a child—was to be more cautious. My father would tell my sister and me the story of Wilhelm Tell. In order to increase the story's drama, he would question whether I would ask him to shoot at the apple on my head to prevent his arrest. I would not, despite my great love for him. I only remarked "such a sad story."

Reading the history and literature of the time between the two World Wars largely impacted on my thinking. We would read Remarque, Kästner, Tucholsky, Brecht, Borchert, Zweig, and Werfel, describing the disaster and tragedies of war. We admired the struggles of Berta von Suttner and Jean Jaures who fought to prevent the outbreak of World War I. Yet, at the same time, we despised Neville Chamberlain and understood that his Appeasement policy only brought disaster.

It was an important mix, helping to create a sense that the struggle for peace had to be multifaceted and combine the disdain of war, education for peace, as well as a deep understanding of the need and the utility of deterrence and if needed, also of force.

When I was nine years old, I decided, when grown up, I would live in Israel. I never changed my mind. On November 2, 1967, the fifty years anniversary of the Balfour Declaration, I made my dream come true and immigrated to Israel.

Suggested Additional Reading

Trying to Understand the Impact of the Holocaust

Eva Hoffman, *After Such Knowledge: Memory, History and the Legacy of the Holocaust*, London 2005 (this is possibly the best description of the impact of Holocaust on the Second Generation, as we did grow up with the traumas of our parents and grandparents).

John Hersey, *Der Wall*, Rowohlt, Hamburg 1950 (Hersey describes the life in Ghetto Warsaw and the heroic struggle of the Warsaw Ghetto Uprising).

Felix Hubalek, *Vom Tag zum Morgen*, Danubia, Wien 1955 (describes in poems the heroic struggle of those Austrians who fought the Nazi regime).

On Jewish History

Haim Potok, *Wanderings: History of the Jews*, Knopf, New York 1978 (tells the story of four thousand years of Jewish history).

Maristella Botticini and Zvi Eckstein, *The Chosen Few—How Education Shaped Jewish History, 70–1492*, Princeton U.P. 2012 (describes the impact of religious learning on the socio-economic development of the Jewish people).

Bernard D. Weinryb, *The Jews of Poland—A Social and Economic History of the Jewish Community in Poland from 1100–1800*, The Jewish Publication Society of America, Philadelphia 1972 (describes the privileges Jewish communities gained in Poland and elsewhere in Central and Eastern Europe; the impact of Anti-Semitism, the first holocaust of 1648–1651, and its impact creating the Jacob Frank, the Hassidic Movement, and Jewish Enlightenment and struggle for Emancipation).

Amos Elon, *The Pity of it All—The Portrait of Jews in Germany, 1743–1933*, Metropolitan Books 2002 (Elon describes the way from Jewish Emancipation via the rise of political Anti-Semitism toward the unfolding tragedy before the holocaust).

The Hashomer HaZair Movement in Vienna After World War II

Heinrich Ehlers, Talma Segal, Arie Talmi (Hg), *Hashomer Hazair—Ein Nest verwundeter Kinderseelen*, Mandelbaum Verlag, Wien 2006 (forty children tell the story of their families, before, during, and after the holocaust, as well as their emerging activism within the youth movement of the Hashomer Hazair).

The History of Europe Until 1945 and the History of Europe After 1945

Hans Kramer, *Die Grossmaechte und die Weltpolitik 1789–1945*, Tyrolia, Innsbruck 1951 (I received this book as a gift from Felix Hubalek and I do not know, why he chose it, or whether it was coincidental. It is a very detailed, over-800-page account of international diplomacy and war, largely focused on the decline of the Habsburg Empire, and a call for the restoration of a "Christian moral code."[4]).

Tony Judt, *Postwar—A History of Europe Since 1945*, Pimlico, London 2005 (this is undoubtedly the most important research written about Europe's history after 1945).

---

[4] Describing the end of World War II, Kramer wrote: "Und dieses Truemmerfeld erstreckt sich ueber die Staaten sowohl der Sieger als auch der Besiegten. Nur der Sieg der christlichen Sittenlehre koennte hier helfen, aber ihre Stimme ist oft der des Rufenden in der Wueste zu vergleichen. …Wenn es ueberhaupt der Welt gegoennt sein wird, zu genesen, so wird dieser Heilungsprozess jedenfalls lange Zeit brauchen und tiefe Narben werden an ihrem Koerper zurueckbleiben" (pp. 829).

Manfred Jenke, *Verschwoerung von Rechts?—Ein Bericht ueber den Rechtsradikalismus in Deutschland nach 1945*, Colloquium Verlag, Berlin 1962 (when, in June 1962, Israel executed Adolf Eichmann, all over Europe, as well as in Austria, Anti-Semitic actions multiplied. We knew that Austria's extreme radical Right was closely connected to the various German groups, and the two major newspaper, National und Soldaten Zeitung and the Deutsche Wochen Zeitung, were widely being read in Austria. Being among the responsible leaders in the Hashomer Hatzair we took action to know ahead of time what right-extreme groups might be planning. We enjoyed full support of the Viennese police force in protecting all activities of our Youth movement.)

3

Experiencing the Unfolding of the Peace Process (1967–1990)

The Six-Day War of June 1967 became a watershed in Israel's and the wider Middle Eastern history. It was also a kind of watershed in my life, immigrating to Israel. For the Palestinian people 1967 symbolized not only another defeat, but also the reemergence of an independent political struggle, under the leadership of the Palestinian Liberation Organization (PLO), Fatah and Yasser Arafat. On November 3, 1991, the enemies, Israelis and Palestinians, would finally meet at the negotiating table, within the supporting framework of the Madrid Conference. In between lay a painful twenty-four years learning process. On the personal level those twenty-four years had prepared me to start the secret negotiations in Norway that would lead the way, to the Oslo Accords. Actually, it was my mother who taught me the first and most important lesson for negotiations.

She was six and a half years old, in September 1914 when she attended first-year grammar school in Vienna. The teacher told her (and the other kids) to go home and pray to God and ask him "to punish England and protect Austro-Hungary as well as the German Reich." Little Lola went home and asked her parents: "What will God do, in case the children in England are told to ask to protect England and punish Austro-Hungary and the German Reich?" When telling us the story, mother would add: "God did answer eventually. He punished both sides."

My Experiences During and Shortly After the Six-Day War

On June 7, 1967 (the third day of the Six-Day War), I took my final exams to obtain the Matura certificate which recognizes successful high school graduation in Austria. The exams covered eight years of learning material that I, never having attended high school, had missed entirely. My mind was in Israel and with the fighting forces. Nevertheless, I passed the exams in English, Latin, and German. On the last exam, Math, I failed.

An Egyptian student was recommended to me as a good math tutor. During our meetings, it was impossible for us not to discuss the situation in the Middle East. Although Israel had now won the war, my tutor insisted that a subsequent defeat was now inevitable. Israel, he asserted, would be drawn more and more into Arab territories, and this would eventually bring about Israel's fall. It would be a replay of Russian military tactics in the war against Napoleon and later against Hitler. I was irritated and thoroughly unconvinced.

In July of 1967, Father, and I traveled to Israel and joined Miriam, who during the war worked as a nurse at Rambam Hospital in Haifa. When we arrived in Jerusalem, I was reminded of my visit to the borderline there in 1954, thirteen years earlier. I, then 9 years old, had tried to cross the barbed wire of the dividing wall of concrete and climb up the wall, where Jordanian soldiers were watching. The man who had accompanied us on that trip pulled me down and spanked me. I was rather astounded that Mother did not protest.

This time, however, the wall of concrete had gone, allowing us a full view of the city wall Sultan Suleiman the Great had built in the sixteenth century. We entered through Yaffa Gate, where the German Emperor Wilhelm II was allowed to ride on a horse into the Old City. And we admired a sign close by, showing the place of the former Austro-Hungarian Post Office, reminding us that the Habsburg monarchy had established a functioning postal service in the Holy Land in the middle of the nineteenth century.

Father introduced us to many of his friends from his own time in the Zionist Youth movement many decades ago. Each one of them greeted us with an unmistakable enthusiasm for the future. "The Arabs will finally make peace with us," they insisted. The father of Miriam's friend Nira Feldmann, a card-carrying member of the right-wing Herut party, told her: "We have now to give all the territories back, and not wait." My sister, surprised at the remark, asked him: "But, you always said that the two sides of the Jordan River, belong to us." His answer still rings in my head today: "I do not give up the claim, but staying in the territories may turn out to become a dangerous trap."

When we traveled to Jericho, we walked inside one of the almost empty refugee camps on its southern outskirts. The Palestinians who had lived there under most dire conditions had to flee a second time, experiencing once more the Palestinian tragedy of dispersal and dispossession. Traveling north along the Jordan River we witnessed the Israeli trauma. On the eastern shore of Lake Tiberias, at Kibbutz Ein Gev, we saw former Syrian fortifications and heard about the many attacks that this Kibbutz had suffered from Syria. Not far away Kibbutz Gadot had been completely destroyed. I wondered whether many threats of the past had come to an end or would be carried forward into the future.

Making Aliya and Studying in Israel

Several days after arriving I started my studies at the Hebrew University. As I never had attended high school, it was for me like being allowed into a forbidden garden, with all too many delicious fruits, I hoped to pick. Like a little boy being given a new toy, I cherished every moment. When there were no lectures, I would sit in the National Library and read far more than the given assignments. In my free time, I would walk with friends to the Old City.

Money was still tight, so I got a teaching job in Ramallah. I was asked to teach Hebrew (the little I knew) to Palestinian physicians. I would travel twice a week in a Palestinian bus from Jerusalem to Ramallah, where I was well received, well fed, and well paid. My students, many of whom were fluent in English, French, and Russian, were quick learners and made tremendous progress. Thus, there were plenty of opportunities to discuss politics. They told me that the Israeli occupation created the opportunity to establish a Palestinian state beside Israel. At the time, I had not developed strong opinions on the question of Palestinian statehood, and I was still unaware of the many complexities. Yet, I understood the need to listen and accept what was being said as important fruit for thought. After one year, the Hebrew of my students was almost better than mine, and I told them with much regret that they would need another teacher.

The Department for Middle Eastern History at Hebrew University very soon became my second home. The older generation of our teachers all came from German or Austrian cultural backgrounds. Professor Gabriel Baer had studied Muslim history in Beirut and was member of the leftist Labor Zionist movement. He taught us mainly social history, in particular the history of land ownership. In many ways, it illustrated the difference between European and Middle Eastern patterns of political and social behavior; the growing cleavages within Egyptian, Palestinian, and other Middle Eastern societies; and the power of the landowning gentry, who became the early leaders of the emerging nationalist movements. We would also discuss why the Fellahin in Egypt would not rise in revolt against their exploiters and why, on the other hand in 1919, the landowners would lead the first revolt against British domination.

A Complicated Chess Game After the Six-Day War

My studies allowed to acquire important knowledge enabling me to put the ideas I heard in Ramallah from my Palestinian students into perspective. At the time, Israel's strategic thinking referred to four major threats the Israeli Government under the leadership of Levy Eshkol were aiming to neutralize.

The first major threat was Egypt's capacity to quickly organize an army and attack Israel every few years. Thus, Eshkol's first aim was to pursue peace negotiations with Egyptian President Gamal Abdel Nasser. The second major threat was an attack from the Jordan River that split the north of Israel from the south, between Tulqarem and Netanya, where Israel's territorial width was only 14 km. Eshkol's second aim was thus to pursue peace negotiations with Jordanian King Hussein bin Talal. The third major threat was the fear of a repeated "domino effect" triggered off by the Syrian Ba'ath regime, pulling Egypt and Jordan also into war with Israel, as had happened during the period that led to the Six-Day War. The fourth and final major threat was that the activities of the PLO will move the international community to question the very legitimacy of Israel.

David Farhi, who taught Ottoman history and would entertain close social contact with us, had become a close advisor of Minister of Defense, Moshe Dayan. We were told (confidentially) that he led the negotiations with the mayor of Hebron, al-Jabari, aiming to create an agreement on Palestinian autonomy. Those efforts failed, due to strong opposition from Jordan. Later we learned that secret negotiations with Jordan failed largely due to strong opposition from Egypt. Thus, it seemed to be evident that Israel needed peace with Egypt first. We also learned of President Nasser's remark, he could not negotiate with an Israeli knife at his throat, and understood that a stalemate situation blocked for the time being every peace seeking effort. A very complicated chess game would have to be played.

The Israeli Government took a most meaningful opening move: On June 19, 1967, the Israeli Government, using both the Americans and Soviets as intermediaries, did present Syria and Egypt with a peace offer. It offered to withdraw from Sinai to the international boundaries with Egypt, and from the Golan to the international border with Syria, in return for direct negotiations, the conclusion of a peace agreement, and acceptable security provisions. Both Syria and Egypt, however, refused. On September 1, 1967, the Arab states gathered at Khartoum and decided on three "no's": no to recognition, no to negotiations, and no to a peace agreement. However, they left the door open to possible arrangements by non-obliging third parties, similar to what had happened after the Sinai War in 1956.

These contradictory positions created a deadlock and induced the United States and the Soviet Union and other members of the international community to adopt UN Security Council Resolution 242, which established the "land for peace" formula.[1] This resolution and the "land for peace" mantra would become key elements in all subsequent peace negotiations.[2]

Prime Minister Eshkol hoping to break the deadlock turned to Jordan. King Hussein, hoping to regain control over the West Bank, engaged. Thus, between December 1967 and May 1969, Israel and Jordan would pursue most serious peace negotiations. Years later, Faisal el-Husseini would tell me that the Israeli offer had been most substantial, and there had even been some indirect contacts with the PLO to achieve acceptance.

Sari Nusseibeh told me that his father had been directly involved in these negotiations also praised the Israeli negotiating offer. And Yaakov Hasan, the leader of the Israel Mapam party, who—as a member of government—was involved in these negotiations, told me that under the premiership of Golda Meir the negotiations had gotten very close to agreement. However, he argued that the unfolding War of Attrition, and the effort of US President Richard

---

[1] Ruth Lapidoth and Moshe Hirsch (ed.), *The Arab-Israel Conflict and its Resolution: Selected Documents*; Nijhoff, Dordrecht 1992, pp. 134.

[2] It should be noted that UN SC Resolution 242 subsequently allowed for three different interpretations: the Israeli interpretationr read "full peace for territories, but not all 'the' territories"; the Palestinian and Arab interpretation read "partial or limited peace for all the territories"; the international reading would suggest "full peace for all territories." Henry Kissinger's comment on Resolution 242 was the following: "The first time I heard one of the staple formulas of the region's diplomacy was at a dinner at the British Embassy in February 1969. Someone invoked the sacramental language of United Nations Security Council Resolution 242, mumbling about the need for a just and lasting peace within secure and recognized borders. I thought the phrase so platitudinous that I accused the speaker of pulling my leg." Henry Kissinger, *White House Years*; Little Brown, Boston 1979, pp. 341.

Nixon to impose an agreement on both sides, had become the major reasons for failure.[3]

Egypt and the Soviet Union tried to break the deadlock by starting the War of Attrition. Israel, with the full backing of US President Nixon, did not back down against escalating Soviet threats.[4] Soviet pilots attacking Israeli targets were shot down by the Israeli air force. When former US President Dwight Eisenhower died February 1970, Nasser sent Mahmoud Fawzi to attend the funeral, indicating that Egypt wanted to end the war. Henry Kissinger, who at the time served as National Security Advisor to President Nixon, would draw the following conclusions:

> But through this turmoil the inherent strength of the American position in the Middle East also gradually emerged. Nobody could make peace without us. Only we, not the Soviet Union, could exert influence on Israel. Israel was too strong to succumb to Arab military pressure, and we could block all diplomatic activity until the Arabs showed their willingness to reciprocate Israeli concessions. If we remained steady and refused to be stampeded, the pivotal nature of our position would become more and more evident.[5]

The chess game had started with old rules that had not worked. Now, in 1970 the new rules of the game had become clear: Israel's military strength had become a most valuable political asset for the United States, to rebuild its influence in the Middle East, and neutralize the Soviet power game there. The Arab leadership, at first in Egypt, and later elsewhere too, understood the United States had—due to Israel's strength—obtained a monopoly over the peace process. The Soviets also understood that the US had gained the upper hand.[6] The stage was set for the peace process to start and pursue Israel's strategic aim of "Egypt First."

What came of it, was an American mediating effort bringing the War of Attrition to an end in August 1970.[7] It was still US Secretary of State William Rogers who led the American mediating effort. The idea was simple:

---

[3] Avi Shlaim, *Lion of Jordan—The Life of King Hussein in War and Peace*; Allen Lane-Penguin, London 2007, pp. 252–320 (Avi Shlaim tells the story of negotiations from the Jordanian perspective. Never being willing to give any credit to the Israeli side, he has refrained from publishing the Israeli proposal).

[4] Henry Kissinger, *White House Years*, Simon and Schuster, New York 1979, pp. 560–575.

[5] Kissinger, *White House Years*, pp. 378–379.

[6] Yevgeny Primakov, *Russia and the Arabs Behind the Scenes in the Middle East from the Cold War to the Present*, Perseus, New York 2009, pp. 125–141.

[7] Compare Kissinger's account with the one given by William Quandt. See William B. Quandt, *Peace Process—American Diplomacy and the Arab–Israeli Conflict since 1967*, the Brookings Institution, Washington D.C. and University of California Press, Berkeley 1993, pp. 159–182.

to commit both parties to a ceasefire, define the supportive conditions, and look forward to the next step. American tactics of doing so created the first pattern of negotiations, which would become the "step-by-step" approach. The template had four components: identifying the common interest at stake on relatively limited issues, providing the conflicting sides with guarantees by the means of side letters, determining technical understandings for implementation, and designing a shared obligation to move on to the next step.[8]

The Yom Kippur War: A Decisive Formative Experience

From discussions I had with my professors 1970, 1971, and 1972, I knew perfectly well that Egyptian strategic intentions had changed. Egypt, now under President Anwar as-Sadat's leadership, wanted to seek peaceful understandings with Israel. In his autobiography, Sadat quotes Nasser saying: "Listen Anwar, whether we like it or not, all the cards of this game are in America's hand. It is high time we talked and allowed the USA to take part in this."[9] In February 1971, President Sadat submitted two proposals. First, a more comprehensive approach for a non-belligerency agreement addressed to the UN Peace Envoy Gunnar Jarring. Second, a "first step" proposal, allowing for Israeli withdrawal from the Suez Canal, addressed to the United States. Israel neither accepted the former nor was forthcoming on the latter. The price to pay was the Yom Kippur War of 1973.

The war costs the lives of over 2600 Israelis, many more wounded, and many more Egyptian deaths and casualties. I was convinced this tragedy could have been prevented. I knew what had prevented an Israeli-Egyptian understanding was the concept of "everything or nothing." Golda Meir—then Prime Minister—wanted an agreement but was afraid that a step-by-step approach would reprieve Israel of decisive negotiation assets in the search for a full peace agreement. Another cause for the war, was Israel's military hubris, the belief to be invincible.

---

[8] The American peace team should definitely be applauded for developing the technique of the step-by-step approach. However, the side letter sent to Golda Meir obliged the United States not to ask for any further Israeli withdrawals before reaching a full peace agreement. Not only did this contradict the step-by-step approach, but it also offered sufficient reason for Golda Meir to oppose President Sadat's peace initiatives before the October/Yom Kippur War of 1973. *See* William B. Quandt, *Peace Process—American Diplomacy and the Arab–Israeli Conflict since 1967*, The Brookings Institution Washington D.C. and University of California Press, Berkeley 1993, pp. 159–182.

[9] Anwar el-Sadat, *In Search of Identity—An Autobiography;* Harper and Row, New York, 1977, pp. 198.

When I met Yossi Beilin years later, I learned that he, as well as Nimrod Novik, Boaz Karni, and many others had experienced the same and drawn the same conclusion: Israel's fate was too dear to us, to leave all the decision-making to the old generation of politicians. We needed to become pro-active in an effective as possible search for peace.

My experience during the war also left a long-lasting impact. When I had immigrated to Israel, I had to give the army all my medical records and, having been hospitalized for one month shortly before I immigrated to Israel, I was not conscripted. Nevertheless, I volunteered at the Jerusalem municipality. I drove every day (alone and unarmed) to different villages in the West Bank and would bring Palestinian teachers to schools in East Jerusalem and Palestinian workers to a bread factory in Jerusalem. In the beginning, I was frightened. But then, I saw the tremendous fear of the Palestinians, far more frightened than myself. They understood that they had been put between the hammer and the anvil: should King Hussein join the war, Jordanian troops would enter from the East, and Israeli troops from the West. It was clear to me that ending the occupation was a shared interest for both Israelis and Palestinians if favorable conditions for both parties were met.

After the war ended later that month, the army did conscript me and others who had all kinds of health difficulties. After the very partial and rudimentary training, I was sent to serve in Gaza to guard the Israeli Defense Forces (IDF) headquarters in the middle of the city. A little Palestinian boy, who must have been only about three years old, came to watch me. I gave him the candies that I had in my pocket, which he gladly took. His sister, who looked only two or three years older than him, suddenly came running toward us. She took the candies away from her brother and threw them at me with obvious contempt and hatred. This little incident, more than any of my academic research, demonstrated to me why the occupation was unsustainable in the long run. Or at least why continuing it could only be possible at an extreme price of inhumanity, for which I hoped Israel would not be willing to pay.

The Foundations of Peace in the Camp David Accords

Israel's victory militarily, in the Yom Kippur War, was perceived by the Israeli public as a defeat; combined with President Sadat's intent to end the war, it, opened the way for negotiations on a step-by-step approach. It allowed the United States to mediate a Disengagement Agreement between Israeli and

Egyptian forces, followed by a Disengagement Agreement between the Israeli and Syrian forces. In September 1975, an Israeli-Egyptian Interim Agreement was concluded, which clearly set both countries on the way to peace.[10] It would take another three years until the Camp David Agreement was signed on September 17, 1978.[11]

By that time, "Peace Now" had become a powerful actor in Israel. Before Prime Minister Menachem Begin would travel to Camp David for the decisive negotiations, 400,000 Israelis (among them my wife Ruthi, six years old Michali, four years old Naomi, just one year old David, and I) would demonstrate hoping for a peace agreement. We celebrated the signing of the Framework for Peace in the Middle East.[12]

Unlike most Israelis, I did read the signed Camp David Accords. At the time, I viewed it as a triumphant piece of art, a great achievement of diplomacy, as well as a document full of ambiguous statements and contradictions. I believed that it opened the way for negotiating peace with all our neighbors (Egypt, Jordan, Syria, and Lebanon) on terms that, to me, seemed very favorable to all. It also prescribed a roadmap for reaching peace with the Palestinian people. The concept of peace was not merely a cold peace, solely with understandings between leaders, but an all-inclusive and comprehensive peace.

It not only allowed for diplomatic relations but also enabled cooperation in many fields of life such as the economy, social affairs, and culture. The price Israel had to pay was to implement UN Security Council Resolution 242. In my view, this made much sense as long as, per the agreement, Israel's security interests were respected. The Camp David Accords provided a gradual approach to solving the Palestinian issue. I thought it made much sense. It would empower the Palestinians under controlled conditions and create the necessary supportive conditions to allow the Palestinians to establish at first a negotiated self-rule regime, creating conditions for permanent status negotiations. Reading the details of the agreement it seemed to be evident that the final result would be to allow the Palestinian people to establish a state of their own, in conjunction with Jordan. I also thought that withdrawing under

---

[10] For negotiations on the step-by-step approach, see Henry Kissinger, *Years of Upheaval*, Little Brown, Boston 1982, ch. 18, 21, and 23.
[11] Harry Hurwitz and Yisrael Medad (eds), *Peace in the Making—The Menachem Begin-Anwar al-Sadat Personal Correspondence*, Gefen Publishing and Menachem Begin Heritage Center, Jerusalem 2011 (for the text of the Camp David Accords and the correspondence between Sadat and Begin. The text of the Agreement and Accompanying letters and statements are on pp. 289–311). *See* Kenneth W. Stein, *Heroic Diplomacy—Sadat, Kissinger, Carter, Begin and the Quest for Arab–Israeli Peace*, Routledge, New York 1999 (for the diplomatic process leading to the conclusion of the agreement).
[12] Quandt, *Peace Process*, pp. 445–456 (the treaty is reprinted here).

controlled conditions from the West Bank and the Gaza Strip, in return for a peace agreement, served Israel's most essential interest of maintaining its Jewish and democratic identity.

However, I also understood the many ambiguities which opened space for future conflict. On the Israeli front, I soon understood that Prime Minister Begin's and the Likud reading of the Camp David Accords was very different from what I hoped for. Camp David was seen and propagated as an agreed blueprint enabling Israel to conclude a separate peace agreement with Egypt. This interpretation of the Camp David Accords was, in my mind, a contradiction to the spirit of the agreement. Nevertheless, it was in line with the text. The text made it very clear that each part of the "Framework for Peace in the Middle East agreed at Camp David" was separate and would be independently pursued, one from the other. Thus, from Begin's point of view of short-range power politics, it made perfect sense to pursue only peace with Egypt and neglect all the other parts of the agreement.

However, the problem was not only neglecting the other parts. The problem was also that Begin hoped that an understanding of Palestinian self-government would allow Israel to expand Israeli sovereignty one way or another also over Judea, Samaria, (collectively the West Bank) and the Gaza Strip. Thus, Camp David was seen by Israel's political Right as offering a carte blanche to engage in a massive settlement effort all over Judea, Samaria, and the Gaza Strip.

On the other hand, listening to President Sadat's speech in the Knesset, it was clear that he aimed to bring about the establishment of a sovereign and independent State of Palestine that lived peacefully beside Israel.[13] The gap could hardly have been bigger and the emerging political conditions in the wider region could hardly have been more counter-productive. The chance to reach an agreement on the Palestinian issue, provided for in the Camp David Accords, was less than slim.

All too soon, I understood that the paradigm created at Camp David in September 1978 was based on three flawed assumptions:

Assumption Number One: It would be possible to achieve an agreement based on two directly contradictory end-game concepts. Israel seeking to expand its sovereignty to Judea and Samaria, while offering self-government rights to the Palestinians. Egypt and the Palestinians were aiming at the establishment of a sovereign independent State of Palestine. With such contradictory negotiating aims, it was difficult to imagine how to define the

---

[13] Hurwitz and Medad, *Peace in the Making*, pp. 15–28 (Sadat's Address to the Knesset of November 1977 is reprinted here).

necessary *zone of possible agreement*. The fact that the PLO and most of the Arab world opposed even the Egyptian approach made it all the more evident that headway would be very difficult to achieve.

Assumption Number Two: Camp David could lead to an agreement that resulted in the "end of conflict" and "finality of claims." Going beyond just Palestinian self-governance, Camp David proposed to solve all five core issues: Jerusalem, refugees, settlements, borders, security, and water. It would soon become clear that, at the time, the common ground on each one of these issues was far too narrow. Only win-lose solutions would be achievable.

Assumption Number Three: Camp David believed that agreement could be achieved based on the formula "nothing is agreed upon until everything is agreed." It became a textbook recipe for perpetual failure.

Thus, the paradigm created at Camp David in 1978 formed a straitjacket that needed to be "loosened" to create sufficient breathing room.

Iran and the Beginning of a Complex Relationship with Chancellor Kreisky

My views in regard to the Camp David Accords were at the time, accurate but irrelevant. Not so, developments in Iran. I was the head of the Iranian desk at the Dayan (then Reuven Shiloah) Center, at the University of Tel Aviv. My account on Iranian developments between 1976 and 1977 was published in the Middle East Contemporary Survey.[14] I wrote then that the social-political coalition that had supported the Shah regime had broken apart. The shah's policies after the rise in the oil price of 1973 had all been counter-productive. His desire to achieve two digital economic growth brought about inflation, widening the gap between poor and rich, causing major migration from rural areas to the cities, causing political and social unrest. I did not foresee Ayatollah Khomeini would return to Iran. Yet, when it happened, I understood what it meant for Israel. An important ally, the shah of Iran, not only of Jerusalem, but of Cairo, had been replaced by a dangerous enemy, Ayatollah Khomeini, who would do everything in his power, to disrupt the evolving peace process.

When Ayatollah Khomeini returned to Iran, February 1, 1979, I was asked to participate in a TV discussion on Iranian events, in Vienna. Chancellor

---

[14] Yair Hirschfeld and Arieh Shmuelevitz, "Iran" in Dishon and Shaked (eds.), *Middle East Contemporary Survey, 1976–77*, vol. 1, Holmes and Meyer.

Kreisky watched the program and (with the help of an Israeli journalist) asked to see me.

By then, I understood the chances of reaching an agreement on Palestinian self-government, as laid out in the Camp David Accords, had gone from rather slim, to completely impossible. Originally, US President Jimmy Carter and Prime Minister Begin hoped King Hussein would join the negotiating effort. However, the king was not willing to accept a Diktat on the conditions for negotiations, he asked 14 questions. Receiving President Carter's answers, the king decided to stay out, and join the Iraqi led "steadfastness front."[15] The Palestinians were not willing to engage, which meant that negotiations had to be led by Egypt as a proxy for the Palestinians and Israel. The strategic interests of Israel and Egypt in this context were most obviously not bridgeable. I explained this as good, as I could to Chancellor Kreisky in our first meeting. He did not question my conclusion. Yet, he wanted to know, if there was anything that could be done, in support of achieving an agreement. We discussed the Israeli political scene, the role of Egypt, and possible positions of Jordan and the PLO.

Kreisky wanted to know whether Shimon Peres or Yitzchak Rabin would be more supportive in trying to bridge gaps and asked me, about the political differences between them. I answered that Rabin wanted a territorial agreement under conditions taking care of Israel's security. Peres, on the other hand, wanted a "functional" agreement, allowing for a division of power between Jordan, Israel, and an emerging Palestinian Self-government over the West Bank and Gaza. Kreisky who had spoken repeatedly with President Sadat knew that the Egyptian president preferred the functional solution, to any territorial agreement. In a territorial agreement, Egypt or the Palestinians would have to give up territory, a functional agreement would allow for concessions that could be later changed.

Kreisky knew how important Egypt is for Israel and wanted to help. He made two suggestions: I would be invited (on my costs, and together with my father) to join an Austrian delegation to Egypt. The Austrians would discuss economic aid to Egypt, and possible side talks might take place to test, the one or other move to improve Israeli-Egyptian economic ties. This paved the way for Austria to invite an Israeli business delegation (from Koor, the Trade Union's industrial conglomerate) and an Egyptian delegation (from one of its leading banks) to Austria, aimed at enhancing trilateral business projects.[16]

---

[15] Quandt, *Peace Process*, annex F, pp. 457–465 (Carter's answers to the 14 questions).

[16] When the two delegations came to Vienna, the Austrian hosts had put an Egyptian and an Austrian flag on the table, but no Israeli flag. The Israeli business delegation walked out. The incident was solved, by taking all the flags off the table.

A second Kresiky suggestion was for me to research the policies of the Israeli Labor Party as well as the European Socialist Parties and prepare a study on the Middle Eastern Policies of the *Socialist International*.[17]

First Experiences in Egypt

Shortly after the signing of the Israel-Egypt Treaty of Peace in March 1979, my father and I joined—as observers—the Austrian delegation to Egypt. It was the first visit of many more to follow. It made me aware of the complexities and the volatility of the peace that had been concluded.

An Egyptian guide showed us around Cairo. In Giza, he showed us one of the former palaces of King Farouk and told us the sad story of the king's gardener. King Farouk, a sexual predator, had dishonored the gardener's wife. The gardener, infuriated at the king, took his gun and shot at him, but missed. The gardener was put on trial and quickly executed. In telling the story, it was clear that the guide wanted to emphasize how indecent, immoral, and illegitimate the King's behavior was. Having made that point, the guide turned around and pointed in the direction of Hotel Mena House, where Israeli-Egyptian peace had been negotiated. He did not say it explicitly, but the meaning was clear. In his eyes, peace with Israel was like the king's deed, indecent, immoral, and illegitimate.

The next day, we visited the Ministry of Food. It was a twelve-floor building. A young boy—possibly 10 years old, managed the lift. He pushed the button for the highest floor and then decided to test his capability to open the doors of the lift exactly at each floor where somebody wanted to exit. It was frightening, as the likelihood of getting stuck appeared to be above 50%. After the meeting, we decided to walk down the stairs, rather than take the lift once more. On every floor, most of the civil servants had left their desks and were in the hallway praying. The power of Islam and the dominance of Muslim leadership in this country were inescapable.

At a second visit to Egypt, the Israeli and Egyptian head of the two business delegations had been both wounded in war. They found out that they had fought in the same place, at the same time, and were both wounded, in their knees. It created a sense of comradeship and shared purpose. The

---

[17] When I finalized my research, the paper was very critical of Kreisky and the European Socialist parties, who I argued, had most substantial interests in the Middle East, but very little power and influence. Yair Hirschfeld, "Schlussbericht: Die Sozialstische Internationale und der Arabisch-Israelische Konflict" *Hirschfeld Khoury-DeConcini Papers, Substack*, July 9, 2023 (originally written in September 1993), https://hkdpapers.substack.com/p/schlussbericht-die-sozialstische (accessed July 9, 2023) (hereafter cited as Hirschfeld, "Schlussbericht," *Hirschfeld Khoury-DeConcini Papers*).

dichotomy of the situation was all apparent. Egypt's Westernized intellectuals and upper classes wanted to conclude peace with Israel and develop close relations, in many spheres, definitely in business and economics. Their approach was backed by the awareness of the terrible damage caused to Egypt by the repeated wars with Israel. On the other hand, the middle and lower classes, mobilized by Islamic groupings, viewed peace with Israel as illegitimate.

It was not too difficult to understand that Sadat's socio-economic policies of *infitah* opening the Egyptian economy to the world would have a major impact. I was told by intellectuals, a Copt businessmen and others, they feared, the internal social gap would grow, and Muslim radical militant fundamentalism would sooner or later undermine the stability of the government of Egypt and peace with Israel.

Back at Hebrew University, I had taken a course with Professor Menahem Milson. For his class, I wrote a paper reviewing Sayyid Qutb's book on Social Justice. Sayyid Qutb became the most revered ideologue of modern militant Muslim fundamentalism. Being executed by President Nasser, he also became a martyr. I also understood very well the great attraction of his ideas to Egypt's poorest class. Talking of the power of "real" Islam, its superiority over Christianity and Marxism, the harmony of society; caring for the needy, the need for "pure" family life, and prohibition of gambling, prostitution, and alcohol all promised a messianic like perfect world in return for militant activism. Thus, having studied these writings, I knew what Mr. Sabongi—the Copt businessmen—and others told me were well-founded fears, based on the realities of Egypt.

Another meeting was with a distant relative of Egypt's Minister of Foreign Affairs, Boutros Boutros Ghali. She was married to an Egyptian diplomat. At a cocktail party, a Palestinian woman berated her for having betrayed the Palestinian cause. She answered that Egypt had fought five wars, its cities had been destroyed, tens of thousands of fathers, brothers, and sons had been killed, and many more wounded, all for a cause that was not Egypt's. The Palestinian woman apologized. Then, Boutros Boutros Ghali's lady relative concluded her story, saying: "then we sat together, and cried together." Her message to me was unmistakable: "We Egyptians want to have peace with Israel, but we still care for the Palestinian people; Israel will have to understand this, and act accordingly."

The Middle East Policy of the Socialist International

I was of course honored that Kreisky asked me to prepare a study regarding the development of a Middle East Policy of the Socialist International. It opened for me the archives of the British, German, and Austrian Labor parties; as well as the archives of the Israeli political parties Mapei (Beth Berl), Mapam (Givat Haviva), and Ahdut Avoda (Ramat Efal) in Israel. The documents I found were fascinating. In London, I learned that the Labor Party offered scholarships to study in England, to leaders of Front for the Liberation of South Yemen (FLOSY) at a time when the Labor Government under Harold Wilson was fighting against them in South Yemen. In Bonn, Germany, I found material describing the diplomatic foreplay of the late 1950s, leading eventually ten years later to Willy Brandt's *Ostpolitik*.

In the autumn of 1957, Nikita Chruchtshov, the Soviet leader, sent letters to the Socialist leaders of the United Kingdom, France, Belgium, Denmark, the Netherlands, Germany, and Norway, inviting them to discuss in Moscow, concepts of disarmament, causing eventually the German Socialist Party to visit Moscow two years later. The important part for me was the fact that the trigger for these discussions was the Soviet reaction to developments in the Middle East. I learned how the strong support of most European Socialist parties for Israel gradual changed after the Six-Day War. Socialist parties in Europe feared that the process of pacification with the Soviet Union achieved by Willy Brandt's Ostpolitik might be endangered by growing tension in the Middle East.[18] Remarkable in this context was a meeting of the Socialist International in Helsinki in 1971. The Finnish delegation fought for a resolution that was strongly opposed by the Israeli delegation. Hoping to comfort Golda Meir, who was present, the Finnish President sung a love song for her, saying his heart was bleeding for the great love he felt for her. It was only partly amusing. The message was clear, something like "our heart is with Israel, but our head—thinking of the Soviet Union, the Cold War and power politics—is not anymore with you."[19]

The final report which I submitted in 1983, described in much detail the ideological and political gap between Israel and Europe's socialist parties and led me to the conclusion, that the dialogue with Europe was of great importance, yet, the diverging US-European interests, made Israel more and more

---

[18] Hirschfeld, "Schlussbericht," *Hirschfeld Khoury-DeConcini Papers*, pp. 3–6.
[19] This incident allegedly greatly irritated Meir, as she described in a report to Lishkat Mapei.

dependent on the United States. That same, I drew another conclusion: only a gradual process was possible.[20]

The study of the Israeli archives was even more enlightening. I would learn of two track-two exercises. During 1957, Ezra Tadmor representing Mapam and Dr. Jamal Sha'er representing the Jordanian Ba'ath party chaired by Antony Wedgwood Benn would engage in peace talks. The initiative for the talks came from the Ba'ath Party. Prime Minister Ben Gurion offered his non-obliging permission for Mapam to test a possible opening for peace. The talks got nowhere. The real intention of the Arab side was to obtain Israeli support for an intended coup to topple King Hussein of Jordan. When in February 1958 Egypt and Syria formed the United Arab Republic, the Ba'ath party engaged in these talks ended the exercise. The Israeli lesson learned was that no harm had been done. Rather, on the contrary, a possible policy option had been tested and been shown to be not sustainable.

Rabin, during his first premiership in 1974–1977, would also allow for a track-two exercise between Arieh Luba Eliav, Matti Peled, and Uri Avneri (on the Israeli side) and Izzam Sartawi and Said Hamami (on the Palestinian side). In January 1977, Izzam Sartawi summed up the peace dialogue in a letter to Chancellor Kreisky. Written on the paper of Hotel Imperial, Vienna (in order to appear unofficial to the PLO), the summary made evident that no common ground had been identified. Sartawi summed up the (deniable) PLO proposal in the following words:

> Very briefly, it can be stated that for the return of the West Bank, Gaza Sector, the Himma and Auja enclaves, a status of non-belligerency can be established between the future sovereign State of Palestine and State of Israel. But for a full state of peace to take place, other issues will have to be settled the most important of which is the Israeli acceptance and implementation of the right of Palestinian refugees to return to their original homes, if they wished to do so or to be compensated if they freely elected not to return.[21]

Israel was being asked to withdraw not only from the territories occupied in 1967, but also from two additional enclaves, not against peace, but against an agreement of non-belligerency, maintaining the demand for all Palestinian refugees who wanted to return to their homes, to be implemented. Rabin sent a letter to Kreisky, thanking him for the effort, as it made him understand

---

[20] Hirschfeld, "Schlussbericht," *Hirschfeld Khoury-DeConcini Papers*, pp. 11–20.
[21] Izam Sartawi, "Letter to Chancellor Kreisky," Hirschfeld Khoury-DeConcini Papers, Substack, July 9, 2023 (originally written on January 27, 1977), https://hkdpapers.substack.com/p/letter-to-chancellor-kreisky (accessed July 9, 2023).

that the option of talking to the PLO could not work.[22] I had no difficulty to explain to Chancellor Kreisky that this was light years away from a hoped-for zone of possible agreement. Instead, what was needed was to obtain Palestinian agreement, to engage in negotiations on the basis of the conditions defined at Camp David (1978).

I learned a lot from these failed track-two efforts. The decisive lesson was to understand the task of the track-two exercise. The aim was not to develop an alternative policy to the policy pursued by the incumbent Prime Minister. The aim was to present the Prime Minister with the pros and cons of an alternative policy and provide the necessary input, to allow him, to decide one way or the other.

Kreisky Pursues My Policy Suggestion

Kreisky explained to me, the key in getting to negotiations was to find ways and means to initiate what he called the "vehicle theory." He explained, it was important to find a way either for the Kingdom of Jordan to lead the way and get the PLO on board; or allow the PLO to become the vehicle also for the inclusion of Jordan in peace negotiations. Because the 1974 Arab Summit had decided to recognize the PLO as "the sole legitimate representative of the Palestinian people," Kreisky argued, King Hussein could not negotiate without a prior consensus from the PLO. However, because the United States and Israel would not recognize the PLO even though they were willing to engage in negotiations with King Hussein, Arafat could not get involved in the negotiating process without King Hussein's assistance. Thus, the question was whether King Hussein would become "the vehicle" for Arafat to get involved in the negotiations or whether Arafat would become a similar vehicle for King Hussein's participation. Kreisky agreed with me that the formation of a Palestinian delegation, representing both: Palestinians allied to Jordan and those allied to the PLO, would be the "hoped-for, obvious way" to get negotiations going. The problem was that neither King Hussein nor Chairman Arafat accepted the Camp David Accords and hence would not support the formation of a Palestinian delegation to start negotiations with Israel, nor would the Palestinians, living in the West Bank and Gaza, dare to take such an initiative.

I suggested to Kreisky how to cut this Gordian Knot. He, as chancellor of Austria, would allow me to invite a Palestinian delegation of economists,

---

[22] Yair Hirschfeld, *Track-Two Diplomacy toward an Israel-Palestinian Solution, 1978–2014*, Woodrow Wilson Center Press, Washington D.C. and John Hopkins U.P., Baltimore 2014, pp. 9–10.

industrialists, and business people from the West Bank and Gaza (representing both Jordanian and PLO interests) to visit Vienna. Kreisky would discuss the possibility of offering economic aid to the Palestinians. Because he was scheduled to visit Jordan that autumn, he could also discuss the concept with King Hussein of Jordan there and follow that discussion first with PLO chairman Arafat, and after with the Israeli government. In return, I would try to obtain the support of Shimon Peres.

Kreisky gave me the "green light" to organize such an event. I knew that Jordan and the PLO had established a joint committee, aimed at offering economic support to the Palestinian inhabitants of the West Bank and Gaza, with the aim to strengthen their "steadfastness" and not be tempted to join negotiations on the basis of the Camp David Accord. I also knew that parallel hereto, the mayor of Hebron, Fahd Qawassme had founded the "Arab Industrial Committee," whose members included Palestinian supporters of Jordan and the PLO. I found a way to meet a member of the committee (Kamal Hassouneh) and presented him an offer he could not (and would not) refuse: "*to meet Chancellor Kreisky in Vienna, and discuss ways and means to obtain economic aid from Austria.*" The delegation arrived at the beginning of September 1980 in Vienna. (Arriving at the airport they looked like Israelis, when later they dressed properly for the meeting, the similarity was gone.) Kreisky was badly prepared for the meeting. He promised too much and created expectations, he could not keep. Nevertheless, he gained confidence of the workability of the proposal I had made. He was interested to discuss a possible follow-up with the Jordanians and his forthcoming visit several weeks later. In Amman, Crown Prince Hassan bin Talal had prepared for him a relevant paper: "Some Suggestions For Aiding the West Bank Economy."

The paper stressed the aim to "*strengthen the attachment of the people of the West Bank to their land, and bolster the structure of the West Bank economy, particularly in agriculture and industry.*" And it stated: "*It is important to point out that any aid given to the West Bank should be linked to Jordan. Much emphasis was put on the need to create credit facilities for the West Bank economy, and establish an Economic Planning Agency (EPA).*"[23]

Returning from Jordan, Kreisky was willing to take the initiative to the next step. He invited me to attend the Conference of the Socialist International in Madrid and sent me to Germany and Denmark, to meet

---

[23] Hassan bin-Talal, "Some Suggestions for Aiding the West Bank Economy," *Hirschfeld Khoury-DeConcini Papers, Substack*, September 22, 2022 (originally written on September 30, 1980), https://hkdpapers.substack.com/p/suggestions-for-aiding-the-west-bank-economy (accessed July 9, 2023).

Socialist counterparts.[24] He put me in contact with Bernt Carlsson, the Swedish General Secretary of the Socialist International, obviously intending to prepare the ground for obtaining the support of Olof Palme. He also put me in contact with Herbert Dingels, the International Secretary of the German Socialist Party, apparently hoping to obtain the eventual support of Chancellor Helmut Schmidt. I traveled to Bonn and Copenhagen. (The father of a student of mine, Herbert Pundik, who edited a daily newspaper in Denmark, "Politiken" prepared a red carpet for my coming.) It seemed possible that a peace-building initiative of the Socialist International, largely along the lines of my suggestions, was getting underway.

The Suggested Socialist International Peace-Building Initiative

When I met Yossi Beilin the first time, he listened most carefully to the stories I told him of Kreisky, the Palestinians and the Jordanian reaction, and some of my experiences in Egypt. He almost forgot to take his younger son Uri from Kindergarten. He asked me to join his political group within the Labor Party and he got me in touch with Shimon Peres. The paper Kreisky had received from Jordan, written by Crown Prince Hassan, served as my entry billet, Peres was fond of the proposed policy concept.

With the help of Yossi Beilin I got the go-ahead from Shimon Peres to work with Kreisky and the Socialist International on preparing an economic development plan for the West Bank and Gaza.

Without my doing, two weeks after I had submitted the proposal to Peres, Elias Freij, the Palestinian mayor of Bethlehem, published in the Washington Post his proposal for a Palestinian Peace Initiative.[25] He suggested that Palestinians "recognize the right of Israel to exist as a sovereign and independent state within defined and internationally recognized borders, on a reciprocal, mutual and simultaneous basis," and he added that an Israeli proposal "to

---

[24] At the airport of Madrid, on the way back, I had also a short meeting with Gro Harlem Brundtland, at the time chairwoman of the Norwegian parliament. I told her of my activities with Kreisky and the others. She was interested, but never followed up. When many years later I met her in Norway, she did not even remember the Madrid encounter, fourteen years earlier. Sometimes efforts to connect people to projects are unsuccessful. But do not let this discourage you from persisting.

[25] Elias Freij "A Palestinian Initiative for Peace," *Washington Post*, February 14, 1982, https://www.washingtonpost.com/archive/opinions/1982/02/14/a-palestinian-initiative-for-peace/12ada36d-ac5e-4682-971f-5ae68e018048/ (accessed July 10, 2023), archived at https://web.archive.org/web/20230712040732/https://www.washingtonpost.com/archive/opinions/1982/02/14/a-palestinian-initiative-for-peace/12ada36d-ac5e-4682-971f-5ae68e018048/.

give us our right to self-determination and to reach it in stages might be considered."[26]

In my still very naïve thinking, Freij's Peace Initiative fitted like hand in glove, with the Initiative I had suggested to Kreisky. Freij had added a decisive political component, I thought would make it worthwhile for the Socialist International, and particularly for Kreisky, Schmidt and Palme, to engage. Freij's suggestion to move in stages would make it possible to negotiate in detail the first phase of an economic development plan and economic empowerment of the Palestinian inhabitants of the West Bank and Gaza. And on the more political components of the proposed approach, I thought there were sufficient gains for both sides, at least to start negotiations.

Nothing the like happened. In June 1982, Israel started a war in Lebanon, and Kreisky dropped the entire idea like a hot potato.[27]

Joining Yossi Beilin's Group "Mashov"

Shimon Peres did not care too much about Kreisky and would ask me to arrange meetings between him and Palestinian leaders from the West Bank. And Yossi Beilin asked me to join his political group within the Labor Party. I was quickly promoted to be in charge of the Palestinian portfolio. It was quite a time-consuming position. I would travel often three times a week to Jerusalem, the West Bank, and Gaza. We met Palestinians from all streets of life and listened to them pro-actively asking questions. Yossi Beilin would come with me to meet political leaders. Naftali Blumenthal, who headed the Histadrut-owned Koor Industries, would join me in meeting Palestinian industrialists and business leaders. Finally, Boaz Karni would join me also in meetings with less prominent people. All these meetings aimed to prepare the confidential dialogue between Shimon Peres and the more conservative pro-Jordanian Palestinian leadership.

I prepared these meetings for Shimon Peres, participated in them, and would also be responsible for the follow-up work.

More importantly, however, was the desire of our small group of activists, to find a way out of the Israeli-Palestinian quagmire. We asked many questions. Yet, in essence, all these questions focused on two complementary policy concepts: First, should Israel withdraw unilaterally from the occupied

---

[26] Freij, "A Palestinian Initiative for Peace."
[27] Keisky accused the Israeli Labor Party under the leadership of Shimon Peres for having offered support to the War in Lebanon and prepared a political move aimed at ousting the Israeli Labor Party from the Socialist International. I criticized Kreisky too heavily, which ended our relationship.

territories to a secure and jointly-recognized border? Second, what would be necessary to convince the Palestinian leadership to negotiate based on the provisions laid out in the Camp David Accords?

The repeated answer we got to the first question was devastating: "*First, we do not believe that Israel will ever unilaterally withdraw; second, if Israel should do so, we Palestinians will first kill each other, and then we will kill you.*" The reference to a secure and jointly-recognized border was completely ignored, leading us to surmise that no Palestinian or Arab leader would ever agree to this. The answer to the second question was much simpler: "*Speak to the PLO.*"

The next question we asked was: what should be done, in case, negotiations would not start? Not unexpectedly we received a most supportive response to the ideas I had discussed with Dr. Kreisky: to introduce measures of economic empowerment of the Palestinians of the West Bank and Gaza, to be combined with a state-building economic development plan.

Yossi Beilin and I took the idea to the Americans. We convinced a young US diplomat, stationed in Tel Aviv, Dan Kurtzer, and he took it to Secretary of State Shultz. Thus, in November 1983, Shultz announced the "Quality of Life" policy, which had the two components that we thought were important: economic empowerment of an optimally united Palestinian leadership, combined with an economic development plan.[28] It did not work. Allowing the Palestinians of the West Bank and Gaza to obtain economic, and accordingly political, power opposed the interests of the three major external stakeholders: the PLO, Jordan, and Israel. All three killed the idea.

Peres' Early Proposals Are Rejected

I remember the first time, I was invited to a meeting in Peres' flat in Ramat Aviv, to attend a meeting with Mayor Rashad ash-Shawwa and his son Mansour from Gaza. It was November 1982. Sonja, Peres' spouse, had prepared a table full of the most delicious food. The two old men were too engaged in their discussion, and I was still too insecure to take a bite, as long as nobody else would do so. Thus, the food remained untouched. The substance of this dialogue was not more constructive. Peres asked Rashad Shawwa to suggest to the Palestinian leadership to accept the Camp David Accords as a basis for negotiations. Shawwa responded with a question: "what would we get out of it?" Peres answered: "You would obtain a veto on what

---

[28] Secretary of State George Shultz, address to the Council of Jewish Federations and Welfare Funds, Atlanta, November 21, 1983.

would happen on the West Bank and Gaza" indicating that this would make it possible to put a hold on settlements. Peres argued that negotiations on Palestinian self-government, proposed in the Camp David Accords of September 1978, were important for creating both a new reality and momentum toward a final peace agreement. On the issue of Palestinian land and water rights, he added that "the best you could achieve would be a joint Israeli-Palestinian administration based on a 50–50 approach," surmising that this would offer the Palestinians the right to veto Israeli expansion.

When I wrote the summary of the meeting, Peres crossed out the word "veto" and replaced it with the word "vote," meaning that, while not absolute, the Palestinians would have a clear say on the issue.[29] Regardless, I thought that this still meant the Palestinians would have a veto on settlement expansion and that they definitely should insist on achieving this in the proposed negotiations. At that time, about 6000 settlers were living in the West Bank. It was one of many historic opportunities lost. With only 6000 settlers living in the West Bank, an Israeli government could afford to agree to a complete settlement stop and possibly even relocate them. Ten years later in 1992 the settlement community had increased to about 90,000 and had gained substantial political clout. Already then, no easy solution was available.

The Americans Reshuffle the Cards

The United States under President Reagan's leadership (1980–1988), actively supported Peres' strategic approach of seeking an agreement with Jordan, and with Jordanian support negotiate Palestinian self-government, as laid out in the Camp David Accords. In April 1987, Peres, having the portfolio of Minister of Foreign Affairs, succeeded in concluding the "London Agreement" with King Hussein. The idea was to convene an International Conference and get negotiations on Palestinian self-government under way.[30] Alas, the Likud Prime Minister, Yitzchak Shamir opposed the agreement and

---

[29] Yair Hirschfeld, "Protocol of Peres and Shawwa Meeting," November 21, 1982, ארכיונים ואוספים אישיים/אוסף יאיר הירשפלד (trans. Archives and Personal Collections/Yair Hirschfeld Collection), ישראל גינזך המדינה /trans. Israel State Archives, Jerusalem.
[30] Avi Shlaim, *Lion of Jordan*, pp. 440–452 (Shlaim describes in much detail the negotiations and the content of the London Agreement).

it fell through.³¹ And Secretary of State Shultz refused to intervene, in order to save the London Agreement.

Several months later the Intifada started. America's Secretary of State Shultz launched another initiative which PM Shamir also rejected.³² When Shamir was asked by the Americans whether he would agree to any agreement on Palestinian self-government, the answer they gathered from his response was "No."³³

In order to "reshuffle the cards" and oblige Israel to fulfill obligations undertaken in signing the Camp David Accords of 1978, the United States decided to speak to the PLO and listen to them. On December 14, 1988, the beginning of an official dialogue between the USA and the PLO was announced.³⁴ In order to pre-empt a possible joint US-PLO proposal the pressure was now on Israel to lay out a policy concept, the Americans could accept.

Rabin, being Israel's Minister of Defense, understood by the summer of 1988, that there was no military solution to the intifada. Only a diplomatic approach offered a way out. Throughout the autumn of 1988 he met Palestinian notables and listened to them every week. He visited Faisal el-Husseini, the leading descendant of the most important aristocratic Palestinian family in prison and let it be known that he wanted to pursue negotiations with him.³⁵

Following the election of President George Bush, and the nomination of his Secretary of State, James Baker III, in 1988, Rabin suggested a four-point plan to allow for negotiations:

(1) Strengthening the peace between Israel and Egypt on the basis of the Camp David Accords;
(2) Establishing peace between Israel and other Arab countries;
(3) Finding a solution to the problem of Arab refugees;

---

³¹ Beilin met Secretary of State Shultz in Helsinki and asked him to convince Shamir to come along, in order to save the London Agreement. Shultz rejected to do so. This had important ramifications for the Oslo negotiations. When the negotiations became official, Peres ordered me to stop reporting to Kurtzer. The result was that the Americans had no idea of progress made in the negotiations in Norway.
³² Quandt, *Peace Process*, pp. 486–487 (the "Shultz Initiative" is reprinted here).
³³ Yair Hirschfeld, private interview with Daniel Kurtzer, January 13, 2012.
³⁴ Quandt, *Peace Process*; appendixes J and K, pp. 488–496.
³⁵ Boutros Abu Manneh, "The Husseynis: The Rise of a Notable Family in 18th Century Palestine," in D. Kushner ed., *Palestine in the Late Ottoman Period: Political, Social and Economic Transformation*, Jerusalem Yad Yizchak Ben Zvi, 1986, pp. 93–108 (an important description of the dominant role of the el-Husseini family in Jerusalem can be found here).

(4) Holding elections in the West Bank and Gaza Strip for a Palestinian leadership which will negotiate an interim agreement for self-government and a subsequent permanent solution.

With some changes, these four points became the Shamir-Rabin Plan and the guiding principles for the Madrid Conference.[36]

Close Bonds with Faisal el-Husseini and Hanan Ashrawi

Beilin and I knew that Rabin had met el-Husseini several times in prison and wanted to work together with him. Thus, I immediately, after his release in January 1989, would meet him and start to prepare what became the Notre Dame Meeting. I suggested, he should come to the meeting with a delegation from all the various groupings of the "inside" PLO".[37] Almost three years later, all the Palestinian participants at the Notre Dame Meeting would become members of their delegation to the Madrid Conference.

I understood from the very beginning that they needed green light from the PLO to go ahead. However, the idea of aiming to start negotiations with the Palestinian West Bank and Gaza leadership, in essence undermined the legitimacy of the PLO. The challenge was to find a way out of that Catch 22 situation. Dan Kurtzer would keep me and Beilin informed about the ongoing US-PLO dialogue in Tunis; I would meet Faisal el-Husseini to receive his account and would discuss with him in detail, Israeli politics, with the aim to explain, what might be possible, and what not. Nevertheless, we remained deadlocked.

Yossi Beilin decided to break the deadlock. A former Dutch Minister of Foreign Affairs, Max van der Stoel offered to arrange a meeting in Den Haag with PLO officials. I went to Paris to prepare and made it very clear that we were—by Israeli law—not allowed to meet the PLO delegation, yet, van der Stoel could go from one hotel to the other, and we could work, on agreed principles. We did this.[38] When knowledge of this meeting became known, Shamir asked Peres to dismiss Beilin. Peres refused.

---

[36] James A. Baker III, *The Politics of Diplomacy—Revolution, War and Peace 1989-1992*, G.P. Putnam's Sons, New York 1995, pp. 119-121 (for James Baker's description and comment of the Shamir Four Point Plan).

[37] The "inside PLO" described members residing in the West Bank and the Gaza Strip.

[38] Hirschfeld, *Track-Two Diplomacy*, pp. 66–94.

Personally, the visit to The Hague had some amusing parts to it. When Beilin and I arrived at Schiphol airport, he was immediately surrounded by a security cordon of armed soldiers. Two tanks moved outside the long corridors alongside us. I was pushed outside the security cordon around Beilin and left apparently exposed to a possible terrorist attack. Beilin camouflaged the meeting in The Hague with a parallel meeting with the Netherland's Ministry of Finance. He discussed various techniques of customs control. Although billed as Beilin's professional assistant, I had no idea and no interest in what they were talking about, but Beilin of course was fluent in the issues involved.

Coming back from the Netherlands' the dialogue with Faisal el-Husseini gained momentum and together we produced at the end of July, a first formula, which had two parts: A Palestinian delegation with eight members from the West Bank, Gaza and Jerusalem, and two members from the outside, was the first part. The Palestinians from the "outside" could be Palestinians who had been exiled by the Israeli Government, hence, Israeli could argue they were part of the "inside," and the Palestinians could say, they were from the "outside." This was not a technical matter. It was substance. The "inside" Palestinians wanted end of occupation and the creation of a State. The "outside" wanted to implement the right of return. Israel could negotiate with the "inside" leadership, who might include, Palestinians who had been in exile and had returned. The Israeli experience was that the World Zionist leadership, who resided outside of Israel, might help here and there, but they would not be given any decision-making power in Israel's affairs. Neither Rabin nor Peres was willing to give the Palestinian Diaspora decision-making power in negotiations with Israel.

It took another seven months of intense diplomatic activities led by Secretary of State, James Baker, by President Mubarak, Rabin and Peres, to convince PM Shamir and his Minister of Foreign Affairs, to accept a more carefully designed formula. Almost for every demand of Shamir or of Arens, to change the formula, I would go to see Hanan Ashrawi and Faisal el-Husseini and get their inputs. Give them to Beilin and Nimrod Novik, and to Peres and discuss it also with Dan Kurtzer. As part of the exercise, early in September 1989, I would arrange a first meeting between Faisal el-Husseini and Hanan Ashrawi with Shimon Peres. Miriam Hoexter, who had studied with me, offered her flat. Peres got lost in the building, but eventually got there. Bystanders thought, Peres was planning to buy a flat there and the prices would go up. It was in this meeting when Faisal el-Husseini convinced Peres to add an important sentence to the emerging negotiating formula, saying: "The Palestinians could consult, with whomever they wanted." It was actually Peres who coined this phrase the first time in an Interview he gave to the Jerusalem Post on September 15, 1989.[39]

It turned out that PM Shamir's and MFA Arens' support for the proposed formula to start negotiations with a Palestinian delegation was not good enough. The Likud Central Committee opposed and the initiative came to a first end. I continued to remain in touch with Faisal el-Husseini and Hanan Ashrawi all through the crisis leading to and during the First Persian Gulf War. And when the war was over, it was Beilin and I, who encouraged the Americans to meet again with el-Husseini and Ashrawi, which led to a meeting between the Palestinian team led by Faisal el-Husseini and Secretary of State James Baker III, at the American Colony, the East Jerusalem hotel, were most semi-secret meetings had taken place.[40]

James Baker III—now—when the first Persian Gulf War was won—was determined to set the Israeli-Arab peace process in motion. He would engage in a complex shuttle diplomacy, aimed at getting everybody, the Egyptians, the Syrians, the Lebanese, Saudi Arabia other Gulf States, Europe, and other members of the international community on board. Beilin, Novik, and I would discuss with el-Husseini and Ashrawi the emerging US-Israeli and the parallel US-Palestinian dialogue and offer advice, when asked for it.[41]

The Madrid Conference

When the Madrid Conference was being convened I was asked by Peres to go there, stay in close touch with the US, European, and Palestinian delegations and report to him about the unfolding events of the Conference. There was some drama: When the Syrian and Israeli delegation exchanged mutual accusations—the Syrian delegation threatened to leave, boasting that nobody else would dare to attend the planned bilateral negotiations, planned for the following Sunday. So I watched the work of the American peace team from Friday November 1, noon, over Shabbat until the late evening of November 2, when they knew, that the Jordanian-Palestinian delegation would attend the bilateral meeting with the Israeli delegation. James Baker, Dennis Ross, Daniel Kurtzer, and the others had pulled all possible strings to assure that the Jordanian-Palestinian delegation would come. Nobody knew

---

[39] Menachem Shalev and Jeff Black, "Spotlight: The Americans are the Critical Link," *Jerusalem Post (International Edition)*, September 15, 1989 (interview with Shimon Peres).
[40] Sari Nusseibeh and Anthony David, *Once Upon a Country—a Palestinian Life*, Halban, London 2009, pp. 338–343.
[41] James A. Baker III, *The Politics of Diplomacy—Revolution, War and Peace, 1989–1992*, Putnam, New York 1995, pp. 411–513.

whether the Syrian delegation would stay, or would leave. In case the Syrians would leave, the Lebanese would leave too. The next morning, the Syrians had packed their suitcases but waited to see if the Jordanian-Palestinian delegation would dare to come. They did. In the evening the Syrian team met with the Israeli team. A month later, in December, multilateral negotiations started in Moscow. The peace process was once again underway.

When, in Madrid, I visited the headquarters of the Palestinian delegation in Hotel Victoria, I saw what the formula "to consult with whomever they want" meant: members of the PLO were everywhere in evidence. Indeed, the entire delegation had been flown to Tunis, to receive instructions from Yasser Arafat. El-Husseini's personal greatness was that in order to get the negotiations going and sustain them he was willing to swallow repeated humiliations by Chairman Arafat.

The Gulf War of January–February 1991 had completely undermined the standing of the PL0 and of Arafat on the regional and global level and upgraded the political importance of el-Husseini. He was given an open door at the White House and everywhere else, while Arafat was not allowed to come yet out of the closet. The picture below, showing el-Husseini and Ashrawi conferring with President Bush in the White House, illustrates more than words can do his important role in ensuring the Palestinian delegation to participate in the Madrid Conference. The story this picture does not tell is that its publication had a substantial—but very negative—impact on the relationship between Arafat and el-Husseini.

Pictured President George H. W. Bush (the father) with Faisal El-Husseini and Hanan Ashrawi

When I met el-Husseini in the night between November 2 and 3, 1991, at the Victoria Hotel in Madrid, I understood the tremendously precarious situation. El-Husseini and the entire Palestinian delegation had just come back from Tunis, where they had been given instructions by Arafat. I was told (by other members of the delegation) that Jamil Tarifi, a Palestinian notable, told Arafat in front of everybody else: "there is a traitor among us who conspires with the Israelis behind our back." He pointed at Faisal el-Husseini. Undoubtedly, this scene was stage-managed on Arafat's instructions.

Before that encounter in Madrid (in the night between November 2 and 3), I had hundreds of hours of meetings with el-Husseini. I never before and never afterward saw him so depressed and exasperated. He had told me before that after the Gulf War the Saudis had offered him an open check and told him to write in any sum he might need to create an organization that would be independent of the PLO. The Saudis deeply resented Arafat's support for Saddam Hussein during the first Gulf War. El-Husseini rejected the Saudi offer. He explained to me that the memory of the events of 1936–39, when one Palestinian faction would fight the other, was reason enough to reject the offer. El-Husseini was probably also afraid of being assassinated, although he always would put his personal interest in second place. Arafat's suspicion of el-Husseini would turn out to become a major impediment for negotiations to come. Internal Palestinian rivalries, and the tremendous internal division of Palestinian society, tended to paralyze any necessary Palestinian flexibility in negotiations. Worse, internal divisions became a major factor enhancing terror.

The above picture showing el-Husseini and Ashrawi sitting together with President George Bush (the father) illustrates that in speaking to the American leadership el-Husseini and Ashrawi were very effective. However, they had very little or no real decision-taking power. For the Israeli negotiating team, this meant that concessions made in a dialogue with el-Husseini and Hanan Ashrawi would create a constructive atmosphere, however, but that they could not themselves make any reliable commitments the Israeli side needed to obtain.

Twelve years of "on the job learning" prepared me, for a decisive next phase. In retrospect, Kreisky taught me many of the important lessons: He opened the world of diplomacy for me; showed me how important analytically accurate innovative ideas could be; and demonstrated the need to be aware of the many pitfalls on the way.

Suggested Additional Reading

Kreisky and Austrian Social-Democracy during the First and Second Republic (1918–1985).

Bruno Kreisky *Zwischen den Zeiten—Erinnerungen an fuef Jahrzehnte*; Siedler, Berlin 1986.

And: *Im Strom der Politik: Der Memoiren zweiter Teil;* Kremayer, Wien 1988.

Kreisky's description of Austrian history and politics was almost identical to the understanding and beliefs of my parents. In many ways his description represents the secular views of the Austrian Jewish community before World War II. After World War II this was not anymore the case.

The Origins of the Israeli-Arab Conflict

Neville Mandel *The Arabs and Zionism before World War I*; University of California P. Berkely, 1976 (Mandel provides a comprehensive and balanced description of the origins of the Israeli-Arab Conflict and efforts to build bridges early on, however, with little success).

David Fromkin *A Peace to End All Peace: The Fall of the Ottoman Empire and the Creation of the Modern Middle East*; MacMillian, London 1989 (Fromkin's account is the most read classic and an essential read for any student of modern Middle Eastern history).

David Ben Gurion *My Talks with Arab Leaders*. Keter, Jerusalem 1997. Ben Gurion's account addresses the depth of the conflict; his account illustrates good will on both sides and lack of capability to turn this into a political reality, due to the fact that the nationalist needs of each side left little room for compromise.

Walid Khalidi (ed.) *All That Remains: The Palestinian Villages Occupied and Depopulated by Israel in 1948;* Institute for Palestinian Studies, Washington D.C. 1992. This book provides a description of the physical extension of the Naqba, the Palestinian Catastrophe of 1947–1949.

The Emergence of Israel and the Palestinian National Identity

Anita Shapira *Israel—A History*; Chicago U.P. 2014; Shapira offers a comprehensive description of the historic developments leading to the creation of the

State of Israel, its long state-building process before 1948, and its internal and external struggles since then.

Rashid Khalidi *Palestinian Identity—The Construction of Modern National Consciousness*; New York, Columbia U.P. 1997. Khalidi's book describes the emergence, the self-denial, and the revival of Palestinian nationalism.

Israeli Foreign Policy After 1967

Michael Brecher *Decision's in Israel's Foreign Policy*; New Haven Yale U/P/ 1975. Brechers offers a detailed account of the dilemmas and decisions of Israel shortly after the Six-Day war of 1967. Any Israeli Peace activist at the time had to read and study Brecher's account, in order to understand what action might be acceptable to Israel's senior decision-makers, and what not.

Yehoshafat Harkaby, *Israel's Fateful Decisions*, Tauris, London 1988. The Hebrew version of this book was published 1986 and had a major impact on the thinking of Beilin, Novik, Karni, and me. Harkaby's message was to reach an Israeli-Palestinian agreement before it would turn into a religious conflict. Today, the book reads as if it were written just now.

Nadav Safran *Israel the Embattled Ally*; Harvard U.P. Cambridge 1978; Safran offers a very comprehensive description of the prolonged traumas and fears of Israeli society and its impact on policies. The book also offers some important insights referring to the first phases of an American led unfolding peace process.

Some Important Palestinian and Israeli Personal Accounts

Hanan Ashrawi *This Side of Peace—A Personal Account*; Simon and Schuster, New York 1995; Ashrawi played a leading role in the ongoing peace effort, particularly between February 1989, when the Israeli-Palestinian dialogue intensified and lead the way to the Madrid Conference, and eventually to the negotiations in Norway in 1993.

Ahmed Qurie (Abu Ala') *From Oslo to Jerusalem—the Palestinian Story of the Secret Negotiations;* Tauris, London 2006. In substance Abu Ala's account does not differ from my narrative. The vantage point, of course, is different. Abu Ala' documents convincingly that the negotiations were led on both sides with the best intentions. Later Israeli and Palestinian accounts accusing the other side to have intentional manipulated the negotiations to fail the other are proven to be wrong.

Robert Slater *Rabin of Israel—Warrior for Peace, 1922–1995*; Harper, New York, 1996; The story of Rabin's life, his peace efforts during his first premiership, 1974–1977; his action as Minister of Defense, during most of the 1980ies, and his commitment to reach an agreement with the Palestinians during his second premiership, 1992–1995, are important reading. A more in-depth description of the unfolding of his relationship with Arafat still needs to be researched and written.

Shimon Peres *Battling for Peace Memoirs*; Weidenfeld and Nicolson, London 1995; Peres tells his life story, the emergence, and development of his political and ideological thinking. Describing the Oslo channel he added some important information that at the time was not known to me.

Yossi Beilin *Israel: A Concise Political History*; St. Martin's Press, New York 1992; During the 1980s Beilin played a major role in starting to re-evaluate, criticize, and change the political narrative and thinking of Israel's founding fathers.

The Role of US Middle Eastern Policies and the Promotion of the Peace Process (1967–1993)

James A. Baker III *The Politics of Diplomacy—Revolution, War and Peace, 1989–1992*; Putnam, New York 1995. For anybody studying the period after the fall of the Berlin Wall, the First Persian Gulf War, and the Unfolding of the Middle Eastern Peace Process, this book is an absolute must. Baker's description of the 1989–1990 effort to get Israeli-Palestinian negotiations going is essential to understand, why, and how our work behind the scenes was so important. His description of the diplomatic effort necessary to bring the relevant Middle Eastern players to the negotiating table at the Madrid Conference; how to turn the Conference into a success; and allow for continued bilateral and multilateral negotiations is not only important for historians, but similarly for policy planners for possible future action.

Henry Kissinger *White House Years*; Little Brown, Boston 1979; chapters. 10, 14, 15, 30, and *Years of Upheaval*; Little Brown, Boston 1982; chapters 6, 11, 12, 13, 14, 16, 17, 18, 19, 20, 21, 22, 23, 24. Kissinger's account of the unfolding of America's Middle Eastern policy between 1967 and 1975 is the decisive source essential to understand the emerging thinking and role of the United States in the Middle East and Israel's contribution to the growth of American influence.

William B. Quandt *Peace Process: Amerian Diplomacy and the Arb-Israeli Conflict Since 1967*; Brookings Institute, Washington D.C. 1998; This is the most quoted classic describing the peace process from its beginning until the conclusion of the Oslo Accords. Quandt represents the classic view of State Department thinking. The book is particularly valuable due to its many appendixes.

Egypt's Role in the Peace-Making Process

Anwar el-Sadat, *In Search of Identity—An Autobiography;* Harper and Row, New York, 1977; President Sadat's autobiography is important reading, although it does not reflect sufficiently his all-dominant role in promoting the peace process from 1970 onward, deciding to go to war, in 1973, and then moving ahead by what he called "bit by bit" leading the way to peace between Israel and Egypt and the conclusion of framework principles for a comprehensive peace in the Middle East. His strategic thinking has impacted on Middle Eastern policies and the peace process, long after he was assassinated in 1981.

Mahmoud Riad *The Struggle for Peace in the Middle East;* Quanton Books, New Yorik 1982; Mahmoud Riad served as Egyptn's Minister of Foreign Affairs, and later as Secretary General of the Arab League. He was critical of President Sadat's peace policy, which makes the reading of his memoirs particularly important.

4

From the Madrid Conference to the Conclusion of Oslo

The Importance of Earned Trust

The two years between the Madrid Conference in October 1991 and the signing of the Israel-PLO Declaration of Principles on the White House Lawn in September 1993 were marked by triumph and success. However, it was the twelve years of apprenticeship prior that provided me with the necessary preconditions for these promising developments:

Firstly, I gained the trust of Shimon Peres and the unwavering support of Yossi Beilin. Additionally, I developed an intimate knowledge and relationship with senior members of Israel's various security authorities. The confidence and credibility I earned through dialogue with Palestinian decision-makers and negotiators were crucial. They shared their negotiating papers, valued my suggestions, and engaged in brainstorming sessions to find solutions to seemingly unbridgeable conflicting interests. Working with Kreisky, I also learned to observe changing power dynamics and the art of diplomacy. Lastly, my friendship with Dan Kurtzer and the resulting dialogue with American leadership proved invaluable.

Several months before the Madrid Conference, the Economic Cooperation Foundation (ECF) was founded. Initially, it was merely an unpaid desk at my home in Ramat Yishai with no budget for action. Nonetheless, I was given the opportunity to put all my experiences into a study commissioned by the European Union titled "Israel, the Palestinians and the Middle East From Dependence to Interdependence." When I submitted the study a year later, it became a key factor in our success.

Eberhard Rhein, the head of the Middle East desk at the European Union in Brussels, held significant decision-making power at the time. After reading my study, he directed those seeking funding from Israel to consult with me first.[1] From that point onward, whenever ECF needed funding, I would travel to Brussels, discuss the proposed project with Rhein in a one-hour session, and receive immediate feedback on funding availability.

The study I prepared for the EU was important not only due to its findings but also for its impact. I was fully aware of the difficulties that lay ahead. The study's opening assumption stated:

> The inherent causes of instability in the Middle East are too strong, as to enable a sudden and complete change from the old political order to a new one. Rather, a long and protracted struggle for a new and more stable order may be anticipated. As banal as it may sound, the success of the forces of pragmatism will depend on finding and implementing pragmatic solutions to existing conflicts, as well as assuring failure of political, terrorist or military tactics of the radical camp.[2]

The study delved into the details of "The Threat of Arab Radicalism and Militant Islamic Fundamentalism." I explained how militant radicalism drew strength from four complementary functions: defending traditional Islamic society, fulfilling social tasks through mosques and their networks where governments had failed, the legitimate desire to replace corrupt and ineffective leadership, and the hope offered to people living in destitution and distress through a messianic message.[3]

I highlighted how these tendencies could easily become a diplomatic threat to Israel. Additionally, I underscored the military threat by referencing Pakistan's and Iran's attempts to develop military nuclear capacities, as well as their stockpiling of chemical and biological weapons.

---

[1] A group of economist from Beer Sheba and the Hebrew University did consult me, and then together with ECF received a grant of many hundred thousand Euro's for what became a foreplay of Israeli-Palestinian negotiations on an economic agreement. When the Israel-PLO Declaration of Principles was concluded, the study had not been completed, and Israeli as well Palestinian participants of the study group became official negotiators. This ended the communication between them. It had a negative impact on the final product, nevertheless Eberhard Rhein remained pleased with the outcome.

[2] The final research report was submitted to the European Commission in September 1992. Yair Hirschfeld, "Israel, the Palestinians and the Middle East: From Dependency to Interdependence," *Hirschfeld Khoury-DeConcini Papers*, Substack, forthcoming (originally written in September 1992), pp. 4, https://hkdpapers.substack.com/p/israel-the-palestinians-and-the-middle-east (hereafter in this chapter cited as Hirschfeld, "Israel, the Palestinians and the Middle East," *Hirschfeld Khoury-DeConcini Papers*).

[3] Hirschfeld, "Israel, the Palestinians and the Middle East," *Hirschfeld Khoury-DeConcini Papers*, pp. 1–4, 139–145.

Moreover, I stressed the importance of understanding the asymmetry of Israeli and Palestinian interests. The Palestinians required significant concessions from Israel, while having little to offer in return, except for the additional legitimacy Israel would gain from engaging in peace-making efforts.

Israel stood to benefit significantly from improvements in its relationships with the wider Arab and Muslim region. This perspective led me to propose a paradigm shift that differed substantially from the one established at the Camp David Accords in 1978. I suggested that the initial step should be to negotiate an agreement on Palestinian self-government, aligning with the Camp David framework.

After that, however, the next focus should be on establishing a Middle Eastern Security Organization (MESO). Instead, the Camp David framework pushed the parties to immediately delve into negotiations on all core issues. Establishing an MESO before this would help to ensure regional security and stability against radical militant forces, which I saw as the largest threat to preserving the negotiations. Additionally, a Middle Eastern Community of Water, Energy, and Tourism (MECWET) should be created to further foster regional cooperation and coordination. Only after achieving these necessary regional understandings would there be a real chance for successful negotiations on the core issues of the conflict.

In an effort to garner support for this idea, I collaborated with Tom Phillips (now Sir Tom Phillips), who was serving in the British Embassy in Tel Aviv as the Deputy Chief of Mission (DCM) at the time. Together, we drafted a paper and selectively circulated it among diplomatic circles. However, the response was predominantly negative. While the US was open to exploring alternative approaches to implementing the Camp David Accords, as a cosigner, they were not willing to adopt an entirely new approach.

The most crucial aspect of the study was outlining three different negotiating options and gathering critical feedback from various Palestinians, as well as Israeli strategists, including civil servants working under Prime Minister Shamir's guidance.

1. The minimalist approach, largely aligned with the Rabin-Shamir Plan, proposed detailed arrangements for elections and agreed-upon actions to support economic development before negotiating the final powers of the self-government agreement.
2. The maximalist approach envisioned negotiating a settlement-freeze agreement initially, followed by the establishment of three working groups focusing on the economy, security, and elections.

3. The compromise model suggested a mechanism for a gradual and orderly transfer of authority to an increasingly empowered Palestinian authority.

The compromise model found acceptance from both sides and served as a blueprint for the subsequent negotiations in Norway. A Palestinian provided valuable input by correcting my text with red ink, replacing certain terms with more acceptable ones, offering the necessary language. Another Palestinian presented me with a chart outlining perceived Israeli-Palestinian negotiating positions, shedding light on the possibilities of gradual compromise. Importantly, without explicitly stating it, the chart demonstrated that while certain Palestinian demands could be postponed, they could not be relinquished entirely.

The chart also illustrated the complexity of the issues that would need to be addressed during the negotiations:

Issue	Israeli position	Palestinian position
The substance of the agreement	Agree on autonomy arrangements	Recognize right to self-determination
Connection between interim agreement and permanent agreement	Interim stage to be open-ended	Interim agreement to be linked to permanent agreement
Terms of reference	No reference to the security council resolutions or to the camp David accords	UN security council resolution 242 and resolution 338 to apply to all territories
Source of authority	Will be military government; Israel will transfer some authority	Palestinian self-government
Powers of self-government	Powers of self-government to be based on full coordination with Israeli and Jordanian governments; residual powers stay with Israel	Unlimited, with any exception to it powers qualified and agreed to
Territorial extension	No territorial dimension	Jurisdiction over all territories of the West Bank, East Jerusalem, and the Gaza strip
Legislative powers	Functional administrative arrangements	Complete legislative and judicial powers

(continued)

(continued)

Issue	Israeli position	Palestinian position
Jurisdiction	Jurisdiction limited to people, not to land and not to natural resources	Full jurisdiction over land, natural resources, water, subsoil, territorial sea, airspace, and all Palestinian inhabitants
Executive power	Limited executive powers only as stated in agreement; Israel maintains residual powers with military government	Full executive power without foreign intervention
Foreign policy	Foreign policy powers opposed for the self-government regime	Foreign policy powers demanded for the self-government regime
Judiciary	Palestinians will have the right to participate in the administration of justice	Fully independent Palestinian judiciary
Police force and security	Responsibility for security stays with Israel, with Palestinians to cooperate on granting public order	Strong Palestinian police force responsible for public order and security
Peacekeeping forces	No room for the UN	UN peacekeeping
Standing committee	Rejection of the standing committee	A five-member standing committee demanded
Date of elections	Israel will not set a date	An election date must be set
Purpose of elections	To establish a twelve-person administrative council	To establish a 180-member legislative assembly
Function of elected body	Exercise limited administrative functions	Exercise the full national and political rights of the Palestinians
Laws defining campaigning for elections	Prepared to negotiate these issues	Demand to rescind all existing orders and regulations which prohibit assembly, movement, participation, and campaigning

(continued)

(continued)

Issue	Israeli position	Palestinian position
Administrative detention and return of deportees	Israel does not relate to this point (under the prime minister, this issue will be negotiated in a different channel)	Demand an end to administrative detention and demand the return of deportees
Participation of Palestinian inhabitants of Jerusalem in elections	Palestinian inhabitants of Jerusalem should not participate; later might vote by proxy	Palestinian inhabitants of Jerusalem can vote and be nominated as candidates

It proved to be an invaluable preparation for the upcoming negotiations.

Rabin Becomes Israel's Prime Minister

We all celebrated Rabin's victory in 1992. During the campaign, he made a significant promise to conclude an agreement on autonomy with the Palestinians within one year. Yossi Beilin managed to include an article in the party platform that outlined conditions for legalizing contacts with the PLO. Prime Minister, Rabin insisted on retaining full control over negotiations with the Palestinians, effectively taking this responsibility away from Peres, who was his Minister of Foreign Affairs.

However, despite their mutual dislike, both leaders understood the need to work together and signed an agreement outlining how they would cooperate. The agreement granted Rabin exclusive control over bilateral negotiations with the Palestinians, while Peres was tasked with overseeing the multilateral negotiations. My role was to collaborate with el-Husseini and Ashrawi in formulating a framework for the multilateral talks.

After numerous meetings, often held at Hanan Ashrawi's home, she handed me a suggested formula, written on a yellow piece of paper, regarding the participation of Palestinians from the Diaspora in the multilateral negotiations. Peres accepted the formula, and I contacted Ashrawi multiple times a day, seeking the final approval. However, it never came. Instead, about a week later, Osama el-Bas, President Mubarak's advisor on Middle Eastern affairs, came to Jerusalem to meet with Peres. He presented a different formula for Palestinian participation in the multilateral talks, one that Arafat had given him. This formula was less favorable to the Palestinians than the proposal I had received from Ashrawi.

The message was clear: Arafat would block any proposal put forth by the internal Palestinian leadership and, in order to make progress, would offer more lenient conditions to facilitate Israeli acceptance. This seemingly minor incident made it evident to Rabin, Peres, and myself that we needed to establish a direct dialogue with Arafat and his people. Rabin, in a public speech at the end of November, compared Arafat to Nahum Goldmann, the leader of the World Zionist Organization. This depiction, vastly different from that of a terrorist, legitimized dialogue with Arafat.

At that time, we realized that the high expectations of reaching an agreement had been unfounded. The negotiations in Washington quickly reached an impasse. I received a detailed Israeli policy paper preparing for the negotiations with the Palestinians.[4] The gap between the parties was too wide, the issues too complex, and neither side had much room for maneuver. It was a classic situation where discreet track-two negotiations were necessary to find a way forward. In every meeting I had, el-Husseini and Ashrawi encouraged me to initiate such a channel.

Rabin's comparison of Arafat to Nahum Goldmann gave me confidence that he would be open to offering his support. I received a paper from Europeans and the Palestinians, written by Abu Ala', on the "Development of the Palestinian Economy and Regional Economic Cooperation."[5] It gave me hope that I might find common ground with him. Terje Larsen, a Norwegian visitor who offered his services to Beilin and me, told me that I would get along well with Abu Ala'. I was curious to see if that would be the case.

Attending a conference on water in Switzerland, I sought advice from Sari Nusseibeh. I expressed to him the challenges we faced as Israelis when dealing with the Palestinians due to internal divisions and infighting, making it nearly impossible to reach understanding. It felt like reaching out to one boat, then another, only to end up falling into the water. Sari suggested that I speak to three key individuals: Arafat, for psychological reasons; Abu Mazen, to get

---

[4] "Draft for Consideration: Informal Concept of the Interim Self-Government Arrangements—Building Blocks for Agreement," September 8, 1992, יוזמת לשיתוף פעולה כלכלי ולהסכם ביניים עם הפלסטינים (trans. An initiative for economic cooperation and an interim agreement with the Palestinians) (folder name), ISA-Privatecollections-NA-001rt7w (new folder identifier), "5821/13–פ" (trans. P 5514/1) (old folder identifier), pp. 148–158, ארכיונים ואוספים אישיים/אוסף יאיר הירשפלד (trans. Archives and personal collections/Yair Hirschfeld collection), ישראל גינוך המדינה (trans. Israel State Archives), Jerusalem, https://www.archives.gov.il/archives/Archive/0b07170688f2f0fd/File/0b07170689eaacf4/Item/090717068a008a7b (accessed June 28, 2023), archived at https://web.archive.org/web/20230712041155/https://www.archives.gov.il/archives/Archive/0b07170688f2f0fd/File/0b07170689eaacf4/Item/090717068a008a7b (hereafter cited as Hirschfeld, "Draft for Consideration," Yair Hirschfeld Collection).

[5] Ahmed Qurie (Abu Ala'), "Statement to the Middle East Peace Multilateral Negotiations; Working Group on Development of the Palestinian Economy and Regional Economic Cooperation," *Hirschfeld Khoury-DeConcini Papers, Substack*, forthcoming (originally written May 11, 1992), pp. 1–10, https://hkdpapers.substack.com/p/statement-to-the-middle-east-peace-negociations.

the PLO organization on board; and Faisal el-Husseini, to gain support from the internal leadership and the people.[6]

Planning a trip to London to discuss a potential ECF project on Israeli-Palestinian labor relations with Terje Larsen, I informed Hanan Ashrawi that I would be willing to meet with Abu Ala'. I asked her to have him contact my cousin's home in Northern London, where I would be staying, so we could arrange a meeting. Ashrawi and el-Husseini informed Akram Haniye in Tunis about the plan. Upon my arrival at my cousin's home, I discovered that Abu Ala' had already made several phone calls. Without seeking permission from anyone, I agreed to meet with him. This meeting was scheduled before my meeting with Terje Larsen, who had shown himself to be trustworthy and had offered us any assistance we might need. He would keep his promise.[7]

The initial meeting with Abu Ala' was friendly, but not more than that. It was friendly enough, however, for us to agree to meet again later that same day, in the evening.[8] I decided to inform Yossi Beilin about the meeting, so I went to see him at the hotel where he was staying. As I arrived at the hotel's entrance, Haim Ramon spotted me and asked what I was doing there, adding "Yair is surely meeting the PLO here." I denied it, of course. Beilin was pleased with my account of the meeting and gave his full support for further engagement. Abu Ala', Afif Safiye, and I then met at the Ritz. It was an evening with a lively dance band, and the music was quite loud, so we had to shout to understand each other.

Abu Ala's description of this second meeting reads as follows: "*My interest and curiosity were excited by the earnestness of Hirschfeld's desire to continue with our meetings, when Hirschfeld suggested a third encounter, I asked where he proposed this should be held. To my astonishment, he replied 'In Oslo, for example' …He suggested that we could have wide-ranging talks with an unrestricted agenda, in which each side could explore the other's position on a range*

---

[6] Sari Nusseibeh and Anthony David, *Once Upon a Country—a Palestinian Life*, Halban, London 2009, pp. 363.

[7] In various accounts it has wrongly been said that the Norwegians arranged the first meeting between Abu Ala' and me. Hanan Ashrawi tells the story as it was. Hanan Ashrawi, *This Side of Peace—A Personal Account*, Simon and Schuster, New York 1995, pp. 267.

[8] Ahmed Qurie (Abu Ala'), *From Oslo to Jerusalem—The Palestinian Story of the Secret Negotiations*, Tauris, London 2006, pp. 39–43. Abu Ala' describing the first meeting writes: "Though caution and reserve dominated the atmosphere, we stayed together for almost two hours. As an uncontroversial opening, Hirschfeld spoke about the impression of my economic paper. We then moved on quickly to the subject of the negotiations taking place in Washington…I felt I had overcome my initial antipathy to the idea of talking to the enemy. I agreed at once, when he suggested that we meet again."

of political, economic and social issues...On the basis of this meeting, my conviction was that these contacts were a joint American-Israeli attempt to achieve a breakthrough at the stalled Washington talks."[9]

We decided to meet in Norway. The following day, I met with Dan Kurtzer and provided him with a detailed account of what had transpired. Kurtzer emphasized the importance of creating connecting lines between all the parties involved. He stressed that any dialogue with the PLO should support the talks in Washington rather than replace them. The negotiation structure established at the Madrid Conference, combining bilateral and multilateral negotiations, needed to be maintained. This would allow the possibility of an unofficial Israeli-PLO dialogue to act as a pacemaker, injecting energy into the peace-making efforts.

Track-Two Negotiations Start in Norway

The track-two negotiations in Norway began after the law prohibiting meetings with PLO officials was repealed in January. Ron Pundik and I traveled to Norway for the meetings, having prepared together in advance. We received a 13-point proposal for an agreement from Ashrawi, but it was clear that there was still a significant gap between the parties. I submitted the paper and ideas how to respond to Peres.[10] I understood that this track-two effort was different from previous ones I had learned about. Instead of merely testing a policy the Israeli government was not interested in pursuing, our aim was to fulfill a policy promise made by Prime Minister Rabin before the elections. I was well aware of the Palestinian demands that Rabin and Peres were not willing to accept, as well as the need to find common ground for an agreement.

However, in order to succeed, it was crucial to ensure that Rabin would not oppose our efforts. There were several delicate balancing acts that needed to be performed:

---

[9] Qurie, *From Oslo to Jerusalem*, pp. 43.

[10] Yair Hirschfeld and Ron Pundak, "Yair Hirschfeld and Ron Pundak to Foreign Minister Shimon Peres," January 14, 1993, "9/6262-פ" (trans. P 6262/9) (old folder identifier), ארכיונים ואוספים אישיים/אוסף יאיר הירשפלד (trans. Archives and Personal Collections/Yair Hirschfeld Collection), ישראל גינזך המדינה (trans. Israel State Archives), Jerusalem, https://catalog.archives.gov.il/wp-content/uploads/2022/12/Hirschfeld-and-Pundak-to-Peres-14-1-1993-P-5825-10-1.pdf (accessed June 28, 2023), archived at https://web.archive.org/web/20230712041910/https://catalog.archives.gov.il/wp-content/uploads/2022/12/Hirschfeld-and-Pundak-to-Peres-14-1-1993-P-5825-10-1.pdf.

- I had to make it clear that whatever commitments I made were of an academic and private nature and did not bind the Israeli government. At the same time, I had to assure the official Palestinian delegation that our discussions were relevant and could pave the way to an agreement.
- I had to reject most of the Palestinian demands and establish "Red Lines" that could not be crossed, while convincing our dialogue partners of our determination to reach understanding.
- It was important to convey to Abu Ala' how we could persuade the Israeli officials to come on board, even though I myself did not know how the discussions would unfold.

To obtain Rabin's approval, Pundik and I wrote a very positive report of the meeting, emphasizing Abu Ala's proposal for a "Gaza First" agreement combined with a "Marshall Plan." As far as I recall, Peres reported the first meeting to Rabin, not at a later stage, and received his approval. I learned later that Rabin did not believe we would be able to break the deadlock. However, he did hope that the dialogue in Norway would allow to renew the Washington talks that had been broken off, without giving in to Hamas' demands that were being seconded by Arafat.[11]

I also learned from later discussions with Major General Uri Sagie, the head of IDF Intelligence at the time, how the (untrue) narrative developed claiming that Rabin was unaware of our discussions in Norway. Israeli intelligence collected information from Palestinian reports about the negotiations, and other senior military leaders were informed. They asked General Sagie to speak with Rabin about it. Rabin, determined to prevent any leaks, informed Sagie that he was aware and instructed him not to report back to the other generals.[12]

We found a relatively simple way to reconcile the need for deniability regarding the relevance of our discussions while establishing the necessary credibility. Before each meeting in Norway, Beilin and I would arrange a meeting between Peres, el-Husseini, and Ashrawi. We ensured that Pundik's and my participation in these meetings was mentioned in the protocols

---

[11] In December 1992, Hamas had kidnapped and murdered an Israeli police officer, Nissim Toledano. Rabin then expelled more than 400 Hamas extremists to Lebanon. This again caused the Palestinians to break off negotiations in Washington. Hamas and Arafat demanded their unconditional return to the West Bank.

[12] Major General (ret.) Sagie, his wife Gila, Ruthi and I, and a group of other friends meet regularly every three-to-four months. Uri Sagie gave all of us a very lively account of Rabin's fear, knowledge of the Oslo talks would spread and his order to keep all the related knowledge the Israeli Intelligence would gather, absolutely secret.

prepared by the Palestinians, which we knew would be sent to Tunis by el-Husseini.

This approach had an important side effect: Abu Ala' would occasionally use Peres' language, and I might echo some of the remarks made by el-Husseini or Ashrawi, thus creating an impression of continuity and alignment between the different parties.

It was clear to me that establishing clear Red Lines and rejecting many of the demands put forward by Abu Ala' were crucial for the success of our negotiations. I knew what to do: turn the other side into the "demandeur." The goal was to position the other side as the one wanting the agreement more, allowing us to state our terms and enable them to achieve what they hoped for.

However, this approach was exactly what Abu Ala' had employed in the initial meeting in Norway. He proposed a "Gaza First" deal connected to a Marshall Plan and economic cooperation projects, aligned with Peres' thinking, with the expectation that this would be the Palestinian concession and, in return, Ashrawi's Thirteen Points, with slight modifications, would be acceptable. This "Give and Take" approach was not workable.

Without knowing exactly how far Rabin was willing to go to reach an agreement, we adopted various approaches to make it clear that the positions I outlined in the discussions represented the optimal concessions the Israeli government might be willing to grant. Our lack of official positions allowed us to act as "advisors" to the Palestinian team, providing them with insights into what might be achievable for them and what might not.

We emphasized that the Party Platform of the Israeli Labor Party indicated what Rabin could agree to and what he could not. We made it clear that Pundik and I, as private individuals, were strong supporters of the Palestinian cause and were dedicated to paving the way for an agreed Two-State Solution, striving to obtain optimal conditions not only for Israel but also for the Palestinians.

To test optimal conditions and proposals, we employed the "waste paper principle," which allowed us to propose ideas, test them internally, and if they faced significant rejection, seek alternative approaches. We also emphasized to the Palestinian team that whatever we collectively came up with, they should be aware that Beilin, Peres, and, most importantly, Rabin might make additional demands. The key was to create a gradual process toward a two-state solution.[13]

---

[13] Early in June 1993, Rabin asked Yoel Singer to review progress that had been made in the negotiations in Norway. I was given fifteen minutes to explain to him what we had achieved. I told him that adopting the principle of gradualism we had solved most problems, and it allowed

The red lines were tested later in August at a critical stage of the negotiations.

On August 6, 1993, after negotiations had been broken off, I was sent to Paris to receive a final "Palestinian proposal." The fact that we had created detailed Red Lines early on made it possible for me to negotiate an entire night with Abu Ala', in order to assist him in submitting a "Palestinian proposal" Rabin and Peres could (and did) accept.

Abu Ala' describes the meeting in Paris, as follows:

> *At this meeting final decisions were supposed to be made concerning all the controversial points that were still outstanding after both sides had conducted their reviews of the latest draft of the Declaration of Principles and its annexes....Much was accomplished during the Paris meeting which lasted for seven hours, but we still failed to reach full agreement on all the outstanding points. However, we felt that the road to agreement was now more open than ever before.*[14]

Defining the process ahead was both necessary and risky. I had to ensure that false expectations were not created that could derail the process at any given moment. We needed to exchange ideas, work on a text, identify common ground, recognize remaining gaps, and think of possible ways to bridge them. This would be the "fact-finding phrase." I understood that Abu Ala's goal was to pave the way for official negotiations with Peres and Rabin, which would be the "breakthrough phase."

Additionally, Rabin and Peres would require proof of the Tunis leadership's commitment to accept decisive Israeli demands, which would be the "legitimizing phase." I assumed that in order for Abu Ala' to ask Arafat to make visible concessions necessary for Rabin and Peres, he needed some form of

---

Israel to transfer only those authorities, that would not undermine Israel's security, but rather would built a partnership with the Palestinians. Singer' argues in his report to Shimon Peres that the concept of the five-year transition period will start immediately with the signing of the Declaration of Principles while gradually transferring powers is extremely positive. However, there is room for improvements in order to deal with issues that were not addressed and to correct the wording. Joel Singer, "Joel Singer to Foreign Minister Shimon Peres," June 5, 1993, "אוסלו 1992–1993" (trans. Oslo 1992–1993), ISA-Privatecollections-NA-001nwgb (new file identifier), "5513/1-פ" (trans. P 5513/1) (old file identifier), ארכיונים ואוספים אישיים/אוסף יאיר הירשפלד (trans. Archives and Personal Collections/Yair Hirschfeld Collection), ישראל גינזך המדינה (trans. Israel State Archives), Jerusalem, pp. 65–66 https://www.archives.gov.il/archives/Archive/0b0717 0688f2f0fd/File/0b071706894b3f8f/Item/090717068976ff6a (accessed June 28, 2023), archived at https://web.archive.org/web/20230712074856/https://www.archives.gov.il/archives/Archive/0b0717 0688f2f0fd/File/0b071706894b3f8f/Item/090717068976ff6a.

[14] Qurie, *From Oslo to Jerusalem*, pp. 232. For my account of the meeting, see Yair Hirschfeld, "Summary of Meeting between Yair Hirschfeld and Abu Ala'," August 6, 1993, ארכיונים ואוספים אישיים/אוסף יאיר הירשפלד (trans. Archives and Personal Collections/Yair Hirschfeld Collection), ישראל גינזך המדינה ן (trans. Israel State Archives), Jerusalem.

reassurance that the unofficial Israeli team's statements in Norway had at least partial authorization. Therefore, during the first meeting, I handed Abu Ala' a small paper with four lines: *fact-finding, partial authorization, legitimization, and breakthrough*. Throughout our discussions, he would repeatedly ask me which phase we were in. Abu Ala' eventually accepted my language of the process.[15]

By establishing these phases, it helped provide a framework for our negotiations and facilitated understanding and communication between the parties involved.

Our Cabin "in the Woods of Norway"

---

[15] Qurie, *From Oslo to Jerusalem*, pp. 111–141.

Hoping for a US Shuttle Diplomacy

Upon returning from the first meeting in Norway, we provided a report to Beilin, Shimon Peres, and Dan Kurtzer separately.[16] Abu Ala' reported to President Mubarak and Osama el-Bas, his Middle East advisor. They were reportedly excited about the progress made and sent Ambassador Ibrahim Shash to advise the Palestinian team on "how to negotiate with Israelis."[17]

Beilin instructed me to prepare a "frisch-misch," which meant reshuffling the cards. I secluded myself in my home in Ramat Yishai for several days and prepared a three-part paper: the Principles of an Israeli-Palestinian Negotiating Plan, a Draft for an Israeli-Palestinian Cooperation and Working Program, and a proposal for "Preparing a Marshall Plan for the West Bank, Gaza Strip, and the Region."

This paper combined ideas I had prepared for the European Union with suggestions made by Abu Ala'. It aimed to use the language of Palestinian empowerment and proposed the establishment of various state-building institutions such as the Palestinian Land Authority, Palestinian Water Administration Authority, Palestinian Electricity Authority, Gaza Port Authority, Palestinian Development Bank, Palestinian Export Promotion Board, and Environmental Authority.

The Draft for an Israeli-Palestinian Cooperation and Working Program (CWP) was a precursor to what would later become Annex III of the Israel-PLO Declaration of Principles, and the third part of the paper became a precursor to what would become Annex IV. As we couldn't agree on the same text for a variety of issues, the document suggested presenting both Israeli (I)

---

[16] Yair Hirschfeld and Ron Pundak, "Report on a Meeting with a PLO Delegation," January 25, 1993, "משא ומתן באוסלו) (ערוץ אחורי) - מאי - ינואר 1993" (trans. Negotiations in Olso (Back Channel) January-May 1993), ISA-Privatecollections-NA-001nwgj (new folder identifier), "5514/1–פ" (trans. P 5514/1) (old folder identifier), ארכיונים ואוספים אישיים/אוסף יאיר הירשפלד (trans. Archives and Personal Collections/Yair Hirschfeld Collection), ישראל גינזך המדינה (trans. Israel State Archives), Jerusalem, pp. 197-203 (the meeting was on January 23, 1993) https://www.archives.gov.il/archives/Archive/0b07170688f2f0fd/File/0b071706894b3f97/Item/09071706897b1fbe (accessed June 28, 2023), archived at https://web.archive.org/web/20230712075802/https://www.archives.gov.il/archives/Archive/0b07170688f2f0fd/File/0b071706894b3f97/Item/09071706897b1fbe.

[17] Yair Hirschfeld and Ron Pundak, "Summarized Support of the 3rd Sarpsborg-Meeting," March 21, 1993, "משא ומתן באוסלו) (ערוץ אחורי) - מאי - ינואר 1993" (trans. Negotiations in Olso (Back Channel) January-May 1993), ISA-Privatecollections-NA-001nwgj (new folder identifier), "5514/1–פ" (trans. P 5514/1) (old folder identifier), ארכיונים ואוספים אישיים/אוסף יאיר הירשפלד (trans. Archives and Personal Collections/Yair Hirschfeld Collection), ישראל (trans. Israel State Archives), Jerusalem, pp. 25-28 https://www.archives.gov.il/archives/Archive/0b07170688f2f0fd/File/0b071706894b3f97/Item/09071706897b1fbe (accessed June 28, 2023), archived at https://web.archive.org/web/20230712075802/https://www.archives.gov.il/archives/Archive/0b07170688f2f0fd/File/0b071706894b3f97/Item/09071706897b1fbe (hereafter cited as Hirschfeld and Pundak, "Summarized Support of the 3rd Sarpsborg-Meeting," Yair Hirschfeld Collection).

and Palestinian (P) versions. The decisive element of the entire exercise was Paragraph 4.

The Palestinian version stated:

> The jurisdiction of the Palestinian Interim Council will cover the Palestinian territories occupied in 1967. Any administrative exception hereto should be discussed during negotiations. Stipulated these exceptions should not prejudice UN Resolutions 242 and 338 and the principles of international law.[18]

The Israeli version read: "The jurisdiction of the Palestinian Interim Council will cover control over land as mutually agreed upon." It was stated that the Israeli team did not accept the Palestinian proposal for paragraph 4, and vice versa, the Palestinian team did not accept the Israeli proposal.[19]

During our first meeting, Abu Ala' had instructed me, in no uncertain terms, not to brief el-Husseini and Ashrawi about our discussions. I understood the importance of strengthening the "inside" leadership politically, diplomatically, and personally. Therefore, I proposed a daring idea of suggesting a US shuttle diplomacy within Jerusalem. Version Four of the text we produced stated:

> It is suggested that the US Secretary of State will go to Jerusalem and will submit to the Government of Israel, on one hand, and to the Palestinian leadership (Faisal el-Husseini and Hanan Ashrawi), on the other hand, an American draft for a DoP (Declaration of Principles); an outline of a proposed Israeli-Palestinian CWP (Cooperation and Working Program); and an outline of a proposed Marshall Plan for the West Bank, the Gaza Strip, and the Region.[20]

Abu Ala' assured us that he would inform el-Husseini and Ashrawi accordingly, and he did. We knew that Warren Christopher, the US Secretary of State, was scheduled to visit the area. Immediately after returning from

---

[18] Yair Hirschfeld and Ron Pundik "The Principles of an Israeli-Palestinian Negotiating Plan (Version 3)," March 21, 1993, "ינואר 1993 - מאי - (ערוץ אחורי) משא ומתן באוסלו" (trans. Negotiations in Olso (Back Channel) January-May 1993), ISA-Privatecollections-NA-001nwgj (new folder identifier), "פ-5514/1" (trans. P 5514/1) (old folder identifier), ארכיונים ואוספים אישיים/אוסף יאיר הירשפלד (trans. Archives and Personal Collections/Yair Hirschfeld Collection), ישראל גינוך המדינה (trans. Israel State Archives), Jerusalem, pp. 29–32 https://www.archives.gov.il/archives/Archive/0b0717 0688f2f0fd/File/0b071706894b3f97/Item/09071706897b1fbe (accessed June 28, 2023), archived at https://web.archive.org/web/20230712075802/https://www.archives.gov.il/archives/Archive/0b0717 0688f2f0fd/File/0b071706894b3f97/Item/09071706897b1fbe (hereafter cited as Hirschfeld and Pundak, "The Principles of an Israeli-Palestinian Negotiating Plan (Version 3)," Yair Hirschfeld Collection).

[19] Hirschfeld and Pundik, "The Principles of an Israeli-Palestinian Negotiating Plan (Version 3)," Yair Hirschfeld Collection.

[20] See Footnote 19.

Norway, I had a meeting with Molly Williamson, the American Consul General.[21]

One day prior to Warren Christopher's visit to Israel on February 22, we arranged a meeting between Shimon Peres, Faisal Husseini, and Ziad Abu Zayyad. Husseini came with a message from Arafat that seemed to reflect the meeting and the atmosphere we had created in Norway. The message read:

> *We are concerned about the peace process, our commitment is so strong. It is important for us, for the region, it is not only the shape of the new world that can help us, we also can help the new world order. As far as we are enemies, but in this peace process there is a partnership, so do not make more problems for both of us. Your credibility and our credibility are linked, if our credibility is hurt, this hurts the peace process, and in turn your credibility among your people. Things can come to concrete steps. Both of us are not completely free to do steps exclusively without consideration of the other side.*[22]

The situation regarding the return of the 400 plus Hamas members exiled to Lebanon posed a challenge. Arafat had empowered el-Husseini to urge Peres and Rabin to allow their return before negotiations could be renewed in Washington. However, our task in Norway, as understood by the Americans and Rabin, was to urge Arafat to take a stand against Hamas and resume negotiations in Washington without resolving the issue first. I was aware of the sensitivity of the deportees issue for the Palestinians, as it brought back memories of the trauma of dispersion. In Norway, Abu Ala' and Hassan Azfour insisted on discussing the issue of the deportees, with Azfour expressing his strong emotions about it.

I hoped that the suggested American shuttle diplomacy could help resolve the situation. In two reports I sent to Yossi Beilin, I proposed that the

---

[21] Looking at my daily schedules from 1992–1993, I have records of individual meetings with Molly Williamson on February 14, at 11 am, Yossi Beilin on February 17, at 8 am, Terje Larsen on February 21, at 7:30 am, and Faisal Husseini on February 21, at 12 pm, and Molly Williamson (again) on February 21 all in the Hilton Jerusalem. I then had a group meeting with Husseini, Yossi, and Peres on February 21 at 2 pm. Later that evening, I met with just Beilin and Peres at 5:30 pm. It was a busy time.

[22] Orient House Staffer, "Minutes for the meeting with SP," February 21, 1993, 2:20 PM, "באוסלו ומתן משא (ערוץ אחורי) - מאי - ינואר 1993" (trans. Negotiations in Olso (Back Channel) January-May 1993), ISA-Privatecollections-NA-001nwgj (new folder identifier), "5514/1–פ" (trans. P 5514/1) (old folder identifier), ארכיונים ואוספים אישיים/אוסף יאיר הירשפלד (trans. Archives and Personal Collections/Yair Hirschfeld Collection), ישראל (trans. Israel State Archives), Jerusalem, pp. 130 https://www.archives.gov.il/archives/Archive/0b07170688f2f0fd/File/0b071706894b3f97/Item/09071706897b1fbe (accessed June 28, 2023), archived at https://web.archive.org/web/20230712075802/https://www.archives.gov.il/archives/Archive/0b07170688f2f0fd/File/0b071706894b3f97/Item/09071706897b1fbe.

US shuttle diplomacy on the Palestinian issue should be based on a prior commitment to six issues:

- An agreement to transfer of authority in the spheres of taxation, tourism, education, health and social welfare;
- Agreement on elections;
- The conclusion of a Palestinian Economic Development Program closely interconnected to a Regional Economic Development Program;
- Agreement on an Israeli-Palestinian Cooperation and Working Program;
- Agreements on rights and responsibilities of Palestinian Interim Council;
- An Israeli obligation in principle to withdraw from the Gaza Strip after two years under agreed conditions of an international trusteeship.

In the second paper I sent to Beilin, I also suggested a detailed division of preparatory work in Israel between the Prime Minister's office and the Foreign Ministry. My aim was to achieve a breakthrough as quickly as possible and continue negotiations at the official level, even if it meant my exclusion. I did hope that Beilin would assign me further tasks in some capacity.[23],[24]

I was not allowed to participate in the meeting between Peres and Christopher on February 22, as it mainly focused on Christopher's shuttle diplomacy between Jerusalem and Damascus. In the final round, President Assad was unwilling to offer any openings for negotiations. Nevertheless, Christopher asked Peres to publicly state that his effort had been successful. Peres did so, against the advice of Beilin and Novik, who argued that indirectly complimenting President Assad would be counterproductive. They believed it would give Assad no reason to adopt a more forthcoming approach, while the Israeli lobby opposed to any withdrawal from the Golan Heights, which was essential for a peace agreement with Syria, would become more vocal in their opposition. I asked Peres why he agreed to praise Christopher's unsuccessful

---

[23] Yair Hirschfeld, "Plan and Timetable for (US-Proposed) Israeli-Palestinian Negotiations," February 26, 1993, "ינואר - מאי - (ערוץ אחורי) משא ומתן באוסלו" 1993" (trans. Negotiations in Olso (Back Channel) January-May 1993), ISA-Privatecollections-NA-001nwgj (new folder identifier), "5514/1-פ" (trans. P 5514/1) (old folder identifier), ארכיונים ואוספים אישיים/אוסף יאיר הירשפלד (trans. Archives and Personal Collections/Yair Hirschfeld Collection), ישראל גינזך המדינה (trans. Israel State Archives), Jerusalem, pp. 126–128 https://www.archives.gov.il/archives/Archive/0b0717 0688f2f0fd/File/0b071706894b3f97/Item/09071706897b1fbe (accessed June 28, 2023), archived at https://web.archive.org/web/20230712075802/https://www.archives.gov.il/archives/Archive/0b0717 0688f2f0fd/File/0b071706894b3f97/Item/09071706897b1fbe.

[24] Abu Ala' wanted the Norwegian Minister of Affairs to discuss the proposed concept with the US Secretary of State. However, I received from Abu Ala a commitment not to report these ideas to the Norwegians yet. I wanted him to do so only after I obtained the go-ahead from Jerusalem. He kept his word.

effort. Peres explained that Christopher needed his praise for internal political reasons in the United States, which he considered more important than immediate progress with the Syrians.

Despite the meetings in Norway, negotiations were blocked due to the deportee question, and the proposal I made to break the deadlock was deemed too complicated to be successful. It seemed that Peres was also not enthusiastic about the idea of another US shuttle diplomacy effort. Instead, a different approach was adopted. The United States and Russia, as cosponsors of the Middle East peace process, extended invitations to Israel, Jordan, Syria, Palestinians, and Lebanon to resume bilateral negotiations in Washington. The ninth round of negotiations was scheduled to continue "in uninterrupted fashion" from April 20 to May 6.[25] Simultaneously, the next rounds for the multilateral working groups were being rescheduled in different locations.[26]

In the week following the invitation, there were indications that the Palestinians, Jordanians, Syrians, and Lebanese would reject the invitation and not attend the negotiations in Washington. It seemed that the delegations might at best only participate in the multilateral negotiations in various cities. Many different players informed me that the US-Russian invitation would be rejected.[27] We were concerned that this would lead to another breakdown of negotiations and a resurgence of violence.

During a meeting in Norway on March 20–22, Beilin, Pundik, and I understood that it was crucial to convince the Palestinian leadership in Tunis to return to negotiations regardless of Hamas' demands backed by Arafat. Beilin instructed me to conclude a joint paper that would pave the way back to negotiations in Washington. Peres, although unaware of Beilin's instruction, shared our concerns about the potential end of negotiations. He instructed me to ask Abu Ala' a question that would make the Palestinians into demandeurs, meaning they would be the ones seeking a return to negotiations. The question was whether and when Chairman Arafat would want to return to Gaza. I knew that Abu Ala' would be determined to pave the way

---

[25] "Invitation to Bilaterals," *Hirschfeld Khoury-DeConcini Papers, Substack*, forthcoming (originally written March 10, 1993), https://hkdpapers.substack.com/p/invitation-to-bilaterals (this is the text of the joint US Russian announcement for bilateral negotiations).

[26] The Water Working group would convene in Geneva, April 27–20; the Economic Development Working Group was to convene in Rome, May 4–5, the Refugee Working Group in Oslo, May 11–13; the Arms Control and Regional Security Working Group in Washington, May 17–20 and the Environment Working Group in Tokyo in late May.

[27] The most reliable input I received was from Sari Nusseibeh on March 16. This was confirmed on March 18 by Alexej Chestakov, a senior member of the Russian foreign service. During the first Lebanon War, Chestakov had hosted Yasser Arafat in the Soviet Embassy in Beirut and, unrelated to that, had since become a friend of mine.

for Arafat's return to Gaza. Peres had discussed this question/proposal with Rabin before, receiving a "yellow-green" go ahead.

We did conclude a joint paper, but to avoid obligating the Israeli government, I insisted on adding a reservation at the top of the document, stating that the joint paper was a "*mutually envisaged Israeli-Palestinian understanding.*" The crucial issue we had to resolve was Paragraph Four on Jurisdiction. The proposed wording read: "*The jurisdiction of the Palestinian Interim Council will cover control over land, as mutually agreed upon.*" Fully aware of the dangers of ambiguous wording, I revised the new text to: "*Jurisdiction of the Palestinian Interim Council will cover West Bank and Gaza Strip land.*"

I made sure to confirm with a phone call to my friend Tom Phillips in Norway, without disclosing the reason, whether the English text was ambiguous enough to argue that it could either cover all the West Bank and Gaza Strip land or only parts of it. In any case, I had previously informed Abu Ala' that if we succeeded and officials joined the channel in Norway, the negotiations might have to start from the beginning.[28]

At the same meeting, important oral understandings were reached. It was agreed that the three documents would be renegotiated in Washington, allowing the Americans to propose ideas to both sides. Additionally, it was decided to maintain contact in Norway as a "crisis management" channel. Abu Ala' proposed the preparation of a "peace propaganda plan" to coordinate public relations activities. The idea of a "Gaza Strip Stabilizing Plan" was raised, along with a commitment to fully demilitarize the Gaza Strip. There was also a suggestion to coordinate the preparation of a Palestinian Investors Conference.[29]

However, upon returning home, the atmosphere turned dramatic and depressing. Shimon Peres was deeply irritated by the fact that we had agreed to conclude a joint paper. He feared that Rabin would assume it was done on his instruction and would dismiss him for going behind Rabin's back.

---

[28] The prospect of restarting negotiations understandably frustrated Abu Ala'. I assured him, however, that restarting wouldn't mean all our previous work had been in vain. To illustrate my point, I told him a joke about Czarist Katharina of Russia. Here is the short version: One night, Czar Katarina summons a Russian solider into her bedchambers. She tells him that she wants him to satisfy her that night, but will only allow him the opportunity if he manages to do it 100 times before the night is over. The solider, excited at the prospect, decides to keep track of his progress by marking his boot after each time. Several hours pass and then Katatrina announces "ok, you've satisfied my 86 times so far." The solider, counting his boot, disagrees and says "Empress, I believe it has been 92 times." But then, just before Katarina begins to argue, he spits on his hand and begins wiping away the marks on his boot. Quite confused, Katarina asks the solider what he is doing. The solider simply remarks "It doesn't matter. We can just start again."

[29] Hirschfeld and Pundak, "Summarized Support of the 3rd Sarpsborg-Meeting," Yair Hirschfeld Collection.

Peres vented his anger on me, but Beilin offered his full support, which was personally important to me. Despite our today's conceptual differences, our friendship remained dear. Nevertheless, by the end of March 1993, I was convinced that the entire effort of fourteen years had ended in failure and would likely lead to an escalation of violence.

Surprisingly, the opposite happened. In a meeting with Dan Kurtzer on April 13, Pundik and I received an encouraging briefing. During Prime Minister Rabin's visit to Washington, President Clinton and his team criticized the negotiating tactics employed by Elyakim Rubinstein, who headed the dialogue with the Palestinians. The Americans argued that the tactics of attrition and lack of progress would inevitably lead to a resurgence of violence. Instead, the Americans suggested that the Palestinians should return to negotiations and put all the outstanding issues on the table. Even if no agreement was reached, this would allow the Americans to propose bridging proposals to both sides. Regarding the negotiations in Sarpsborg (Norway), Kurtzer emphasized the importance of maintaining the channel as a confidence-building measure. However, the US administration was cautious and would not legitimize the Norwegian channel.[30] Kurtzer added that Secretary of State Warren Christopher rejected receiving Jan Egeland, the Norwegian Deputy Secretary of Foreign Affairs, in Washington. Nevertheless, it was understood that the support of PLO Tunis was crucial for achieving an agreement, which is why the "Gaza First" approach, agreed upon by Abu Ala', was significant.[31]

Rabin Takes Control of the Renewal of Negotiations in Washington and Oslo

President Clinton's criticism of the official Israeli negotiating tactics, and pointing out progress that had been made in Norway, influenced Rabin to take full control of negotiations, both in Washington and Norway, while leaving Peres a relatively free hand to promote the process. I was asked by Peres to submit a proposed strategy based on our meetings in Norway. My recommendations were simple: renegotiate the Declaration of Principles. Abu Ala' had informed me privately that further substantial concessions would be

---

[30] Kurtzer, in referring to the US peace team, said: "regarding the PLO, they are more catholic than the Pope."
[31] Yair Hirschfeld and Ron Pundik, "Meeting with Daniel Kurtzer," *Hirschfeld Khoury-DeConcini Papers, Substack*, forthcoming (originally written on April 13, 1993), https://hkdpapers.substack.com/p/meeting-with-daniel-kurtzer.

made to accommodate Rabin and Peres if we could reach a breakthrough and continue negotiations with senior Israeli officials. I suggested pursuing negotiations on three parallel channels: in Washington to allow the Americans to propose bridging proposals, in Oslo to offer necessary support, and in Jerusalem with el-Husseini to primarily focus on economic issues.[32]

On Sunday, April 25, Peres briefed Pundik and me about the official Israeli negotiating team's presentation of a "package" to the Americans for the Palestinians, which included the proposal to control 60% of the West Bank. He emphasized the need to expand negotiations in more detail on economic issues, indicating that the discussions in Norway were valuable and could provide an area where the Americans could play a supportive role. Peres informed us that President Mubarak had suggested expanding the "Gaza First" approach to include Gaza and Jericho. We were surprised that Abu Ala' had not mentioned this at all. I mentioned that it not only made sense but also provided a legitimate reason for the Israeli team to request substantial changes to the concluded paper.

Peres then discussed the issues covered in the joint "envisaged" Sarpsborg paper in great detail. He opposed the paragraph allowing for elections to the Palestinian Interim Council in Jerusalem, stating that voting would be acceptable, but Palestinian Jerusalemites should not be eligible for election. He criticized the paragraph related to possible arbitration and insisted on changing it. He wanted clarification on the meaning of basing participation in elections on the population register of June 4, 1967, indicating that it needed to be modified.

Furthermore, Peres expressed his support for negotiations aimed at a more comprehensive agreement if the Palestinians agreed to create a Jordanian-Palestinian Confederation. He suggested supplementing it with a trilateral economic cooperation agreement between Israel, Palestine, and Jordan, modeled after the Benelux Agreement that laid the foundations for European cooperation after World War II. Peres emphasized the importance of including Uri Savir, the young Director General of the Ministry of Foreign Affairs, in the process and preparing necessary understandings with Abu Ala' regarding the multilateral negotiations. He proposed forming a confidential brainstorming group under his leadership and asked Pundik and me to suggest other participants for these deliberations.[33]

---

[32] Yair Hirschfeld and Ron Pundik, "Proposed Back-Channel Negotiating Strategy" *Hirschfeld Khoury-DeConcini Papers, Substack*, forthcoming (originally written on April 22, 1993), https://hkdpapers.substack.com/p/proposed-back-channel-negotiating-strategy.

[33] Yair Hirschfeld and Ron Pundik, "Meeting with Shimon Peres on April 25, 1993," April 25, 1993, " אוגוסט - מאי - אוסלו 1993" (trans. Oslo–May–August 1993), ISA-Privatecollections-NA-001nwgh (old folder identifier), "5513/7-פ" (trans. P 5513/7) (new folder identifier),

Two days later, on April 27, the Palestinian delegation returned to Washington for negotiations. It was evident that the work we had done in Norway had achieved the desired outcome that Rabin had hoped for. From that point on, Rabin directed and controlled every step in both Washington and Norway, while allowing Peres to remain at the forefront. Peres formed a small and intimate working group that included Uri Savir, Avi Gil, Yossi Beilin, Shlomo Gur, Pundik, and me. Peres briefed us on his meeting with US Ambassador to Israel, Sam Lewis, and wanted us to explore in more detail the possibility of a trilateral Jordanian-Palestinian-Israeli economic cooperation structure.

He instructed us to discuss it first with the Palestinians and then present the idea to the Americans. Uri Savir was assigned to discuss understandings in the multilateral negotiations with Abu Ala'. Savir informed us that the Americans wanted to establish a joint fund with the Europeans to finance Palestinian state-building projects. Peres emphasized the importance of always including a necessary regional component that would also connect Israel to the broader region. It was all very promising news. However, there was a caveat: Peres instructed Pundik and me to wait and not return to Norway for the time being.[34]

We had previously informed Abu Ala' and Larsen that if negotiations were to resume, we would return to Norway a few days later. Without specifying a date, Abu Ala', along with Azfour and el-Kurd, arrived in Oslo at the end of that week. I discussed this with Ruthi at home, and she expressed that not going to Oslo now would be seen as a grave insult. Abu Ala' had delivered what we had asked for, and now he would be left alone in the cold? We imagined the conversation Abu Ala' might have with Arafat upon returning home, and what Arafat would say to him. It was evident that Abu Ala' would transform from a staunch supporter of seeking a peaceful understanding with Israel to a staunch opponent, and Arafat would likely conclude that the two of us, Israeli academics, had deceived him. Hassan Azfour, who reported to Abu Mazen, would likely add fuel to the fire. And Maher el-Kurd would probably inform Arafat that the "two academics" had good intentions, but

---

ארכיונים ואוספים אישיים/אוסף יאיר הירשפלד (trans. Archives and Personal Collections/Yair Hirschfeld Collection), ישראל גינוך המדינה (trans. Israel State Archives), Jerusalem, pp. 179–180, https://www.archives.gov.il/product-page/2696943 (accessed June 28, 2023).

[34] Yair Hirschfeld and Ron Pundak, "Meeting with Shimon Peres on April 27, 1993," April 27, 1993, "אוסלו - מאי - אוגוסט 1993" (trans. Oslo–May–August 1993), ISA-Privatecollections-NA-001nwgh (old folder identifier), "5513/7-פ" (trans. P 5513/7) (new folder identifier), ארכיונים ואוספים אישיים/אוסף יאיר הירשפלד (trans. Archives and Personal Collections/Yair Hirschfeld Collection), ישראל גינוך המדינה (trans. Israel State Archives), Jerusalem, p. 181, https://www.archives.gov.il/product-page/2696943 (accessed June 28, 2023), archived at https://web.archive.org/web/20230712075856/https://www.archives.gov.il/product-page/2696943.

Rabin and Peres never intended to reach an understanding with the PLO in Tunis.

We decided to express our concerns to Peres. He asked me what I proposed, and I suggested, "Allow Ron and me to go to Norway and inform Abu Ala' that we are 'not' coming due to several unresolved issues. However, we are committed to continuing the Norwegian channel." This meant that Abu Ala' would maintain his role in paving the way for Arafat's return to Gaza. Peres agreed. Pundik and I flew to Norway, this time to Oslo, with Peres' full approval, as planned. Years later, Abu Ala' told me that our arrival in Oslo three days after the resumption of talks in Washington was the decisive confidence-building moment for him.

Abu Ala' provided us with a detailed account of how Arafat had imposed the decision on the Palestinian delegation to return to Washington. He said:

> The entire delegation was against the chairman's decision. Ghassan al-Khatib and Samir Abdallah boycotted the decision. Haidar Abd al-Shafi was strongly against it. Another strong group against it came from Gaza: the people around Dr. Zakaria al-Agha. Hanan Ashrawi was against the resumption of negotiations. Saeb Erekat warned to write his memoirs, rather than to go to Washington.[35]

Interestingly, in Abu Ala's memoirs, he dedicated twenty-six pages to the April 30-May 1 meeting in Oslo, describing his "optimism," "concerns," and "growing pessimism" in detail. His account reflects the two achievements we had made in our track-two effort. On the Israeli side, we had achieved what we had hoped for: Track-two had transformed into a fully government-directed back-channel. The "official" Israeli delegation had not yet arrived in Oslo, but it was evident that we were moving in that direction, giving Abu Ala' reason for "optimism."

On the Palestinian side, we had gained enough standing to request additional concessions from the Palestinians before the officials joined, leading to the breakthrough. I needed additional legitimizing moves: coordinating Israeli-Palestinian positions in the multilateral talks on water in Geneva, economic cooperation in Rome, and refugees in Oslo. And most importantly, for Rabin, it was crucial that the PLO would send el-Husseini to Washington to lead the Palestinian team there. This gave Abu Ala' cause for "concern." Being aware that the Israeli official delegation would make new demands also caused Abu Ala' to feel "pessimistic."

---

[35] Abu Ala' made this statement to me on April 30, 1993.

In Oslo, a dangerous incident occurred when the head of the US delegation to the multilateral talks attempted to extract information from Terje Larsen. He pushed Larsen to acknowledge that secret talks with the PLO were taking place. It was a tactic known as "fishing," where you claim knowledge to confirm suspicions. Instead of responding with uncertainty and promising to investigate, Larsen admitted that secret talks were indeed underway. Concerned about the situation, Larsen immediately informed Pundik and me, and we promptly relayed the incident to Jerusalem. I was instructed to cease briefing Dan Kurtzer, and Christopher was not willing to be briefed either. From that point on, the Americans were kept in the dark about the dramatic events unfolding in Oslo.

The following day at 6:30 a.m., Abu Ala' proudly woke me up to inform me that el-Husseini was on his way to Washington to lead the Palestinian delegation there. He had delivered, and we had achieved the breakthrough we had been working toward.

The Official Back-Channel Negotiations Get Underway

On May 20, 1993, Uri Savir, the Director General of the Ministry of Foreign Affairs, became the head of the official Israeli delegation to the negotiations in Oslo. Several weeks later, Yoel Singer joined the team. It was evident that Savir represented Peres, while Singer represented Rabin. Pundik and I not only became full members of the official negotiating team but also played important supportive roles. I had prepared Abu Ala' extensively for what would transpire, and he knew that certain parts of the initial negotiating plan would need to be revised. Rabin had instructed Singer to make minimal changes, as he believed that negotiations on the practicalities would follow the Declaration of Principles. Nonetheless, Singer sought more clarity and posed about thirty questions to Abu Ala'. The commitment to "Gaza First" served Israeli interests, the promise of Arafat's return to Gaza served Palestinian interests, and it helped ease the acceptance of the changes Singer requested.

Arafat's had sent this message to Peres months earlier:

[I]n this peace process there is a partnership, so do not make more problems for both of us. Your credibility and our credibility are linked, if our credibility is hurt, this hurts the peace process, and in turn your credibility among your people. Things can come to concrete steps. Both of us are not completely free to do steps exclusively without consideration of the other side.

4 From the Madrid Conference to the Conclusion of Oslo

It became a useful mantra for Pundik and me to defuse confrontations during ongoing discussions. My primary task during the official negotiations was to help preserve the Red Lines established at the outset and to calm Abu Ala' when he became agitated by Singer's numerous questions. Singer's inquiries primarily focused on the daily management of Palestinian self-government and the necessary coordination with Israel. Singer added an Annex on Elections and an Annex on the withdrawal from Gaza. The original Article 6 of the March 21, 1993 (Fourth Version) Sarpsborg Document was dropped. It had read:

> In order to guarantee optimal economic development and growth, immediately with the signing of this DOP, a Palestinian Land Committee and a Palestinian Water Administration Committee will be established.
>
> The Palestinian Land committee and the Palestinian Water Administration Committee will be given immediate powers as mutually agreed upon. A coordinated land and water resources development plan will be negotiated between the Palestinian Land Committee and the Palestinian Water Administration Committee on the one, and the Government of Israel on the other side.[36]

What I had in mind was to renew the suggestion made by Shimon Peres to Gazan Mayor Rashad Shawwa, in November 1982 (see above) to allow the Palestinians to have a veto/vote on land development in the West Bank and Gaza, and hereby limit possible future settlement expansion.[37]

I did not protest the fact that this paragraph was dropped. I did not think I had the power to do so. The second important idea that was dropped was the idea to establish after the Israeli military withdrawal an international trusteeship to administer the Gaza Strip. It would have prevented much of the abuse that happened later. Although I knew that Peres opposed the idea of the trusteeship, I did make an effort to translate the concept into action. On June 3, 1993, I wrote a detailed proposal based on discussions I had had with Abu Ala'. The idea was to reach full understandings on all the following items; Abu Ala' had suggested to me to prepare their suggestions on all the

---

[36] Yair Hirschfeld and Ron Pundak, "The Sarpsborg Document," March 20, 1993, "יוני - ינואר - אוסלו 1993" (trans. Oslo–January–June 1993), ISA-Privatecollections-NA-001nwge (box identifier), "5513/4-פ" (trans. P 5513/4) (folder identifier), ארכיונים ואוספים אישיים/אוסף יאיר הירשפלד (trans. Archives and Personal Collections/Yair Hirschfeld Collection), ישראל גינוך המדינה (trans. Israel State Archives), Jerusalem, pp. 16, https://www.archives.gov.il/archives/Archive/0b0717 0688f2f0fd/File/0b071706894b3f92/Item/090717068976ff68 (accessed June 28, 2023), archived at https://web.archive.org/web/20230712080220/https://www.archives.gov.il/archives/Archive/0b0717 0688f2f0fd/File/0b071706894b3f92/Item/090717068976ff6 (hereafter cited as Hirschfeld and Pundak, "The Sarpsborg Document," Yair Hirschfeld Collection).

[37] This concept was also largely in line with the official "informal" paper I had received in autumn 1992. Hirschfeld, "Draft for Consideration," Yair Hirschfeld Collection.

points raised, allowing to create together a comprehensive Stability Program for Gaza. The handwritten paper, where I listed the issues to be dealt with, read:

"Understandings"
1. Prepare a coordinated Peace P.R. Effort. (Uri Savir supported this).
2. Prepare an Israel-Gaza Stability Plan to include:
(a) Proposed security measures to establish a Palestinian Police Force of 30,000; (everybody opposed);
(b) Proposed regulations of labor mobility;
(c) Necessary infrastructure (construction);
(d) Proposed regional planning;
(e) Sea Port Development;
(f) Immediate economic projects;
(g) Development of trade;
(h) (supporting) social organization networks (to counter-balance the Hamas organisations);
3. After (Israeli) withdrawal from the Gaza Strip, it will be completely demilitarized. A Joint Israeli-Palestinian Security Programme will be worked out.
4. The trusteeship for Gaza should be joint US-Egypt-Jordan under UN auspices; (a final Palestinian positions will be presented to at the next meeting)[38];

Among the entire group Peres had gathered to brainstorm on how to pursue the ongoing negotiations, I remained the only vote, in favor of the proposed approach. In order to find another way to achieve a similar result, I wrote the next day a proposal to Terje Rod Larsen, to organize a simulation game, to prepare for the first and a second "100 Days Programme"; FAFO (the research institute of the Norwegian Trade Unions) and ECF would organize the simulation and invite other participants as needed.[39]

---

[38] Yair Hirschfeld, "Understanding" (handwritten), June 6, 1993, יוזומת לשיתוף פעולה כלכלי ולהסכם ביניים עם הפלסטינים (trans. An initiative for economic cooperation and an interim agreement with the Palestinians) (folder name), ISA-Privatecollections-NA-001rt7w (new folder identifier), "5821/13-פ" (trans. P 5514/1) (old folder identifier), pp. 95-100, ארכיונים ואוספים אישיים/אוסף יאיר הירשפלד (trans. Archives and personal collections/Yair Hirschfeld collection), ישראל גינוך המדינה (trans. Israel State Archives), Jerusalem, https://www.archives.gov.il/archives/Archive/0b07170688f2f0fd/File/0b07170689eaacf4/Item/090717068a008a7b (accessed June 28, 2023), archived at https://web.archive.org/web/20230712041155/https://www.archives.gov.il/archives/Archive/0b07170688f2f0fd/File/0b07170689eaacf4/Item/090717068a008a7b.

[39] Yossi Beilin in preparation of the 1984 and 1988 elections had gathered such teams to prepare for the first 100 days of hoped for Peres Government. It meant that we had some experience in how to do this. Yair Hirschfeld, "Preparing Two 100 Day Programmes for the Interim Period" (handwritten) June

This proposal was similarly rejected. And I was told to convince Abu Ala' to drop the idea of a trusteeship for Gaza. It took me exactly one-and-a-half minutes, explaining that instead of the international trusteeship the Palestinian Council would have direct control over the region. These are probably the one-and-a-half minutes of my life, I have most regretted, ever since.[40]

A week later June 10, 1993, Joel Singer took full control of the negotiating process, mainly by asking questions. As Abu Ala' answered these questions, we did relatively quickly bridge remaining gaps and achieved almost full understanding by July 6, 1993. At that point, I reported to Norwegian Minister of Foreign Affairs Juergen Holst that a comprehensive agreement seemed imminent.

However, the Palestinian team wanted to test whether the official Israeli negotiators would agree to further demands that exceeded the Red Lines established months earlier. As a result, negotiations were temporarily halted for most of July. I was then sent alone to Paris to assist Abu Ala' in presenting a "Palestinian proposal" necessary to resume negotiations. Once negotiations were back on track, I was given the opportunity to refine the text of the Israeli-Palestinian Cooperation and Working Programme (CWP) into Annex III and the "Marshall Plan for the West Bank, Gaza Strip, and the Region" into Annex IV.

After returning from Paris, it took an additional two weeks and two days until the night of August 23–24 when Abu Ala' and Uri Savir would sign the Declaration of Principles in the presence of Shimon Peres.

4, 1993, יוזמת לשיתוף פעולה כלכלי ולהסכם ביניים עם הפלסטינים (trans. An initiative for economic cooperation and an interim agreement with the Palestinians) (folder name), ISA-Privatecollections-NA-001rt7w (new folder identifier), 5821/13-פ" (trans. P 5514/1) (old folder identifier), pp. 101–108, ארכיונים ואוספים אישיים/אוסף יאיר הירשפלד (trans. Archives and personal collections/Yair Hirschfeld collection), ישראל גינוך המדינה (trans. Israel State Archives), Jerusalem, https://www.archives.gov.il/archives/Archive/0b07170688f2f0fd/File/0b07170689eaacf4/Item/090717068a008a7b (accessed June 28, 2023), archived at https://web.archive.org/web/20230712041155/https://www.archives.gov.il/archives/Archive/0b07170688f2f0fd/File/0b07170689eaacf4/Item/090717068a008a7b.

[40] Hirschfeld and Pundak, "The Sarpsborg Document," Yair Hirschfeld Collection (article 13 read: "*Not later than the end of the second year of the interim-peiod, Israeli military forces will withdraw completely from Gaza, in the spirit of partial implementation of 242 and 338. The Israeli withdrawal will be fully coordinated with the Palestinian Interim Council. After the Israeli withdrawal from Gaza, a trusteeship will be established, as agreed upon between the Government of Israel and the Palestinian Interim-Self Government*").

Each Player Had Their Role

In the Israeli team, each member had an important role to play, although these roles have been misunderstood by the public. Rabin's leadership was decisive, as he allowed Peres to oversee the track-two negotiations and provided detailed leadership throughout the entire process starting from the end of April. It was Rabin's authority and courage that made the Oslo process possible. Peres, often referred to as "the father" of the Oslo process, agreed to the formula that allowed the Palestinian delegation to consult with whomever they wanted, paving the way for PLO involvement in the negotiations. Offering Arafat the opportunity to return to Gaza was a crucial factor in reaching an agreement. Peres shaped the content and tone of the negotiations through his discussions with el-Husseini and Ashrawi. His presence in Sweden to conclude the negotiations and participation in the informal signing ceremony in Oslo in August 1993 helped bring everything together.

Yossi Beilin, had during the 1980ies convinced Peres as well as the Labor Party of the need to reach an agreement with the Palestinians, and if necessary with the PLO. His political leadership and backing made it possible for me to achieve the necessary understandings that made the Oslo process possible.

My network of relationships and the trust I had built over fourteen years with various Palestinian power brokers played a crucial role in the success of the process. This foundation allowed us to discuss outstanding issues, gain insights, draft an understanding, and choose appropriate language. Actively listening and testing nuances of support or opposition enabled sustained dialogue.

Yoel Singer became the pivotal negotiator from June onward, and his influence is evident throughout the final text. He played a key role in the exchange of letters that led to the mutual recognition between Israel and the PLO. Singer recognized some of the practical flaws in the initial negotiating plan, deleted some important ideas, and successfully concluded a comprehensive agreement.[41]

Uri Savir's role was decisive when the Israeli team broke off formal negotiations in July in response to a Palestinian move aimed at testing Israeli concessions that I was unwilling to make. Savir rejected many Palestinian

---

[41] I would later question his strategic approach, when the Oslo II agreement of September 1994 was concluded. Beilin and I opposed the idea of dividing the West Bank territory into A, B, and C areas. With hindsight we know today, that this division has become a major obstacle for reaching an understanding, leading the way irreversibly to a two-state agreement.

demands but maintained a close personal dialogue with Abu Ala'. His technique of breaking off formal negotiations while keeping channels open should serve as a model for future negotiators.

Ron Pundik provided valuable input in thinking through the negotiating process and anticipating Palestinian demands and arguments. His commitment to peace was unwavering, and his untimely death was a significant loss.

On the Palestinian side, Abu Ala' was the decisive negotiator. He skillfully packaged our suggestions and proposals for Arafat and Abu Mazen. Until June, Maher el-Kurd, Arafat's economic advisor, would write almost verbatim protocols. During the team's return to Tunis from Geneva, they would often revise and refine the protocols to effectively present them to their leaders. Abu Ala' would then privately meet with Arafat in Tunis to clarify any discrepancies between the written protocols and the demands of the Israeli team.[42]

The Norwegian team played a crucial and meaningful role in the negotiations. They provided vital support by hosting the meetings on their territory and ensuring their confidentiality. Although they did not participate directly in the negotiations, they acted as intermediaries and facilitated communication between us and the Palestinians during periods when official meetings were not taking place. Despite having only partial information, their involvement helped overcome remaining obstacles.

Unlike the United States, which had significant interests in the Middle East, Norway's primary interest was to assist in the success of the peace process. Their commitment and impartiality earned them great recognition and respect on the international stage. Following the Oslo Accords in 1993, Norwegian diplomats took on important roles in broader international efforts to promote peace and stability.

Overall, Norway's contribution was substantial, and they reaped significant rewards, both in terms of international recognition and the opportunity to play a prominent role in the future peace initiatives.

---

[42] Mahmoud Abbas (Abu Mazen), *Through Secret Channels—the Road to Oslo: Senior PLO Leader Abu Mazen's Revealing Story of the Negotiations with Israel*, Garnet Publishing, Reading 1995.

Suggested Additional Reading

Learning to Negotiate

Leigh Thompson *The Mind and Heart of the Negotiator;* Prentice Hall, London 1998; Thompson's book is most recommendable for studying negotiations. Most useful is her advice to identify the "Focal Points" of the Conflict and negotiations at first; test, whether "A Zone of Possible Agreement" is achievable; prepare the "BATNA" the Best Alternative to No-Agreement; and define the "Reservation Point" understanding under what conditions is it essential to move from hoping to reach an agreement, to the best other alternative.

Bernard S. Mayer Beyond Neutrality—Confronting the Crisis in Conflict Resolution; Jossey-Bass, San Francisco, 2004. Mayer explores the role of mediation. The importance of his study is to question common understandings. His central finding is summed up in one sentence: "But conflict is a process and system, and resolution is not always a timely or useful goal" (p. 119).

James Sebenius, Nicholas Burns and Robert Mnookin Kissinger the Negotiator—Lessons from Dealmaking at the Highest Level; Harper-Collins, New York 2018. At the end of the book are fifteen useful lessons. I found more important the description, how and when Kissinger built local, regional and international coalitions to support his negotiating effort.

Hussein Agha, Shai Feldman, Ahmed Khalidi and Zeev Schiff Track II Diplomacy—Lessons learned from the Middle East; MIT Press, Cambridge, 2003. It is a useful description of the methodology of track-two negotiations, based largely on the experience we gained in Norway, and later in Sweden.

Memoirs

Mahmoud Abbas (Abu Mazen) Through Secret Channels—The Road to Oslo: Senior PLO Leader Abu Mazen's Revealing Story of the Negotiations with Israel' Garnet, Reading 1995; Abu Mazen's description of the unfolding negotiating process provides most important insights on the Palestinian perspective; earlier attempts and causes of their failure. The protocols of discussions between Abu Ala' and me (pp. 119–141) are only partly accurate. In order not to irritate Abu Mazen and maintain his continued support, the Palestinian team to Norway, rewrote the protocols, staying in Geneva on the way back to Tunis.

Ron Pundak Secret Channel—Oslo—the Full Story, Yedioth Ahronot, Tel Aviv, 2013 (Hebrew) Pundak describes the negotiating process as he experienced it. Whereas, from my point of view, the process of trial and error between 1980 and 1993 was an integral part of the entire narrative, for Pundak, his account of history started when he joined ECF in 1992.

Uri Savir The Process—Behind the Stage of Historical Decision-making; Yedioth Ahronot, Tel Aviv 1998; (Hebrew) Also for Savir the Oslo Process started when he joined the negotiations in May 1993.

Analytical Accounts of the Oslo Process

Daniel Kurtzer (ed.) Pathways to Peace—America and the Arab–Israeli Conflict; Palgrave MacMillan, New York 2012; The book includes six important contributions: Avi Gil's article "Israel's Strategic Dilemmas: Don't wait for the dust to settle; Act Now"; Samih Al-Abid and Samir Hileleh 's "Palestine as a Partner in Peace"; Yossi Alpher's "Israel and the US Role"; Ghassan Khatib "Constrained and Now Corrosive: How Palestinians view the US Role"; Gershom Gorenberg "the Other Negotiator: The Israeli Public at the Peace Table," and Robert Malley "The Peace Process and the Palestinian National Movement." These different accounts offer important insight over the complexity of the process, and the sensitivities of Israelis and Palestinians.

Abdel Monem Said Aly; Shai Feldman, Khalil Shikaki Arabs and Israelis—Conflict and Peacemaking in the Middle East; Palgrave MacMillan, New York 2013. This is a most important book, presenting the Israeli, Palestinian and Egyptian perception regarding the history of the conflict and the peacebuilding process. The book should be taught in every university and high school of the Middle East and possibly also elsewhere. Chapters 7 and 8 deal with the Oslo negotiations and offer important insights.

5

The Oslo Process of Trial and Error Unfolds

The 1990s were marked by hope and the struggle for a better future, but they were also years of trial and error. We found ourselves in uncharted territory, still carrying the wounds of the past. Unfortunately, we underestimated the power of those who opposed peace and lacked sufficient understanding of the challenges that lay ahead. It was clear that we were in for a tough ride.

An Awkward Beginning to the Tough Ride Ahead

In late August 1993, news leaked about a secretly negotiated agreement between Israel and the PLO. Almost instantly, a race for fame and recognition erupted. This race started among and between the Norwegian team and soon spread to the Israeli team. Naively, I failed to grasp the implications. Peres and Savir were concerned that Beilin, Pundik, and I would take all the credit. Peres even tried to prevent our invitation or participation in the signing ceremony on the White House Lawn. For months, he advised everyone not to provide any funding for ECF. Nevertheless, the Ebert Foundation funded our flights and accommodations to Washington, and Israel's Ambassador to Washington, Itamar Rabinowicz, included us on the guest list for the signing ceremony.

Realizing the need to rebuild a working relationship with Peres, I came up with a suggestion. I proposed to Prof. Aliza Shenhar, the rector of the University of Haifa, that we offer Peres and the UN Secretary-General Boutros Boutros Ghali an Honorary Doctorate in New York and turn the event into a fundraising opportunity for the university. It worked. While waiting for the ceremony to begin, dressed in formal academic attire, Peres asked me to share something about Boutros Boutros Ghali. I informed him that Boutros Boutros Ghali was a Copt. Historically, Copts played a significant role in tax collection and landownership registration.

In 1910, Boutros Boutros Ghali's grandfather, under British rule, served as Prime Minister and was assassinated by a Muslim fundamentalist fanatic. After the Yom Kippur War, Boutros Boutros Ghali became a driving force for peace. He invited an American social psychologist, Stephen Cohen, to Cairo to advise President Sadat and himself on negotiating with Israel. Peres listened attentively. When it was time for him to speak after receiving the Honorary Doctorate, he delivered a brilliant speech based on the limited information I had shared. It was unbelievable that Peres hadn't prepared the speech beforehand. The main goal of my efforts had been achieved: we were able to reestablish our communication and working relationship.

I also made attempts to build a working relationship with Rabin and his associates. However, the enmity between Rabin and Peres persisted. On the day Rabin and Peres received the Nobel Prize, during lunch, Peres spent over an hour criticizing Rabin. He explained to the four of us, who shared lunch with him, why he believed direct election of the Prime Minister would be a grave mistake for Israel. He couldn't publicly take a stance that Rabin would perceive as a personal attack. Alongside the analytical part of his arguments, Peres peppered his remarks with bitterness toward Rabin's way of thinking and acting. Nevertheless, when Rabin was tragically assassinated, Peres mourned deeply for his former rival.

Looking back, the numerous personal rivalries became a significant obstacle to pursuing a coordinated peace-building policy. I was particularly concerned about the rejection we faced when we proposed initiating the "peace propaganda plan" suggested by Abu Ala'. The explanation we received sounded rather awkward to me: it was deemed essential to lower Palestinian expectations in the upcoming negotiations, and implementing a "peace propaganda plan" would legitimize various Palestinian demands that we wished to hold back until the final phase of the negotiations.

The Continuing Riddle of Arafat

Among all of us, Uri Savir was particularly concerned about what would happen when Arafat returned to Gaza. Beilin asked me to prepare a presentation, which turned out to be one of the most awkward lectures I have ever given. In the late 1950s, Arafat gathered a group of Palestinian militants and founded Fatah, one of several Palestinian factions. Each faction had its own leadership, independent sources of funding and weapons, and received support from different Arab governments. The Arab League initiated and founded an umbrella organization to control these factions, allowing Egypt, Saudi Arabia, Syria, or another Arab country to guide the Palestinian struggle instead of allowing the Palestinians themselves to lead.[1]

Despite having limited power, Arafat achieved two significant accomplishments. He became the unquestioned leader of not only Fatah but also the PLO, effectively controlling other Palestinian organizations as well. He also managed to establish the PLO as an entity capable of making independent decisions while still receiving substantial funding from most Arab governments. Remarkably, he achieved this without ever having a legally sanctioned monopoly over the use of force or control over revenues.

To me, this power structure seemed somewhat similar (though not entirely) to that of the Qajar family, who ruled Iran from 1795 to 1925. For 130 years, the Qajars lacked control over their own army (with the only armed forces, the "Cossacks," being controlled by Russia) and had no monopoly over the use of force. They also had no organized revenue system and exerted little control over the revenues of other powerful figures in different regions of Iran. The Qajars maintained their grip on power through various means: employing divide-and-rule tactics, pitting tribes, clans, and families against each other; resorting to brutal violence against individuals, executing members of one family while allowing others to maintain influence; and applying arbitrary and capricious law enforcement.

They practiced arbitrary protectionism, granting concessions to certain individuals or groups in a kind of "musical chairs" game where privileges could be taken away at any moment. The small governmental structure of civil servants often succumbed to intentional corruption, allowing complete dependence on the whims of the Shah. Revenue was often raised through "suggested donations." During Nasr ed-Din Shah's visit to England, the English aristocracy found amusement in recounting the story of the Shah advising Crown Prince Edward to "kill the Duke of Kent because he is so rich and powerful."[2]

Historians are taught early on that drawing comparisons like the one I was making can be dangerous and misleading. However, the many stories I had heard from Palestinians in the West Bank, Gaza, and Norway struck a familiar

---

[1] Alan Hart, *Arafat—A Political Biography*, Sidgwick and Jackson, London 1984 (and revised 1994).
[2] Shaul Bakhash, *Iran: Monarchy, Bureaucracy and Reform under the Qajars, 1858–1896*, London, Ithaca Press, 1978.

chord. We were aware of numerous instances where Arafat had resorted to violence and engaged in various forms of corruption. The conclusions I reached were contradictory: while we had to support Arafat in establishing his rule upon returning to Gaza, we also had to provide him with the means to do so. In the medium or long term, the goal should be to encourage the Palestinian Authority to establish a monopoly over the use of violence, implement a transparent tax and revenue system, combat corruption, and establish a functioning rule of law. However, in the months to come, such aspirations seemed unattainable.

In hindsight, my negative assessment was not far from the truth, and my hope for change was at least partially misplaced. We had hoped to transform the revolutionary spirit and mindset of the PLO into a state-building endeavor. However, we were unaware of the uphill battle that awaited us. There was much goodwill on the Israeli side and an understanding that an effective Palestinian state-building effort was not only in the Palestinians' interest but also a crucial Israeli interest. Nevertheless, we underestimated the challenges. Israeli security authorities were involved in negotiations to prepare for Arafat's return to Gaza and ensure an orderly transfer of authority as agreed upon. Economists were discussing financial arrangements, customs, and revenue issues, which led to the signing of the Paris Protocol.[3] Our intention was to reach a comprehensive agreement on permanent status and resolve all outstanding core issues of the conflict in one full swoop. However, I recognized that this could only be achieved step by step, with a clear understanding of the desired destination.

A small yet significant incident, which occurred shortly after the signing ceremony on the White House Lawn, provided me with a glimpse of what was to come. Beilin, with Rabin's knowledge, asked me to propose to el-Husseini that we hand over most of the data and documents of the Civil Administration to him and the "technical committees."[4] This was meant to facilitate an orderly transfer of authority. After more than a week, el-Husseini informed me that they would "not accept documents from Israel while still under occupation." He knew perfectly well that this statement was outrageous. Arafat had denied permission to do so aiming to diminish the power

---

[3] Arafat's return to Gaza, and the subsequent transfer of power, was organized through Cairo Agreement, which was signed on May 4, 1994. The Paris Protocol was signed before this, April 26, 1994. It was then reincorporated into the Cairo Agreement, and again into the Oslo II Agreement of September 1995.

[4] Sari Nusseibeh describes the work of the Technical Committees in his autobiography under the heading "A Shadow Government." Arafat subsequently replaced the "Technical Committees" with PECDAR (Palestinian Economic Council for Development and Reconstruction). Sari Nusseibeh and Anthony David, *Once Upon a Country—a Palestinian Life*, Halban, London 2009, pp. 353–363.

and influence of the "technical committees," which were under el-Husseini's and Sari Nusseibeh's control. The urgency of state-building actions had to take a backseat to Arafat's political whims. The larger issue at hand was the escalation of a vicious cycle of terrorism.

The Challenges Ahead

The Battle Against Terror is Lost

Before Arafat's Return to the Territories

One month after the signing ceremony on the White House Lawn, Beilin travelled to Tunis to attend another multilateral meeting. Pundik and I planned to meet Arafat. The purpose was to discuss how best to prepare for Permanent Status negotiations. While sitting beside Arafat, he sweetened my tea with excessive honey. It was he who initiated a discussion on how to deal with Hamas. He stated that he would employ five complementary tactics: co-opting many Hamas members, especially those in lower ranks; dividing them by holding elections; cutting off their financial resources from abroad; delegitimizing them internally; and using force only as a last resort. At the time, this sounded promising. However, we didn't fully grasp what Arafat was hinting at between the lines. He intended to employ every possible tactic to counter Hamas and Jihad and would resort to violence only when absolutely necessary.

Between September 13, 1993 (the signing ceremony) and the end of February 1994, Hamas and Jihad carried out 22 acts of terror, resulting in the deaths of one or two Israelis each time. These frequent acts of terror, occurring four to five times per month, provoked a response from Israeli Jewish militants.[5] On February 25, 1994, a Jewish physician named Baruch Goldstein murdered 29 Palestinians while they were praying at the Ibrahimi Mosque/the Tomb of the Patriarchs, holy to Muslims and Jews alike, in Hebron. This brutal act not only alarmed the Palestinian people and leadership but also the entire Arab and Muslim world. Peres, among other actions, sent Pundik and me to discuss possible coordinated Israeli-Palestinian measures with Maher el-Kurd, who had a close personal relationship with

---

[5] Jewish Virtual Library, "Comprehensive Listing of Terrorism Victims in Israel," https://www.jewishvirtuallibrary.org/comprehensive-listing-of-terrorism-victims-in-israel (accessed July 11, 2023), archived at https://web.archive.org/web/20230712075538/https://www.jewishvirtuallibrary.org/comprehensive-listing-of-terrorism-victims-in-israel.

Arafat. The three of us were convinced that a decisive action was needed. We suggested closing down the Romanov House in Hebron and relocating other Jewish presence to nearby Kiryat Arba. Peres agreed with our suggestions and promised to discuss them with Rabin. However, upon returning from Rabin, Peres became convinced it couldn't be done.

Many years later, Brig. General Efraim Sneh, who was then in charge of the Civil Administration over the West Bank, revealed to me that he had convinced Rabin that the price of evacuating Jewish residents from Hebron would be too high.[6] Instead, negotiations led to the establishment of the Temporary International Presence in Hebron (TIPH), an international observation unit. However, TIPH's mandate did not allow for effective intervention. Thus, a vicious cycle of Palestinian terror provoking Jewish terror, and Jewish terror escalating Palestinian terror began to unfold.

Arafat's Return to Gaza

Arafat's return to Gaza was poorly planned. Before his arrival, he met Warren Christopher and managed to irritate him. Arafat would interrupt Christopher when strategic issues were being discussed, causing frustration and reluctance. Nonetheless, Christopher reported to Rabin about ten minor confidence-building demands raised by Arafat, including the right to purchase helicopters from Greece. Rabin prepared responses to all ten issues, but Arafat insisted on addressing other matters.[7] Upon arriving in Gaza, Arafat smuggled weapons in his car, causing significant irritation. The situation quickly deteriorated.

Hamas and other groups in Gaza feared that their power base would be eroded. Additional acts of terror occurred on July 7 and 25, August 2 and 26, and September 4. In October, two significant acts of terror shook Israeli society. Israeli soldier Nachshon Waxmann was kidnapped and, after an IDF siege, murdered, garnering widespread media attention. On October 19, bus No. 5 exploded in the center of Tel Aviv, killing 22 Israelis. Before attending the Nobel Prize Ceremony in Norway on December 10, four more acts of terror took place on November 11, 19, 27, and 30.[8]

---

[6] Yair Hirschfeld, private interview with Efraim Sneh, January 10, 2012.

[7] Yair Hirschfeld meeting with Dan Kurtzer on August 22, 1994, 13.00–14.00 at Department of State, Washington.

[8] Jewish Virtual Library, "Comprehensive Listing of Terrorism Victims in Israel" (when large Israeli and Palestinian delegations arrived to attend the Nobel Prize Peace Ceremony in Oslo, Israeli right-wing demonstrators had come to demonstrate as loud as possible against the Oslo Accords. The day we arrived was Friday. Peres walked from the hotel to attend Friday Service at the local Synagogue. All the way, demonstrators shouted at him their slogans. On the way back from the synagogue he was so irritated and fell, and needed medical treatment).

Arafat had limited control over power and lacked the means to confront Hamas. He also faced financial constraints in buying support and stabilizing the situation. Three weeks after Arafat's return to Gaza, I wrote a paper to Beilin suggesting various measures to strengthen Arafat's economic capacity. One of the suggestions was to create an Emergency Fund and coordinate the efforts of supportive non-governmental organizations. I also proposed seeking support from the US, the EU, and Japan to establish a functional banking system in Gaza and the West Bank.[9] Rabin appointed Yossi Ginnossar, a Shabak officer, to initiate an ongoing dialogue with Arafat, including financial and economic understandings. Peres approached the Americans, the EU, and the Norwegians for their support and involvement. I specifically focused on working with the Dutch Government.[10]

On November 18, I sent Peres and Beilin a report emphasizing the urgency of the situation. The next day, Saturday, November 19, hell broke loose in Gaza.[11] A clash between Arafat's forces and Hamas supporters occurred while attempting to suppress a Hamas demonstration. Pundik and I arrived in Gaza on November 21 to report on the situation. Explosions could still be heard as we crossed the entrance into Gaza at 10:00 am.

Instead of meeting Arafat in the city center as planned, we were taken to a fish restaurant on the beach, where Nabil Shaath welcomed us. To pass the time, Nabil Shaath gave us an informed lecture on the Russian economy, arguing that the abundance of oil and gas income had hindered essential economic reforms and would eventually lead to adverse consequences. It seemed that we were on the verge of creating a similar curse on the Palestinian economy by relying heavily on aid funds. We sent a report on the dismal situation to Peres at 7:00 pm later that same evening.

This clash occurred at a time when Arafat was ill-prepared. Hamas activists had prepared for a demonstration against Arafat. The police force tried to confiscate loud-speakers and other equipment, causing the Hamas activists to attack the police violently. In response, the police opened fire. During the

---

[9] Yair Hirschfeld, "Economic Issues (with political repercussions)," July 17, 1994, ארכיונים ואוספים אישיים/אוסף יאיר הירשפלד (trans. Archives and personal collections/Yair Hirschfeld collection), ישראל גינוך המדינה (trans. Israel State Archives), Jerusalem.

[10] Yair Hirschfeld, "Report of Meeting with Dutch Minister of Foreign Affairs van Mierlo," September 13, 1994, ארכיונים ואוספים אישיים/אוסף יאיר הירשפלד (trans. Archives and personal collections/Yair Hirschfeld collection), ישראל גינוך המדינה (trans. Israel State Archives), Jerusalem.

[11] Yair Hirschfeld, "Report warning about the Urgency of the Situation in Gaza," November 18, 1994, ארכיונים ואוספים אישיים/אוסף יאיר הירשפלד (trans. Archives and personal collections/Yair Hirschfeld collection), ן ישראל גינוך המדינה (trans. Israel State Archives), Jerusalem.

clash, loyalist forces under Arafat's command killed at least 12 Hamas and Jihad activists and injured around 200 activists.[12]

At first, the clash convinced Hamas and Jihad to restrain their activities against the emerging Palestinian governmental authorities, creating a temporary atmosphere of stability. However, Arafat's fear of another confrontation led him to avoid confronting Hamas, thus giving them an almost free hand to commit acts of terror against Israel.[13]

We made efforts to mobilize Palestinians to take action and put an end to the series of terrorist acts. El-Husseini, Abu Ala', and Ahmed Tibi were supportive and helped arrange a meeting with Arafat on December 29, 1994. My objective was to persuade him to confront Hamas and stop the acts of terror. However, he responded with anger, shouting at me, stating that he would handle internal opposition within the Palestinian community in his own way and would not be dictated to by us. He believed that Israelis should address their own internal problems. Less than two months had passed since the clashes in Gaza in November, and it was clear that Arafat had no intention of engaging in further violence with Hamas.[14] The consequences were devastating. On January 22, 1995, two explosions near Netanya claimed the lives of 22 Israelis, severely undermining the initial strong support for Oslo.[15]

The Increasing Threat of Jewish Militant Radicalism

Although we were aware of the danger posed by right-wing Jewish militant opposition, we greatly underestimated its severity after the signing of the Oslo Accords. In 1995, Hassan Azfour provided me with a protocol detailing secret meetings between Palestinian and settler leaders. The meetings were organized and overseen by Yossi Alpher, a former Mossad member. Alpher published the dialogue years later.[16] In these meetings, participants from both sides would share their personal stories, including their childhood experiences, upbringing, and ideological development. The narratives of the

---

[12] Division for Palestinian Rights, "Chronological Review of Events—Relating to the Question of Palestine;" The United Nations, September 30, 1994, https://www.un.org/unispal/document/auto-insert-203944/ (accessed July 11, 2023), archived at https://web.archive.org/web/20230712080515/https://www.un.org/unispal/document/auto-insert-203944/.

[13] Y. Shabath, *Hamas and the Peace Process*; Jerusalem, Givat Zeev, 2010, pp. 139–150 (for a detailed description of Hamas and Jihad activities against Arafat, after he entered Gaza in July 1994).

[14] In earlier meetings with Arafat he had been most forthcoming and supportive and he would offer most useful analytical comments about his own thinking, and sometimes also about the way Hafez Assad, whom he hated, was acting. This time, he shouted.

[15] Shabath, *Hamas and the Peace Process*, pp. 199–232.

[16] Yossi Alpher, *And the Wolf Shall Dwell with the Wolf: The Settlers and the Palestinians*, Hakibutz Hameuchad, 2001 (Hebrew).

settlers were remarkably similar. They had all grown up in religious youth movements, supported peace policies, and admired left-wing Kibbutz movements that produced military heroes. However, everything changed after the events of June 1967.

They had always dreamed of returning to the Jewish ancestral land in Judea and Samaria, viewing it as part of a divine plan. The establishment of the State of Israel in 1948 and the subsequent return to Judea and Samaria gave meaning to the Holocaust and paved the way for the anticipated redemption prophesied centuries ago. With this hope in mind, they moved to these areas with the intention of fostering friendly relations with the Palestinian residents. However, they encountered hostility and violence, which eventually escalated into terrorism, making their lives challenging. When terrorism initially targeted settlers in Judea, Samaria, and Gaza, or the soldiers serving there, the settlers felt isolated. However, when terror attacks reached Tel Aviv, Afula, and Hedera, they realized that the Israeli public might join them in opposing the Oslo Accords. As a result of the acts of terror, former supporters of the accords became opponents, including influential army commanders like Moshe (Bugi) Yahalon and Amos Gilead, who had the ability to influence many others. This shift in public sentiment fueled Jewish right-wing militant radicalism and contributed to the atmosphere that ultimately led to the rabbinical ruling sanctioning the assassination of Yitzchak Rabin.[17]

At the end of September 1995, the Oslo II Agreement was signed between Israel and the PLO, establishing the Palestinian Authority in Ramallah and granting it authority over Gaza and most of the West Bank. This agreement served as the political motivation for escalating protests against Rabin. On October 5, 1995, a demonstration with over 20000 participants took place at Zion Square in Jerusalem's city center. Rabin was depicted as an SS Officer, and people chanted "Rabin is a traitor." Netanyahu, the leader of the Likud opposition, stood on the balcony without taking significant action to prevent the demonization of Rabin. Despite a warning from the Israeli Secret Service (Shabak), he refused to call for an end to the militant protests. One month (minus one day) after the Zion Square demonstration, on November 4, 1995, Rabin was assassinated, causing immense pain and sorrow that still lingers.

When reading the protocol of meetings between settlers and Palestinians several months prior to Rabin's assassination, I noticed a certain sense of political realism and a desire to find common ground with Rabin's government. To test the waters, I contacted one of the ideological leaders, Israel Harel. When

---

[17] Moshe Yahalon, *The Longer Shorter Path*, Gefen, Jerusalem 2020. See Ehud Sprintzak, *Brother against Brother: Violence and Extremism from Altalena to the Rabin Assassination*, Simon and Shuster, New York 1999.

Rabin was assassinated, Harel expressed his condolences genuinely. I facilitated a meeting between him and Peres to discuss coordinated action. The discussions seemed friendly and constructive, but in the end, the commitments made by the settlers were often not upheld. It wasn't just my experience but that of senior IDF officers responsible for operations in the West Bank and Gaza. Settler leaders would justify breaking commitments by saying that for "the sake of God, we are allowed to lie."[18]

Since then, we have lost several subsequent battles. In 2017, I visited Israel Harel at his home in Ofra, accompanied by Paul Pasch, the head of the Ebert Foundation. Harel proudly showed us around, including the school, kindergarten, and meeting hall, and he pointed out that there was enough space around Ofra for another 300 to 400,000 Jewish settlers. Palestinian presence in the area appeared to be non-existent. The situation worsened as a nearby settlement, Amona, built on privately owned Palestinian land, was evacuated months before our visit. Harel took us there and explained that the Amona settlement provided protection against potential terror attacks for the residents of Ofra. He pointed to the nearby Palestinian village beyond Amona.

The political realism that seemed to be in place in 1995 when it seemed that an Israel-Palestine understanding under Rabin's leadership was possible had given way to reinforced messianic hopes among militant settlers.

The Failure of Palestinian State-Building Efforts

In discussing Palestinian state-building with numerous Palestinian counterparts, our hope was that Palestinians would follow the Israeli model of state-building. The Jewish population and leadership in Palestine, known as the Yishuv, had established most essential state institutions long before the proclamation of the State of Israel in 1948, under the British Mandate from 1921 onward. They had carefully built the administrative, legal, physical, and institutional infrastructure in preparation for the future state. The only aspect not established before 1948 was a monopoly on the use of force.[19]

However, by 1993, we had learned lessons that indicated the Palestinian development might take a different path. Early attempts to promote the economic empowerment of Palestinians in the West Bank and Gaza were hindered by the political interests of the PLO, Jordan, and Israel, all seeking

---

[18] Yair Hirschfeld's private interview with Major General Kaplinsky on June 8, 2002.
[19] Anita Shapira, *Israel—A History*, Brandeis U.P., Boston 2012.

to exert control over the area. In a study I presented to the European Union in 1992, I wrote:

> During the late 1960ies and the 1970ies as well as during the mid 1980ies economic growth in the West Bank and the Gaza Strip brought about increasing Palestinian dependency upon Israel and Jordan. In the beginning, improved conditions of welfare contributed to political stability; however, increasing awareness of the insecurity of prosperity, particularly at times of political stagnation, tended to create radicalizing rather than moderating effects.[20]

When examining the economic growth figures between 1968 and 1987, the year the Intifada began, a striking picture emerges: Palestinian GDP increased from $131 million in 1968 to $1,783 million in 1987.[21] It becomes evident that economic growth alone was not a cure-all but instead exacerbated the conflict, delaying an inevitable, and likely violent, confrontation.

In my 1992 report to the EU, I highlighted the crucial role of Israeli administrative and security controls over the West Bank and Gaza Strip, which resulted in significant dependencies in all infrastructure matters, such as road networks, transportation, electricity, and water infrastructure, all relying on Israel. It became clear to me that breaking free from these dependencies would only be achievable through an ongoing dialogue and cooperation between Israel and the Palestinians. While the Palestinian physical infrastructure required years of construction, the population still relied on Israel for water, electricity, and transportation. I had hoped to address these issues in Annex III, the "Protocol on Israeli-Palestinian Cooperation in Economic and Development Programs," and Annex IV, the "Protocol on Israeli-Palestinian Cooperation Concerning Regional Development Programs."[22]

Despite goodwill from all sides, the obstacles were immense. When Arafat arrived in Gaza, the immediate concern was to generate income. To accomplish this, Rabin agreed to the establishment of a "private bank account" and the creation of monopolies on cement, gasoline, and other goods. This

---

[20] Hirschfeld, "Israel, the Palestinians and the Middle East: From Dependency to Interdependence," *Hirschfeld Khoury-DeConcini Papers, Substack*, forthcoming (originally written in September 1992), p. 23, https://hkdpapers.substack.com/p/israel-the-palestinians-and-the-middle-east.

[21] United Nations Conference on Trade and Development, "Palestinian External Trade under Israeli Occupation," New York, 1989, https://unctad.org/system/files/official-document/rdpseud1_en.pdf (accessed July 11, 2023), archived at https://web.archive.org/web/20230712080615/https://unctad.org/system/files/official-document/rdpseud1_en.pdf.

[22] Mahmoud Abbas, *Through Secret Channels—The Road to Oslo: Senior PLO Leader Abu Mazen's Revealing Story of the Negotiations with Israel*; Garnet, Reading 1995, pp. 231–234.

approach contradicted the promotion of a functioning economy but guaranteed Arafat a monthly income of $20 million. Maher el-Kurd, who was Arafat's economic advisor, reported this figure in a meeting we had in Paris, in 1996.[23] The ongoing security situation, characterized by persistent and escalating terror, made any investment in the Palestinian economy highly risky. Additionally, Rabin's attention was divided between internal opposition, negotiations with Palestinians, Jordan, and Syria, and maintaining a close alliance with the USA. Despite the challenges, Rabin remained committed to developing a functional partnership with Arafat, understanding that ongoing confidence-building measures were more important than reaching far-reaching agreements that neither side was ready to sustain.

Arafat, on the other hand, focused on rebuilding his power base in Gaza and the West Bank and overseeing negotiations with Israel. It was difficult for him to abandon the political habits he had developed over three decades of revolutionary struggle. His control mechanisms, manipulation of administrative structures, fostering a sense of insecurity among his subordinates, and divisive tactics were counterproductive to constructive state-building efforts. Furthermore, the Palestinian rank and file had grown accustomed to revolutionary behavior, expecting pensions and avoiding payment for utilities. Clan interests often prevailed over rational economic considerations. Similarly, Israeli government authorities aimed to maintain influence and control over economic affairs in the occupied territories, showing little inclination for cooperation with their Palestinian counterparts.[24]

It wasn't all negative, though. The Paris Protocol established cooperation mechanisms, particularly the Joint Economic Committee (JEC), managed by the two Ministers of Finance. While it offered an effective structure for solving emerging problems, it lacked a well-thought-out strategy to encourage Palestinian state-building and end dependencies on Israel.

At the time, we were aware of the numerous drawbacks that arose from complete dependency on donor funding and the monopoly system. In Paris, during a meeting with Maher el-Kurd in early January 1996, he informed me that Arafat had established a committee chaired by el-Kurd. Arafat had agreed to abolish the monopoly system and had given the green light to collaborate with Israel on implementing the items outlined in Annex III and Annex IV of the Declaration of Principles. At that time, Beilin served as Minister of

---

[23] Yair Hirschfeld, "Meeting with Maher el-Kurd," January 8, 1996, ארכיונים ואוספים אישיים/אוסף יאיר הירשפלד (trans. Archives and personal collections/Yair Hirschfeld collection), ישראל גינוך המדינה (trans. Israel State Archives), Jerusalem (hereafter cited at Hirschfeld, "Meeting with Maher el-Kurd," Yair Hirschfeld Collection).

[24] Compare with Yazid Sayigh, *Armed Struggle and the Search for State: The Palestinian National Movement 1949–1993*, Clarendon Press, Oxford 1997.

Planning and had the authority to oversee the implementation of cooperation programs.[25] We felt a sense of optimism, but it only lasted a few weeks before the terrorist acts of early 1996 put an end to those plans.

As a result, the efforts toward Palestinian state-building were replaced by increasing security restrictions and a heavy reliance on substantial donation funds, which provided enough income to forgo essential economic institution building and reforms necessary for constructing the State of Palestine.

Learning to Navigate Uncharted Territory

Finalizing a Blueprint for a Permanent Status Agreement

During our initial meeting with Arafat in October 1993, we requested him to nominate two counterparts who would work with Pundik and me to develop a blueprint for a Permanent Status Agreement. It wasn't until August of the following year that we began the work with Hussein Agha and Ahmed Khalidi. Hussein Agha is Shi'ite and descends from both the royal Iranian Qajar family and Ayatollah Khorassani. Ahmed Khalidi comes from an esteemed Jerusalem family, with his father being recognized as one of the most important Palestinian historians. A young revolutionary, Yasir Arafat, sought guidance from Khalidi's family when Ahmed was a child. Khalidi's mother is the daughter of former Lebanese Prime Minister Riyad as-Sulkh. Agha and Khalidi became acquainted at the age of six in grammar school in Beirut and later joined the Fatah movement as youths. They were sent to London for their studies, with the intention of preparing them for future diplomatic tasks, and they maintained close relationships of trust with both Arafat and Abu Mazen.

With the support of the Swedish government (specifically the Olof Palme Institute), we held regular meetings, often twice a month, to develop an initial blueprint for a Permanent Status Agreement. The majority of the work was carried out by the four of us, but on several occasions, Yossi Beilin and/or Nimrod Novik would join us, as well as Nabil Shaath and Hassan Azfour from the Palestinian team. In order to prepare for the negotiating sessions in Sweden, the ECF organized several workshops covering the various issues that needed to be addressed. On security matters, we consulted with generals representing different schools of thought on security matters. On Jerusalem, we consulted rabbis, city planners, historians, and foreign

---

[25] Hirschfeld, "Meeting with Maher el-Kurd," Yair Hirschfeld Collection.

experts on Jerusalem.²⁶ On legal affairs and refugees, we sought the expertise of Ruth Lapidoth, one of Israel's most recognized experts in international law. On water, we collaborated with Shaul Arlozoroff and discussed possible approaches with Eran Feitelson and Marwan Haddad, who later produced a final report of their work.²⁷

On Tuesday, October 31, 1995, the four of us—Agha, Khalidi, Pundik, and I—presented an agreed-upon text to Yossi Beilin and Abu Mazen at the ECF office in Tel Aviv, located at 22b Daphne Street. Both Beilin and Abu Mazen offered their full support. After the meeting, I drove Abu Mazen to Herzliya, where he stayed with the Egyptian Ambassador Bassiouni in his residence. During the journey, Abu Mazen expressed his belief that "we shall get there" and made a supportive gesture with his hands, indicating that we might encounter pushbacks from both sides along the way. While we understood that these were not official negotiations and held no binding commitments, we had reached a complete understanding that the document we had produced should serve as an agreed-upon terms of reference for both sides.

I still firmly believe today that we had every reason to be proud of the document.²⁸ When presented to President Clinton (referred to as the "Stockholm Document" by Agha, Khalidi, Pundik, and myself to claim authorship), he reportedly suggested, "let us change the title and sign it." However, we were well aware that the political leadership on both sides was not yet prepared for the suggestions we were making.

Six weeks prior to finalizing the document, on September 11, at 8 p.m. in the evening, I had a meeting with Arafat. Ferdinand Lacina, the Austrian Minister of Finance (also the former chief of staff to Chancellor Kreisky) and Patricia Kahane, the daughter of a Jewish tycoon who had befriended Arafat, were present. After exchanging pleasantries with his Austrian guests, Arafat turned to me and said "Yair, I know you are working with Yossi Beilin and Abu Mazen on a concept for a Permanent Status Agreement. I suggest you should *not* conclude the agreement. It is too early and the positions are too

---

[26] Yair Hirschfeld, "Report: Paris Seminar in Jerusalem (13 May 1995)," May 17, 1995, ארכיונים ואוספים אישיים/אוסף יאיר הירשפלד (trans. Archives and personal collections/Yair Hirschfeld collection), ישראל גינוך המדינה (trans. Israel State Archives), Jerusalem.

[27] Eran Feitelson and Marwan Haddad, "Joint Management of Shared Aquifers—Final Report," *The Palestine Consultancy Group—East Jerusalem and the Harry S. Truman Research Institute for the Advancement of Peace—the Hebrew University of Jerusalem;* December 1995, pp. 1–35.

[28] "The Beilin-Abu Mazen Document: Framework for the Conclusion of a Final Status Agreement Between Israel and the Palestine Liberation Organization," Jewish Virtual Library, October 31, 1995, https://www.jewishvirtuallibrary.org/the-beilin-abu-mazen-document (accessed July 11, 2023), archived at https://web.archive.org/web/20230712080948/https://www.jewishvirtuallibrary.org/the-beilin-abu-mazen-document.

much apart." In my diary from 1994 to 95, I also recorded Arafat emphasizing that if we were to conclude the document, it would cause a divide between our group with both Rabin and Peres. A week earlier, Arafat had made the same remark to Yossi Beilin.

We were well aware that Peres opposed the territorial concept, as he had expressed to Beilin on several occasions. In order to minimize Peres' opposition, we insisted on including Article One, Paragraph 1/c, which stated that *"both sides continue to look favorably at the possibility of establishing a Jordan-Palestine Confederation, to be agreed upon by the State of Palestine and the Hashemite Kingdom."* However, we knew this was too vague for Peres. Additionally, we were aware that Rabin, at best, would be hesitant. In his speech to the Knesset on October 5, 1995, he opposed the creation of a Palestinian State. He said:

> We view the permanent solution in the framework of State of Israel which will include most of the area of the Land of Israel as it was under the rule of the British Mandate, and alongside it a Palestinian entity which will be a home to most of the Palestinian residents living in the Gaza Strip and the West Bank. We would like this to be an entity which is less than a state, and which will independently run the lives of the Palestinians under its authority.[29]

Rabin's approach was to build a partnership with Arafat despite the difficulties involved and gradually move forward, allowing Israel to maintain security and political control where necessary. Over time, I realized that this was the only feasible strategy. It did not aim to create a "permanent solution" but rather to sustain an ongoing process of trust-building and peace.

It wasn't only Arafat, Peres, and Rabin who indicated their reluctance to conclude what we were suggesting. The analytical description of the Palestinian and Israeli political systems provided by Sari Nusseibeh during the Jerusalem seminar in Paris in May 1995 struck me. Nusseibeh argued that it would be better if Likud, rather than the Labor Party, led the Israeli Government. The Labor Party, particularly its left-wing, wanted to move too quickly, creating excessive pressure on the Palestinian political structure, which would struggle to keep up. There would also be significant opposition within Israel. Nusseibeh believed that if Likud were in power, progress could be made gradually, and the Labor Party, especially its left-wing members, could offer

---

[29] Yatzhak Rabin, "Speech to Knesset on Ratification of Oslo Peace Accords," Jewish Virtual Library, October 5, 1995, https://www.jewishvirtuallibrary.org/pm-rabin-speech-to-knesset-on-ratification-of-oslo-peace-accords (accessed July 11, 2023), archived at https://web.archive.org/web/20230712081307/https://www.jewishvirtuallibrary.org/pm-rabin-speech-to-knesset-on-ratification-of-oslo-peace-accords.

practical support to the Palestinian side, allowing for the building of necessary supportive networks and advancing the process.

Nusseibeh's remarks both alarmed and comforted me. He was the first to raise the concerns that Arafat, Peres, and Rabin would later express. At the same time, his message conveyed the need for time to build a sufficient majority, bring Likud on board, and address the issue of violence on the Palestinian side. It was not merely comforting, but also a challenge for us to pursue.

Netanyahu Continues the Oslo Process with Our Support

Netanyahu's electoral victory came as a feared and expected shock. However, it became evident that we needed to adapt to the new circumstances. To do so, I took three steps. Agha had previously met Dore Gold, who was appointed by Netanyahu to handle the Palestinian portfolio. Ron and I persuaded our Swedish friends to cover the expenses of Agha's meetings not only with Dore Gold but also with Netanyahu whenever it seemed beneficial. Agha engaged in frequent discussions with Netanyahu and, to a greater extent, with Dore Gold, exploring ways to move forward.

Recognizing the dire economic situation in Gaza and the West Bank, Maher el-Kurd asked me to arrange a meeting between him and the newly appointed Israeli Minister of Finance, Dan Meridor. I approached the EU ambassador to Israel, Jean-Paul Jesse, to host the meeting. Meridor not only agreed but also offered support to alleviate the economic crisis and proposed organizing an investment conference for the Palestinian territories at the College of William and Mary in the United States. A third step involved facilitating a working relationship between Faisal el-Husseini and the incoming Minister of Internal Security, Avigdor Kahalani. To accomplish this, Beilin convinced Kahalani to appoint our friend, Ami Glusker, as his Director General.

Unfortunately, these efforts proved unsuccessful. Although we secured full support from Dan Meridor, who proposed holding an investment conference for the Palestinian territories at the College of William and Mary in Williamsburg, Virginia, the Palestinians canceled their participation at the last moment. This occurred in late December, just as Israeli-Palestinian negotiations on what would become the Hebron Protocol reached a crucial stage. The Palestinians feared that the Williamsburg Conference would alleviate political pressure on the Israeli negotiating team and thus decided to call off the conference. This cancellation happened merely three days before it was scheduled to begin, causing a significant financial loss of over $100,000 to the College of William and Mary.

Our failure to establish a functional working relationship between Kahalani and Faisal el-Husseini was even more detrimental. Netanyahu did not permit Kahalani to meet with Faisal el-Husseini. As no ongoing dialogue between the Israeli Minister for Internal Security and el-Husseini was maintained, the predictable disaster of the opening of the Hasmonean Tunnel could have been, but was not prevented.

However, some of our other efforts yielded partial success. We enjoyed unrestricted access to the newly appointed Minister of Foreign Affairs, David Levy, and I developed a friendship with Dore Gold. We also had similar access to the American peace team and used the information gathered in our meetings with various stakeholders to advocate for our ideas. In preparation for the Clinton-Netanyahu-Arafat Summit in Washington, on October 1, 1996, I prepared a two-page memorandum for Aaron Miller and Dan Kurtzer. It outlined anticipated Israeli positions, Arafat's expected reactions and demands, and listed ten proposed economic relief measures that should be implemented.[30]

Over the next three years, Beilin, Novik, and Ramon would establish a supportive structure to influence ongoing negotiations and policy discussions. They would meet regularly, often once or twice a month, with Abu Mazen and/or Saeb Erakat at the residence of the Egyptian Ambassador Bassiouni, assisting them in defining realistic expectations for the ongoing negotiations. Additionally, they would maintain contact with relevant Israeli, American, and Egyptian decision-makers.

Beilin achieved another crucial success by concluding a "Joint National Platform" with prominent members of Likud, as well as members of Gesher and Zomet, two other right-wing parties in January 1997. In my opinion, this agreement was the decisive success we needed. It would enable us to heed Sari Nusseibeh's advice and gradually move toward an Israel-Palestine two-state solution while garnering sufficient support from each side to accept and uphold the necessary concessions.[31]

Despite facing significant challenges, Netanyahu and Arafat surprisingly found common ground. In January 1997, they successfully reached agreements on the Hebron Protocol and the Note for the Record. In October

---

[30] Yair Hirschfeld, "Memorandum to Aaron Miller," October 1, 1996, ארכיונים ואוספים אישיים/אוסף יאיר הירשפלד (trans. Archives and personal collections/Yair Hirschfeld collection), ישראל גינזך המדינה (trans. Israel State Archives), Jerusalem.

[31] Yair Hirschfeld, *Track-Two Diplomacy toward an Israel-Palestinian Solution 1978–2014*; Woodrow Wilson Center Press, Washington D.C. and John Hopkins U.P., Baltimore 2014, pp. 195–196.

1998, the Wye River Agreement was signed.[32] Then, following the explicit proposal of Beilin and Novik, Netanyahu and Arafat agreed to establish four parallel dialogue channels:

(1) the "Mahmoud Abbas-David Levy" channel, which coordinated four committees on security cooperation, further Redeployment preparations, settlement restrictions and Permanent Status arrangements;
(2) the "Erekat-Danny Naveh" channel, which was responsible for general coordination mainly between the Israeli and Palestinian government ministries on both sides;
(3) the "Abu Ala'-Yizchak Molcho" channel, which considered the core issues of the conflict including Jerusalem and refugees; and
(4) the "Yasser Arafat-Netanyahu" channel, which supervised all activities and all other issues.

The Oslo Process was still alive.

Preparing an Agreement on Jerusalem, Refugees, and Security

Jerusalem

We established various working groups to address different aspects. One group comprised Israeli and Palestinian planners who developed preliminary guidelines for a 25-year Master Plan for city planning. We also commissioned policy papers on topics such as the Holy Sites and the social welfare needs of both Israeli and Palestinian residents. Through intimate dialogues with el-Husseini, who represented the PLO's Jerusalem portfolio, we explored potential agreements on Jerusalem in incremental phases rather than focusing solely on the permanent resolution. One interesting challenge was deciding the location for the Palestinian Parliament building, which we successfully advocated for its construction in the outskirts between Abu Dis and Ezariyyeh, where it remains vacant to this day.

There were reasons for optimism regarding Haram ash-Sharif/Temple Mount as well. In 1998, Sephardic Chief Rabbi Bakshi Doron issued a religious ruling acknowledging the management of the Temple Mount by Islamic dignitaries. In July of the same year, ECF organized a workshop in Milan with

---

[32] Dennis Ross, *The Missing Peace—The Inside Story of the Fight for Middle East Peace*; Farrar, Straus and Giroux, New York 2004, pp. 415–459.

the participation of the Deputy Mufti of Jerusalem and Rabbi Shmuel Sirat. During the workshop, the Deputy Mufti inquired if it was true, according to Jewish belief that the Temple would descend from heaven. Rabbi Sirat responded, "Yes, on the Day of Judgment." To this, the Vice Mufti replied, "On the Day of Judgment? This is fine with me." This exchange suggested that, if mutual fears could be minimized, an understanding regarding the Holy Sites might also be achievable. However, Rabbi Sirat added a caveat, stating, "You have to understand that no Israeli government can relinquish sovereignty over the Temple Mount before the Day of Judgment."

Refugees

I believed that actions outside the negotiation room should precede the signing of a final agreement. Arafat provided some reason for optimism in this regard. With the assistance of Maher el-Kurd, I explored an important idea suggested by US diplomat Michael Metrinko, who was responsible for allocating US aid to Palestinian refugees in the Occupied Territories, Jordan, Syria, and Lebanon. Metrinko, aware of the significant obstacles faced by Palestinian refugees in Lebanon, asked me to inquire whether Arafat would support a scheme allowing them to immigrate to the United States. If Arafat showed preliminary support, Metrinko hoped to push this idea in Washington. Maher el-Kurd returned with a positive response from Arafat, conditioned on the US offering at least 100,000 Palestinian refugees a program for immigration (at the time, the estimated Palestinian refugee population in Lebanon was 198,000).[33] The second condition was to keep the initiative as low-profile as possible. Arafat's response was straightforward: "If the US is willing to relieve me of dealing with this problem, fine." This indicated Arafat's willingness and interest in pursuing pragmatic approaches.

As part of our work on the refugee issue, ECF arranged visits for Israelis to refugee camps and for refugees to Israel. Those who participated in this program tended to experience a change in perception. Israelis, who typically denied any responsibility for the Palestinian refugee question, became aware of the problem and increasingly inclined to participate in broader programs aimed at rehabilitation. Similarly, refugees who visited Tel Aviv and Jaffa began to recognize that realities had significantly changed, and the idea of "returning" was no longer in their best interest.

---

[33] This statistic is from a confidential, unpublished report by FAFO titled "A Framework for the Negotiations on the issue of Palestinian Refugees—A Practical Approach to Enhance the Acceptability and the Implementability of a Possible Agreement.".

Security

Official negotiations between Israeli and Palestinian security authorities resulted in a common draft agreement on all relevant bilateral security issues in December 1997. Netanyahu had authorized the negotiation of this agreement to address what he referred to as the "danger of revolving doors," which meant that terrorists would move in and out of prison, and support for security cooperation with Israel could change rapidly. The draft agreement was concluded in a single night of negotiations.

On the Israeli side, the negotiations were led by Major General Shlomo Yanai and Brigadier Generak Shlomo Bromo, who was head of the Strategic Planning Department of the IDF. On the Palestinian side, they were led by General Jibril Rajoub and General Tirawi. However, Netanyahu later retracted his support and insisted the document should remain unsigned. Nevertheless, the existence of an officially prepared draft agreement provided encouragement.[34]

Initiating a Wide Range of People-to-People Activities

Under Pundik's and my leadership, and with ample funding from various sources, a wide range of People-to-People activities were initiated. Joint Israeli-Palestinian hubs were established in the areas of health, led by the Brookdale Institute. In environmental issues Pundik led a joint hub competing with two other joint Israeli-Palestinian organizations. In the field of research, members of al-Quds University collaborated with senior Israeli researchers across various disciplines. The Rothschild Foundation established a hub focused on education and reconciliation. Additionally, regional cooperation between Jenin, Haifa, Gilboa, and the Beit Shean Region served as a practical model for fostering good neighborly relations.[35]

---

[34] Yair Hirschfeld's private interview with General Brom on September 6, 2022. The text of the unsigned agreement has been classified and remains unavailable. The agreement obliged Palestinian security cooperation but at the same time limited possible action of Israel's security agencies.

[35] ECF, "A Strategy to Promote People-to-People Activities in the Middle East—Israel-the Palestinian Authority-Jordan-Egypt," January 1997, יוזמת לשיתוף פעולה כלכלי ולהסכם ביניים עם הפלסטינים (trans. An initiative for economic cooperation and an interim agreement with the Palestinians) (folder name), ISA-Privatecollections-NA-001rt7w (new folder identifier), "5821/13–פ" (trans. P 5514/1) (old folder identifier), pp. 28-46, ארכיונים ואוספים אישיים/אוסף יאיר הירשפלד (trans. Archives and personal collections/Yair Hirschfeld collection), ישראל שטאט ארכיוון (trans. Israel State Archives), Jerusalem, https://www.archives.gov.il/archives/Archive/0b0717068 8f2f0fd/File/0b07170689eaacf4/Item/090717068a008a7b (accessed June 28, 2023), archived at https://web.archive.org/web/20230712041155/https://www.archives.gov.il/archives/Archive/0b0717 0688f2f0fd/File/0b07170689eaacf4/Item/090717068a008a7b.

Warning Signs

The Danger of Ambiguity

I hadn't been involved in the negotiations for the Oslo II Agreement, but I had numerous discussions about its concept and wording with negotiators and individuals on both sides of the Israeli-Palestinian divide. It became clear to me that each side interpreted the agreement based on their own hopes and expectations.

The problematic paragraph was Article XI, specifically paragraphs 1 and 2:

Article XI Land

1. The two sides view the West Bank and the Gaza Strip as a single territorial unit, the integrity and status of which will be preserved during the interim period.
2. The two sides agree that West Bank and Gaza Strip territory, except for issues that will be negotiated in the permanent status negotiations, will come under the jurisdiction of the Palestinian Council…[36]

The Israeli interpretation of Article XI/1 and 2 was that it allowed for territorial compromise, which led Barak to believe later on that he could offer a 67:33 percent division of the West Bank to the Palestinians under its terms. On the other hand, the Palestinian interpretation was that this was irrelevant. They assumed, with some justification, that when the time came for permanent status negotiations, previous agreements would hold little or no relevance. The decisive factor would be the need to reach a new agreement. Convinced that time and international law were on their side, the Palestinians believed that the demand for a 100% territorial agreement was an internationally recognized condition that would eventually be accepted. If Israel did not agree, they would repeatedly say "no."

Security Warnings

I understood that the Oslo agreements would eventually compel Arafat to take effective action against Hamas. Allowing Hamas and Jihad terrorism to persist would force Israeli security forces to take forceful action that Arafat

---

[36] "Israeli-Palestinian Interim Agreement on the West Bank and the Gaza Strip," September 28, 1995, United Nations Peacemaker, Article XI (p. 16), https://peacemaker.un.org/sites/peacemaker.un.org/files/IL%20PS_950928_InterimAgreementWestBankGazaStrip%28OsloII%29.pdf (accessed July 11, 2023), archived at https://web.archive.org/web/20230712081143/https://peacemaker.un.org/sites/peacemaker.un.org/files/IL%20PS_950928_InterimAgreementWestBankGazaStrip%28OsloII%29.pdf.

could not prevent. In the eyes of the Palestinian people, he would be seen as powerless while Hamas would gain dominance. To prevent such a situation, I believed Arafat would need to demonstrate that the PLO was the sole legitimate representative of the Palestinian people and take the necessary steps to suppress Hamas and Jihad terrorism, either independently or in cooperation with Israel's security forces. We had discussed this scenario several times.

However, during the 1990s, Rabin allowed for a third option. Arafat was given the opportunity to exploit acts of terrorism by Hamas and Jihad to obstruct negotiations when it served his interests and seek further concessions. Concerned about this possibility, I opposed Rabin's slogan of "to fight terror, as if there were no negotiations, and to negotiate, as if there was no terror." It made it too tempting for Arafat to resort to violence when he did not achieve what he wanted through negotiations. Instead, I believed that Israel should halt negotiations in response to acts of terror and insist on enhancing security cooperation. I tried to convince Beilin, Pundik, and many others through quiet discussions. However, they all argued that "stopping negotiations" would reward Hamas and Jihad. They believed the Israeli Defense Forces (IDF) could handle the terrorism issue, while I was convinced that it was Arafat who needed to take action and should be compelled to do so.

My reasoning overlooked the fact that Rabin and Arafat's political timetables were not synchronized. When Rabin needed Arafat to act, he was not ready to do so. Four months after Rabin's assassination, the situation had deteriorated to a point where Arafat decided to take action. It was on Sunday morning, March 3, 1996, when I was attending a meeting at Fathi Arafat's office to discuss health cooperation. Just a week earlier (February 25), there was a suicide attack on bus 18, resulting in the deaths of 26 Israelis. While I was at Fathi Arafat's office, we received news of another attack on bus 18. Among the 19 people killed was the son of Tamara and Nahum Barnea. Tamara was working with ECF and Fathi Arafat on health cooperation. She called me to express her determination to continue working for peace despite her personal tragedy. While I was still at the office, Arafat called and wanted to talk to me, asking me to relay a message to Peres that he would now give the order to fight Hamas and Jihad with whatever was necessary. The same message was conveyed to Peres through various channels.

Under the command of Ami Ayalon and Yuval Diskin, Israeli security forces and Palestinian security forces led by Muhammad Dahlan cooperated in attacking the military infrastructure of Hamas and Jihad. Palestinians also advised Pundik and me to suggest that Israel implement severe economic and other punitive measures temporarily to make it clear to the Palestinian public that terrorism would not achieve its goals.

We had frequent discussions on security issues with Palestinian counterparts responsible for security affairs. Jibril Rajoub explained the Palestinian perspective, stating:

> When there is progress in the peace process, security cooperation with Israel allows the PA to take action against militant radical groups. Then, any act of terror only puts sticks in the wheels of a forward movement. However, when there is stagnation in the peace process, security cooperation is seen by our people as a means to prolong occupation. We are perceived to be collaborators with the enemy, similar to the position General Haddad of South Lebanon, whose collusion with Israel would then turn him into a traitor in the national Lebanese perception.[37]

The situation presented both promising and problematic aspects. The promising part was that there was a Palestinian commitment to security cooperation. However, the problematic part revolved around what would happen if progress did not meet Palestinian expectations or if the Palestinians rejected essential Israeli requests. Would the resulting stalemate legitimize a return to "armed struggle" in the eyes of the Palestinians? Would it lead to a renewed alliance between Fatah, Hamas, Jihadist movements, and their regional supporters?

Muhammad Dahlan and Hassan Azfour provided a clear answer to this question during their conversation with Novik in February 1998. They stated that "violence was the only realistic response against an unfolding US-Israeli conspiracy against the Palestinians."[38]

This warning highlighted the potential for a renewal of violence if negotiations on permanent status reached an impasse and did not meet all Palestinian demands. Since every Israeli government preparing for permanent status negotiations would coordinate with the United States, a failure to meet Palestinian demands could lead to a resort to violence.

Based on these observations, my personal conclusion was straightforward: Yasir Arafat would be the most decisive actor in the upcoming permanent status negotiations. Simply anticipating his behavior based on a comparison

---

[37] Jibril Rajoub would repeatedly make this statement to most members of ECF. He has maintained until today a very close friendship with Brigadier General Dov Sadaqa. In a workshop in Houston he would discuss the entire security complex of relations in much detail with Israel's Lieutenant-General Amnon Lipkin Shachak.

[38] Nimrod Novik, "hamifgash hameshushah" (trans. The Meeting of the Six), February 3, 1998. Quoted in Hirschfeld *Track Two Diplomacy*, p. 193 and fn. 28.

with the Qajar dynasty in Iran was not sufficient. We needed a deeper understanding of Arafat's thinking and actions in order to prepare appropriately for the permanent status negotiations.

Suggested Reading

Understanding Arafat and the Palestinian National Movement

Ronit Marzan *Yassir Arafat—The Rhetoric of a lone Leader*; Resling, Tel Aviv 2016; Marzan describes the buildup of Arafat's militant rhetoric at first, and then his effort to adopt a very different rhetoric, preparing the Palestinian national movement for compromise and a peace-building process with Israel. It is absolutely essential reading.

Yezid Sayigh *Armed Struggle and the Search for State: The Palestinian National Movement, 1949–1993;* Clarendon Press, Oxford 1997. Sayigh's monumental work offers a detailed and analytical understanding of the successes and failures of the Palestinian national movement. He hints at the difficulties that emerge in the transformation of a militant and fighting revolutionary movement to a state.

The Economic Challenge of State-Building

Steven Lobell and Norrin Ripsman (ed.) *The Political Economy of Regional Peacemaking*; Michigan U.P. Ann Arbor 2016. The entire collection of articles addressing the issue in different areas is of great value. My Foreword describes the experience gained in Palestine, while responding to five central questions, the donor community should always keep in mind. Another important contribution is Marie-Joelle Zahar's article "Making Peace with Non-state Armed Actors".

Toufic Haddad *Palestine Ltd. Neoliberalism and Nationalism in the Occupied Territory*; Tauris, London 2016; This is a well-documented, and well informed, but biased account. Although I personally tend to disagree with the conclusions drawn, the data and analysis presented are extremely useful to serve a future professional dialogue, on what to do, and what not to do, in order to build a prosperous Palestinian economy.

Yezid Sayigh and Khalil Shikaki, "Strengthening Palestinian Public Institutions," Council on Foreign Relations Press 1999 (this is the report of an independent task force sponsored by the Council on Foreign Relations).

The Challenge of Terrorism

Y. Shabath *Hamas and the Peace Process—To What Extent does Hamas Act to Undermine Reconciliation*; Jerusalem-Givat Zeev 2010. Shabath describes in eleven chapters the Hamas ideology, its political objectives, and its reactions to ongoing events—the Oslo Process, the Treaty of Peace with Jordan, the withdrawal from Gaza and a potential peace with Syria. It is obligatory reading.

Martha Crenshaw "Terrorism and Global Security" in Chester A Crocker et al. (eds) *Leashing the Dogs of War—Conflict Management in a Divided World*; United States Institute of Peace Press, Washington D.C. 2007; pp. 67–82.

Learning from the Irish Conflict

Brendan O'Brien *The Long War—the IRA & Sinn Fein*; the O'Brian Press, Dublin 1993. O'Brian described the political dilemma of the IRA (Ireland Republican Army) during the early 1970ies. Terror without any hope for change caused opposition to the national struggle within the catholic Northern Ireland community. In order to sustain wide community support a parallel negotiating process became essential. However, when the nationalist political demands were not met, the use of terror, became again a decisive instrument, for pursuing the hoped for outcome. The division between the IRA and Sinn Fein then solved the problem; when negotiations would not lead to the hoped for result, terror acts would aim to achieve the necessary reset; while then again returning to negotiations might allow to achieve the necessary headway. Seen from an Israeli perspective this created a serious challenge for the negotiation effort with the PLO and the simultaneous struggle against the terror acts of Hamas and Jihad.

Jewish Militant Radicalism Leading to the Assassination of Rabin

Ehud Sprinzak *Brother Against Brother: Violence and Extremism in Israeli Politics from the Altalena to the Rabin Assassination;* Simon and Schuster, New York, 1999. Sprinzak's description of Jewish religious militancy was then and is even more today obligatory reading. Understanding the historical development and the causes of Jewish violent militancy directed against Jews and Arabs in Israel and Palestine is not enough. Political action and related research is needed to overcome this threat to Israeli and Palestinian society.

Ongoing Negotiations, Disagreements, and Agreements (1993–1999)

Mahdi F. Abdul Hadi (ed). *Documents on Palestine –From Negotiations in Madrid to the Post-Hebron Agreement Period;* Passia, Jerusalem 1997; offers a multitude of documents, including speeches, as well as a description of achieved agreements throughout these years, with an additional description of day-to-day events. The collection of these many documents clearly illustrates the success story of the Oslo process during these years, in spite of the many difficulties and set-backs. Of particular interest for understanding the PLO position on the first Oslo Accord is the PLO Executive Committee Statement on the Declaration of Principle, Tunis, 12 September, 1993, pp.143–144.

Raphael Cohen-Almagor, *Resolving the Israeli-Palestinian Conflict: A Critical Study of Peace Mediation, Facilitation and Negotiations between Israel and the PLO* (New York and Cambridge: Cambridge U.P. (forthcoming). Cohen-Almagor's description of the unfolding of the Oslo process, after the conclusion of the Declaration of Principles, and throughout the 1990s provides an excellent account of the successes rather than the failures of the Oslo process, during these years.

An American Description of Events during the First Netanyahu Government (1996–1999)

Dennis Ross *The Missing Peace—The Inside Story of the Fight for Middle East Peace*, Farrar, Straus and Giroux, New York 2005. Chapters 13–19. Ross provides a detailed description of the American negotiating effort during these years.

Addressing the Final Status Issues: Jerusalem, Refugees, Borders, Settlements, Security, Water

Aharon Klieman *Compromising Palestine—A Guide to Final Status Negotiations*; Columbia U.P. New York, 2000. Having failed 1995, 2000, 2001, 2008 and 2014, to conclude successfully an Israeli-Palestinian Final Status Agreement, this book, is an important guide to the issues that have to be negotiated. It may be of assistance for future policy planning either to pursue a final status agreement, or if not, seek a best alternative to such an agreement.

6

From Hope Under Netanyahu to Disaster Under Ehud Barak

Adapting the Israeli Approach to Arafat's Strategic Behavior

During my leadership at ECF, our primary goal was to prepare for final status negotiations. Understanding the strategic mindset of Palestinian leader Yasser Arafat was crucial. To gain insights into his thinking, I sought the assistance of my friend Zuheir el-Menasreh, a significant Palestinian figure known for his unique relationship with Arafat. While serving within the PLO, El-Menasreh had been appointed the Governor of Jenin, the head of Palestinian Preventive Security, and later the Governor of Bethlehem. El-Menasreh belonged to a small minority within the PLO who could openly express disagreement without fearing backlash from Arafat.

I approached him to gain a better understanding of Arafat's strategic thinking. He shared a conversation he had witnessed between Arafat and Robert Mugabe during a diplomatic trip to Zimbabwe years ago. Arafat emphasized the importance of first controlling both the flow of financial resources and also multiple armed groups. He then stressed the need to develop two different grand-strategies and maintain their independent viability. This allowed for a constant assessment of which strategy yielded the best results and the ability to switch between them if necessary.

In the context of the Israeli-Palestinian conflict, I interpreted Arafat's approach as aiming to pursue peace negotiations while keeping the option of armed struggle open, possibly in collaboration with groups like Hamas, Jihad, or Iran. The specific concern was Arafat's ability to swiftly deploy an armed struggle if he was dissatisfied with the progress in negotiations.

In order to keep Arafat on the peace-track ECF focused on four interconnected projects:

Preparing a Code of Conduct

The initial step was to establish Arafat's commitment, at least publicly, to peace through negotiations. Our Palestinian partners in the Stockholm channel proposed that we ask Arafat to present a code of conduct for the negotiation process. The opportunity arose in 1998 when he was invited to Stockholm to commemorate the 10th anniversary of the US-PLO dialogue's inception.

Sten Andersson, the Swedish Minister of Foreign Affairs, played a crucial role in initiating the dialogue in 1988. At the commemoration event, he aimed to not only celebrate the achievement but also advance the process. Taking advantage of this opportunity, the ECF team, Pundik, and myself, and our Palestinian counterparts Agha and Khalidi, prepared a speech for Arafat titled "Moving from the Logic of War to the Logic of Peace." With Andersson's support, Arafat delivered the speech word for word and emphasized the certain phrases exactly as Agha and Khalidi had directed.

To establish that he (and the Israelis) were committed to the path toward peace, Arafat declared that:

> We see that our first task is to undertake a qualitative change in our political discourse. This means the transition from the logic of war and confrontation to the logic of peace in our mutual dealings. For actions and words that may be appropriate to the era of war and confrontation can no longer be useful or appropriate in the era of peace and cooperation…There can be no alternative to resolving the disputed issues between the two sides except through negotiations.[1]

Arafat also demanded that Israel commit to a two-state solution before further progress could be made. He acknowledged the primary importance of security conditions and expressed the Palestinian side's willingness to consider arrangements that respected Palestinian sovereignty.[2]

This speech was well-received in Israel, garnering positive responses from the press and the majority of Knesset members. What was needed would be

---

[1] Yasir Arafat, "Address to the Swedish Parliament, Stockholm 5 December 1998" in *Journal of Palestine Studies* 28, No 3. April 1999.
[2] Arafat, "Address to the Swedish Parliament.".

to negotiate the Code of Conduct in a way that would oblige both parties—with international endorsement—to sustain "the Logic of Peace" and refrain from violent action.

Trouble was twofold: returning from Sweden to the Middle East, Arafat made again most militant statements, in clear contradiction to "the Logic of Peace." We failed to convince the incoming Barak Government to engage on negotiations on the proposed "Code of Conduct."

Supporting Palestinian Economic Growth

We did not think that support for economic growth could stand alone. Nevertheless, economic growth was an essential building stone on the way to dealing with the more political issues.[3] Thus, in collaboration with the Norwegians, we assembled a team of Israeli and Palestinian economists to design a strategy for future economic relations, known as the Economic Permanent Status (EPS) project.

David Brodet, who had negotiated the Paris Agreement as the Director General of the Ministry of Finance in 1994, led the Israeli team. Maher el-Kurd, Arafat's economic advisor, led the Palestinian side. The concept developed for the project involved three tiers:

- The first tier defined a shared vision of political separation and economic cooperation. The vision was based on a partnership for growth and development, especially of the Palestinian economy.
- The second tier defined guidelines in key areas of economic relations: trade relations, investment, labor, and currency issues. It addressed institutional support structures, as well as considerations for the environment, natural resources, and long-term developments. It also outlined the development of an Israeli Economic Assistance Program, a dispute settlement mechanism, and, most critically, security policies.
- The third tier concentrated on transforming the existing Interim Period economic regime into the envisioned EPS model. It also outlined the

---

[3] Norrin M. Ripsman, "The Economics of Peacemaking: Lessons from Western Europe and the Middle East" in: Steven E. Lobell and Norrin M. Ripsman (eds) *The Political Economy of Regional Peacemaking* Michigan U.P., Ann Arbor 2016, pp. 23–34 (for an analytical evaluation of the role and the constraints of economics in peacemaking) and pp. ix-xv (my foreword). See Toufic Haddad, *Palestine Ltd.—Neoliberalism and Nationalism in the Occupied Territory*, Taurus, London 2016 (this provides important information about the Palestinian economy. However, his thesis that Israel would intentionally prevent Palestinian economic development is untenable and completely disregards the impact of political and security events, as much as existing Palestinian shortcomings).

necessary conditions for transitioning towards a final Permanent Status Agreement.

Ultimately, the EPS agreement was signed between the two project teams in 1999. It was followed up in meetings with the World Bank and the IMF in Washington. However, Arafat asked Mohammad Shtaiyeh to review the document, who opposed it, due to internal political turf battles.[4]

Preparing Trilateral Security Understandings

Together with Gilead Sher, who later became Barak's chief negotiator, we began planning to combine regional security understandings with would-be security arrangements between Israel and Palestine. We based our approach on two key assumptions:

A. Israel's primary security borders are the northern and eastern borders of Jordan. To strengthen these borders against potential attacks from other countries through Jordan, such as Syria from the north or Iraq from the east, Israel, Jordan, and the USA would cooperate.
B. Many security challenges, including terrorism, missile attacks, and military invasions, could not be effectively addressed solely through bilateral Israeli-Palestinian arrangements. They would be better managed within a trilateral structure involving Jordan.

In 2000, King Abdullah II and Prime Minister Barak accepted and supported our approach. However, the Palestinians withdrew their initial commitment and agreement.[5]

---

[4] ECF, "The EPS Model—A Possible Set of Israeli-Palestinian Economic Understandings," *Hirschfeld Khoury-DeConcini Papers, Substack*, forthcoming (originally written 1999), pp. 1–56, https://hkd papers.substack.com/p/the-eps-model. See John Lyndon et al., "Long-Term Strategy to Create Conditions for Peace: Recommendations for the Implementation of the Nita M. Lowey Middle East Partnership for Peace Act" Alliance for Middle East Peace (ALLMEP), January 2021, https://www.allmep.org/wp-content/uploads/2021/04/MEPPA-Implementation.pdf (accessed July 11, 2023), archived at https://web.archive.org/web/20230712082211/https://www.allmep.org/wp-content/uploads/2021/04/MEPPA-Implementation.pdf.

[5] ECF, "Integrated Security Arrangements Between Israel, Jordan and the Palestinian State—The Need, Main Characteristics and the Possible Participation of Third Party Forces," *Hirschfeld Khoury-DeConcini Papers, Substack*, forthcoming (originally written 1998), pp. 1–56, https://hkdpapers.sub stack.com/p/integrated-security-arrangements.

Preparing People-To-People (P2P) and Government-To-Government (G2G) Cooperation

A fourth strategic component aimed at preventing Arafat from adopting a strategy of militant resistance, was to develop People-to-People activities on several levels: cooperation between youth and youth seemed essential for the future; addressing specific issues as health, culture, environment, and scientific research by initiating cooperation between professionals served to identify and pursue shared interests, while creating cooperative networks, was another approach. We also initiated strategic cooperation between the two police forces, which actually was based on a Government-to-Government Cooperation. Most of these activities were interrupted by the Second Intifada of 2000–2005. More recently the Alliance for Middle East Peace (ALLMEP) has revived many of these activities.[6]

From my personal point of view, the most important activity, was "Cooperation North." It combined grass-root people-to-people activities, with cooperation between Local Councils (municipalities) and coordination between related governmental actors.

In 1997, during a workshop initiated by the Ebert Foundation, the Governor of Jenin el-Menasreh and I realized the potential for broader cooperation. The market for goods from the Jenin Governorate was primarily Israel, making economic cooperation mutually beneficial. Palestinian merchants were selling most of their goods and services to Israelis, who were invited to enter the Jenin area and make purchases there. Estimates indicated that this trade pattern provided over $150 million for Palestinian income.

Danni Atar, the mayor of the neighboring Gilboa municipality, supported cooperation. He understood that economic relations would also offer important advantages to his whole municipality, which also included Arab villages. Families on the Israeli side had relatives on the Palestinian side. It created a human network for business and other relations. In a dialogue with all concerned actors, we first defined principles for cooperation. We then agreed to establish four joint work groups focusing on economic cooperation, regional infrastructure planning and construction, civil security, and human resources development and education.

The project, known as "Cooperation North," included the Jenin Governorate on the Palestinian side, the Haifa, Gilboa and Emek HaMaayanot

---

[6] Yair Hirschfeld and Sharon Roling, "The Oslo Process and the People-to-People Strategy," in *Development, Community and Conflict, 2000 43/3; pp. 23–28*, The Society of International Development, London.

municipalities on the Israeli side. We aimed to transform the borders into venues for cooperation and trust-building measures rather than barriers that foster hostility. The Gilboa municipality was the close by neighbor to the Jenin Governorate. The Emek HaMaayanot municipality opened the way to the Jordanian border and offered to widen agricultural cooperation. The Haifa Municipality and the Haifa harbor, opened access to the West; while the University of Haifa, and the Technion offered possibilities for cooperation on a wide range of needed research and scientific options. Most important was the plan to establish a laboratory to ease the upgrading of Palestinian agricultural exports to Israel and beyond. A joint Steering Committee oversaw the project, and a joint office was established in the Governorate building in Jenin. On February 15, 1999, a signing ceremony took place in Haifa municipality, involving the three mayors and the governor.

Our next step was to create an industrial park in the Jenin area. To facilitate this, we successfully convinced the Israeli government to unilaterally change Area C to Area B. Working groups on infrastructure worked on improving water supply and recycling sewage, as well as road and railway connections to further enhance cooperation and development in the region. A work group on civil security effectively fought crime on both sides of the border. The work group on human resources development aimed to coordinate professional training between the administrative staff of municipalities on both sides of the divide and encourage sport and cultural activities between youths.

Remarkably, personal connections were forged with members of the refugee camp in Jenin. A young boy from the camp became friends with an Israeli Bedouin social worker. This social worker, in turn, organized a visit by an almost exclusively female delegation consisting of Israeli psychologists, social workers, occupational therapists (including my wife Ruthi), teachers, and kindergarteners to the refugee camp. During the visit, they discussed ways to improve physical conditions, upgrade equipment, and enhance teaching methods. In return, a delegation from the refugee camp, accompanied by their husbands, paid a visit to Kiryat Tivon. Then, the Israeli group brought important equipment to the refugee camp, to assist early child education.

An ECF Report describes in much detail people-to-people work carried out. Furthermore, a theoretical model for good neighborly relations was submitted to the EU. It proposed five complementary layers:—on the border itself; between the bordering districts; on a larger regional basis impacting the border districts; the connection to Jordan and via Haifa west-ward, and third party involvement and support.[7]

In summary, these four strategy components were an integral part of ECF's aim to keep Arafat on the peace track, and prevent him to changing over to his second strategy of returning to violence. The proposed "code of conduct" aimed to foster a supportive atmosphere for negotiations. The EPS Agreement offered conditions for substantial Palestinian economic growth and development, while granting full sovereignty over their economic policies. The trilateral Israel-Palestine-Jordan security package aimed to establish the necessary security framework. The people-to-people activities sought to generate bottom-up support and legitimacy for the leadership's peace efforts.

In retrospect most of these efforts failed: The idea of creating safety networks before negotiations was opposed to Prime Minister's Barak concept of "everything or nothing". Nevertheless, the strategic logic remains valid and should be reintroduced and adapted to changing circumstances.

ECF Influence in Barak's Peace Administration Proved Futile

Several months before the elections, I traveled with Gidi Grinstein to Egypt to meet with Ambassador Dan Kurtzer for a brainstorming session. Gidi Grinstein, who was a project director at ECF, coordinated the work on Economic Permanent Status (EPS) with David Brodet and on Security Permanent Status (SPS) with Gilead Sher. We compiled a two-and-a-half-page report summarizing the meeting with Kurtzer. At the beginning of the report, Dan Kurtzer expressed the urgency to finalize negotiations before January 20, 2001, while President Clinton was still in office. This appealed to Barak. With the support of Clinton he hoped to reach an agreement as soon as possible.

Subsequently, with the assistance of David Brodet and Gilead Sher, we made concerted efforts to convince Barak to include Gidi Grinstein in his policy planning team. This allowed Gidi Grinstein to become a member of the "Peace Administration." In an effort to maximize our influence, Gidi

---

[7] ECF, "Israel-Palestinian Cross-border Economic Cooperation in the Northern West Bank—A Good Neighborly Relations (GNR) Model," *Hirschfeld Khoury-DeConcini Papers, Substack*, forthcoming (originally written 2016), https://hkdpapers.substack.com/p/israel-palestine-cross-border-cooperation.

received the ECF computer, along with all the work we had done, to challenge other members of the Peace Administration and hopefully have our prepared policies adopted and implemented.[8]

However, our hopes were shattered as Barak not only disregarded ECF's advice but also dismissed most inputs from the Peace Administration. The consequences of Barak's actions were far-reaching. When he assumed office, the peace process, despite its flaws and setbacks, was still intact. However, by the time Barak left office in February 2001, mistrust and terror had become the norm, and the Israeli-Palestinian partnership had crumbled. While it is essential to acknowledge Arafat's deplorable contribution to this disaster, Barak undoubtedly played a significant role in its occurrence.

Ehud Barak's Initial Policy Approach

Barak employed a high-pressure negotiation tactic, operating on the principle of "everything or nothing." His strategy involved initially dampening Palestinian expectations, followed by presenting an irresistible offer. He believed that if Arafat rejected the deal, it would enhance Israel's standing in the region and the international community, exposing the Palestinian rejectionist stance as the main obstacle to an agreement. Barak's assumption was that time would eventually favor Israel.

At Wye River, Netanyahu had committed to enlarge area A by 1 per cent and Area B by 12%, hereby decreasing Area C by 13%, but when Netanyahu left office, the IDF had only withdrawn from 2%.[9] Upon assuming office, Barak contacted Arafat to convey his decision to explicitly postpone the implementation of the understandings reached in the Wye River Memorandum.[10]

---

[8] All the policy planning work ECF had carried out between 1996 and 1999 was taken with Grinstein to serve Barak's negotiating team. Other members of the Peace Administration would regularly consult with the entire ECF team. Grinstein prepared a day-to-day record, divided into five chapters: 1. May 5—September 10, 1999 (until the conclusion of the Sharm el-Sheikh Memorandum; 2. September 11–November 7, 1999 (the dialogue on the formal track); 3. November 8, 1999-April 15, 2000; (little progress before Sweden); 4. April 15-July 10 (From the talks in Sweden to Camp David); 5. July 11, 2000-February 5, 2001 (to the fall of the Barak Government). For any future research regarding peace negotiations under Prime Minister Barak, this material is of great importance. Gidi Grinstein (with Ari Afilalo), *Lessons in Peace-Making—30 Years of the Oslo Process;* Gefen Publications, Jerusalem

[9] "The Wye River Memorandum," October 23, 1998, https://web.archive.org/web/20010715073548; https://www.knesset.gov/docs/wye_eng.htm (accessed July 12, 2023).

[10] For a detailed description of Barak's thinking and action, see Grinstein, *Lessons in Peace-Making.* Grinstein explains that Barak needed time to pursue negotiations on the Syrian track.

Additionally, he disregarded track-two negotiations, including those involving Pundik and myself, stating his unwillingness to engage in unofficial discussions like those held in the woods of Norway. In September, the Sharm el-Sheikh Protocol was signed, committing Barak to finalize a Framework Agreement by February 2000. However, he disregarded this commitment, prioritizing negotiations with Syria instead.

Barak's approach, coupled with concerns about him and Clinton imposing an agreement, fueled Palestinian anger and contributed to the outbreak of the Second Intifada, resulting in the breakdown of negotiations. The notion of either reaching a complete understanding or nothing at all reflects a perilous approach that paves the way for disaster. It hindered Arafat's ability to pursue a negotiated agreement and pushed him towards an alternative strategy of violence and terror; which does not relieve Arafat of his responsibility of having destroyed the peace process.

Hanan Ashrawi, then the Palestinian Legislative Council representative for Jerusalem, offered a description of how Barak's approach to Permanent Status negotiations with the Palestinians was perceived:

> Very few people question Barak's determination to pursue and achieve a peace treaty with the Palestinians (and even the Syrians for this matter). The question is in his vision of "peace" and his misguided notion that he can single-handedly design a process, control the conduct of negotiations, select the Palestinian negotiators, dictate the substance and the time frame, redefine the role of the sponsors (the US) and the international community, and impose the outcome unilaterally….The vast gap between Barak's concept of peace and the minimal level of Palestinian rights and legality cannot be solved by a forced or dictated version.[11]

The Several Delusions of Barak's Approach to Negotiating

When Ashrawi penned these lines in November 1999, they may have appeared overly critical. Yet, over the subsequent seven and a half months, her assessment of Barak's and Clinton's approach became increasingly accurate. Most of Barak's tactics proved counterproductive. He was not interested in collaboration with the Palestinians, but rather in dictating to them. This

---

[11] Hanan Ashrawi, "Unilateral Peace?" Miftah, October 30, 1999, http://www.miftah.org/Display.cfm?DocId=112&CategoryId=1 (accessed July 11, 2023), archived at https://web.archive.org/web/20230712082558; http://www.miftah.org/Display.cfm?DocId=112&CategoryId=1.

approach reflected a lack of respect towards his negotiating partners and did not engender a spirit of cooperation.

His failure to adjust his strategy in the face of its continued failure was more than just a miscalculation. It bordered on a complete delusion of the actual events he was presented with. His perspective seemed completely detached from reality. Here I have highlighted what I find to be the four most egregious "delusions" he pursued:

The Delusion of an Unprepared Summit

When studying how to prepare for summit meetings in a negotiation process, the Kennedy-Khrushtchew Summit Meeting in Vienna in 1961 is often referenced. Kennedy's lack of preparation and inadequate briefing about the situation in Iran gave Khrushtchew the impression that major concessions could be pressured. This led to the Cuba Crisis of 1962, which nearly escalated into World War III. The lesson learned is to never go unprepared into a summit meeting. Unfortunately, Barak and Clinton did not learn this lesson. Aaron Miller described shortcomings of preparing for the Summit in much detail.[12]

The Delusion of Negotiating like in the Persian Bazar

Barak's initial territorial proposal, which demanded the annexation of 33% of the West Bank, faced rejection. Subsequently, he revised his offer multiple times, gradually eroding his own red lines "into pink lines." This approach only served to raise expectations rather than diminish them. Miller commented that the "urgency caused Barak's redlines to turn pink time and again, signaling a weak and wily Arafat that he would get more from the Israelis simply by holding out for more. How could the summit be a 'moment of truth,' …when 'every redline' was changed in favor of the next."[13]

---

[12] Aaron David Miller, *The Much Too Promised Land–America's Elusive Search for Arab-Israeli Peace*; Bantam New York 2008, pp. 295–309. He describes President Clinton's approach as follows: "But that was how Bill Clinton approached the summit and acted throughout the two week conference: he never developed or asked for either a strategy to maximize the chance for success or a backup plan to minimize the impact of failure; I might add, we (the US peace team) did not give him one" (p. 298). Miller describes the many shortcomings under the following headlines:"No Sustained Strategy", pp. 300–301; "No Negotiating Text", pp. 302–303; "Not Enough Time" pp. 303–304; "Illusions About Closing" pp. 304-305; "No Arab Support" pp. 305–307; "No Plan B" pp. 307–309.

[13] Miller, *The Much Too Promised Land*, p. 297.

The Delusion of Rejecting "Backward Negotiations"

In June 1999, Moty Cristal, a member of the Peace Administration, proposed a more effective approach known as "backward negotiations." The idea was to start with the Beilin-Abu Mazen Understanding offering Arafat statehood, turn him into the demandeur, while defining the supportive conditions and Palestinian concessions needed to secure the essential majority in the Knesset, possibly moving gradually forward. Later that autumn, Gilad Sher, who served as de facto chief negotiator for Barak, met with Agha and Khalidi in London, and they suggested the same approach. Sher and later Ben Ami supported the idea, but Barak rejected it.[14]

The Delusion of Playing in Domestic Palestinian Politics

When intense negotiations began in Stockholm in April 2000, Barak and US National Security Advisor Sandy Berger bypassed Abu Mazen and instead engaged in negotiations with Abu Mazen's personal enemies, Muhammad Dahlan and Hassan Azfour. When Agha was asked why this happened, this was his response:

> Because they thought they will have shortcuts with others; they played the dangerous game of domestic Palestinian politics. The American team and Barak's calculation was to identify the future leaders of the Palestinians and to deal almost exclusively with them. It was a fatal mistake; their estimations were completely divorced from the realities of Palestinian politics.[15]

Sher was aware of this mistake and asked Novik and me to intervene with Abu Mazen. We did, and Abu Mazen requested a meeting with Barak to prepare understandings before the planned summit. Both requests were politely rejected. Not having prepared the Summit at Camp David properly, negotiations there turned into a "dialogue of the deaf." Israeli negotiators would make concessions to Palestinian negotiators who lacked the legitimacy and power to offer the necessary quid pro quo.

---

[14] Gilead Sher, The Israel-Palestinian Peace Negotiations, 1999–2001, Routledge 2006.
[15] Raphael Cohen-Almagor, "History of Track-Two Negotiations: Interview with Hussein Agha," in *Israel Studies*, pp. 47–72; vol. 26, No. 1, Spring 2021.

The Delusion that the Substance of the Offer of "All or Nothing" Could NOT be Rejected and There Would be No Need for "Plan B"

Barak was convinced that decreasing expectations early on, and subsequently "putting all the goodies on the table," in regard to territories, Jerusalem, and even refugees, would convince Arafat to accept the proposed deal. And if not, he would prepare for unilateral disengagement.[16] President Clinton went all along with Barak's strategic approach. He wrote about the proposed agreement:

> It was historic: an Israeli government had said that to get peace, there would be a Palestinian state in roughly 97 percent of the West Bank, counting the swap, and all of Gaza, where Israel also had settlements. The ball was in Arafat's court. I was calling other Arab leaders daily to urge them to pressure Arafat to say, yes. They were all impressed with Israel's acceptance and told me Arafat should take the deal....On the twenty-ninth, Dennis Ross met with Abu Ala', whom we all respected, to make sure Arafat understood the consequences of rejection....I still didn't believe Arafat would make such a colossal mistake.[17]

Knowing and understanding the dire consequences of Arafat's rejection, makes it inexcusable, no Plan B allowing Arafat to go along, had been officially prepared.[18]

My Ignored Warnings

By June 2000, I had worked with Beilin for 20 years. Throughout those years, I had never written a protocol of phone discussions with him. However, on June 10, I felt compelled to do so. Reading the protocol now, I realize how evident it was to me that permanent status negotiations were heading toward

---

[16] First plans for unilateral disengagement were planned during Rabin's premiership of 1992–1995, but rejected due to high costs involved. June 2000, Barak ordered the Peace Administration to plan for unilateral withdrawal, but never followed up. Gilead Sher and Uri Sagi based on the work that had been done, published a plan for unilateral withdrawal in 2002, which eventually became a forerunner of Sharon's Disengagement Plan of 2004–2005. For an interactive database of the Sher-Sagi Plan, see ECF, "Sher-Sagi Plan (2002)," October 19, 2014, https://ecf.org.il/issues/issue/1024 (accessed July 11, 2023), archived at https://web.archive.org/web/20230712082943; https://ecf.org.il/issues/issue/1024.

[17] Bill Clinton, *My Life*; New York, Knopf 2004, p. 938.

[18] See Dennis Ross, *The Missing Peace—The Inside Story of the Fight for Middle East Peace*, Farrar, Straus and Giroux, New York 2004, pp. 650–709 (reading Ross's account makes one at first sight question the wisdom of the American peace team).

a disaster. Palestinian violence had already begun in May, and Barak's government had lost the majority in the Knesset. The leak of secret negotiations in Stockholm to the Lebanese press caused the Palestinian team to block any progress. Instead of reaching out, Clinton and Barak intended to intensify pressure on the Palestinians, hoping for a decisive moment. The idea of asking Arafat to come to Camp David and ignore his opposition was already in the air, although not yet decided upon.

In response to Beilin's calm request, I prepared two papers. The first paper, titled "Preliminary Guidelines for a 1000-Day Program for a Barak-led Government," aimed to convince Barak to look beyond the end of the Clinton administration and develop an action plan for his entire term. It addressed four issues following Israel's withdrawal from Lebanon:

1. Stabilizing Israel's northern border with international assistance;
2. Creating the reality of a two-state solution without finalizing agreement on all core issues of conflict[19];
3. Proposing a program for National Unity to bridge religious, ethnic, and socio-economic gaps within Israel, which I believed was essential to help solve central issues of conflict with the Palestinians; and
4. Developing an agreed-on trilateral United States-Egypt-Israel understanding on how to reach a long-term strategy for comprehensive peace in the Middle East.

I never received any feedback, not from Beilin or anyone else. My suggestions were fundamentally opposed to Barak's thinking, as he solely focused on the Palestinian track based on his "everything or nothing" approach.

The second paper suggested a two-phase approach for a Permanent Status Agreement. Novik read the paper and rewrote it as "Building a Corridor to Peace." He faxed the paper to Barak's home and received an angry phone call from him about ten minutes later. Barak prohibited Novik from showing the paper to anyone, stating that he had it all figured out and believed it would be impossible for Arafat to say "no." Barak saw the paper as creating an escape route for Arafat, which would undermine his well-thought-out strategy. When Nimrod asked what would happen if Arafat did say "no," Barak did not answer.[20]

---

[19] We knew at the time that Arafat wanted to proclaim the State of Palestine unilaterally. A major diplomatic effort was undertaken to prevent that. I also thought that such a unilateral action would create a dangerous situation. However, Arafat's interest to do so provided the possibility to discuss with him the conditions necessary to allow him to proclaim the State of Palestine and commit to negotiations on all outstanding issues.
[20] Yair Hirschfeld's private interview with Nimrod Novik on January 25, 2012.

About ten days later, one day before the Camp David Conference began, my fears worsened. Arafat's reluctance to attend the conference was overruled by the Americans, who offered a vague promise not to blame him if no success was achieved. It served as a free ticket for Arafat's intended rejectionist approach.[21]

Preparing the Camp David Summit of September 1978, the basic quid pro quo had been in place. Nothing the like had been achieved in preparation of the July 2000 Camp David Summit. Barak believed that he could make concessions on Jerusalem in exchange for concessions on the refugee issue. However, this was merely an illusion, as Arafat was unwilling to give up either. The night before Camp David, I expressed my concern to my sister, stating that "Barak was jumping from an airplane without a parachute."

By this point, Novik and I had convinced Beilin that Camp David was destined to fail. Beilin handed Barak a closed envelope and instructed him to open it and pursue a Plan B if negotiations at Camp David proved unsuccessful. However, upon returning from Camp David, Barak returned the unopened envelope to Beilin.

Efforts to Prevent Disaster

The Camp David Summit was an utter failure. In an attempt to salvage the situation, the Americans changed their strategy. Previously, they had blindly followed PM Barak's advice, but now they sought to please Arafat and bring him on board. Recognizing Barak's willingness to make concessions on Jerusalem, the focus shifted (primarily but not exclusively) to the issue of refugees. Pundik and I were invited to discuss potential formulas with Rob Malley at his holiday retreat in Evian on Lake Geneva.

Malley explained a refugee formula that the American peace team was considering, one that effectively allowed for increased Palestinian demands for the return of refugees to their former homes in Israel. In my view, this was a recipe for continued friction and conflict. No Palestinian government would be able to resist pressure from the Palestinian Diaspora to minimize demands for a return to Israel, and no Israeli government would be willing to comply. I made it clear that accepting such a formula would lead to renewed conflict and compelled me to publicly call on Barak not to sign.

I argued that the Americans had unquestioningly endorsed Israeli positions on Permanent Status issues during the first half of 2000, putting the

---

[21] Miller, *The Much Too Promised Land*, p. 69.

Palestinians in a no-win situation. It would make no sense now to adopt the opposite position and propose ideas that crossed the most critical Israeli red lines. Rob Malley later informed me that following our discussion, the American peace team revised the refugee formula they had prepared.

Upon returning from Evian, Boaz Karni and I engaged in separate meetings with Hanan Ashrawi, aside from the official meetings of the Israeli, Palestinian, and American peace teams. While the official teams were bound by the Clinton-Barak demand to seek an end to the conflict and a comprehensive agreement, we had the privilege to think outside the box.

Arafat desired to be recognized as the founder of the State of Palestine, and Barak sought a two-state solution. In 2000, the proposed deal was to allow Arafat to become President of the State of Palestine under conditions controlled by Israel, with full support from the international community. In fact, Arafat made such a suggestion, albeit too late. This proposal, consisting of five handwritten pages, Arafat had dictated to Hanan Ashrawi was presented to Boaz Karni and me on September 25, 2000 (prior to the outbreak of violence). The essence of the proposal included:

> An understanding that would allow him to declare the State of Palestine optimally on November 15, 2000, but no later than January 1, 2001. The Palestinians would view the 1967 ceasefire lines as the temporary border, but understood that the final border would only be defined by negotiations and by agreement with Israel. It was essential that Israel recognize the Palestinian State. However, the Palestinians would not commit themselves to "end of conflict," but rather to "resolve all outstanding issues peacefully, being committed to nonviolence.[22]

Additionally, three substantial demands and several smaller demands were included, such as municipal elections in Jerusalem, an end to financial support for Israeli settlements, and a minimum of 11% further redeployment. Arafat also proposed that passages to Jordan and Egypt be controlled and monitored by an international peacekeeping force rather than the Palestinians themselves.[23]

This was not a "take it or leave it" proposal but a request to negotiate necessary conditions for the establishment of the State of Palestine before discussing its final borders with Israel. The benefits for Arafat were twofold: he would be celebrated as the historical Palestinian leader who paved the way for the State of Palestine, and on a national level, such an agreement

---

[22] Hirschfeld, *Track-Two Diplomacy*, pp. 246–247.
[23] Hirschfeld, *Track-Two Diplomacy*, pp. 246–247.

would confirm the two-state solution as the outcome of Israeli-Palestinian peace negotiations.

The gain for Israel was equally significant. Essentially, the State of Palestine would be established in Areas A and B, which constituted 42% of the West Bank territory, along with an additional 11% of the requested redeployment. While the de facto temporary borders of the State of Palestine would encompass the Gaza Strip and 53% of the West Bank territory, Arafat needed to claim that the 1967 ceasefire line would become the final border allowing both parties to negotiate a territorial agreement that would include swaps and other arrangements.

I did not know at the time, but I learned several years later that Othniel Schneller had been given the authority to work with Jamil Tarifi and in collaboration with Israeli and Palestinian governmental ministries to establish a coordination and cooperation structure for civil and economic affairs. Arafat was willing to accept a territorial understanding for the recognition of a Palestinian state with provisional borders. This, combined with the civil and economic cooperation understandings prepared by Schneller and Tarifi, provided a crucial foundation for a controlled state-building process, subject to other arrangements we had prepared in detail.

It is impossible to know for certain whether the cautious strategy my colleagues and I had developed would have yielded different results at the time. Policy planning and track-two understandings, even if signed, are often formulated behind closed doors, away from political pressures and actions that can derail progress. However, we do know that Barak's alternative approach led to disastrous outcomes. To draw relevant policy conclusions today, it is important to examine the fallacy of his strategic approach.

By mid-June 2000, it was evident that a disaster was foreseeable. We not only foresaw it but also provided warnings and suggestions in a timely manner, urging a change of strategy. Barak's approach, in retrospect, aligns with Barbara Tuchman's concept of "March of Folly."

A poignant statement came from my granddaughter, Naama. Born just two days after Barak's landslide victory, she remarked she had to grow up in a time of terror and repeated wars, following the failure of the peace process. The optimism of the 1990s, in spite of all their difficulties had pasted.

The Salvage Attempt

At the end of Barak's government, it became apparent that most of our policy hopes and assumptions had been shattered, and a new chapter needed to be written. Many of us, including myself, felt it was crucial to maintain the network of personal and political relationships built over the past two decades. Preserving the model of cross-border cooperation that we had established held particular significance.

In early October 2000, a visit to Arafat by Israeli mayors, myself, and el-Menasreh was planned to discuss ways to upgrade and expand the cooperation structure to a national level and extend it to other areas. However, the eruption of violence led to the cancellation of the meeting.

Creating an area of security, stability, and good neighborly relations before the Second Intifada began was relatively easier. The real challenge emerged when violence engulfed the region. From early October 2000 to the beginning of May 2001, it seemed that progress could be made. We not only maintained the structure of cooperation but also preserved economic links and prevented further escalation. Palestinian terrorists would occasionally start fires in the Gilboa mountain ridge, but Governor el-Menasreh promptly dispatched the fire brigade to extinguish them.

Quiet cooperation persisted for seven months until a turning point. El-Menasreh informed me that, under pressure, he had allowed a major demonstration to march toward the Israeli border. He requested that the IDF not interfere and asked for the demonstration to be called back to Jenin to continue protesting within the city.

I relayed this information to the IDF, who emphasized the importance of full coordination with el-Menasreh's security forces to prevent dangerous disturbances. I failed to convince the IDF that el-Menasreh was right, but instead convinced el-Menasreh to maintain ongoing coordination. Unfortunately, this resulted in a disastrous outcome. The continuous coordination between the security forces led to complacency and reduced alertness.

Neither side noticed that the demonstrators were nearing the settlements of Ganim and Kadim. Eventually, a breakdown in nerves led to gunfire, resulting in the killing of seven Palestinian members of their own security forces, allegedly by Israeli shooters. El-Menasreh successfully called the demonstrators back to Jenin, preventing further catastrophe. However, the incident had a severe impact as the slain Palestinian security force members belonged to influential Great-Families seeking revenge.

Following this incident, Jenin transformed from an area of security, stability, and good neighborly relations into the most dangerous hotbed of the

Intifada. It subsequently became a target of Israeli military attacks. Despite the violence, we persisted in maintaining minimal coordination and cooperation to mitigate further damage. When our office equipment was destroyed during an Israeli attack, we sought funding to replace it through the Ebert Foundation and the European Union, receiving their support.

In response to a series of suicide terror attacks, Israel launched Operation Defensive Shield in late March 2002. The battle for Jenin resulted in the deaths of 52 Palestinians and 23 Israelis. Parts of the refugee camp were leveled by Israeli bulldozers, creating what is now known as "ground zero." During this time, we maintained close dialogue with Governor el-Menasreh and engaged in activities beyond our usual scope. The three municipalities appealed to private donors and raised funds to provide essential goods such as flour, sugar, and clothing for adults and children. I led a delegation from all three municipalities to meet Governor el-Menasreh and deliver the collected supplies. I also paid a condolence visit to close friends in a nearby Kibbutz who had lost their son in Jenin while attempting to minimize casualties on both sides.

Operation Defensive Shield severely weakened the Palestinian security forces throughout the West Bank, particularly in the Jenin area. Jihadist groups and various family-based irregular troops assumed control, terrorizing the civilian population and replacing the previous security order with the rule of the gun. After Governor el-Menasreh had to leave the area, an incident occurred that could be considered absurd. An international observer from Germany was attacked by irregulars but managed to secure his car in time to repel the bullets. He called General Baruch Spiegel from inside the car, who arranged an escort for him to leave Jenin and return to Israel. Weeks later, the culprits contacted our German friend and requested a meeting to apologize for the incident. This incident highlighted the loss of the Jenin-Gilboa area as an island of security, stability, and good neighborly relations.

Despite the setbacks, we persisted in our efforts to maintain or reestablish functioning security cooperation between Israeli and Palestinian counterparts. The work of General Dov Sedaka, my friend and head of the IDF civil administration in the West Bank during the Second Intifada, and General Jibril Rajoub remained crucial. Although they were unable to prevent further acts of violence, they maintained the ability to collaborate and consider new beginnings.

I remained convinced of the importance of maintaining a close dialogue with our Palestinian counterparts. In July 2002, Arafat dismissed Rajoub and appointed Zuhair el-Manasreh as head of the Palestinian Preventive Security Forces. Three weeks later, el-Manasreh shared his action plan with me, as well as American and Israeli officials. His plan involved restructuring the Palestinian security forces and negotiating understandings that would allow the Palestinians to regain control based on the security provisions in place before September 28, 2000, the start of the Intifada.

El-Manasreh believed it was mutually beneficial to create a stable and positive atmosphere that would facilitate the rebuilding of the Palestinian security system. He recognized the need to disarm and arrest irregular forces within the Palestinian territories. He also aimed to engage in dialogues with extremist groups in the mosques, while cutting their sources of financing and limiting their public activities.

He emphasized the importance of mobilizing the Palestinian people in a collective effort to enhance security. He acknowledged that the anarchic situation, where small armed groups dominated and terrorized the civilian population, necessitated a public campaign for security. El-Manasreh initiated dialogues with various political committees in each area and sought Israeli cooperation.[24]

I reported the details of the meeting with el-Manasreh to the relevant political and military authorities. The response varied from lukewarm to unfriendly, but I realized that el-Manasreh's efforts were destined to fail. Even though he aimed to create broad Palestinian consensus, the wounds caused by the Second Intifada, where violence was launched against an Israeli government offering support for the establishment of the State of Palestine and other significant concessions, were too deep to allow a return to the previous status quo.

However, in the years following 2005, we witnessed some positive developments. Mayor Atar of the Gilboa area constructed a fence along the cease-fire line to prevent Palestinian incursions. Despite the hostilities, the memory of good relations persisted. Cooperation projects resumed from 2005 onward. ECF successfully convinced the IDF to reopen the Jenin area for Israelis to purchase goods and services as before. Initially, this privilege was extended only to Israeli Arabs due to concerns about potential attacks against Jews. Consequently, the Jenin economy recovered and thrived more than other Palestinian areas, leading to the initiation of several cooperation projects.

Through these experiences, I realized the vulnerability of conflict transformation activities such as the Cross-Border Cooperation Agreement. Many achievements were lost due to the reemergence of violence. Nonetheless, my conclusion, reached several years later, was to persevere in the search for

---

[24] Yair Hirschfeld, "Notes of Meeting with al-Manasreh," *Hirschfeld Khoury-DeConcini Papers*, *Substack*, forthcoming (originally written August 1, 2002), https://hkdpapers.substack.com/p/meeting-with-zuhair-el-manasreh.

conflict transformation measures while seeking the essential "Take Off-Point" necessary to move forward, in the hope of making achievements gained, irreversible.

The Need and Weakness of Track-Two Policy Planning

The events that unfolded during Barak's premiership vividly demonstrated the inherent ineffectiveness of track-two policy planning. I first became apprehensive when Barak appointed Shlomo Ben Ami as Minister of Foreign Affairs. On that occasion, Beilin gave me a somewhat qualified compliment, saying, "Yair, you have more knowledge and experience than Shlomo Ben Ami. However, he has had the courage to publicly fight for his convictions, and you are paying the price for never having done so." This simple remark encapsulated the limitations of track-two work. Politicians with less knowledge and differing experiences might be willing to listen to suggestions, but even with the best intentions, the implementation would often distort the proposed strategic concept.

I have previously described the rules and lessons that need to be observed in order to achieve the desired results. I have found success when access to decision-makers is not a sporadic one-day event but is based on an ongoing close working relationship. This allows for a shared process of suggesting policies, receiving feedback, and obtaining permission to proceed with the follow-up. However, both the leadership and their senior government advisors tend to keep external actors at a distance. As a general rule, they neither share information nor pass on the information provided by me or other track-two and back-channel actors. They minimize any useful input and emphasize mistakes or failures while engaging in efforts to discredit us.

Without continuous and unrestricted access to the leadership, very little can be achieved. If such access is available, the following recommendations should be considered (although they are not exhaustive). The fundamental process to strive for is developing an agreed-upon concept with the other side, followed by building a broad coalition to create the capacity for implementation. To develop an agreed concept, your partners need unfettered access to their leadership. It is crucial that the concept addresses the key issues at the heart of the negotiations.[25]

---

[25] Leigh Thompson, *The Mind and Heart of the Negotiator*, Prentice Hall, New Jersey 1998, pp. 18–19.

When building a successful coalition, it is important to consider the overall effort and not just focus on your "own" channel. Understanding the complexity of multitrack diplomacy is essential, as is maintaining a well-thought-out flow of information with central actors, including third parties. This enables the creation of a "butterfly effect," where others contribute to a supportive environment.

If the coalition-building effort proves successful, it is vital to anticipate any deliberate blockages or crisis situations that either side may create for tactical reasons. In such circumstances, fallback options must be prepared. Even if all these steps are accomplished, the ultimate success still depends entirely on the final decision of the leadership. Hence, my most important advice is prepare yourself to sustain failures. Nevertheless, do not give up. Mid- and long-term strategic thinking has to be pursued in close cooperation with the political leadership, but far away from daily pressures. Track-two planning therefor, in spite of all its weaknesses, remains essential.

Suggested Additional Reading

The Account of Israeli Negotiators

Gilead Sher *Israeli-Palestinian Peace Negotiations, 1999–2001—Within Reach*; Routledge, New York 2006. It is a very fair and honest account of the Israeli official negotiating approach, which was completely dominated by Prime Minister Barak and left Gilead Sher, being his chief-negotiator, very little space for maneuver.

Gidi Grinstein *Lessons in Peacemaking—30 Years of Oslo* Gefen Publishing House, Jerusalem, 2023. Grinstein was a very successful project director in ECF. When he became a member of the Peace Administration established by Prime Minister Barak in the summer of 1999, he received all the preparatory work the ECF team had carried out, in preparation of Final Status negotiations. Being the personal assistant of the chief negotiator Gilead Sher, he experienced the unfolding of the negotiations. He told me that by April 2000 many months before the total failure, he foresaw the unfolding disaster, however, he was not in a position to prevent it.

Shlomo Ben Ami *Scars of War, Wounds of Peace: The Israeli-Arab Tragedy*; Weidenfeld & Nicholson, 2005; this is another account of the failure of the 1999–2001 peace negotiations.

All these accounts offer little hope and add to a determinist atmosphere of the path to failure.

The Account of a Member of the American Peace team

Aaron David Miller, *The Much Too Promised Land—America's Elusive Search for Arab–Israeli Peace*; Bantam, New York 2008 (this is by far the best American account of the 1999–2001 peace effort, and its failure. Miller points out all the many shortcomings of the joint Barak-Clinton strategy, and the lack of understanding what the repercussions might be).

A Joint US-Palestinian Account

Rob Malley and Hussein Agha "Camp David: The Tragedy of Errors", *The New Yorker*, The Review of Books, August 9, 2001. The basic argument made is that in any negotiations not only the content of the proposed agreement is of importance, but similarly the supportive political circumstances.

A Very Short and Concise Palestinian Account

Sari Nusseibeh, *Once Upon a Country—A Palestinian Life*, Halban London 2009; pp. 422–427; Nusseibeh suggested that "*by prior agreement of the two sides, Palestinians could declare a state with their ideal borders, and Israel could simultaneously recognize an independent Palestinian state in the borders Israel deemed best. The two sides could then enter into negotiations to bridge the difference between the two borders. That way, at least we could keep the 'peace process' alive.*" As this did not happened, he understood what would be happening, and did happen, was war. (The second "intifada" lasted from 2001 to 2005).

The Importance of People-to-People Activities

Endersen Lena C., *Contact and Cooperation, the Israeli-Palestinian People-to-People Program*, FAFO Institute for Applied Social Science, 2000. Lena Endersen was in charge of officially overseeing the various People-to-People Activities. Her report remains very valuable.

An Important Theoretical Input

Kelman Herbert C., "The Interdependence of Israeli and Palestinian National Identities: the Role of the Other in Existential Conflicts" in: *Journal of Social Issues,* Fall 1999; vol. 55, no. 3 pp. 581–680. Kelman gathered for many years Israeli and Palestinian personalities of influence—from academia, the government, the security services—and worked with them on peace-developing concepts. He hereby created an important cadre of peace activists. His work is being continued after his death, by the Herbert Kelman Institute in Vienna, Austria.

7

The Need to Rethink Possible Action

The Three Most Important Building Blocks for a Peace Policy Fall Apart

The new millennium brought forth numerous traumatic events and challenges. On October 12, 2000, two Israeli soldiers were publicly lynched in Ramallah, while the Palestinian security forces, who had promised protection, failed to intervene. That same evening, my daughter Naomi got married, but the joy of the occasion was overshadowed by the tragedy in Ramallah.

The breakdown of Israeli-Palestinian relations extended far beyond that incident. The joint patrols, symbolic of political and security cooperation, suffered a severe blow when a Palestinian member shot and killed his Israeli colleague. This act shattered any notion of collaboration, and further tragic events followed.

Three significant developments compelled a reassessment of the entire process. The breakdown of Israeli-Palestinian cooperation and the emergence of conflicting narratives regarding the peace process hindered future negotiations for decades to come. The foundations of the Israel-US alliance, as I understood them, were shifting, and American support for an effective Israeli peace policy was waning for an extended period. Additionally, the rise of Islamic militant terror outside the Israeli-Palestinian conflict had a profound impact on any peace efforts, likely lasting for decades.

The Breakdown of the Shared Israeli-Palestinian Narrative for Peace-Seeking

Following the breakdown of security cooperation, a shared narrative for peace-seeking and peace-making also unraveled. The Palestinian narrative had a valid foundation, arguing the Israeli side was exploiting agreements to expand settlements, suggesting a lack of an Israeli genuine intent to reach an agreement.

Similarly, the Israeli narrative had its own foundations. An Israeli peace government had negotiated in good faith and made substantial concessions to the Palestinians.[1] However, in response, the Palestinians launched a war against the Israeli government and people, causing immense human and material damage. Prime Minister Ehud Barak succinctly captured this sentiment with his statement, "The Palestinians are no partner for peace."[2] This narrative, originating from Israel's left, became dominant in subsequent years.

These conflicting narratives emerged following the failed Camp David Summit in July 2000, continued through subsequent negotiations ever since. Ariel Sharon's election as Prime Minister on February 6, 2001, opened a new phase, in a complex search for security, deterrence, stability, and a way to peace. The day after Sharon's election, my mother passed away, leaving me uncertain about how to continue her pursuit of a better world.

The US Understanding of and Support for Israeli-Peace Making Falters

Now violence ruled the day. Under these conditions I hoped to halt or limit Israeli settlement expansion. In April, an international commission led by Senator Mitchell presented its report on the causes of the intifada, including a recommendation to "freeze all settlement activity, including the natural growth of existing settlements."[3]

---

[1] Miguel Moratinos, "Document for Taba Negotiations," *Ha'aretz*, February 14, 2002 (originally written January 2001).

[2] Compare with Gidi Grinstein (with Ari Afilalo), *Lessons in Peace-Making—30 Years of the Oslo Process;* Gefen Publications, Jerusalem. Grinstein argues that Barak added that the "Palestinians are no partner for peace *at this time.*" Barak would tell Dennis Ross that "it is either peace or war." Dennis Ross, *The Missing Peace—The Inside Story of the Fight for Middle East Peace,* Farrar, Straus and Giroux, New York 2004, p. 773.

[3] George Mitchell et al., "Sharm El-Sheikh Fact-Finding Committee Report," U.S. Department of State, April 30, 2001, https://2001-2009.state.gov/p/nea/rls/rpt/3060.htm (accessed July 11, 2023), archived at https://web.archive.org/web/20230712083827/https://2001-2009.state.gov/p/nea/rls/rpt/3060.htm.

However, the formulation chosen by the commission proved counterproductive. The settlement leadership accused them of attempting to restrict settler families from expanding, which led to increased settlement activity. It became evident that Sharon's government would not comply, the United States would not enforce the recommendations, and the Palestinian government found itself in a no-win situation. They could not accept less than what the Mitchell Commission demanded and had a valid excuse to reject a renewal of negotiations.

In discussions with US Consul General to the Palestinian Authority, Jeff Feltman, I explained the Senator Mitchell approach would and could not succeed. Instead I proposed the creation of a stringent and effective monitoring structure and taxation of US donations to settlers amounting to hundreds of millions of dollars. However, Feltman argued that the US was willing to condemn settlements but preferred to be "easy on monitoring." This response was disheartening, suggesting that the US cared more about diplomatic declarations than the realities on the ground and their implications for the peace process. As a matter of fact, the atmosphere in the White House had changed.[4]

For two decades, I had admired and relied on US peace-making efforts in the Middle East, particularly in the Israeli-Palestinian arena. Dan Kurtzer was a close friend, and figures like Joseph Sisco, Richard Murphy, Henry Kissinger, and James Baker were my "heroes." However, over time, admiration turned into growing criticism. I criticized Bill Clinton's unwavering support for Barak and his flawed understanding of Arafat's political behavior and decision-making, despite warnings from his own team.

Yet, the situation went from bad to worse. The shock of 9/11 made it clear that the world had changed. During my visit to Washington in 2002, I found much of what I saw highly frustrating. Just as many Israelis had been overly jubilant about the military victory in the Six Day War, most Americans I met were overly confident about their military success in Afghanistan. To make matters worse, a group of influential Neo-Cons led by Donald Rumsfeld and Paul Wolfowitz pursued ideas that were detached from reality and

---

[4] Feltman did not tell me that the mood in the White House had changed. The incoming advisor for Middle Eastern Affairs of the National Security Council, working in the White House, made the following comment on the Mitchell Report: "the report took a stance of total moral relativism between terrorism and Israeli settlements....On one side, murder; on the other, housing: To the Mitchell fact-finding committee, the moral responsibility was equally shared. Where the new administration could go with this report remained unclear." Eliott Abrams, *Tested by Zion—The Bush Administration and the Israeli-Palestinian Conflict*, Cambridge U.P. New York 2012, p. 7.

highly damaging.[5] They firmly believed that the United States could use its armed forces to bring democracy to the Middle East. Yet, I couldn't comprehend how they could ignore the historical lessons that Napoleon's military campaigns had led to totalitarian regimes in Spain, Italy, Austria, Germany, and Russia during the twentieth century.[6] It baffled me how anyone could believe that a US military occupation could bring democracy to the Middle East.

At the time, Admiral Amy Ayalon and Sari Nusseibeh attempted to convince members of Congress, the Senate, and the US administration that the notion of democratizing the Middle East was a dangerous vanity, but their efforts were in vain. I met Liz Cheney, who oversaw people-to-people projects promoting the concept and rules of democracy in the Department of State. I sought funding for cross-border cooperation projects and political analysis, which ECF eventually received from US-AID. However, I later discovered that nobody in Washington bothered to read what we had to say.

Around the same time, President Carter awarded a prestigious prize to Terje Larsen for his contribution to the Oslo Accords. Surprisingly, neither Yossi Beilin, Ron Pundik, nor I were invited to the ceremony. In response, I wrote a letter to Carter, and his response was that we could attend the ceremony as part of the audience if we paid for our own tickets. It was a deeply insulting experience. What was even worse was that Carter's actions reflected a form of white supremacist thinking, suggesting that only "educated" individuals from the northern parts of the globe were capable of making peace, while the "natives" were deemed incapable. This combination of ignorance and arrogance justified a condescending approach by American politicians and diplomats in dictating what Israel, the Palestinians, and others should do.

However, my confidence was somewhat restored when I met James Baker III and Ambassador Djerejian in Houston. Despite being strong supporters of

---

[5] Pierre Bourgois, "The PNAC (1997–2006) and the Post-Cold War 'Neoconservative Moment,'" *E-International Relations*, February 1, 2020, https://www.e-ir.info/2020/02/01/new-american-century-1997-2006-and-the-post-cold-war-neoconservative-moment/ (accessed July 12, 2023), archived at https://web.archive.org/web/20230712084354/https://www.e-ir.info/2020/02/01/new-american-century-1997-2006-and-the-post-cold-war-neoconservative-moment/ (excerpt from an article originally published (in French) in *Politique américaine*, n° 31, pp. 173–198, November 2018). See their writing at "Project for the New American Century," United States Library of Congress Web Archive 2002, https://www.loc.gov/item/lcwaN0011283 (accessed June 12, 2023), archived at https://web.archive.org/web/20230712084358/https://www.loc.gov/item/lcwaN0011283.

[6] In his monumental work on "the Origins of Totalitarian Democracy," Talmon described the transformation of ideological radicalism of the French revolution toward popular supported totalitarianism. Preparing the second volume of his work, he discussed in class the next phase, when Napoleon's troops invaded most of Europe, creating in its counter-reaction, militant nationalism. See J.L. Talmon, *The Origins of Totalitarian Democracy*; London, Secker and Warburg 1952.

the Bush Administration, they shared my criticisms, particularly concerning the policies of the Neo-Cons and Donald Rumsfeld. This gave me some hope and prevented me from becoming too pessimistic. However, months later, the Americans invaded Iraq, and I began to understand that the American presence in Iraq and Afghanistan would change the established rules of the game. Throughout the latter half of the twentieth century, Israel's military capabilities had neutralized Soviet influence in the region, allowing the United States to gain dominant influence. The Six Day War (1967), the War of Attrition (1968–1970), and the Yom Kippur War (1973) were all fought by Israel, and its victories played a crucial role in persuading Arab leaders to turn away from Moscow and seek American support. The rule was simple: Israel fought, while the United States relied on diplomacy to increase and maintain its influence. However, with American boots on the ground, the rules of engagement were changing, and I foresaw trouble ahead.

The Rethinking Process Got Underway

We faced a challenge in dealing with the rise of worldwide Islamic terror. Having read Sayid Qutb in the late 1960s, I had long understood that militant Islamic fundamentalism was a force to be reckoned with. The events of 9/11 only confirmed that Islam-based terrorism would remain a significant threat to the West for a long time to come. If I had previously believed that an Israel-Palestinian peace agreement would stabilize the Middle East, it was now evident that negotiations and signing an agreement would not halt militant Islamic attacks against the West and Israel. In fact, it might even provoke a renewed escalation. I hoped we could minimize the damage, but we needed to learn how to achieve this.

Thus, the process of rethinking had begun. We faced a crucial question: Should we stick to our ideological convictions or adapt to changing circumstances? If we chose to adapt, how should we proceed? I remained convinced that an Israel-Palestine peace agreement still made sense for several reasons: It would strengthen Israel's Jewish-democratic identity, provide regional and international legitimacy to both Israel and Palestine, help form a broad coalition against radical militants, and allow Israel and its allies to maintain the moral high ground, which would be crucial if a new conflict were to erupt.

My second reaction was one of caution. We had just witnessed the tragic consequences of failed negotiations. Could we really bridge the gap on all core conflict issues and reach an agreement on "end of conflict" and "finality of claims"? This issue was extensively discussed in ECF. Eylon

Yavetz, a new member of ECF, presented a paper titled "Deficiencies in the Israeli-Palestinian 'Permanent Status Strategy' and Initial Recommendations." He argued that the deep-rooted narratives developed over a century of conflict made bridging the gap nearly impossible. Furthermore, both Israelis and Palestinians were still trapped in the daily reality of occupation and terrorism, with little improvement throughout the negotiations. Instead of a comprehensive conflict-resolution approach, Yavetz suggested a process-oriented approach that involved gradual partition, physical separation, capacity building, confidence-building measures, economic packages, security arrangements, and educational programs.[7]

Yavetz's paper sparked major conflicts within ECF. Boaz Karni vehemently opposed Yavetz and wanted to dismiss him immediately, while others saw him as a renegade. However, I defended Yavetz and argued that his analytical approach was legitimate. Although I didn't fully agree with Yavetz's conclusions, I still believed in giving it a second try. I aimed to engage in solution-oriented dialogue with the Israeli right wing and form a broader internal Israeli coalition to support another attempt at an Israel-Palestine two-state solution, including agreement on finality of claims and end of conflict. Addressing the three battles we lost in the 1990s—terrorism and security threats, Israel's national religious radicalism, and creating conditions for Palestinian state-building—was crucial. The combination of these factors created a vicious circle of violence, radicalism, poverty, despair, and revanchist attitudes. We needed to find a way to break the impasse.

Seeking Ways and Means to Break the Vicious Circle of Crises in a Protracted Conflict

In my search for theoretical writings on breaking the cycle of repeated crises in protracted conflicts, I came across the teachings of John Paul Lederach, which resonated with me. Lederach explained how protracted conflicts reignite themselves, as Yavetz described in his ECF paper. Lederach proposed that defining a shared vision of a better future and designing steps to achieve it was essential to overcome the setbacks inherent in protracted conflicts. It required recognizing that quick fixes were not possible and that sustained

---

[7] Eylon Javetz, "Deficiencies in the Israeli 'Permanent Status Strategy' and Some Initial Recommendations," *Hirschfeld Khoury-DeConcini Papers*, *Substack*, forthcoming (originally written in February 2002), https://hkdpapers.substack.com/p/deficiencies-in-permanent-status-strategy (Javetz submitted the 20th draft of this paper to ECF).

peace work was necessary to break the cycle of violence. The task of peacemakers, therefore, was not merely to have an agreement signed but to initiate necessary structural changes. A top-down dialogue with and among leaders was crucial to connect short-term needs with a long-term vision. However, emerging understandings also needed legitimacy from grassroots actors.

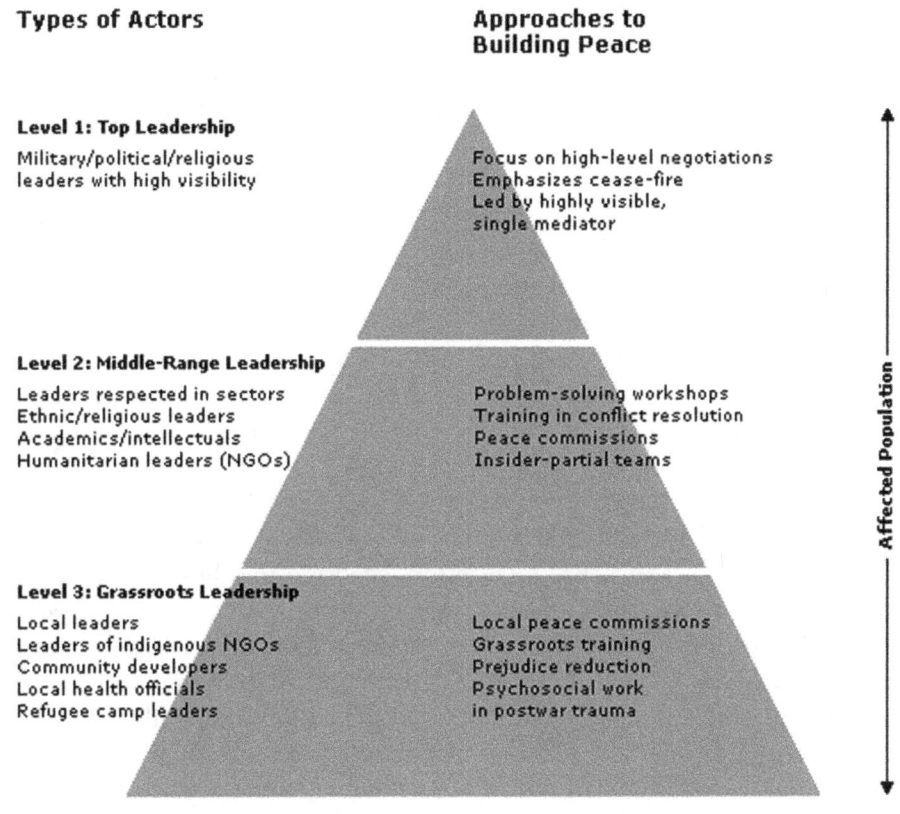

Derived from John Paul Lederach, *Building Peace: Sustainable Reconciliation in Divided Societies* (Washington, D.C.: United States Institute of Peace Press, 1997), 39.

Lederach's Pyramid illustrates his theoretical approach as follows:

- Bottom-up work with grassroots leadership serves two purposes: providing political leadership with legitimacy to reach and sustain an agreement and enabling continued peace-building activities at the grassroots level in case of failed negotiations.
- Middle-out work involves experts and various leadership groups planning negotiations, establishing initial understandings on a track-two level, and

guiding bottom-up work. This middle-out peace work helps connect the top-down and bottom-up approaches.

- Top-down action is essential to create the decisive moment of change, referred to as "money time." Leadership must make decisive decisions and secure supportive majorities. I aimed to translate Lederach's teachings into action by maintaining close access to the Israeli government, Palestinian leadership, and diplomats.[8]

To address the top of Lederach's pyramid, I supported a Six Point Understanding reached by Amy Ayalon, the former commander of the Israeli Navy, and Sari Nusseibeh:

1. "Commitment to a two-state solution.
2. Negotiating borders based on the 1967 lines with territorial swaps.
3. No settlers remaining in Palestinian territory.
4. Delineating Jerusalem borders along ethnic lines.
5. Allowing Palestinian refugees to return to Palestine.
6. Commitment to the end of conflict. These six points provided a direction while allowing leadership flexibility to build the necessary political capital for progress.[9]"

We believed that ECF excelled in the middle of Lederach's pyramid. Our relentless efforts in conceptualization, coalition-building, and capacity-building were directed at defining the end-game based on the Ayalon-Nusseibeh principles. Simultaneously, we addressed the three major battles we had previously lost concerning security, Israeli and Arab militant radicalism, and Palestinian state-building. Although it was a tedious task, only toward the end of the first decade of the twenty-first century significant partial successes

---

[8] Lederach's work as important and instructive it is, is not free of journalistic superficialities, particularly when he refers to the Oslo negotiations. He quotes Larsen and Yuul of having created an intimate atmosphere by making "them to feel easy in a pleasant house…they slept under the same roof, and took all their meals together" (pp. 133). It misrepresents the creation of supportive measures to improve a constructive atmosphere. The truth is that what really mattered was the fact Beilin, Karni, I, and others had under the supervision of Shimon Peres built a trust relationship with the Palestinians over 13 years before we came to Norway. The idea that with good food and comfortable housing such an atmosphere can be created, is non-sense. John Paul Lederach, *Building Peace: Sustainable Reconciliation in Divided Societies*, Washington, D.C., Unites States Institute of Peace Press 1997.

[9] "The Nusseibeh-Ayalon Agreement," *United States Institute for Peace*, July 2002, https://www.usip.org/sites/default/files/file/resources/collections/peace_agreements/nusseibeh_ayalon.pdf (accessed July 12, 2023), archived at https://web.archive.org/web/20230712085421/https://www.usip.org/sites/default/files/file/resources/collections/peace_agreements/nusseibeh_ayalon.pdf. For Ami Ayalon's account of his cooperation with Sari Nusseibeh, see Ami Ayalon, *Friendly Fire—A Memoir*; Steerforth Press, New Hampshire 2020, p. 177.

were achieved: A functioning Israeli-Palestinian security cooperation was introduced and sustained; under the premiership of Salam Fayyad, progress regarding Palestinian State-building was accomplished, and a religious-secular dialogue unfolded.

The challenge was how to change attitudes through bottom-up work, which many others were involved in. My experience in Vienna showed me that rational explanations were not enough, and I referred to this as the "Dieter Hoffman conundrum." Dieter, a school friend, listened to my stories and explanations about the Holocaust but ultimately said, "What you say is convincing. Still, my father died believing in the Nazi ideology. If I were to think differently, I would not be loyal to him."[10] I discussed this with Andre Zaaiman, a brilliant strategist from South Africa,[11] who directed my attention to a seemingly unrelated book on "Commitment-Led Marketing," specifically Chapter Nine titled "Working with the African National Congress—Applying a commitment-led approach to political marketing."[12] We explored two conversion models to change the opinions of non-believers. The first model involved traumatic experiences that would lead to a complete 180° change, like communists becoming anti-communists or religious fanatics becoming apostates. In our situation, this seemed to suggest that conversion would be brought about by war or another equally dramatic event, which I hoped would never occur. The second model referred to a situation where a married man would live with his mistress for years. The conversion moment would come when he had to choose between staying with his wife and ending the relationship with his mistress or getting divorced and marrying the other woman. In the Israeli-Palestinian context, it was clear what this meant. We needed to convince the Israeli public that it would be impossible to maintain the Jewish-democratic identity of the state of Israel while continuing the occupation. We had to choose one or the other. Bottom-up work was necessary to persuade the Israeli right wing that allowing for Palestinian statehood was essential for sustaining our own identity, and parallel understandings had to be reached on the Palestinian side as well.

---

[10] Compare with Vamik Votan, *Bloodlines—From Ethnic Pride to Ethnic Terrorism*, Farrar, Straus and Giroux, New York 1997.

[11] Andre Zaaiman was a descendent of a leading Boer family of South Africa. After having graduated from the Officer's Academy with excellence he strongly opposed the Apartheid regime, and cooperating with the ANC had to leave South Africa. He became a close advisor to Thabo Mbeki.

[12] Jan Hofmeyr and Butch Rice, *Commitment-Led Marketing—The Key to Brand Profits is the Customer's Mind*, John Wiley & Sons, New York 2000, pp. 243–258.

Putnam's Double Game Theory

Lederach's pyramid and the study of conversion models made it evident that extensive work had to be conducted separately in each of the two conflicting societies. Putnam's "double game theory" provided the necessary theoretical explanation, emphasizing the pursuit of negotiations on the home front as much as with the adversary or enemy.[13] In my mind, this meant marginalizing militant radicals and seeking common ground with pragmatic forces within the Israeli settler leadership.

After Barak lost his majority in the Knesset on June 8, 2000, it became clear to me that he had largely lost the internal legitimacy to agree to concessions in the hoped-for agreement. The dramatic failure of the peace negotiation effort highlighted the importance of building a bridge with pragmatic representatives from Israel's right wing who understood the necessity of achieving a two-state solution. I first met Othniel Schneller, the former Secretary General of the Settler movement (Yesha) in 2000. Despite our political and ideological differences, Schneller and I had more in common than met the eye. We both grew up in Zionist youth movements, Hashomer Hatzair and Bnei Akiva, during our formative years, aspiring to create a better world and believing in our ability to achieve it. Schneller had made attempts to reach out to the Israeli left with limited success, while I had also tried to engage with the Israeli right without much progress. Schneller had been involved in peace negotiations and worked closely with Palestinian and Jordanian counterparts. We were both convinced that any way forward in the peace process needed to be based on creating a "sufficient majority."

Together, we prepared a joint document stating that the basic objective of the diplomatic-political process and negotiations for peace with Palestinians and other Arab neighbors was to ensure the continuation of Zionism in the twenty-first century while maintaining the Jewish-democratic identity of the State of Israel. We developed a code of conduct for defining agreements and committed to "agree to disagree" within Israeli society. We acknowledged the interests of the settler community in designing Israel's final borders while supporting the partition of Eretz Yisrael. Security issues were discussed, including Israel's independent deterrence policy, cooperation with third parties, peace with Egypt and Jordan, and the pursuit of peace with Syria and Lebanon. We called on global powers to guarantee the safety and stability of the Hashemite Kingdom of Jordan.

---

[13] Robert D. Putnam, "Diplomacy and Domestic Politics: The Logic of Two-Level Games," in *International Organization*, vol. 42, no. 3 (Summer 1988), pp. 427–460.

Strengthening Israel's relationship with the international community was in its best interest, and we viewed renewing negotiations with the Palestinians as a means to achieve this goal. We anticipated international support in ensuring Israel's safety, combating terrorism, and establishing good neighborly relations for peace-building. We emphasized that the welfare of the Arab–Israeli community was a clear interest aligned with Jewish tradition and Zionist ethos. Detailed solutions for the refugee problem and reaching essential understandings on Jerusalem were also addressed in the document. It took us another three years to publish it.[14]

Beilin and I Pursue Different Approaches

In 2001, a group organized by Beilin traveled with a sizable Palestinian and Israeli delegation to South Africa. In Cape Town, we spent a full day with South African President Thabo Mbeki, accompanied by a senior South African delegation who shared their experiences from the armed struggle and negotiation years. Our objectives were twofold: to learn from the South African experience and lay the groundwork for coordinated Israeli-Palestinian action. However, Beilin and I drew contrasting conclusions from our weeklong meeting with South African negotiators representing both the ANC and the former Apartheid regime.

Beilin identified with the South African political objective of the exercise, which aimed to help the Israeli and Palestinian delegations reach an acceptable agreement. On the other hand, I aligned with the South African strategic approach of always cultivating and sustaining a "sufficient majority." This approach had proven essential for developing a viable peace-finding process and ultimately reaching the necessary agreement. I also recognized that while Thabo Mbeki was president, South Africa intended to foster a broader peace coalition in Israel by supporting the peace camp led by Beilin and seeking backing from more centrist and right-wing actors, such as Zippi Livni and Ehud Olmert.

Upon returning from South Africa, it seemed logical for Beilin and me to work separately in a complementary manner. Beilin would focus on preparing a blueprint for an Israeli-Palestinian agreement, while I would make efforts to broaden political support within Israel. At the time, amid the tremendous losses caused by the second intifada, public sentiment in Israel leaned toward

---

[14] Yair Hirschfeld and Othniel Schneller, *Gesher shel Niyar*, Maariv, Tel Aviv 2006 (Hebrew). See Othniel Schneller and Yair Hirschfeld, *A Bridge of Paper*, Sifriat Maariv, Tel Aviv 2005 (Hebrew).

retaliation rather than outreach. After the Palestinians rejected the Beilin-Abu Mazen Understanding, the Clinton Parameters, and the Taba proposals (mentioned above), I questioned the wisdom of offering further concessions that the Israeli public was unwilling to accept. I feared it would create friction in Israel and undermine the endeavor to establish a sufficient majority for a more modest peace-seeking approach. Thus, Beilin and I, while still working together and respecting each other, found ourselves on a confrontational path.

Initially, we believed and hoped that maintaining a coordinated complementary strategy was possible. In 1999, ECF facilitated an exchange of political ideas between Likud Members of the Knesset and Jordan, which included Zippi Livni as a participant. Under Sharon's government, she became the Minister for Regional Cooperation. In that role, she sought my assistance in connecting with Palestinians, Jordanians, Egyptians, and other regional stakeholders.

Following my suggestion, Livni also met Andre Zaaiman, a close advisor to Thabo Mbeki who had collaborated with ECF for three years and made the South African meeting possible. Years later, during a meeting with Tamar Zandberg and her partner Zaki, Zaki acknowledged that despite my (negative) "right-wing" leanings, I had played a role in convincing Livni to move away from the right wing and toward the peace camp.

In an effort to support the Ayalon-Nusseibeh principles, I proposed that Amy Ayalon accompany me to South Africa to meet President Mbeki. Andre Zaaiman assured his support. Upon arriving in Pretoria, we first met with South Africa's Deputy Minister of Foreign Affairs, Aziz Pahad. His task was to prepare us for the meeting with President Mbeki, test our arguments, and inform us about the effectiveness of our points.

Ayalon and I successfully passed the initial tests. Subsequently, we had a one-hour meeting with Thabo Mbeki, passing the second test and gaining reassurance of supportive action. Only then were we asked to spend several hours with a consultative forum consisting of senior ANC members and former leaders of the Apartheid regime. This was the crucial test: we had to secure their support. Once again, we succeeded. It was a captivating illustration of what the South African notion of creating and maintaining a "sufficient majority" entailed. It went beyond merely achieving a one-time parliamentary majority; it involved establishing an enduring "sufficient majority" throughout an ongoing governmental decision-making process.

In Israel, I realized that Beilin perceived my support for Amy Ayalon as hostile. He was working on what would become the Geneva Accord, intending to override the Ayalon-Nusseibeh principles and provide a detailed blueprint for peace.[15] I found his anger unjust and resented the division among the Israeli left wing, with Beilin, Ayalon, and a third approach led by Gilead Sher and Uri Sagie proposing unilateral action. I couldn't understand why we couldn't develop a united approach. We remained friends, but I had to defend my right to think and act differently.

A year later, after the conclusion of the Geneva Accords, I wrote a lengthy letter to Beilin explaining my opposition. I compared the effort to crossing a wide river without a bridge, questioning the legitimacy, responsibility, and capability to implement an agreement. I emphasized the danger of dividing the Israeli left and centrist forces unnecessarily. With most groups in the Labor Party opposing the proposed conditions, I argued that the Geneva Accords relied on a precarious isolated minority in the Knesset. Furthermore, the accords created unrealistic expectations among the Palestinian peace camp regarding official negotiations with any Israeli government. I was unaware of how damaging this would turn out to be.

Our difference of opinion had organizational consequences. Beilin intended for the Geneva Initiative to become the primary focus of ECF's actions. I firmly objected, stating that it would only happen "over my dead body." Consequently, a separate organizational structure was created to pursue the Geneva Accords. Later, while attending a conference in Lake Como, Italy, my wife Ruthi and I took a train ride to Geneva to visit my sister. On the train, Zippi Livni called me to inquire about Beilin's conclusion of the Geneva Accord. I responded, "I am on my way to Geneva, but I am not involved in that effort, and I oppose it."

Many years later, in a conversation with Zaher el-Khouri, a strong supporter of the Geneva Accord and a founding member of the "Israeli-Palestinian Peace Coalition," I asked him why the Palestinians rejected Olmert's peace proposal. His immediate response was that it was a "take it or leave it" offer, without giving Abu Mazen time to reflect. I disputed this, noting that after the initial rejection, Olmert sent Pundik to meet with Abu Mazen asking him to propose changes necessary for obtaining his agreement. Pundik returned empty-handed. El-Khouri then mentioned that the Geneva Accords suggested a 1.9% territorial swap, whereas Olmert proposed a 6.3% swap (similar to the proposed swap of the Beilin-Abu Mazen Understanding).

---

[15] "The Geneva Accords: A Model Israeli-Palestinian Peace Agreement," *Geneva Initiative*, October 12, 2003, https://geneva-accord.org/wp-content/uploads/2019/04/The-Geneva-Accord_-Full-Text.pdf (accessed July 12, 2023), archived at https://web.archive.org/web/20230712085912/https://geneva-accord.org/wp-content/uploads/2019/04/The-Geneva-Accord_-Full-Text.pdf.

Taken aback, I wondered if he understood the difference between an official offer from the Prime Minister of Israel and a track-two understanding supported by a small minority within the Israeli political system.

El-Khouri's response was even more frustrating: "*Yair, the Geneva Accord had the support of many generals and the international community. We believed the generals represented Israel's 'deep state,' and we knew we had international support for our demands.*" In my view, there couldn't have been a more devastating judgment on the Geneva Accords.

Beilin and I have both made efforts to maintain our friendship and mutual respect, but not without significant challenges. We hoped to sustain the dual structure of ECF working alongside the Geneva Accord Office, but it caused division within ECF and led to personal and organizational friction. It took me far too long to eventually resign from my position as ECF's president.

In contrast to the Geneva Accord, I pursued a policy concept that aimed to build a sufficient majority for the two-state approach. I aimed to go beyond freezing settlement expansion and gradually reverse the trend, progressing step by step toward an ongoing process of conflict transition and resolution, ultimately hoping to leading the way to a Permanent Status Agreement, as well as agreed progress on the way. In order to make this possible and suggest necessary security policies we studied the relevant literature on the utility of force, the evolvement of a security strategy, and how to promote a grand strategy seeking peace rather than a mere military victory in war.

Suggested Additional Reading

In Search for Security During the Second Intifada and After 9/11

B.H. Liddell Hart *Strategy;* Meridian London 1991; Second Revised Edition (revisiting Liddell Hart meant to go back to basics; important is Liddel Hart's distinction between "Strategy" and "Grand Strategy"[16]).

Rupert Smith *The Utility of Force—The Art of War in the Modern World*; Penguin, London 2006 (Smith takes the teaching of Liddell Hart right into the beginning of the twenty-first century. He addressed most of the issues relevant to the Israeli-Palestinian situation: using force amongst the people; being always aware of the impact of militant measures on the political outcome; of acting within the law; with and among the media).

---

[16] He writes "For the role of grand strategy—higher strategy—is to co-ordinate and direct all the resources of a nation, or band of nation, toward the attainment of the political object of the war… while the horizon of strategy is bounded by the war, grand strategy looks beyond the war to the subsequent peace" (p. 322).

United Kingdom Ministry of Defense Joint Doctrine Publication 2–40 *Security and Stabilization: the Military Contribution*; November 2009 (the British Army takes Rupert Smith's theoretical teachings a substantial step further. Discussing the "stabilization of fragile states" a mutually circular reinforcing tri-fold intervention is being suggested: Building Human and National Security should be employed to stimulate Economic and Infrastructure development; and this again should strengthen the Capacity and Legitimacy of the (fragile) government; while the growing legitimacy of government, would strengthen human and national security and economic and infrastructure development, and so on).

All of these theoretical findings were pursued by defining the Quartet Benchmarked Roadmap and its implementation during the first decade of the twenty-first century.

Testing Again the Idea of a Trusteeship

Jarat Chopra and Jim McCallum, Amjad Atalah and Gidi Grinstein "Planning Considerations for International Involvement in the Israeli-Palestinian Conflict" https://csl.armywarcollege.edu/usacsl/publications/PCII.pdf (accessed July 12, 2023), archived at https://web.archive.org/web/20230712090138/https://csl.armywarcollege.edu/usacsl/publications/PCII.pdf.

Testing Theoretical Options of the Creation of States

James Crawford *The Creation of States in International Law*, Clarendon Press, Oxford, 1979; particularly Part Two: pp. 173–297 (a great variety of options are discussed there, such as explicit grants of independence; gradual devolution; the concept of a federation, or confederation and other forms of political union; problems of recognition; forms of self-government and more).

Re-evaluating People-to-People Activities

Shira Herzog and Avivit Hai *The Power of Possibility: The Role of People-to-People Programs in the Current Israeli-Palestinian Reality* Economic Cooperation Foundation (ECF) and Friedrich Ebert Foundation; Herzliya 2005, https://library.fes.de/pdf-files/bueros/israel/04093.pdf (accessed July 12, 2023), archived at https://web.archive.org/web/20230712090313/https://library.fes.de/pdf-files/bueros/israel/04093.pdf (Herzog and Hai discuss the need for a legitimization strategy in protracted conflict; the importance of capacity building, of political and a-political cooperation, the importance of coordinated uni-national work and more).

The Reshaping of American Policy in the Middle East

Daniel Kurtzer et al., the Peace Puzzle—America's Quest for Arab–Israeli Peace, 1989–2011; Cornell U.P. Ithaca and London, and United States Institute for Peace, Washington D.C. 2013; chapter four: "George W. Bush Reshapes America's Role' pp. 154–190 (this is a concise description of America's response to the shock of 9/11 and its impact on the Middle East).

Emerging Changes in Europe

Tony Judt Postwar—*A History of Europe Since 1945*, op.cit., Part Four: After the Fall: 1989–2005 and Epilogue: From the House of the Dead—An Essay on Modern European Memory, pp. 637–831 (the two chapters on "the European way of life" and the "modern European Memory" are of particular importance for understanding European policies toward Israel).

Emerging Changes in Russia's Foreign Policy

Andrei P. Tsyganikov (ed.), *Routledge Handbook for Russian Foreign Policy*, Taylor and Francis Group, Milton Park, Abingdon, Oxon and New York 2018, specifically:

Elena Kropatcheva, "Power and National Security," pp. 43–59,

John Beryman, "Geopolitics in Russian Foreign Policy," pp. 60–78 (one section of the paper is entitled: "From Cold Peace to a new Cold War: The Putin Years, 2000–2017" and describes Russia's growing fear of NATO expansion all too close to Moscow, Petersburg, and Kaliningrad; the sense of being pushed to the periphery of world politics, and Putin's willingness to take military action. Beryman, writing in 2017, stresses the importance of Ukraine for Russian strategic thinking).

Luke March, "Nationalism," pp. 79–98, and

Valery Konyshev and Alexander Sergunin, "Military," pp. 168–181 (the last sentence of this essay reads: "It should be noted that the 'hybrid warfare' tactics and strategy blur the boundaries between real and virtual wars, and bring both sides to the brink with all its dangerous consequences.").

8

Maintaining the Struggle for a Two-State Solution Under Sharon and Olmert (2001–2009)

Rebuilding Jewish–Arab Relations at Home to Foster Close Working Relationship with Sharon's Government

In February 2001, Arik Sharon achieved a decisive victory in the elections. His primary objective was to demonstrate to the Palestinian leadership that violence would not yield favorable results. Sharon did not believe in a two-state solution. His objective was to negotiate an Interim Agreement that did not commit to, nor dismiss, a two-state solution. The underlying idea was to offer the Palestinians a state-like structure encompassing 40% or more of the West Bank territory and the Gaza Strip. Omri, Sharon's son, proposed this idea to Abu Mazen, who predictably rejected it. Subsequently, Vice Prime Minister Peres discussed the proposal with Abu Ala' leading to the development of a plan connecting the Interim Phase to the endgame, facilitating a gradual progression towards a two-state solution. However, Sharon rejected this concept, temporarily halting further exchanges. Simultaneously, he aimed to stabilize the Jewish–Arab relationship within Israel following the violent clash between Israel's Palestinian citizens and the Israeli police in October 2000. During Barak's tenure, the ECF team and I collaborated extensively with the Israeli National Security Council to enhance government relations with the Arab sector. With the assistance of Andre Zaaiman, we initiated a dialogue involving the Israeli Arab leadership, the Shabak, and the heads of police, as part of the preparations for the Orr-Commission's work.[1]

Additionally, I reached out to Rabbi Brian Lurie from San Francisco, and together we organized discussions with representatives of the Jewish Federations of the United States. This led to the establishment of the Inter-Agency Task Force on Israeli-Arabs, which has since been dedicated to supporting Jewish–Arab cooperation projects in Israel. Avivit Hai, a project director at ECF, played a significant role in ensuring the success of these endeavors.[2] While other organizations may have been better equipped for this field, the most favorable outcome was the development of close working relations with the incoming Sharon government.

Violence Replaces Diplomacy

ECF and I found ourselves in high demand from various parties: the incoming Sharon-led government, the Palestinians, the Israeli Palestinian Arab leadership, the Americans, the EU, as well as other international actors, particularly from the Netherlands and Canada, NATO, and numerous non-governmental organizations. In a context where official Israeli-Palestinian relations had deteriorated, and violence prevailed, the maintenance of established informal networks became exceedingly valuable.

The underlying idea was to offer the Palestinians a state-like structure encompassing 40% of the West Bank territory and the Gaza Strip. Omri, Sharon's son, proposed this idea to Abu Mazen, who predictably rejected it. Subsequently, Vice Prime Minister Peres discussed the proposal with Abu Ala', leading to the development of a plan connecting the Interim Phase to the endgame, facilitating a gradual progression towards a two-state solution. However, Sharon rejected this concept, temporarily halting further exchang.[3]

Violence and political uncertainty characterized the period. On June 1, 2001, a terrorist attack in Tel Aviv claimed the lives of 21 young people.

---

[1] Yair Hirschfeld private interview with Eivval Gileady on August 2, 2012 (General Gileady headed the Strategy Planning Department of the IDF).

[2] Immediately after the workshop we had organized under Andre Zaaiman's chairmanship, the "National Commission of Inquiry into the Clashes Between the Security Forces and Israeli Citizens of October 2000" was formed. Its members were: Theodore Orr, Judge of Israel's Supreme Court; Hashim Khatib, District Court Judge, and Ambassador Professor Shimon Shamir. They submitted their report on September 2, 2003.

[3] "Ten Years of the Orr Commission—Recommendations," Inter Agency Task Force on Israeli Arab Issues, September 2003, https://www.iataskforce.org/sites/default/files/resource/resource-1256.pdf (accessed July 12, 2023), archived at https://web.archive.org/web/20230712090828/https://www.iataskforce.org/sites/default/files/resource/resource-1256.pdf.

German Minister of Foreign Affairs, Yoshke Fischer, happened to be staying in a nearby hotel at the time. Fischer recounted his discussions with Arafat and showed him his notebook, declaring that he would erase the Palestinian leader's contact information if significant action against terror was not taken. This compelled Arafat to adopt an 11-point program aimed at ending terrorist activities.[4]

However, it failed to prevent Arafat from planning a resurgence of militant action. On January 3, 2002, the Israeli navy intercepted the MV Karine A, a Palestinian ship loaded with weapons from Iran. At the end of March, another act of terror occurred, resulting in the murder of 29 Israelis who were observing Passover at the Park Hotel in Netanya. Several days later, the IDF launched Operation Defensive Shield, which effectively incapacitated the Palestinian security forces. The Jenin refugee camp experienced significant destructions during this operation.

This chaos led to total anarchy, with former members of various Palestinian security forces terrorizing the population. The EU appointed Alastair Crooke, a former MI5 agent, as their security expert, marking the inception of what would become the European security group. Alastair Crooke collaborated closely with ECF, particularly with Boaz Karni.

Testing the Option of Internationalizing Security

Restoring security was a top priority for everyone involved. The EU established a security unit to collaborate with the Palestinians and Israelis, aiming to rival the CIA. We engaged with both parties. In Israel, ECF formed a team to study internationalization and the concept of trusteeship, drawing lessons from Macedonia, Kosovo, Afghanistan, East Timor, and the Marshall Islands. Additionally, I maintained contact with the Palestinians who were keen to learn more about internationalization, mirroring the interest shown by the Israelis in visiting Macedonia and Kosovo.

After confirming the interest of Israelis and Palestinians, I pursued two complementary approaches. I consulted with Andre Zaaiman about Palestinian conditions and proposed his visit to the West Bank to prepare the Palestinians for a trip to South Africa. The objective was to discuss strategic options with President Thabo Mbeki, coordinating efforts with us on the

---

[4] ECF, "Report on Meeting with German Foreign Minister Joschka Fischer," *Hirschfeld Khoury-DeConcini Papers*, Substack, forthcoming (originally written October 26, 2001), https://hkdpapers.substack.com/p/meeting-with-foreign-minister-joschka-fischer.

other side.⁵ The second approach involved collaborating with Robert Serry, responsible for conflict prevention in NATO, along with the Canadian Peace Envoy to the Middle East, Jill Sinclair, and the Ebert Foundation. Serry, Sinclair, and the Ebert Foundation organized a study visit to Macedonia and Kosovo.⁶ The group I assembled included Major General Danny Yatom, former head of Mossad, Brigadier General Baruch Spiegel, Colonel Ron Shatzberg, an unnamed Brigadier General trusted by Netanyahu, Micky Drill, and myself.⁷

Our visit to Skopje and later Kosovo was met with great hospitality. The conflict prevention structure in Macedonia impressed us, with senior ambassadors from the US, EU, and Russia working closely alongside NATO headquarters. This ensured effective coordination of military and diplomatic conflict prevention on a daily basis. NATO troops assisted villages on both sides of the demographic divide, aiding in infrastructure development as needed. In times of clashes, NATO troops positioned themselves in between the conflicting parties. During our helicopter ride in Kosovo, we witnessed heartbreaking scenes of destruction. We were taken to a Serb enclave within an Albanian village, protected by NATO tanks. Movement between places for Kosovan Albanians and Kosovan Serbs seemed entirely impossible.⁸

Upon returning from Macedonia and Kosovo, I discussed emerging ideas with Zuheir el-Menasreh and held a separate meeting with Hani el-Hassan, one of the founding fathers of the Fatah movement.⁹ They wanted to explore a "cease-fire implementation strategy for stability creation."¹⁰ Fatah's Revolutionary Council had decided that Fatah must assume control of the Al Aqsa brigades, former security forces that terrorized the Palestinian population. Fatah would disarm these individuals, apprehend them, and provide

---

⁵ Yair Hirschfeld, "Note to Andre Zaaiman," *Hirschfeld Khoury-DeConcini Papers*, Substack, forthcoming (originally written August 11, 2002), https://hkdpapers.substack.com/p/note-to-andre-zaaiman (I describe in the email the internal power relations within Palestine).

⁶ Robert Serry organized in June 1989 the proximity talks between Beilin and I on the Israeli and a PLO delegation, in Haag. We met again at the Madrid Conference, and remained in contact. Yair Hirschfeld, "Correspondence with Robert Serry," *Hirschfeld Khoury-DeConcini Papers*, Substack, forthcoming (originally written August 20-25, 2002), https://hkdpapers.substack.com/p/correspondence-with-robert-serry.

⁷ Yair Hirschfeld's private interview with Ron Shatzberg on August 9, 2022.

⁸ Years later, Naftali Bennett's plan to annex Area C reminded me of Kosovo. Implementing Bennett's plan would subject Israeli settlements and Palestinian villages to a similar siege.

⁹ At the beginning of 2002, at a time when the Karine A was captured by Israel troops, Arafat had nominated Hani el-Hassan to liaise with Israeli security forces. I had a first meeting with him on January 30, 2002 (my calendar).

¹⁰ Yair Hirschfeld, "Meeting with Zuheir el-Menasra," *Hirschfeld Khoury-DeConcini Papers*, Substack, forthcoming (originally written 4 February 2003.), https://hkdpapers.substack.com/p/meeting-with-zuheir-el-menasra (hereafter cited at Hirschfeld, "Meeting with Zuheir el-Menasra," *Hirschfeld Khoury-DeConcini Papers*).

monthly stipends to their families during imprisonment. This effort aimed to establish unified command over Palestinian security forces under the Ministry of Interior's responsibility, with support and necessary supervision from the international community. Similar measures were deemed necessary for financial management and the electoral process. El-Menasreh stressed the need for elections "within civil society, as well as for Fatah, local government, and a constitutional assembly."[11]

To explore potential Israeli-Palestinian security coordination and draw insights from the South African experience, Andre Zaaiman, with my assistance, organized a visit by an Israeli Security Group to Johannesburg and Cape Town. The conference we attended was incredibly fascinating. Although the agenda suggested "exchanging experiences," most of the time, over two days, the military wing of the ANC and representatives of the Apartheid government security forces shared their experiences. They vividly described their unfolding military strategic thinking and how both sides would interpret and anticipate each other's actions, ultimately motivating them to seek reconciliation. At the conclusion of the conference, the two delegations were received by President Thabo Mbeki.[12] The discussions made it evident that military power had limitations and that understanding, negotiations, and transforming realities were the only viable path forward. Equally impressive was the account of how community work was organized on the ground.[13]

---

[11] Hirschfeld, "Meeting with Zuheir el-Menasra," *Hirschfeld Khoury-DeConcini Papers*.

[12] It was the first time that the ANC military wing and the Apartheid security members discussed the former military struggle between them. We asked for the protocol of the discussion and never received it. We did receive the list of participants: Israeli Security Group, 14–17 February 2003. The members of the South African team were: Minister Lindwe Sisulu, Minister Charles Noakula, Minister Valli Moosa; Minister Ronnie Kasrils; Minister Jeff Rabebe; Deputy Minister Aziz Pahad; Deputy Minister Bridget Mabandla; Speaker Frene Ginwala; former Minister Pit Botha; former Minister Leon Wessels, former Minister Roelf Meyer; Mr. Mike Louw and Dr. Niel Barnard; in addition: Deputy President Jacob Zuma; Minister Mosis Lekota and Minister Oenuyell Maduna; the Middle East Task Team and NIA Logistics and Security; former Security officials: General Constat Viljoen, Lt.General George Meiring; Lt. General Wessel Kritzinger; Major General Chris Thirion; Major General Joffel van der Westhuizen; Gert Opperman; Commissioner Andre Pruis and Commodore Johan Retief. The Israeli delegation was headed by Lt. General Amnon Lipkin-Shachak; other members were: Major General Alik Ron; Major Gen. Gideon Scheffer; Major Gen. Yossi Hen; Major Gen. Danny Rothschild, Major Gen. Uri Simhoni; Major General Shay Avital; Brigadier Gen. Iftach Spector; Pini Meidan former security advisor to Prime Minister Barak; and Yair Hirschfeld.

[13] Susan Collin Marks, *Watching the Wind—Conflict Resolution During South Africa's Transition to Democracy*, United States Institute of Peace Press, Washington D.C. 2000. See Jeremy Seekings, *The UDF—A History of the United Democratic Front in South Africa, 1983–1991*, David Philip Publishers, Claremont 2000.

Seeking Economic Relief and Development for the Palestinian Territories

We were aware that security alone, even with significant international support, was not enough. Economic assistance and a political path were also necessary. I regularly discussed this with Zippi Livni, who served as Minister of Regional Cooperation in Sharon's Government. As she lacked connections to Palestinians, Jordanians, or Egyptians, she sought my help. I assisted in arranging meetings, occasionally participating and providing advice. I also connected her with Andre Zaaiman, whose strategic thinking impressed her. Meetings typically took place at her office, but sometimes at her home in Zahala. Shortly after Operation Defensive Shield, Livni proposed organizing a donor relief program and suggested I discuss it with Dan Kurtzer, the US ambassador to Israel at the time. In the following months, I visited the United States three times, in May, October, and November.

During my May visit, I had a crucial meeting with Liz Cheney, Deputy Assistant Secretary of State for Near Eastern Affairs, who was responsible for the economic portfolio and US-AID. These meetings paved the way for a lasting cooperation between ECF and successive heads of US-AID in Israel and Palestine, such as Larry Gerber, Jim Bever, Howard Sumka, David Harden and Michael Harvey. ECF played a leading role in planning and liaising, working with Palestinian counterparts and experts to develop economic relief and development plans for Gaza and the West Bank. Additionally, our capacity to facilitate communication between various stakeholders including the IDF, Israeli ministries, the PA, the World Bank, the IMF, US-AID, the EU, and the German and Dutch delegations was crucial.

Based on our study of the South African experience, we recognized the importance of community work on both the Israeli and Palestinian sides. In October and November, Grinstein and I visited Boston to explore potential collaboration with Harvard University. We met with Prof. Robert Mnookin to discuss engaging with Israel's settlement community and helped organize a workshop in Israel with key settler leaders. Othniel Schneller presented a detailed paper proposing "settlement consolidation," suggesting the concentration of settlements into blocks and the relocation of other settlements into these blocks, with the aim to prepare for Israeli-Palestinian negotiations seeking an agreed two-state resolution.[14]

---

[14] Sanford Gallanter, "Settlement Consolidation Project," *Harvard University*, December 7, 2002 (unpublished). Othniel Schneller submitted to us two papers he had written with similar ideas. See Othiel Schneller, "Izuv mchadash shel Mapat hahityashvut byeshaa—mehkar (The Renewed

Hoping to Recreate a Political Horizon

While actively pursuing security and economic rehabilitation, we did not overlook the need for a political path forward. Nimrod Novik proposed a three-phased approach during the first half of 2001, which later became the conceptual precursor to the Quartet Benchmarked Roadmap for Peace in the Middle East. We discussed these ideas with various individuals on the Palestinian side, including Hani el-Hassan, Saeb Erakat, Maher el-Kurd, and others, who sought an escape from the cycle of violence. We engaged in discussions with the American peace team to analyze what went wrong, referring to it as the "WWW project" (What Went Wrong). Only Marwan Barghouti conveyed to Rob Malley that Palestinian violence would persist until the end of the occupation.[15] Workshops organized by Robert Serry, Jill Sinclair, and Ed Djerejian served as platforms to discuss these ideas.

In June 2002, we received a confidential paper from the Germans, which presented an initial version of what eventually became the Quartet Benchmarked Roadmap.[16] The German proposal included a more stringent international monitoring and oversight function than the final Roadmap. It took approximately another year until the Quartet announced the final "Benchmarked Roadmap."[17] Personally, I was not fond of the specified deadlines and concerned that the Roadmap would remain a mere diplomatic gesture. However, it proved otherwise. It took some time to establish a Quartet implementation structure on the ground. Former World Bank President James Wolfensohn was assigned to address the political and economic aspects of the Roadmap, while US General William Ward was tasked with security reform in the PA and promoting Israeli-Palestinian security cooperation. Both relied heavily on the support provided by the ECF team and myself.

Consolidation of the Settlement Map in Judaea and Samaria)," January 28, 2003 (unpublished) (the other paper he had written in 1989) (Hebrew).

[15] Yair Hirschfeld meeting with Rob Malley on April 26, 2001. Marwan Barghouti told Malley that violence would continue until it would bring about the end of occupation.

[16] "German Non-Paper," June 26, 2002 (confidential and unpublished).

[17] The best description of the diplomatic work leading to the formulation of the Quartet Roadmap is given by Marwan Muasher. Marwan Musher, *The Arab Center—The Promise of Moderation*, Yale University Press, New York 2008, pp. 176–198.

Emerging Threats from the Region

During my visits to Washington in 2002, I observed a dangerous complacency among American political and military leaders following the relatively easy victory in Afghanistan. This complacency led to a misguided sense of confidence that a similar military action in Iraq would also be smooth. Ambassador Djerejian shared recommendations from his team regarding Iraq, which included a substantial increase in US troops and the need to rebuild Iraqi state infrastructure, such as the military and oil fields, along with preparing a Marshall Plan for the region.

Unfortunately, Secretary of Defense Donald Rumsfeld took the opposite approach. I was particularly concerned about the potential negative repercussions for Israel. I feared that the American complacency would fail to understand Iran's regional fears and its aspirations for regional hegemony. The American encirclement of Iran through its presence in Iraq, Afghanistan, Central Asia, and the Persian Gulf initially frightened the rulers in Tehran. As a result, they sent an appeasing message to Washington via the Swiss Embassy and conveyed a similar message to Israel through the ECF.[18] The offer included stopping efforts to develop nuclear military capacity and ceasing arms deliveries to Hamas. The Swiss message reached Jim Larocco at the Department of State, but he requested an official direct proposal from Iran instead of an unofficial message from an undefined source.[19] Whether there was a realistic opportunity to end Iran's military nuclear buildup and minimize its support for Hezbollah and Hamas remains unknown.

The Iranian threat perception of encirclement was only half of the story. The other half involved Iran's enhanced regional hegemonic aspirations resulting from the American invasions of Afghanistan and Iraq. The danger that Saddam Hussein's Iraq posed to Iran was now in the past. The US invasion provided Iran with additional means to influence Iraqi politics in support of the Shiite population, as well as extending its reach through Iraq to Syria and Lebanon, ultimately reaching the Mediterranean.[20]

It was evident that these developments posed a significant threat to Israel. Iran would do everything in its power to prevent the formation of a strong US-Israel-Arab coalition. Their strategy included providing military training,

---

[18] A former M16 operator, Alastair Crooke, sent the message to Boaz Karni who informed the relevant Israeli authorities. Boaz Karni remembers that the Iranian source was the chairman of the majlis, Mr. Larijani.

[19] Yair Hirschfeld private interview with Boaz Karni on August 12, 2022.

[20] For a very comprehensive description of Israel's majority and politically relevant perception of the Iranian threat, see Dore Gold, *The Rise of Nuclear Iran—How Tehran Defies the West*, Regnery Publishing, Washington D.C. 2009.

arms, including missiles, and funding to non-state proxies like Hezbollah, jihadist groups, and Hamas. The intention behind assisting Hezbollah in building a large missile arsenal capable of targeting any place in Israel was to deter Israel from activating the Begin Doctrine, which advocated attacking Iran's nuclear military buildup. These Iranian initiated actions were accompanied with genocidal language, demanding "Death to Israel".[21]

The Second Phase: Sharon's Unilateral Disengagement Policy

In late 2003, Sharon announced his "Unilateral Disengagement Policy," which involved withdrawing from the Gaza Strip, evacuating all settlements there, and removing five settlements from the northern West Bank. According to Dov Weissglas, who handled negotiations with the Americans, Sharon also proposed evacuating 17 settlements with 15,000 inhabitants from the West Bank. The Americans rejected the idea, which in hindsight, was another missed opportunity. The second mistake was Sharon's refusal to negotiate the "unilateral disengagement" with the Palestinians and instead seeking assurances from President Bush, which he received.[22]

From ECF's perspective, the timing of Sharon's announcement was opportune. Even without prior knowledge of Sharon's move, we had already undertaken the necessary preparatory work. Our standing with the Israeli government was stronger than ever before. We had the trust of Zippi Livni and enjoyed her confidence. This was invaluable, as she had the full confidence of Sharon. We had collaborated with the National Security Council, established close personal relationships with senior leaders in Israel's security authorities, worked closely with US-AID, received support from Ambassador Ed Djerejian and the James Baker Institute for Public Policy, and maintained a friendship with the American ambassador, Dan Kurtzer. Additionally, together with Othniel Schneller, I initiated an ongoing working dialogue with the settler leadership.

---

[21] F. Wehrey et al., *Dangerous but Not Omnipotent: Exploring the Reach and Limitations of Iranian Power in the Middle East*, Rand Corporation, Washington D.C. 2009. The full study most evidently demonstrated the aggressive nature of Iranian politics and its danger to the stability of pro-Western Arab states, as well as Israel. The executive summary of the study—aiming to be "politically correct," denied most of the rather threatening findings documented in the report.

[22] Dov Weissglas, *Sharon-Prime Minister*, Yedioth Ahronot, Tel Aviv 2012 (Hebrew), pp.155–257 (particularly p. 227). Ehud Yaari told me years later that he had initiated track two negotiations with Chairman Arafat, and Arafat was willing to support the "unilateral" approach, but Sharon rejected their suggestions.

With such favorable circumstances, we were uniquely positioned to coordinate Israeli-Palestinian economic development, security cooperation, and the revival of the peace process.

Attempting to Coordinate Israeli-Palestinian National Interests

The Economy

At the request of the National Security Council, we took on the task of coordinating economic efforts with the Palestinians and the international community. Our goal was to facilitate an orderly transfer of assets left behind by Israel and encourage the international community to support the jumpstart of a strong economic growth in the occupied territories. The World Bank assigned different economic sectors to various nations, with each country taking responsibility for specific areas of development. For example, the Netherlands would support Palestinian agriculture, Denmark would focus on fishing, the EU would assist with construction and housing, the USA would contribute to industry and labor, and so on.

Based on this division of responsibilities, in collaboration with the Palestinian NGO al-Mustaqbal, we developed a plan for the orderly transfer of goods and infrastructure in each area. In the Northern West Bank, for instance, the Netherlands would transform the settlement of Homesh into an agricultural research center, while Austria would establish tourist-based community centers in Ganim and Kadim. In the Gaza Strip, Gush Kativ, which housed most of the settlements, would be turned into a Middle Eastern tourism center, with Austria overseeing tourism and the Netherlands promoting the continuation and improvement of high-tech agriculture left behind by Israel. Other settlements would be repurposed for urban development, parks, and industrial parks, with various countries involved in these projects.[23]

To promote this concept, we organized a workshop in Herzliya and invited Shimon Peres and Salam Fayyad, who was still serving as the Minister of Finance at the time. We coordinated the plan closely with Itamar Yaar, Deputy Head of Israel's National Security Council, and received full support

---

[23] ECF, "Tochnit tlatzdadit lemaavar musdar shel nekhasim" (A Trilateral Plan for the Orderly Transfer of Assets), *Hirschfeld Khoury-DeConcini Papers*, *Substack*, forthcoming (originally created in preparation for a meeting in December 2004), https://hkdpapers.substack.com/p/trilateral-plan-for-orderly-transfer-of-assets.

from Deputy Prime Minister Shimon Peres. Peres even suggested including military buildings and installations in the transfer, with the exception of Jewish cemeteries and synagogues. However, the Quartet Office, led by James Wolfensohn representing the international community, made the decision to have the assets destroyed instead, based on the Palestinian Authority's demand to uphold international law, which deemed economic actions by the occupying force in occupied areas as illegal. This resulted in the destruction of the assets left behind, creating an image of war and destruction instead of the anticipated construction and economic growth. It was a wasteful outcome, both in terms of American and European tax money and our hopes for a better future.

James Wolfensohn was personally upset about this decision, and he donated $600,000 from his personal funds to support ECF's efforts. Together with additional funds raised, ECF, under the leadership of Boaz Karni, purchased greenhouses from the settlers who were leaving. ECF owned the greenhouses for just a minute before transferring them to the Palestinian government.[24]

Security

ECF established a security team led by Brig. General Dov Sedaka (Fufi), which worked closely with Jibril Rajoub. We prepared policy papers on various aspects of security cooperation and arranged meetings between Lt. General Amnon Lipkin-Shachak and the Palestinian Minister of Interior, General Nasr Yussuf, based on our findings. These efforts were successful in planning for the orderly coordination of settlement evacuations. Table exercises were conducted between the IDF and Palestinian Security Forces to prevent any Israeli-Palestinian friction during the actual evacuation.

General Nasr Yussuf requested that the IDF remain in Gaza to allow the Palestinian governmental security forces to rebuild their presence and control. However, Sharon rejected this demand, and the consequences of that decision would prove detrimental to what followed.[25]

---

[24] The transfer was legally overseen by the law office of Herzog Fox Neeman Tel Aviv.

[25] In the meeting held between General Nasr Yussuf and General Lipkin-Shachak, General Yussuf asked also for the supply of Israeli arms to the Palestinian Authority. Lipkin-Shachak denied this request, saying that most of Israeli earlier arms supplies had been smuggled or sold on the "free market" or even to terrorist groups. (We did not record this meeting for fear of leakage; quoted from my memory). Sharon's point of view was explained to me by General Giladi, who had planned the Disengagement, being head of the IDF Strategy Department. Yair Hirschfeld private interview with Evval Giladi on July 10, 2011.

Creating a Political Horizon—Getting Back to Roadmap Implementation

In our efforts to create a political horizon and advance the implementation of the roadmap, we engaged in ongoing discussions with various stakeholders, including the United States, Germany, the European Union, and others. The ECF took on the task of detailed planning to facilitate the withdrawal from settlements in the Northern West Bank, envisioning it as a major state-building project that could serve as a model for future settlement evacuations and relocations.[26]

Throughout 2005, I was part of a group led by Othniel Schneller, Aviad Friedman, and Pini Meidan. Aviad Friedman, a close friend of Omri Sharon and director of the daily Maariv newspaper, often engaged in late-night discussions with Prime Minister Sharon on various topics. Pini Meidan, a former foreign policy and security advisor to Barak, also played a role in our discussions.

Based on repeated discussions and input from Prime Minister Sharon, we developed a disengagement map with four categories of settlements. The blue settlements, located west of the security fence, were intended for annexation to Israel sooner rather than later. The yellow settlements, located east of the fence but close to it, were intended for annexation upon the conclusion of a final agreement. The green settlements, situated near Palestinian towns and villages along the North–South West Bank ridge, were planned for evacuation and relocation within the "blue" settlement blocs. The red settlements, mainly along the Jordan River, were designated for relocation only if a satisfactory arrangement could guarantee Israeli security interests along the Jordan River.

The main idea behind the "four-colored" map was to change the dynamics and use a second unilateral disengagement as a catalyst to return to bilateral negotiations. Later, I learned that Prime Minister Sharon had even more comprehensive plans, combining significant settlement relocations with supportive political actions.[27] However, on January 4, 2006, he fell into a coma, effectively leaving the political scene forever, long before his death in

---

[26] ECF, "Report on ECF Seminar: Disengagement of the Northern West Bank," *Hirschfeld Khoury-DeConcini Papers, Substack*, forthcoming (originally written 2001), https://hkdpapers.substack.com/p/disengagement-of-the-northern-west-bank (the ECF team and I, the following international actors participated: Jill Sinclair (Canadian Embassy); Barry Southern (Ward Team); Edward Djerejian (Baker Institute); Christian Berger (EU); William Taylor (US Embassy); Orit Gal (IDF), David Brodet).

[27] Yair Hirschfeld private interview with Evval Giladi on July 10 2011 (Giladi had worked closely together with Sharon on these plans).

2014. Unfortunately, the battle to "turn the tide" and use unilateral disengagement as a catalyst for permanent status negotiations was lost. Instead of promoting negotiations, the unilateral disengagement had the opposite effect.

The Mistakes that Strengthened the Most Radical Elements in the Settlement Community

Before the settlement evacuations took place, I visited Gush Katif with my sister, Miriam, to engage with the people there. We were met with polite hostility. The residents firmly believed that the disengagement would not happen due to rabbinical prophecies. They refused to cooperate with the disengagement authority, rejected restitution payments, and did not plan for their future relocation. I hoped to convince them, to prepare for successful relocation, with the support of the Israeli government and reminded them that according to Jewish law, a prophecy that doesn't come true would be punished later on.

As the summer approached, rabbinical leaders called on religious soldiers to disobey orders. This directive mobilized retired generals, colonels, and other senior military officials to assist in the evacuation. The involvement of these military leaders, who had previously commanded many of the settlers during their military service, created a sense of authority and respect, leading to a relatively peaceful evacuation.

However, in hindsight, the disengagement scenes of the summer of 2005 were perceived by the public as a tremendous sacrifice by the settlement community. Instead of security and stability, Gaza eventually fell under the rule of Hamas, and its military branch posed a constant threat to nearby Israeli villages and towns. Strategically, the supply of rockets and missiles from Iran enabled Hamas to create a new and persistent threat that subsequent Israeli governments have struggled to address.

Furthermore, the sense of instability was reinforced by the lessons learned from the 2005 disengagement. Radical rabbinical leadership developed the concept of "price tag," which involved provoking and committing acts of violence against Palestinian targets to preempt any potential evacuation or relocation of settlements. This tactic also included violent resistance against IDF actions taken to counter illegal settlement expansion. The "price tag" policy did not hesitate to resort to killing Palestinians, Israeli peace activists, or even soldiers if the threat of settlement evacuation grew.

Overall, the mistakes made during the disengagement process inadvertently strengthened the most radical elements within the settlement community, leading to increased instability and escalating cycles of violence.

Postscript: Lessons Learned Show the Value of Multilateral-Coordinated Unilateral Move

Despite the challenges and mistakes encountered during the disengagement process, I believe it would be a mistake to disregard the value of multilateral-coordinated unilateral moves. Even today, such an approach holds advantages for both sides and could help change the reality on the ground on the path toward a two-state agreement. It allows the Palestinians the advantage of not having to accept the legality of settlements or give up their demands for future negotiations. For Israel, it provides an opportunity to "turn the tide."

We learned five lessons: Israeli unilateral action had to be fully coordinated with the Palestinian Authority; it was essential to allow the Palestinian leadership to take the credit for Israeli withdrawals; security cooperation had to reach beyond the immediate moves and allow the Palestinian Authority to take control and establish law and order. This again was an essential precondition for the orderly transfer of non-movable real estate, in line with a regional and internationally supported investment plan for economic growth. Finally, a commitment of both sides to return to negotiations would be essential.

Olmert's Government, 2006–2009

Following the incapacitation of Prime Minister Sharon in January 2006, Ehud Olmert formed a new government in March. Initially, both Olmert and Tzipi Livni, who became the Minister of Foreign Affairs, intended to initiate a second unilateral disengagement, largely in line with Sharon's plans. However, the Palestinian elections in January 2006 resulted in a majority representation of Hamas in the Palestinian parliament. Consequently, the decision was made to refrain from a second unilateral disengagement that would involve the evacuation and relocation of settlements.[28]

---

[28] Compare with Elliot Abrams, *Tested by Zion—The Bush Administration and the Israeli-Palestinian Conflict*, Cambridge, Cambridge U.P. 2013, pp. 119–157. Abrams describes a long discussion he had with Saeb Eraqat on the elections. He quotes Eraqat saying: "Don't interfere with our internal business. We want the Hamas to participate, we will beat the hell out of them, and we will win"

Two months prior to the Palestinian elections, I submitted a Trilateral Action Plan for Roadmap Phase One Implementation to the Baker Institute and Ambassador Djerejian. The plan aimed to enable close cooperation between the international community, the Government of Israel, and the PA in creating secure conditions for the intended second phase of disengagement and the relocation/evacuation of numerous settlements. I explained that the Government of Israel would not return to bilateral negotiations "until the PA can establish a functional government, retain a monopoly of violence and create stability. A trilateral security plan would strengthen the legitimacy of the PA and help to overcome bottlenecks."[29]

In line with this approach, I tried to convince the Palestinians to postpone the scheduled parliamentary elections. I suggested that President Abbas should ask Hamas to participate in a joint effort to end the ongoing state of anarchy and reestablish law and order, thereby creating the necessary stability for holding elections. However, despite predictions of a landslide Hamas victory from within ECF, international pressure, including from the United States, prevailed, and Abbas did not dare to postpone the elections.

ECF commissioned a paper to assess the impact of Hamas's victory.[30] The paper outlined five immediate targets: preventing Hamas participation in terrorist acts, sustaining the functioning of existing Palestinian security forces to maintain stability, separating Hamas political and security forces in Gaza from those in the West Bank, securing international humanitarian support for the PA, and working toward a fully unified and coordinated international approach to Hamas. To engage with Hamas, the paper emphasized the need for the group to accept three conditions: refuting the 1988 Hamas Charter calling for the destruction of Israel, recognizing the State of Israel, and ending all acts of terrorism. It was suggested that these demands be put forward while maintaining cooperation with the PA.

A serious internal discussion took place within ECF on how to react to the situation. Boaz Karni proposed maintaining indirect contact by cooperating

---

(pp. 152). From the Israeli legal point of view this was problematic. The elections were defined in the Oslo II Agreement of September 1995. In order to participate in the elections, Hamas would have to accept and recognize the Oslo Agreements, which it did not do. Within ECF Boaz Karni prophesized accurately a Hamas victory.

[29] "Trilateral Action Plan for Roadmap Phase 1 Implementation," *Israeli-Palestinian Working Group Policy Paper*, James A. Baker III Institute for Public Policy, Rice University, November 16, 2005, https://www.bakerinstitute.org/research/trilateral-action-plan-for-road-map-phase-i-implementation (accessed July 12, 2023), archived at https://web.archive.org/web/20230712092201/https://www.bakerinstitute.org/research/trilateral-action-plan-for-road-map-phase-i-implementation.

[30] "Tarkhishej Hitkadmut efshariim im nizachon hahamas bbchirot" (trans. Scenarios of Possible Action after the Hamas Victory in the Elections), *Hirschfeld Khoury-DeConcini Papers, Substack*, forthcoming (originally written shortly after January 15, 2006), https://hkdpapers.substack.com/p/scenarios-of-possible-action-after-hamas-victory (author asked to remain unnamed for their security).

with Alastair Crooke. Nimrod Novik suggested dividing the three conditions into different phases, demanding an immediate cessation of terrorism while allowing time for Hamas to accept the other two demands. The discussion revolved around the Arab idiom: whether it made more sense to have Hamas inside the tent and risk their actions negatively impacting the situation or keep them outside the tent, fearing their potential disruptions.

Before taking a clear position, I wanted to listen and scheduled a meeting with Hamas ideologue Hassan Yussuf. However, before the meeting could take place, TV Channel One wrongly reported that I had already met with him, which caused a dramatic and unexpected chain of events. Palestinian friends and counterparts who were close to me phoned angrily, threatening to cut off all relations, while others simply ignored my calls. The message was clear: any serious dialogue with Hamas would question the position of the PLO and PA as the sole legitimate representatives of the Palestinian people, as established by the Arab Summit Conference in October 1974. It became evident that creating a Zone of Achievable Agreement with the PLO and PA was challenging enough, and having Hamas "in the tent" would render it impossible.

After Hamas violently seized control of the Gaza Strip from June 10–15, 2007, General Mansur Abu Rashed of Jordan, in coordination with the Jordanian Security Services, facilitated a meeting between Ron Shatzberg, myself, and a representative from the Jordanian Muslim Brethren movement. Their message was clear: the various Muslim Brethren movements in Jordan, Palestine, Egypt, and other parts of the Middle East operated in coordination to ultimately control the entire region. **Their primary objective was to strengthen and maintain Hamas' grip on the Gaza Strip, regardless of the cost.** At the time I did not fully grasp the gravity of this statement. **It meant that the military wing of Hamas would maintain under all conditions the capacity to attack Israel, at any given moment, in order to prevent any political process that might allow the Palestinian Authority to regain control over the Gaza Strip.** It would lead to successive wars on Gaza; and it would undermine the possibility to prepare for economic investment, growth and development.

While I had the luxury of exploring policy options without time constraints, Prime Minister Olmert and his Minister of Foreign Affairs faced the immediate challenge of responding to Hamas' victory in the January 2006 elections to the Palestinian parliament. They considered pursuing a second Disengagement agreement but ultimately rejected it, choosing instead to prepare for Permanent Status negotiations.

The Rise and Fall of the Agha-Khalidi-Brodet-Hirschfeld Negotiating Channel

The Agha-Khalidi-Brodet-Hirschfeld Negotiating Channel experienced its rise and fall during this period. Shortly after assuming office, Zippi Livni and Vice Prime Minister Haim Ramon requested David Brodet and me to explore potential understandings with Agha and Khalidi that could revive the peace process. Swiftly, the four of us (Brodet, Agha, Khalidi, and I) formulated a seven-point understanding, which outlined the following:

1. *The ultimate goal of the political process is the creation of a free, independent, democratic, sovereign, viable, secure, and contiguous Palestinian state, living side by side with Israel in peace and security;*
2. *Future Israeli withdrawals from the West Bank are part of a process of ending the occupation;*
3. *The final borders between the two states and other outstanding issues will be determined by negotiations (this will include agreed-upon land swaps);*
4. *No progress in the political process is possible without mutual and reciprocal security for the Israeli and the Palestinian peoples;*
5. *Progress in the political process should include measures to provide for economic viability and independence for the Palestinian people;*
6. *Jerusalem is a city holy to all three monotheistic faiths, and freedom of access to holy sites shall be guaranteed (the political future of Jerusalem will be determined by demographic considerations); and*
7. *A fair and equitable resolution of the Palestinian refugee problem shall be agreed upon with due consideration to the concern of both parties.*[31]

In May 2006, Agha and Khalidi traveled to Strasbourg to discuss these seven principles with Abu Mazen, who fully supported them. The same text was later presented to PM Olmert and Minister of Foreign Affairs Livni, who agreed to the first five points but rejected points six and seven. President Abbas, in response, emphasized the importance of the agreed-upon process rather than the specific wording. This understanding paved the way for a successful meeting between Abu Mazen and Livni in June 2006 at Sharm el-Sheikh.

---

[31] This paper was original submitted to the Baker Institute for Public Policy. Yair Hirschfeld, "Second Year Report," *Hirschfeld Khoury-DeConcini Papers, Substack*, forthcoming (originally written October 12, 2007), https://hkdpapers.substack.com/p/second-year-report (hereafter cited as Hirschfeld, "Second Year Report" *Hirschfeld Khoury-DeConcini Papers*).

Due to the abduction of Gilad Shalit on June 25, 2006, and the subsequent war with Lebanon in July 2006, official contacts and the work of our group of Four were interrupted for several months. Efforts to resume negotiations stalled until the Hamas takeover of Gaza and the formation of a new Palestinian government led by Salam Fayyad. The Economic Cooperation Foundation (ECF) had previously collaborated with Fayyad during his roles as the head of the Palestinian IMF branch and Minister of Finance. Contacts aimed at improving security and implementing measures to enhance the economic situation in the West Bank resumed.

Agha, Khalidi, Brodet, and I maintained contact and continued our deliberations. In July 2007, shortly after the formation of the Fayyad Government, Agha and Khalidi submitted a two-and-a-half-page document endorsed by Abbas, which outlined detailed terms of reference for the envisioned Permanent Status Negotiations.[32] However, Olmert, Livni, and Ramon rejected the paper. Our challenge was to find ways to address the political needs of both sides and bridge the substantial gaps.

I recognized that the existing gaps were significant:

- The Palestinian leadership sought explicit language stating Israel's obligation to "end the occupation" and withdraw from all territories occupied after June 4, 1967, while the Israeli leadership preferred vague language to minimize internal opposition and maintain negotiation flexibility.
- The Israeli leadership required clear language denying the right of Palestinian refugees to return to sovereign Israeli territory, whereas the Palestinian leadership sought ambiguous language allowing them to argue for the principle of the "Right of Return" with potential limitations on its implementation.
- While the Palestinians aimed for clear language ensuring full sovereignty rights over the Haram ash-Sharif in Jerusalem, no Israeli government could relinquish unlimited sovereignty over the Temple Mount/Haram ash-Sharif.
- The Palestinian leadership needed assurance that all Israeli settlements in the West Bank would be evacuated, as occurred in Gaza, while the Israeli leadership intended to discuss "relocations into settlement blocks" and allow most settlers to remain in their homes.
- The Israeli leadership needed to demonstrate that security arrangements would create a secure and stable environment without the threat of violence, while the Palestinian leadership desired full sovereignty over all

---

[32] Hirschfeld, "Second Year Report," *Hirschfeld Khoury-DeConcini Papers*, pp. 9–11.

their territory and maintained the right to resist if Israel failed to fulfill its obligations.

Recognizing the existing gaps, Brodet and I prepared a counter-proposal to the Agha-Khalidi Paper. We suggested a three-part approach: a Declaration of Commitments, a menu of confidence-building measures, and a timeframe for concluding negotiations on territory. We aimed to seek regional and international endorsement, as well as oversight for this proposed approach.[33] I was confident that the Seven Commitments we proposed would be a game changer, including a (1) viable Two-State Solution, (2) timeframe for negotiation of final borders, (3) secure and stable environment, (4) performance-based phased implementation, (5) transition from war to peace logic, (6) Third Party Role, and (7) solution on Jerusalem, Holy Places, and Refugees to end the conflict. This counter-proposal offered bilateral, regional, and international support for establishing the State of Palestine while providing Israel with supportive security conditions and a code of conduct necessary for phased implementation and fair negotiations.

We were informed that PM Olmert made handwritten changes on the text on September 29, 2007, but we never received the corrected version. Agha and Khalidi requested some changes, and after discussions, we produced a joint text on October 9, 2007, intending to test its acceptability and conclude it at the next meeting. We hoped to submit this text to Secretary of State Condolezza Rice, who would then share it with the parties, allowing them to express their reservations while moving forward.[34]

Ramon was interested not only in our achievements but also in the rejected demands. Agha and Khalidi opposed including a reference to the Bush letter to Sharon from April 2004, which emphasized accepting realities on the ground when negotiating territory. Our demand to recognize Israel as a "Jewish and democratic state" was rejected, citing contradictions with the Palestinian historical narrative. However, they did agree to the following text:

---

[33] Hirschfeld, "Second Year Report," *Hirschfeld Khoury-DeConcini Papers*, pp. 9–12.
[34] Hirschfeld, "Second Year Report," *Hirschfeld Khoury-DeConcini Papers*; pp. 15–19. See the report David and I originally prepared for Vice Prime Minister Haim Ramon. David Brodet and Yair Hirschfeld, "hitkadmut hamagaim legibush mismach Annapolis" (trans. Progress in the Dialogue Aimed at Reaching an Annapolis Document), *Hirschfeld Khoury-DeConcini Papers, Substack*, forthcoming (originally written on October 22, 2007), https://hkdpapers.substack.com/p/dialouge-aimed-at-reaching-an-annapolis-document (hereafter cited as Brodet and Hirschfeld, "hitkadmut hamagaim legibush mismach Annapolis," *Hirschfeld Khoury-DeConcini Papers*).

Israel views itself as a Jewish and democratic state, Palestine views itself as a democratic part of the Arab Nation and the Islamic world[35]

Regarding Jerusalem, the division between Jewish and Arab neighborhoods was accepted, and we aimed to include specific parts of Arab neighborhoods under Israeli sovereignty to ease the geographic division. The text originally read:

In principle, Arab neighborhoods will come under Palestinian sovereignty.[36]

Agha and Khalidi insisted on deleting "in principle," in order to make it evident that Arab neighborhoods of Jerusalem, where Jewish inhabitants would also reside, would become part of the Palestinian capital.

While I believed these issues were solvable, the warning we received about growing opposition in the territories was concerning. I was asked to speak to Abu Ala' to minimize potential opposition from his camp. During the meeting with Abu Ala', we discussed the territorial agreement and the planned "give and take." He proposed a 2.4% territorial swap, with the Palestinians granting Israel most of the security demands in return. I conveyed to Abu Ala' that, despite good intentions, the Olmert government could not and would not agree to those terms. Instead, I suggested considering a more ambiguous formula on territory in exchange for enlarging Palestinian control in Area C. I reported to Vice PM Ramon that Abu Ala' "might" accept such a proposal.[37]

A week later, Brodet and I sent a detailed report to Minister of Foreign Affairs Zippi Livni. We suggested adopting one of three options: a more or less inclusive and ambiguous Declaration of Principles; an agreed (substantial) transfer of administrative Palestinian control over Area C, or the possibility of preparing a US Declaration that both sides could accept with necessary reservations.[38]

---

[35] Brodet and Hirschfeld, "hitkadmut hamagaim legibush mismach Annapolis," *Hirschfeld Khoury-DeConcini Papers*.

[36] Brodet and Hirschfeld, "hitkadmut hamagaim legibush mismach Annapolis," *Hirschfeld Khoury-DeConcini Papers*.

[37] Yair Hirschfeld, "Sikum pgisha shel Yair im Abu Ala' bnosej hachanot lkrejveidat Annapolis" (trans. Summary of Meeting between Yair and Abu Ala' on the Subjects of Preparations for the Annapolis Conference), *Hirschfeld Khoury-DeConcini Papers*, *Substack*, forthcoming (originally written on October 28, 2007), https://hkdpapers.substack.com/p/subjects-of-preparations-for-annapolis. One month after the Annapolis Conference, Abu Ala' suggested exactly what we had discussed at the end of October, a substantial move in regard to Area C. See Abrams, *Tested by Zion*, pp. 271.

[38] The report was originally submitted to Minister of Foreign Affair Zippi Livni. David Brodet and Yair Hirschfeld, "Divuach al hidabrut btrack II khachana leveidat Annapolis" (trans. Report of

8 Maintaining the Struggle for a Two-State Solution … 183

By November 2007, I noticed several clear warning signs. Understanding the need for double-game negotiations according to the Putnam thesis, the opposition to the emerging understanding became visible on both sides. Two months earlier, Vice PM Ramon gave an interview describing the possible emerging understandings.[39] The day before the interview was published, Othniel Schneller informed me about a rebellion against Olmert led by ten members of Kadima, including prominent leaders. They opposed Olmert's approach and threatened to bring down the government, forming an alternative right-wing coalition under Netanyahu's leadership, in coordination with Liebermann's Yisrael Beiteinu, Shas, and other religious and nationalist parties. Schneller announced his views publicly on the same day as Ramon's interview.[40]

I knew that Schneller and the political forces he spoke for were willing to commit to a two-state solution, create an open-ended process, and change realities on the ground, which was supportive of allowing a Two-State solution to become viable. I also knew from meetings with Samih el-Abed, who was responsible for the portfolio on territory in negotiations with Israel, and Samir Huleileh, who was responsible for the economic portfolio, that they preferred supporting the expansion of Palestinian administrative control in defined Area C territories instead of making any decisive compromise on a final territorial agreement. Following internal politics in Israel and Palestine, sensing the emerging public mood, and understanding the tremendous gap in expectations was most worrisome. As preparations for Permanent Status negotiations were running high, I imagined in my nightmares two fast cars driving in great speed against each other, trying to test which side would "chicken out" first. Aiming to prevent this, Brodet and I discussed with the Palestinians a five-point safety construct, in line with Othniel Schneller's and his right-wing colleagues' demands:

1. The permanent status negotiations would be open-ended, indicating that at no given date, a bottleneck situation would occur;
2. As long as no new agreement was concluded, both parties committed to respect agreements signed;

---

discussions of track II in preparation of the Annapolis Conference), November 7, 2007 (confidential and unpublished). See Hirschfeld, "Second Year Report," *Hirschfeld Khoury-DeConcini Papers*.
[39] Nahum Barnea and Shimon Shiffer, "Ramon Draws a Map," *Yedioth Ahronot—Satuday Supplement*, September 7, 2007 (Hebrew).
[40] Othniel Schneller, "Consensus Now, Peace Later," Maariv, September 7, 2007. One month later (October 7, 2007), Schneller shared a paper with me, titled "The Key for Supporting the Declaration at the Summit Depends on What it Does Not Say" (unpublished). See Hirschfeld, "Second Year Report," *Hirschfeld Khoury-DeConcini Papers*, pp. 51–52.

3. Both sides commit themselves to roadmap implementation, enabling the creation of a two-track-negotiating effort, one track on the core issues of permanent status, and the second track on roadmap implementation;
4. Both sides commit themselves to agree on an action plan to prepare for change on the ground to prepare for the sustainability of a two-state solution; and
5. The involvement of a third party, to monitor the peace process and offer economic and political support and assist in creating at a secure environment was being welcome.[41]

President G.W. Bush and the American peace team were fully aware of the emerging difficulties. In a meeting at the White House between President Bush and Prime Minister Olmert, November 26 2007, difficulties were being discussed, while Bush remarked: "If you had not convinced me that a Palestinian state is possible, we would not be here." And he added: "I am not here to force you and the Palestinians to do something. I won't cram it down your throat."[42]

Several days later the US Government convened an international conference in Annapolis, Maryland, to officially renew the Israeli-Palestinian Permanent Status negotiations. A three-level negotiating structure was created, with twelve committees addressing topics such as the economic relationship, the environment, state-to-state relations, border crossings, legal issues, prisoners, and the culture of peace. Negotiations on the core issues of the conflict were managed confidentially by Tzipi Livni and Abu Ala', while Olmert and Abu Mazen pursued a one-to-one dialogue alongside this.[43]

PM Olmert's Peace Proposal is Rejected

Olmert was determined to reach a Permanent Status Agreement and had extensively discussed relevant issues with Abu Mazen for over 12 months. Olmert's personality, marked by dignity, respect, and hospitality, contributed to a positive atmosphere. In September 2008, he presented his proposal to Abu Mazen. It included a 100% territorial deal based on the June 4, 1967 lines with agreed swaps. Olmert suggested incorporating 6.3% of the West Bank's major settlement blocs into Israel's territory, with a 5.8% swap and

---

[41] Hirschfeld, "Second Year Report," *Hirschfeld Khoury-DeConcini Papers*, pp. 14–15.
[42] Abrams, *Tested by Zion*, p. 253.
[43] Compare with Condolezza Rice, *No Higher Honor—A Memoir of My Years in Washington*, New York, Broadway 2011, pp. 600–605, 613–621.

acceptance of safe passage between the West Bank and Gaza as the remaining 0.5%.[44] Jerusalem would be divided according to Jewish and Arab neighborhoods, with a joint committee responsible for administering the Holy Places. On the refugee issue, a limited number of refugees would be allowed to return to Israel for a five-year period.[45]

Abu Mazen rejected the proposal three times: initially in September, then when requested changes were suggested by Pundik, and finally in December when President Bush asked for reconsideration. In January, Olmert approached me, sharing that Abbas was unwilling to support the proposal. Instead, Olmert planned an alternative approach, backed by Presidents Bush and Mubarak. They would support Israeli unilateral actions to pave the way for the envisioned two-state solution. He then coined the phrase "Coordinated multilateral unilateralism" defining his intended strategy. Olmert believed he could have achieved success if he had remained in power. At the time, I knew it was too late, as it was evident, Olmert would have to serve a prison sentence. Many years later I discussed these events with him. During our meeting, he expressed bitterness, referring to the difficulty for Abu Mazen to accept the "end of conflict" and "finality of claims" and stating that he would have addressed those concerns if he had known. He added, "They killed Rabin, but I was eliminated in a more cruel manner."[46]

Abu Mazen's rejection of the deal reflected his lack of power to agree on territory, the refugee issue, and Jerusalem. Many Palestinians believed a better deal could have been achieved regarding territory, and families with land in the 6.3% area intended for annexation by Israel would strongly oppose it. The refugees were not consulted, and their opposition, along with leading Palestinians from the Diaspora, would be significant. Various Arab and Islamic groups would condemn the proposed agreement concerning Jerusalem.

While Abu Mazen rejected the offer, Olmert lost the majority in the Knesset and faced internal power struggles within his own party, Kadima. The gap between Israeli and Palestinian positions on achieving the "end of conflict" and "finality of claims" was too wide to bridge. The tragedy was that the principle of "nothing is agreed upon until everything is agreed upon" was applied, leading to the loss of important understandings and agreements reached in the twelve negotiating committees.

---

[44] This was almost fully identical to the map Ron Pundik prepared in 1995 and was then accepted as the agreed territorial component of the "Beilin-Abu Mazen Understanding."
[45] Grant Rumley and Amir Tibon, *The Last Palestinian—The Rise and Reign of Mahmoud Abbas*, Prometheus Books, New York 2017, pp. 119–154.
[46] Meeting with Ehud Olmert at 16.00–17.00 on June 30, 2021 in his office in Tel Aviv.

Personally, I had to come to terms with the unfortunate outcome I had predicted and tried to prevent. Emotionally, it weighed heavily on me, knowing that I had emphasized the importance of reaching the "Take Off-Point" months earlier. Rationally, this experience has guided my thinking and actions ever since.

Understanding What Would Be Needed to "Get Israeli-Palestinian Negotiations to the 'Take Off-Point'"

The Emerging Concept

At the end of March 2008, I submitted a 47-page paper entitled "Getting Israeli-Palestinian Negotiations to the 'Take Off-Point'" to USAID-OTI. In Chapter One, "Political Developments inside Israel," I discussed "Olmert's Continued Domestic Vulnerability and Steadfastness." In Chapter Two, "Internal Developments in the Palestinian Authority," I discussed "Abbas' Continued Domestic Vulnerability and Steadfastness.'[47] The simple conclusion was that neither side was politically able to reach and sustain a Permanent Status Agreement. From my meeting with Abu Ala' early in November 2007, I was worried about the conflicting expectations as well as the absence of an agreement on a workable "Give and Take" for both sides. I was convinced that coordinated action on the ground, under enhanced security cooperation, creating the physical, administrative, and attitudinal conditions for the creation of a viable and contiguous State of Palestine, living in good neighborly relations with all its neighbors, was essential. This should lead to official negotiations on territory, while addressing Jerusalem and Refugees could be postponed.

Supportive Action Gets Underway

The formation of Salam Fayyad's government in June 2007 was a most positive potential game changer. Fayyad dedicated his time to building

---

[47] The report covered the period December 2007 to mid-March 2008 and had to offer a political evaluation as part of a comprehensive "Research on Movement and Access." Reading this report today from hindsight and comparing it to my "Second Year Report," written six months earlier (October 12, 2007), it is evident that in the autumn of 2007 my analytical understanding of evolving developments was still very unclear, while by March 2008 I had no doubts anymore—in spite of my admiration for Olmert—of the dangers ahead.

and reforming the Palestinian state institutions and getting the Palestinian economy back on track. His approach was to improve the situation on the ground, creating the social capital necessary to provide the leadership with the legitimacy necessary for conflict resolution. After the November 2007 Annapolis Conference, Secretary of State Condoleezza Rice appointed a special mission to monitor roadmap implementation, first under General Frazer and later under the command of General Paul Selva. In order to promote regional security cooperation, she appointed General James Jones, who would work closely together with General Keith Dayton, while the ECF team and I personally would also work closely with them. To ease Palestinian trade, access, and movement, we developed three "economic corridors" in cooperation with the IDF, connecting Nablus with Jenin and Jalame in the North, Jerusalem with Jericho and the Allenby Bridge in the East, and Hebron with Tarqumiyya in the South.[48]

To create a functioning tripartite security and stability structure, we suggested a "Jenin First Concept." General Dayton's training of Palestinian security forces and oversight functions would allow for rebuilding direct security cooperation between the Israeli and Palestinian security forces in a supportive triangle configuration.[49] We criticized and challenged the IDF's anti-terrorist strategy, assisted USAID in gathering all relevant Israeli security authorities to minimize roadblocks and blockages, helped reinstate Israeli-Palestinian security cooperation, and facilitated the handover of security responsibility to Palestinian forces in specific areas. Finally, in the summer of 2008, a meeting with General James Jones, Gilad Sher, Baruch Spiegel, and me, followed by the resulting General Jones-Barak meeting, kicked off necessary steps for the successful renewal and upgrading of Israeli-Palestinian security cooperation that has lasted to this day, even beyond October 7, 2023, more or less.

Around the same time, the ECF team and I, along with a representative from the Jerusalem municipality, visited the Shu'afat Refugee Camp within the borders of Jerusalem. Due to restrictions on Palestinian police activity and Israeli police hesitancy to enter, the camp had become a hub for crime and hereto related destructive Israeli-Palestinian cooperation. This situation motivated us to form a coalition to improve the conditions. The United Nations

---

[48] Hirschfeld, *Track-Two Diplomacy*, pp. 316–319.

[49] Dayton was fully aware of his task to challenge both sides to cooperate, while insisting painstakingly on direct Israeli-Palestinian bilateral cooperation. Hirschfeld, *Track-Two Diplomacy*, pp. 319–321.

office of the Camp blocked these activities fearing it would undermine their standing.[50]

The Lasting Legacy of Bush and Olmert: Understanding the Importance of the Phased Roadmap Approach

The failure of the 2008 Permanent Status negotiations was a crucial lesson, marking the third failure in the peace process. The previous failures included the acceptance and subsequent rejection of the Beilin-Abu Mazen Understandings and the Barak-Arafat negotiations. PM Olmert made significant efforts to create the necessary conditions and support for President Abbas to agree to and implement the proposed agreement, which aimed to establish the State of Palestine with its capital in Jerusalem and address other core conflict issues.

However, the lasting legacy of President Bush and PM Olmert lies in the phased roadmap approach, which showed a way forward. Under President George Bush's leadership, the Quartet powers produced the Benchmarked Roadmap for Peace in the Middle East. Secretary of State Rice created mechanisms for monitoring, oversight, and implementation. The nominations of General Keith Dayton (2005), General James Jones, and General Frazer (later General Paul Selva) provided a supportive framework for Palestinian security reform, regional involvement, and a comprehensive political, security, and economic framework.

Fayyad, as Minister of Finance from 2003 to 2007 and later as PM, paved the way for revitalizing the Palestinian economy. His initial actions included standardizing income and expenses and creating budgetary transparency. He established a unified payment system for all security officials, ending Arafat's system of rival warlords and enabling a unified chain of command within the Palestinian security forces under the slogan: "one homeland, one law, one gun."[51]

---

[50] Young refugee leaders wanted to act independently of the UN provided action there and we wanted to assist them in getting necessary funding and building a supportive coalition for implementation. Eventually we were told that the UNRWA locals opposed these activities, not being willing to give up their non-effective monopoly. ECF, "Project on the Rehabilitation of the Shu'afat Refugee Camp," *Hirschfeld Khoury-DeConcini Papers, Substack*, forthcoming (originally written December 26, 2007), https://hkdpapers.substack.com/p/rehabilitation-of-the-shu'afat-refugee-camp.

[51] Reuters, "Palestinian Premier to Unveil his vision of Independence", *Haaretz Online*, August 25, 2009, https://www.haaretz.com/2009-08-25/ty-article/palestinian-premier-to-unveil-his-vision-of-independence/0000017f-db94-d856-a37f-ffd495a80000?_amp=true (accessed July 12, 2023), archived at

Despite limited support from Palestinian and Israeli leadership, Fayyad's comprehensive state-building efforts provided an opportunity for progress. By the end of 2008, it became evident what didn't work, what did work, and what needed to be done: Attempting to reach a Permanent Status Agreement in one go, after multiple failures, would only lead to further disappointment, violence, and the strengthening of anti-peace elements.[52]

What worked was an intensified effort of Palestinian state-building in cooperation with Israel, supported by international oversight and monitoring embedded in wider regional cooperation. Detaching state-building from the Permanent Status negotiation strategies was crucial. The United States had sufficient influence to make it clear that state-building preceded permanent status negotiations. The decisive "Take-Off Point" would involve designing supportive conditions for a mutual commitment to achieve an Israel-Palestine Two-State solution. What was still needed, was an intense track-two Israeli-Palestinian brainstorming effort, to identify, how best to identify and reach the envisaged Take-Off Point.

Suggested Reading

The Costs of the Second Intifada and the Construction of the Separation Fence

Yeshayahu Folman *The Story of the Security Fence—Life Repudiation Indeed?* Carmel Publishing, Jerusalem 2004 (Hebrew); originally the Israeli Left planned for the Fence on the 1967 cease-fire line or nearby. During Rabin's second premiership—after some detailed planning—the idea was dropped, due to its high costs. Israel's Right opposed the idea, as it meant to out-fence the settler community from Israel and designate the border unilaterally. However, Palestinian terror and massive thefts during the first two years of the Second Intifada created major public pressure to build the fence.

---

https://web.archive.org/web/20230712093609/https://www.haaretz.com/2009-08-25/ty-article/palestinian-premier-to-unveil-his-vision-of-independence/0000017f-db94-d856-a37f-ffd495a80000?_amp=true.

[52] Salam Fayyad, "Why I'm Building Palestine," *Foreign Policy*, November 29, 2019, https://foreignpolicy.com/2010/11/28/why-im-building-palestine-2/ (accessed July 12, 2023), archived at https://web.archive.org/web/20230712093924/https://foreignpolicy.com/2010/11/28/why-im-building-palestine-2/. See Abdel Monem Said Aly, Shai Feldman, and Khalil Shikaki, *Arabs and Israelis—Conflict and Peacemaking in the Middle East*, Palgrave Macmillan, New York 2013, pp. 414–415. See also Tony Blair's team, "Note on Quick Impact Projects," November 8, 2007 (confidential and unpublished).

International Court of Justice *Advisory Opinion Proceedings On: Legal Consequences of Construction of a Wall in the Occupied Palestinian Territory;* Palestine Written Statement (30 January 2004) and Oral Pleading (23 February 2004). And,

Abdel Monem Said Aly, Shai Feldman, Khalil Shikaki *Arabs and Israelis* op.cit. Chap. 11, pp. 361–396 describes the political causes and impact of the intifada on the Israeli and Palestinian domestic scene and the different perceptions of the development, seen from the Egyptian, the Palestinian and the Israeli vantage point.

Understanding Prime Minister Sharon's Strategy

Dov Weissglas *Arik Sharon—Prime Minister—A Personal View*; Yedioth Ahronot, Tel Aviv 2012; Weissglas was Sharon's most intimate advisor and in charge of leading his dialogue with the United States. His description of Sharon's strategic approach as well the description of the Israeli-US negotiations leading to the Disengagement from Gaza and evacuation of five settlements from the Northern West Bank is an essential reading.

Adapting to Rising Security Threats

INSS—*The Middle East Strategic Balance, 2005–2006*; Sussex Academic Press, Brighton, the Institute for National Security Studies, Tel Aviv, 2006; Part I provides a Strategic Assessment of the Middle East; Part II, compares the Military Forces in the region. Mark Heller analyses the failure of the US policy aimed at creating democracies in the Middle East, and describes the rising importance of Identity policies. Several contributions address the rising threat of Iran and its capability to obtain the bomb; another contribution addresses "the Iraqi quagmire"; the situation in Syria and Lebanon. Reading the compilation of the different articles in this volume is essential in order to understand the Israeli perspective and strategic thinking at the time.

Ondrej Beranek (ed.) *Europe, the Middle East, and the Global War on Terror—Critical Reflections*; Peter Lang, Bern 2012, The different articles in this volume, when compared with the INSS study, illustrate the emerging conflicting and converging perspectives as seen from Israel and the West.

The Rethinking of the Political Process

Marwan Muasher *The Arab Center—The Promise of Moderation*; Yale U.P. New Haven 2008. Muasher served as the first Jordanian ambassador to Israel and later as Jordan's Minister of Foreign Affairs. His description of preparing the Arab Peace Initiative (2002) and then the Middle East Road Map (2003) is the most authoritative, as he played a leading role in preparing both of these initiatives. The book has also five important appendixes.

Elliott Abrams, *Tested by Zion—The Bush Administration and the Israeli-Palestinian Conflict*, Cambridge U.P. 2013 (Abrams served during these years in the White House, being the senior advisor on Middle Eastern affairs).

Condoleezza Rice *No Higher Honor—A Memoir of My Years in Washington*; Broadway Paperback New York 2011. Rice served from 2001 to 2005 as President George W. Bush's national security advisor, and from 2005 to 2009 as Secretary of State. The descriptive and analytical narratives of Abrams and Rice provide an important insight regarding the development of the US Middle Eastern policy during the first decade of the twenty-first century.

Ehud Olmert *Search for Peace—A Memoir of Israel*; Brookings Institution Press, Washington D.C. 2022. Olmert describes his effort, as Prime Minister of Israel, to conclude a peace agreement with President Abu Mazen. Under Olmert's guidance peace negotiations were pursued on three levels: Intimate meetings between Olmert and Abu Mazen at Olmert's residence, dealing with the entire complex of the relationship; A parallel dialogue between the Palestinian Prime Minister Abu Ala' and Israel's Minister of Foreign Affairs, Zippi Livni on the core issues of conflict, and 12 working groups, addressing all the practical issues.[53].

Udi Dekel, Lia Moran-Gilad *The Annapolis Process: A Missed Opportunity for a Two-State Solution*; INSS, Tel Aviv, 2021. Udi Dekel headed the Israeli team of the twelve committees, which makes his contribution particularly valuable. In Chapter 2, the points of agreement and disagreement on all negotiated issues are being described. Agreement in regard to many issues discussed was achieved. However, the Palestinian insistence on the principle nothing is agreed upon until everything is agreed upon turned the entire exercise into a complete failure. Nevertheless, understandings reached then, particularly on the practical issues dealt with, might serve to form a first agreement for a new beginning.

---

[53] The 12 working groups were on: Water, Economic Relations, Culture of Peace, State-to-State relations; Healthcare, Tourism, Archaeology, Agriculture, Infrastructure, Communications, the Border Crossing Points, and Environmental Quality.

9

The Netanyahu-Obama Years: 2009–2017

The Growing Gap of Perceptions

During 2002 and 2003 following the US invasions of Afghanistan and Iraq, I became all too aware that the rules of engagement between Israel and the United States were changing, and I feared the consequences: US-Israeli interests in the Middle East would cease to be complementary; diverging and conflicting strategic needs would undermine the US capacity to support a reality-based peace-building process. US initial policies directed against the Soviet occupation of Afghanistan had empowered militant Jihadist forces. Now, when the United States would plan to withdraw forces from the area, Washington would have to isolate the most militant groups, but come to terms with several of Israel's worst enemies. It foreboded little good. I also understood, the evident gap of strategic interests divided the Jewish community in the USA. Right wing supporters of the Republican Party and the Christian fundamentalists would support Israel's counter-productive settlement policy, whereas my progressive Jewish friends would either be completely alienated, or support policy proposals no Israeli Government, even with the best intentions, could deliver. When on our family vacation on Lake Tiberias I read Yoshua Cohen's book "The Netanyahus" the growing gap of perceptions became most evident.[1]

Cohen's depiction of a past meeting of Netanyahu's father and a Jewish American professor sheds light on the growing divide. He highlights how

---

[1] Yehoshua Cohen, *The Netanyahus*, Fitzeraldo Editions, London 2021.

American Jews consider the sensitivities of their non-Jewish colleagues, sometimes tainted by anti-Semitism. In contrast, Netanyahu's father behaves aggressively, firmly believing to counter the all-powerful forces seeking the destruction of Jews. Cohen most clearly illustrated the widening gap between Netanyahu's Israel and the liberal Jewish community in the United States, leaving the Israeli peace camp caught in the middle.[2]

Cohen's book reminded me of Karl Popper's teachings on how perception and beliefs shape reality. Throughout the eight years of Obama's presidency, this gap in understanding realities grew significantly.

During Obama's presidential campaign, there was no divide. My family and friends admired Obama's brilliance and identified with his ideals. The entire Hirschfeld clan celebrated his victory in November 2008, captivated by his autobiographical account in "Dreams of My Father" and his programmatic book, "Audacity of Hope." Each and every Obama speech was a piece of art that addressed the many hopes and beliefs my sister and I had grown up with. We shared Martin Luther King's dreams of freedom, justice, and humanity. We believed in fighting for those ideals wherever injustice occurred. Obama's election filled us with hope and reassurance that the world was moving toward a better future, one in which I aspired to contribute.

A Challenging Start: Olmert's Failed Peace Effort, Gaza, and Iran

It was President George Bush, not Obama, who made two significant decisions that contributed to the growing divergence of interests between Washington and Jerusalem: the withdrawal from Iraq and participation in the P5 + 1 talks with Iran.[3]

By November 2008, it was clear that Prime Minister Olmert's peace efforts faced repeated rejections from President Abbas. As had happened before, the failure of a peaceful solution gave place to the resurgence of violence. In early 2008, Iran and Russia began supplying rockets to Hamas. Following the US presidential elections, Hamas ended the "calm" period in mid-December 2008, leading to increased rocket attacks on Israeli civilians.

Despite multiple Israeli protests to the United Nations, there was no international response to these attacks. Operation Cast Lead launched by the

---

[2] I share most of Yoshua Cohen's criticism, but not his detached disdain. I am convinced a more sympathetic understanding is warranted.

[3] The P5 + 1 countries are a group of nations working together on the Iran Nuclear Deal. The countries include the five permanent members of the United Nations and Germany.

Olmert-Livni government—lasting for 22 days—ended just two days before Obama's inauguration. Three weeks later, Israeli elections paved the way for Netanyahu to return to power. The Obama-Netanyahu years would be dominated by a growing gap not merely of perceptions and interests, but also of policies. While vital to Israelis, these policy differences held lesser importance for the American public.

Months earlier, in July 2008, President Bush authorized William Burns to participate in a P5 + 1 meeting in Geneva, discussing potential international understanding on Iran's nuclear development program. This aligned with Obama's intentions, as Burns described: *"[Obama] advocated direct, unconditional engagement with adversaries."*[4] This signaled to Tehran that time was on their side. It being evident that the United States would be withdrawing from Iraq resulted in the resurgence of al-Qaeda and the strengthening of jihadist movements in the Middle East. Israel found itself isolated in its struggle against Iran and its proxies' and radical competitors' aggressive actions.

From Washington's perspective, the reality looked quite different. Realignment with the Muslim world seemed opportune for a smooth withdrawal from Iraq. Obama's initial visits to Turkey and Egypt aimed to build an alliance with a moderate, modern, and pluralistic political Islam, countering autocracies, theocracies, and extremist movements in the region.

In his speech at Cairo University, Obama expressed his hope to build an alliance with "*a model of moderate, modern, and pluralistic political Islam and an alternative to the autocracies, theocracies, and extremist movements that characterized the region.*"[5]

Recalling the experiences of the 1990s, I recognized the need to connect with religious Jewish and Muslim leaders. However, I had doubts about the overly simplistic view of fundamentalist Muslim movements in the Middle East. I feared that Obama's actions would lead to unintended consequences, for which Israel would pay the price. My immediate concern was sustaining the path toward a two-state solution despite Olmert's failed peace efforts.

---

[4] William J. Burns, *The Back Channel—American Diplomacy in a Disordered World*, Hurst and Company, London 2019, pp. 345 (in order to understand the US policy approach under Obama, it pays to read the entire chapter, entitled "Iran and the Bomb: The Secret Talks," pp.337-387).
[5] Barack Obama, *A Promised Land*, New York, Crown-Random House 2020, pp. 346–347.

First Disappointments

When Obama became President, I had a clear "to-do list." My top priority was to sustain the progress made by Prime Minister Fayyad and the important work carried out by Generals Jones, Dayton, and Selva.[6]

I was pleased with Obama's appointment of General James Jones as National Security Advisor, hoping it signified a commitment to continue the roadmap implementation established by President Bush and Secretary of State Rice. This included strengthening Palestinian security capacities, improving Israeli-Palestinian security cooperation, enhancing regional security collaboration, and supporting Prime Minister Fayyad's state-building efforts. We, along with the Italian Government, sought broad regional support for these goals and organized a workshop titled "The Arab Peace Initiative: Coordinating Support for Palestinian State-Building."[7]

However, my visit to General Jones at the White House revealed his isolation from the president's inner circle. It seemed that President Obama's policy was "Anything But Bush,' disregarding the advice of General Jones, which ultimately led to his resignation in October 2010. Additionally, the Obama Administration launched a negative campaign against the accomplishments of General Keith Dayton and his team, despite their successful efforts to build a unified Palestinian security force and foster Israeli-Palestinian security cooperation. Some influential members of the Democratic Party even campaigned to end General Dayton's service.[8]

Later that month, I decided to organize a strong coalition to support the Dayton mission and Prime Minister Fayyad's state-building efforts, hoping that Washington would listen to its own representatives and senior international actors on the ground. I held a meeting at my home in Ramat

---

[6] Yair Hirschfeld, "Seeking a Fresh Start (Milestone no. 6: Wider Political Horizon Report)," *Hirschfeld Khoury-DeConcini Papers*, *Substack*, July 9, 2023 (originally created on January 13, 2010), pp. 37–44, https://hkdpapers.substack.com/p/seeking-a-fresh-start (accessed July 9, 2023) (hereafter cited as Hirschfeld, "Seeking a Fresh Start," *Hirschfeld Khoury-DeConcini Papers*).

[7] Participants in the workshop included Anwar Majed Eshki from Saudi Arabia, Ambassador Hesham Youssef and Ezzedine Choukri Fishere from Egypt, Jibril Rajoub, Nassr Tahboub and Samih el Abed from Palestine, General Mansur Abu Rashed and General Mohamed Shmeisani from Jordan, David Brodet, Dov Sedaka, Shlomo Brom, and Yair Hirschfeld from Israel (others included Abdullah Ali Sabig, Ahmed Temsah, Omar Nahar, and Ibrahim Shaker). I also had invited John Ging, who was the director of UNRWA in Gaza at the time. "The Arab Peace Initiative: Coordinating Support for Palestinian State-Building with an Integrate Top-Down and Bottom-Up Approach," Workshop, Milan, July 1–4, 2010.

[8] Steven White and P.J. Dermer, "How Obama Missed an Opportunity for Middle East Peace," *Foreign Policy*, May 18, 2012, https://foreignpolicy.com/2012/05/18/how-obama-missed-an-opportunity-for-middle-east-peace/ (accessed July 12, 2023), archived at https://web.archive.org/web/20230528093529/https://foreignpolicy.com/2012/05/18/how-obama-missed-an-opportunity-for-middle-east-peace/.

Yishai, attended by several prominent figures, including US Ambassador James Cunningham, UN Peace Envoy Robert Serry, UK Ambassador Tom Phillips, head of USAID Howard Sumka and others. General Baruch Spiegel, who was well connected within the IDF and David Brodet, well connected to Israel's economic establishment, were also present. We aimed to prevent Dayton's dismissal and garner more support for Fayyad's work. Unfortunately, our collective voices were ignored.

Photos

In the upper picture, from left to right, we see US ambassador to Israel, James B. Cunningham; UN Peace Envoy to the Middle East, Robert Serry; Yair Hirschfeld; General Keith Dayton; his assistant Colonel Steven White; General Baruch Spiegel, and David Brodet.

In the picture below, we can see United Kingdom Ambassador Tom Phillips (center left) engaged in a conversation with the Head of the Israel-Palestine USAID office, Howard Sumka (far right).

General Dayton was dismissed as the USSC for Israel and the Palestinian Authority at the end of October 2010. US ambassador James Cunningham, who had also been appointed by the Bush administration, left the next year in May 2011. The internal Washington political game was powerful. Later, the Obama Administration did not prevent the dismissal of Prime Minister Fayyad by President Abbas.

I remained skeptical of Senator Mitchell's appointment as President Obama's peace envoy. In a previous meeting in 2003, I had warned Mitchell about the pitfalls of a total settlement freeze, which proved to be true. The freeze imposed by Mitchell on Prime Minister Netanyahu for ten months led to increased settlement activities afterward and provided President Abbas with an excuse to avoid peace negotiations.[9]

Iran—My Concerns Turn into Substantial Worries

The gap between the US and Israel regarding Iran's threat was immense for valid reasons. Israel faced a real danger, with long-range missiles paraded in Tehran and calls for the "Death of Israel." Additionally, Iran provided financial, political, and military support to Hezbollah, the Jihadist movement, and occasionally Hamas, creating a twofold threat of unpredictable terror and rocket attacks. The most alarming aspect was Iran's pursuit of nuclear military capabilities alongside religious messianic militancy.

Although the American leadership was aware of these dangers, they could overlook the emerging threats against Israel by emphasizing Israel's right to self-defense. This allowed policymakers in Washington to perceive Iran as a potential ally needed for the safe withdrawal of American troops from Iraq.

The international atmosphere had shifted. In February 2010, I attended the "7th Worldwide Security Conference" in Brussels, organized by New York's East West Institute. I was asked to speak on the "Economic Crisis: Radicalization and Risk Management."[10] However, it was a day earlier, during the workshop on "Nuclear Commission Report Proliferation Dilemmas: The ICNND Report and the case of Iran" that I came head-to-head with the Iranian representative to the P5 + 1 negotiations.

---

[9] In *The Peace Puzzle*, Kurtzer describes the ineffectiveness and the counter-productive results of the 10 months settlement freeze that Senator Mitchell succeeded in imposing. Daniel Kurtzer et al., "*The Peace Puzzle—America's Quest for Arab–Israeli Peace, 1989–2011,*" Ithaca, Cornell U.P. 2013, pp. 248–254 (section titled "Elusive Quest for a Settlement Freeze").

[10] Other participants on the panel were David Young of Oxford Analytica, Peter Neumann of International Centre for the Study of Radicalization NS Political Violence, David Gordon of Global Macroanalysis, and Vladislav Inozemtsev from Moscow.

The Iranian representative had launched vitriolic accusations against Israel. Given my academic background on Iran, I expressed a deep admiration for the country and its people. It was clear to me that Iran and Israel sincerely feared each other. Given this situation, I argued that the best option was to find a way to diffuse these fears and create a mutual sense of safety for both the Israeli and Iranian people. But none of this dissuaded him from turning his back to me and dismissing me as a "war criminal." About 10 of the representatives from the US and European participating in the discussion knew me and my record seeking peace. None raised their voice in my defense. In fact, an Italian EU representative actually apologized to the Iranian speaker for "the undue interference of this Israeli."

This incident vividly demonstrated Israel's potential isolation and bolstered Prime Minister Netanyahu's fear-mongering policy. The following day of the conference brought further anxiety. I spent time with Sundeep Wakselaar from Mumbai, who had played a role in diffusing tensions between India and Pakistan. He shared with me the details of the Mumbai terror attacks in 2008. The Pakistani group Lashka-e-Taiba had targeted the Nariman House of Chabad, specifically aiming to attack and kill Jews. I still remember him distinctly saying "the Nariman House was in a difficult place to find, but they wanted to demonstrate their dedication to killing Jews." Sundeep believed that the Pakistani intelligence instigated the attack.

This information prepared me to fully appreciate the keynote speech by the Pakistani Minister of Foreign Affairs and the subsequent presentation by the former chairman of the Pakistani Joint Chiefs of Staff Committee. During their speeches, Sundeep commented:

> If there will be a second terror attack on India, we will strike back, and in response the Pakistanis might throw a nuclear bomb at us. Yet, even more dangerous are the Chinese. They do not have any morals. Anything is possible in their first attack, should they decide to do so.

We both pondered the implications of President Obama's outreach to stabilize the Muslim world, namely Iran, Turkey, and the Muslim Brotherhood in Egypt. We respectively worried how it would affect stability in India and Israel.

Turkey

At the beginning of Obama's presidency, Israeli-Turkish relations were already in crisis. In an attempt to salvage the relationship, a public meeting between Peres and Erdoğan was planned at the Davos World Economic Forum in January 2009.

I had a long and close friendship with the Turkish Ambassador to Israel, Namik Tan. We have cooperated on a variety of issues over the year. Tan and his predecessor, who held a very senior position in the Foreign Office in Ankara, were interested in preventing the deterioration of Israel-Turkey relations. I was thus part of a joint Israeli-Turkish team to prepare for the Erdoğan-Peres dialogue. We designed guidelines for both leaders that aimed at preventing confrontation. Peres kept to the agreed guidelines, Erdogan did not. Instead, Erdoğan sought confrontation during the discussion panel, causing Peres to respond. Erdoğan walked out.

To pacify the Turkish leader, Peres phoned him and suggested that they become friends again. Instead of agreeing, Erdoğan made a public statement and claimed Peres had issued an apology which Erdoğan would not accept. Erdoğan had chosen a confrontational course. His aim was to position Turkey as the protector of Hamas in Gaza and undermine Egyptian influence in the region.

Rather than alleviating the crisis, Obama's speech to the Turkish Parliament further fueled tensions. During the speech, Obama had failed to set clear boundaries for Erdoğan and instead offered unquestioned support. Afterwards, another Turkish friend told me:

> Yair, Obama must know he cannot offer a carte blanche to Erdoğan. How has he missed to understand that he has to draw, at the beginning, very clear red lines that the Turkish government must not trespass?[11]

---

[11] Obama writes this on his relations with Erdogan: "Recep Tayyip Erdogan and his Justice and Development Party had swept into power in 2002-2003, touting populist and often overly Islamic appeals, it had unsettled Turkey's secular military-dominated political elite. Erdogan's vocal sympathy for both the Muslim Brotherhood and Hamas in their fight for an independent Palestinian state, in particular had also made Washington and Tel Aviv nervous. And yet, Erdogan's government thus far had abided by Turkey's constitution, met its NATO obligations, and effectively managed the economy even initiating a series of modest reforms with the hope of qualifying for EU membership. Some observers suggested that Erdogan might offer a model of moderate, modern, and pluralistic political Islam and an alternative to the autocracies, theocracies, and extremist movements that characterized the region. This set a pattern for the next eight years. Mutual self-interest would dictate that Erdogan and I develop a working relationship." Obama, *A Promised Land*, pp. 346–347.

Obama's later accounts showed clearly his perception of Erdoğan as a close ally, despite subsequent events. In contrast, thirty years earlier, Kreisky recognized the significance of Israel's relationship with Egypt, a lesson that Obama seemed to overlook.

Following the Gaza war in December 2008-January 2009, efforts were made to stabilize the situation by engaging Egypt and forming an Israeli-Palestinian Authority-Egyptian-Arab coalition. The objective was to strengthen President Abbas's legitimacy.[12] ECF, with support from the Italian Government, organized workshops involving participants from Egypt, Jordan, Palestine, Saudi Arabia, and Israel. The discussions focused on stabilizing the ceasefire, establishing monitoring mechanisms, preventing misunderstandings, facilitating civil reconstruction, and gaining wider Arab support.[13]

The reopening of the Gaza-Egypt border crossing was one of the primary successes of these workshops. ECF's General Baruch Spiegel had worked with the European Union Border Assistance Mission (EU-BAM) to Rafah, which allowed for the flow of people, goods and services between Gaza and Egypt. After the Hamas take-over of Gaza in June 2007, the EU-BAM mission was frozen.

The idea, proposed by ECF, was endorsed by the Israeli Ministry of Defense and welcomed by the governments of Israel, Palestine, Egypt, and the EU.[14] In May 2010, the Rafah Crossing between Gaza and Egypt was reopened with the agreement of the Israeli Government and the Palestinian Authority. The EU extended the mandate for the European Union Border Assistance Mission to Rafah.[15] Israeli-Palestinian-Egyptian cooperation, with Arab and EU support, had begun to stabilize the situation in Gaza.

---

[12] We cooperated on this issue specifically with Palestinian General Jibril Rajoub, who supported President Abbas and had strong links to Israel's security authorities and was a close friend of General Sedaka.

[13] Hirschfeld, "Seeking a Fresh Start," *Hirschfeld Khoury-DeConcini Papers*, pp. 39–40.

[14] At the workshop held in Milan, General Anwar Eshki from Saudi Arabia submitted a related policy paper aimed a pacifying the situation in Gaza. General Jibril Rajoub (Palestine) spoke about the need for Egyptian, Jordanian and Saudi political support to strengthen President Abbas and push for an agreement with Hamas. Generals Mansur Abu Rashed and Shmeisani represented Jordan. Eshki's report was attached the seminar paper that was produced at the end of the workshop, but the paper remains unpublished. Anwar Eshki, "The Establishment of Palestinian Self-Rule (Autonomy) in Gaza – An Intermediate Step to Achieve the Ultimate Solution for Peace between the Arabs and Israel," Middle East Center for Strategic and Legal Studies, Jedda January 17, 2010 (unpublished).

[15] Wikalat al-anba al-filastinija (WAFA), "EU Extends Mandate of EUBAM Rafah," December 31, 2015 (originally written May 19, 2010), http://english.wafa.ps/Pages/Details/109134 (accessed July 12, 2023), archived at https://web.archive.org/web/20230712042139/https://english.wafa.ps/Pages/Details/109134.

However, Erdogan aimed to undermine Egyptian influence. The "Free Gaza Movement" and the IHH Humanitarian Relief Foundation, with concealed governmental support, organized the "Gaza Freedom Flotilla" in May 2010. The flotilla, consisting of six ships carrying construction materials and humanitarian aid, attempted to break the Israeli blockade. Despite Israeli Navy's offer to inspect the cargo and allow a third party to transfer the aid from Ashdod into Gaza, the flotilla refused. The Israeli military boarded the ships, being attacked with iron bars, Israeli soldiers killed nine Turkish nationals, and injured many more.

While blaming Obama alone for the incident may be unfair, his unwavering support for Erdogan and opposition to Mubarak's Egypt created an environment where Erdogan felt empowered to act without restraint. The combination of these factors contributed to renewed violence.

Egypt and Gaza: Spreading Destabilization

Since March 1979, I visited Egypt frequently. ECF maintaining strong connections with Egyptian security authorities who influenced Egypt's policies towards Israel and the Palestinians. Nimrod Novik, ECF's chairman, had particularly close ties to various Egyptian power centers, including Omar Suleyman's son-in-law, a key figure in Egypt's security services. In the summer of 2010, during a trip to Cairo on a private plane, Suleyman's son-in-law discussed growing opposition to President Mubarak's nepotism and socio-economic issues. The son-in-law told us that a movement to overthrow Mubarak was likely in the near future.

In January 2011, the Arab Spring reached Egypt. My own son-in-law, Itai Vered, was almost killed while reporting on the mass demonstrations from Tahrir Square. Many Americans, including President Obama, welcomed this as the arrival of liberal democracy. Obama, publicly demanded President Mubarak to resign.[16] I couldn't help but recall the discussions in 2003 about bringing democracy to Iraq through US intervention. It also reminded me of Geneive Abdo's book, *No God but God—Egypt and the Triumph*

---

[16] Obama's commentary in his memoirs referring to Egypt reads: "Most of all, we worried about the autocratic, repressive nature of nearly every Arab government—not just the lack of true democracy but also the fact that those who held power seemed entirely unaccountable to the people they ruled" (pp. 637). Then, "the most powerful and cohesive force in the country was the Muslim Brotherhood, the Sunni-based Islamist organization whose central objective was to see Egypt—and the entire Arab world -governed by sharia law. Thanks to its grassroots organizing and charitable work on behalf of the poor (and despite the fact that Mubarak had officially banned it), the Brotherhood boasted a substantial membership. It also embraced political participation rather than violence as a way of advancing its goals" (pp. 643–644). Obama, *A Promised Land*.

of Islam.[17] Abdo described how political Islam had, long before the Arab Spring, controlled the "universities, the professional syndicates, the professional middle classes." Understanding this and remembering my previous studies on Sayyid Qutb, it seemed evident how this would evolve.[18]

Political Islam had no real experience and professional knowledge in government. It seemed to me likely that when the Muslim Brotherhood took power, clashes with liberal forces and the army would follow. The oppressive nature of political Islam was already evident in Gaza since 2007, but at least Egypt had an army to counter its rise.

This is what had happened in Iran at the start of the twentieth century. In 1905, an originally liberal revolution was overturned by the religious leadership, leading to mutual assassinations and a civil war. This eventually allowed the army to take power in 1921. This was exactly what would happen in Egypt.

In May and June 2012, Egypt held presidential elections, and the result was initially unclear. With the support of the US embassy in Cairo, the electoral committee announced Muhammad Morsi, the Muslim Brotherhood candidate, as president.[19] From an Israeli perspective, Morsi's rise to power posed a significant problem. It was evident that his government would support Hamas and potentially seek to end the 1979 Peace Treaty. However, initially, Morsi showed no interest in confronting the US or Israel, and the old security forces remained in control.

Nevertheless, Hamas believed they could rely on Egyptian support and initiated a military confrontation in November 2012. The US sought a ceasefire with Turkey and Qatar's assistance, but even Morsi resisted this. Our ECF network played a crucial role, with Nimrod liaising with Egyptian security, General Spiegel coordinating with the Israeli government and army, and me

---

[17] Geneive Abdo, *No God but God—Egypt and the Triumph of Islam*, Oxford U.P. 2000.

[18] Sayyid Qutb, *Social Justice in Islam* (translated by Hohn B. Hardie), Islamic Publications International 2000. I read the book in Arabic and wrote a book review as a seminar paper 1970. See Yair Hirschfeld, "A Review of: Social Justice in Islam by Sayyid Qotb," *Hirschfeld Khoury-DeConcini Papers, Substack*, forthcoming (originally created in May 1970), https://hkdpapers.substack.com/p/review-of-social-justice-in-islam-by-sayyid-qotb. See also "haachim hamuslimim bulam haaravi vebkehilot islamiot bmaarav europa" (trans. The Muslim Brotherhood in the Arab World in Muslim Communities in Europe"), Israeli Meir Amit Center for the Knowledge of Intelligence and Terror, December 26, 2011, pp. 1–63, https://www.terrorism-info.org.il/Data/pdf/PDF_11_049_2.pdf (english) (accessed July 12, 2023), archived at https://web.archive.org/web/20230712095523/https://www.terrorism-info.org.il/en/17806/.

[19] Yossi Beilin was told that the real voting results had been different, and the victory was given to Morsi, out of fear of unrest. Yossi Beilin, "Morsi didn't win the elections," *Israel Hayom*, August 18, 2013, archived at https://web.archive.org/web/20130818152944/http://www.israelhayom.com/site/newsletter_opinion.php?id=5395. Obama perceived the 2011–13 developments in Egypt via the prism of his Cairo speech. See Obama, *A Promised Land*, pp. 638.

maintaining contact with Robert Serry and Jeff Feltman.[20] Serry was the UN Peace Envoy to the Middle East and Feltman, who had become a UN official advised Secretary of State Hillary Clinton. Eventually, Feltman helped broker a fragile ceasefire. We presented two proposals outlining the Gaza ceasefire parameters and the positions of Israel, Egypt, and Hamas.[21]

Although ECF intended to offer an economic package for Gaza to stabilize the ceasefire, the fundamental problem remained: Hamas's military wing's *raison d'etre* was the ability to attack Israel at any time. This deterred major economic investments. Robert Serry negotiated the "Gaza Reconstruction Mechanism" after the 2014 military round, providing minimal support to the Gazan economy without changing the volatile power dynamics.

In July 2013, the Egyptian army ousted President Morsi, leading to divided American voices on whether to take action against the coup. Lt. General Moshe (Bugi) Yahalon, Israel's Minister of Defense, told me that he had convinced his US counterpart, and apparently President Obama, to offer support to the incoming Egyptian government.[22]

Seeking to Understand and Overcome the Gap of Interests and Perceptions

By early 2010, it became clear to me that crucial elements necessary for an Israel-Palestine Permanent Status agreement were missing. The Palestinian leadership lacked the willingness and capacity to meet the conditions required by Israel to achieve a comprehensive agreement. Neither Turkey, Iran, nor the various proxies (Hezbollah, Jihad, Hamas) were willing to cease violence or accept any deal. Arab states were reluctant to impose their will on the Palestinians and engage with Israel. They instead opted to increase demands and push US mediators away from a "Zone of Achievable Agreement." Both the Israeli government and public had lost faith in the possibility of a comprehensive agreement, and bridging the gap between religious Jewish and Muslim leadership proved too challenging.

---

[20] Yair Hirschfeld, "Correspondence with Jeff Feltman," *Hirschfeld Khoury-DeConcini Papers, Substack*, forthcoming (originally written November 20-21, 2012), https://hkdpapers.substack.com/p/correspondence-with-jeff-feltman (specifically my message at 10:55 AM on November 19, 2012, his message at 11:04 AM on November 20, 2012, my message a 11:30 AM on November 20, 2012, and my message on November 21, 2012) (hereafter cited as Hirschfeld, "Correspondence with Jeff Feltman," *Hirschfeld Khoury-DeConcini Papers*).

[21] Hirschfeld, "Correspondence with Jeff Feltman," *Hirschfeld Khoury-DeConcini Papers* (specifically the two attachments I sent at 3:22 PM on November 28, 2012).

[22] The very good news was that the US administration was willing to listen and change its former approach. Yair Hirschfeld, private interview with Moshe (Bugi) Yahalon, February 10, 2022.

In Washington, emerging policy ideas suggested the enforcement of an Israel-Palestinian Permanent Status Agreement upon the parties involved. In March 2010, Dan Kurtzer and Robert Malley testified in front of the Senate Committee on Foreign Relations. Almost exactly one year later, in March 2011, U.S. General David Petraeus, testified in front of the Senate Committee on Armed Services. Each of their testimonies, although specifically General Petraesus's, highlighted the "insufficient progress toward a comprehensive Middle East peace."[23]

General Petraeus warned that Israeli-Palestinian tensions often led to violence, fostering anti-American sentiment due to perceived favoritism towards Israel. Arab anger over the Palestinian issue hindered strong partnerships between the US and Arab governments, weakening moderate regimes while providing an opportunity for militant groups like al-Qaeda to exploit the situation. It sounded, as if Israel was driving a wedge between the US and the Arabs. Imposing under US leadership an Israel-Palestine Permanent Status Agreement, might ease or even solve the situation.

General Petraeus presentation described very clearly the American perception of the reality created by the US military involvement in the Middle East. The easiest line to take was to accuse Israel for the difficulties the US army was confronted with:

> The enduring hostilities between Israel and some of its neighbors present distinct challenges to our ability to advance out interests in the AOR. Israeli-Palestinian tensions often flare into violence and large-scale armed confrontations. The conflict foments anti-American sentiment, due to a perception of U.S. favoritism for Israel. Arab anger over the Palestinian question limits the strength and depth of U.S, partnerships with governments and peoples in the AOR and weakens the legitimacy of moderate regimes in the Arab world. Meanwhile, al-Qaeda and other militant groups exploit that anger to mobilize support. The conflict also gives Iran influence in the Arab world through its clients, Lebanese Hisballah and Hamas.[24]

In my view, Israel was paying the price for American action, and not the other way round. And I was sure, the US leadership had neither the capacity, nor the necessary political will to impose an agreement. Moreover, I thought any outside imposed agreement would not stand. It would not end militant

---

[23] David Petraeus, Testimony before the Senate Armed Services Committee, March 15, 2011, http://www.isaf.nato.int/images/stories/File/Transcript/Petraeus%2003-15-11.pdf (accessed July 12, 2023), archived at https://web.archive.org/web/20130221111947/http://www.isaf.nato.int/images/stories/File/Transcript/Petraeus%2003-15-11.pdf.

[24] Petraeus, "Testimony Before the Senate Armed Services Committee," pp. 12.

fundamentalist violence. If imposed on Israel, it might rather invite further Arab demands and aggression; if imposed on the Arab states and the Palestinians, radical militant forces might gain the support of more moderate groups and take action to unravel an agreement. The challenge was to deter radical militant Islam, not to appease them. Instead it seemed easier to assert pressure on Israel.

Dan Kurtzer's previous testimony, defined the conditions the US should assert its pressure on Israel:

> *1. A. The U.S. should consider starting negotiations on borders, since an agreement on borders would frame and resolve many other issues.*
> *B. If the U.S. decides on a borders-first approach, it should lay out the following principles to underpin the negotiations:*
> *i. A borders/territory agreement should reflect the equivalent of 100 percent of the territory occupied in 1967.*
> *ii. There should be territorial swaps of equal size and quality based on a 1:1 ratio.*
> *iii. There should be equitable sharing/allocation of shared resources (water, minerals, etc.)*
> *iv. The negotiations on territory should focus on a narrow definition of settlement blocs which hold the largest concentration of settlers.*
> *v. The negotiations should avoid as much as possible impacting on Palestinian daily life, should ensure territorial contiguity and the viability of Palestinian state, and should not include population swaps.*
> *vi. Borders-first negotiations will need to be complemented by simultaneous final status negotiations on Jerusalem.*
> *2. Throughout the negotiations process, the U.S. would need to decide on a proactive, interventionist U.S. role in order to narrow gaps and bridge differences.*[25]

Kurtzer—I thought quite unnecessarily—outlined detailed conditions for such a territorial agreement reflecting the thinking of the dogmatic Israeli peace camp.[26] It made it exceedingly difficult, if not impossible, for any

---

[25] "Middle East Peace: Ground Truths, Challenges Ahead," March 4, 2010, Hearing Before the Committee on Foreign Relations United States Senate One Hundred Eleventh Congress Second Session, Senate Hearing 111-648, *The U.S. Government Publishing Office*, https://www.govinfo.gov/content/pkg/CHRG-111shrg61686/html/CHRG-111shrg61686.htm (accessed July 12, 2023), archived at https://web.archive.org/web/20230712043615/https://www.govinfo.gov/content/pkg/CHRG-111shrg61686/html/CHRG-111shrg61686.htm, video of testimony (and Kurtzer's and Malley's individual transcripts) at https://www.foreign.senate.gov/hearings/middle-east-peace-ground-truths-challenges-ahead.

[26] Kurtzer did not suggest that the United States should impose an agreement. Nevertheless in a book he authored together with Scott Lasensky, William Quandt, Steven Spiegel and Shibley Telhami, he wrote an entire paragraph under the title "Israelis and Palestinians are tough negotiators, and thus

Israeli government to minimize opposition from Israel's pragmatic Right and the settler community. Consequently, I considered the outlined conditions to be prohibitive. The conditions outlined for a territorial agreement contradicted a fundamental rule of negotiations, which is to present the problems and allow negotiators to develop multiple solutions instead of starting with a proposed solution.

I am aware of the counterargument: detailed conditions were deemed essential to convince the Palestinian leadership to engage in negotiations. However, based on my discussions with Palestinian counterparts, I found that this was not the case. The Palestinian leadership was divided into two groups: those opposing any agreement and refusing to accept any essential Israeli demands, and those genuinely interested in reaching an agreement and willing to explore a variety of potential solutions.

In my view, the way we led the Oslo negotiations provided a necessary model for American involvement. Israelis and Palestinians, optimally in coordination with supportive Arab inputs, had to determine what was possible and what was not. Once we reached an understanding, American support helped build a vital regional and international coalition, crucial for supporting the peace effort. In this regard, US guidelines for our peace effort needed to be minimal. When seeking an agreement on territory, the necessary guideline was simple: base negotiations on the June 4, 1967, lines and allow for swaps and other arrangements. Kurtzer, on the other hand, added too many conditions, narrowing the negotiating space for both sides.

In spite of all of this during Obama's second term, Kerry persuaded Netanyahu and Abbas to allow their representatives, Yizchak Molcho and Hussein Agha, to negotiate and draft a comprehensive agreement. The resulting "framework document" impressed President Obama, who described it as "a piece of art."[27] Progress was particularly notable regarding territorial and refugee issues. Netanyahu was willing to accept the formula included, stating that "*the new secure and recognized border between Israel and Palestine will be negotiated based on the 1967 lines with mutually agreed additional other components.*"[28]

---

the United States must be equally tough" concluding at the end of this paragraph: "Thus the end game of negotiations—always the hardest part—is where the greatest amount of U.S. resolve and determination will be necessary with both sides." Kurtzer et al., *The Peace Puzzle*, pp. 276.

[27] Yair Hirschfeld, private interview with Hussein Agha, April 2021. See Grant Rumley and Amir Tibon, *The Last Palestinian—The Rise and Reign of Mahmoud Abbas*, Prometheus Books, New York 2017, pp. 192–193.

[28] Secretary Kerry made a second attempt to reach President Abbas' agreement and added (without the endorsement of Netanyahu) additional Palestinian demands to the proposed document. Nevertheless, Abbas rejected also the second document. Yair Hirschfeld, private interview with Hussein Agha, November 2022. See Rumley and Tibon, *The Last Palestinian,* pp. 188 and fn. 36, 38.

However, while the document represented a step forward on the learning curve, it also contained unachievable elements and omitted crucial factors. Gaining the support of religious leadership and the general population would have required to give up the demand for end of conflict and finality of claims. Furthermore, Arab states did not offer their support, and regional opposition remained strong. A practical formula for implementing agreements had not been developed, and a coordinated strategy among willing parties to combat terrorism was not on the horizon. Consequently, when Abbas, like Arafat in 2000, requested time for contemplation, it effectively amounted to rejection. Instead, Abbas signed a Reconciliation Agreement with Hamas, signaling an end to negotiations.[29] After Barak and Olmert, Netanyahu was offering his support for a Two State Agreement experiencing another rejection of the Palestinian leadership.

Our Cautious Recommendations Ignored

As Obama's first term concluded without progress in the peace process, I hoped that with the assistance of Ambassador Ed Djerejian, and possibly James Baker III, we could propose the ideas shared by Samih el-Abed and me to the incoming post-2012 elections administration. The James Baker III Institute for Public Policy published our report titled *"Re-engaging the Israelis and the Palestinians: Why an American Role in Initiating Israeli-Palestinian Negotiations is necessary and how it can be accomplished."*[30]

At the core of our proposal were two innovative ideas at the time: first, the guiding principle for negotiations should be "what shall be agreed upon will be implemented," replacing the failed principle of "nothing is agreed upon until everything is agreed upon." Second, negotiations should proceed in two parallel tracks: a "fast track" addressing state-to-state issues for substantial on-the-ground state-building and a "graduated track" where areas of sufficient

---

[29] Rumley and Tibon, *The Last Palestinian*, pp. 193. See Jack Khoury and Barak Ravid, "Hamas, Fatah Sign Reconciliation Agreement," *Haaretz*, April 23, 2014, https://www.haaretz.com/2014-04-23/ty-art icle/hamas-fatah-sign-reconciliation-agreement/0000017f-ec86-dc91-a17f-fc8fc5f40000 (accessed July 12, 2023), archived at https://web.archive.org/web/20220928064828/https://www.haaretz.com/2014-04-23/ty-article/hamas-fatah-sign-reconciliation-agreement/0000017f-ec86-dc91-a17f-fc8fc5f40000.

[30] Edward P. Djerejian, "Re-Engaging the Israelis and the Palestinians: Why an American Role in Initiating Israeli-Palestinian Negotiations is Necessary and How It Can Be Accomplished," *Conflict Resolution Program*, James A. Baker III Institute for Public Policy, Rice University, March 13, 2013, https://www.bakerinstitute.org/research/re-engaging-the-israelis-and-the-palestinians-why-an-american-role-in-initiating-israeli-palestinian (accessed July 12, 2023), archived at https://web.archive.org/web/20230712101035/https://www.bakerinstitute.org/research/re-engaging-the-israelis-and-the-palestinians-why-an-american-role-in-initiating-israeli-palestinian.

agreement could be negotiated and implemented to facilitate consensus on longer-term issues.³¹

Our recommendations also included defining a "political horizon" with Terms of Reference for an acceptable end state for both parties.³² I believed that the principles developed by Agha, Khalidi, Brodet, and myself at the start of our deliberations in 2006 could achieve the desired outcome. Samih el-Abed and I requested a meeting with either Secretary Kerry or his chief advisor, Martin Indyk, through Ambassador Djerejian. While Djerejian met with Indyk shortly after Secretary Kerry's confirmation on February 1, 2013, our request to meet Kerry or Indyk was rejected. Apparently, Indyk had attempted to persuade Secretary Kerry to adopt a gradual approach, but it was unsuccessful.³³

Based on my experience in Washington, US policymakers listened to our concerns and policy proposals. However, I recognized that the personal clash and mutual distrust between Obama and Netanyahu, along with their conflicting worldviews, created insurmountable obstacles. It was a lose-lose-lose situation, and I felt the Israeli peace camp was caught in the middle. Despite offering a substantial financial security package of over $35 billion to address Israeli concerns, without a mutually agreed strategic understanding, tensions continued to rise as Iran and its proxies escalated violence against Israel. While financial and military support from the United States was welcomed, without addressing conflicting interests strategically, it only widened the perception gap and heightened tension.³⁴

---

[31] Djerejian, "Re-Engaging the Israelis and the Palestinians," pp. 7.

[32] Djerejian, "Re-Engaging the Israelis and the Palestinians," pp. 7.

[33] Rumley and Tibon, *The Last Palestinian*, pp. 187.

[34] It may be useful to visit Henry Kissinger's evaluation. He says the "debate should move beyond theoretical speculation. If there is to be an improvement of relations with the Iranian Islamic regime, it seems elementary to link it with abandonment of the export of revolution by force and subversion, a curb on terror, and an end to interference in the Middle East peace diplomacy. Simultaneously, progress must be made with respect to Iran's acquisition of missiles and nuclear weapons." Henry Kissinger, *Does America Need a Foreign Policy? Toward a Diplomacy for the 21st Century*, Simon and Shuster, New York 2002, pp. 199 (see also pp. 196–200).

Hoping for a Religious-Led Peace: Opportunities and Threats

The Opportunity: Negotiating Non-Negotiable God-Ordained Commands

In 2009, a group of young religious peace activists established "Talking Peace" (Siach shalom). Their mission was to facilitate ongoing dialogues between religious and secular Israelis, as well as Muslim religious leaders, to develop a Judaism- and Islam-based strategy for achieving peace. Over more than a decade, the "Talking Peace" group engaged in multiple dialogues with radical Israeli rabbinical leaders following Rabbi Yehuda Zvi Kook (1891–1982). These included the "Merkas haRav" in Jerusalem and other influential rabbis such as Rabbi Smotrich, Rabbi Dov Lior, and Rabbi Zvi Yehuda's disciples, including the leaders of the Jewish Zionism party.

Other peace activists, including Ofer Zalzberg, Roi Ravitzky, and Rabbi Michael Melchior, focused their efforts on theoretical research to inform future action.[35] Ofer Zalzberg's PhD dissertation explored how to negotiate non-negotiable commands, or protected values, that religious Jews and Muslims believe are ordained by God. The protected Jewish and Muslim religious values clash one with the other as they relate to the question of sovereign control of territory. The demand for Jewish sovereignty is based on the teachings of Rabbi Moses Ben Nachman (the Ramban), who emphasized the Jewish obligation to live in Eretz Yisrael and prevent the land from becoming desolate.[36]

Rabbi Zvi Yehuda further argued that full sovereignty was necessary to achieve this goal. However, several related questions offer some room for maneuvering: Can Israeli security oversight be seen as asserting sovereignty? Does the commitment to prevent barrenness necessitate full sovereignty? Can agreements with Arab nations and Israeli allies facilitate Jewish immigration to Israel? And can an agreement without finality of claims allow for additional demands? Similar considerations exist on the Muslim side, where religious

---

[35] *Israel & Palaestina / Zeitschrift fuer Dialog*, vol. II, 2021 (German), specifically: Ofer Zalzberg, "The Israeli-Palestinian Conflict and Efforts to Resolve It: A Worldview Analysis," pp. 7–23; Ofer Zalzberg, "Beyond Liberal Peacemaking: Lessons from Israeli-Palestinian Diplomatic Peacemaking," pp. 24–30; Michael Melchior, "Establishing a Religious Peace," pp. 33–44; and Daniel Roth, "Insider Religious Mediators Advancing Religious Peace in the Context of the Israeli-Palestinian Conflict," pp. 44–47.

[36] Ofer Zalzberg, *Non-Negotiabiity in Conflict: Religious Zionist Attachments to Land and Temple in the Israeli-Palestinian Conflict*, Trinity College Dublin, School of Religion, Irish School of Ecumenics 2023, http://www.tara.tcd.ie/handle/2262/102998 (accessed July 12, 2023), archived at https://web.archive.org/web/20230712102137/http://www.tara.tcd.ie/handle/2262/102998.

teachings emphasize Muslim sovereignty over Jerusalem and Palestine. While both sides cannot renounce their claims to sovereignty, they recognize the acceptability of temporary realities on the ground. Therefore, religiously sanctioned progress can be made through Palestinian state-building, "temporarily" refraining from settlement expansion based on religious law, and accepting temporary lease arrangements.

The militant demands of Rabbi Zvi Yehuda Kook's followers are tempered by other rabbinical leaders such as Benny Lau, Yuval Cherlow, Yoel Bin Nun, and Rabbanit Adina Bar Shalom, who are committed to pursuing a religiously grounded peace. Benny Lau, aware of the influence of religious and social gatherings in synagogues on political opinions, prepared discussion papers for these sessions, linking each week's Torah portion to the "command to seek peace."[37] Yuval Cherlow highlighted Israel's security interest in pursuing peace, referencing Rabin's "three-circle approach" that emphasized concessions to the Palestinians for regional Arab and US support against threats like Iran. Years earlier, Yoel Bin Nun, a friend of Rabin, provided us with the necessary rulings for reaching an agreement on Jerusalem during an extensive meeting. Adina Bar Shalom, the daughter of Rabbi Ovadia Yosef (the founder of Shas), offered both genealogical and political weight, particularly among the Israeli religious Sephardic community.

Many participants in these efforts were also involved with the David Hartman Institute in Jerusalem, conducting research, compilation, and teaching of Jewish political thinking. Notably, they produced three volumes of "Jewish Political Tradition," edited by Michael Walzer, Menachem Lorbeerbaum, Noam J. Zohar, and Yair Lorberbaum.[38] In my view, the most important part of this monumental work was the discussion in volume two regarding the concept of being "the chosen people." The expression of gratitude to God for having "chosen us" is recited by religious Jews in prayers, often multiple times a day. This concept, as documented in volume two of the Jewish Political Tradition, refuted the dangerous aberration of "Jewish Supremacy" advocated by Rabbis Yizchak Shapira and Dov Lior, which legitimized crimes and promoted a religious-fascist worldview.[39]

---

[37] It is called Project 922. Every Friday a part of the Torah is being read and discussed in each Synagogue. Rabbi Benny Lau has a radio program discussing each Friday before prayers the relevant parts of the Torah.
[38] Michael Walzer, Menachem Lorberbaum, Noam J. Zohar and Yair Lorberbaum (eds), *The Jewish Political Tradition,* Yale U.P. New Haven and London, 2000, vol. I ("Authority"); 2003, and 2018, vol. III ("Community").
[39] Michael Walzer, Menachem Lorberbaum, Noam J. Zohar and Yair Lorberbaum (eds), *The Jewish Political Tradition,* vol. II ("Membership"), pp.3–82 ("Introduction");.

Additionally, I studied the teachings of Rabbi Eliezer Berkovits, who argued in an article on "Jewish Sovereignty" that "God's plan for mankind" involved the re-establishment of Israel in the land of its ancestors. This perspective, based on the belief that events such as the Holocaust, the founding of the State of Israel, the Six-Day War victory, and the conquest of Judea and Samaria are part of "God's Plan," serves as a prelude to the redemption of the Jewish people and, ultimately, humanity as a whole.[40] However, in his essay "On the Return of Jewish National Life," Rabbi Berkovits wrote:

> Let us thank God that we were not the masters but only pariahs of these great civilizations; that we had no share in their criminal inhumanities. We have often been trampled on, but let us thank God that it was not we who trampled upon justice, decency, freedom, and human dignity whenever it suited our selfish purposes. Let us be grateful to the exile; it has freed us from the guilt of national existence in a world in which national existence meant guilt. We have been oppressed, but we were not oppressors. We have been killed and slaughtered, but we were not among the killers and slaughterers.

And he concluded:

> But woe unto us if the degeneration of the exile should lead us to a Hebrew nationalism along the European patterns...Are we to erase two thousand years of Jewish history and render sterile all the sacrifice and numberless Jewish generations? Such a relapse would imply that the whole of exile was a meaningless tragedy. Let us think again before we seek to make the changeover from exile to Eretz Yisrael. Not every form of Eretz Yisrael is worth the trouble, and many a form could be unworthy of Judaism.[41]

These teachings offer hope for those pursuing a religiously formulated peace. This hope is further reinforced by developments beyond the realm of peace activism, such as Pope Francis' role in promoting interfaith dialogue and the efforts of political and religious leaders in the United Arab Emirates, Saudi Arabia, Jordan, and Egypt to encourage a more moderate Islam and foster Jewish-Muslim dialogue. Prominent Muslim intellectuals, like the late Sheikh Abdallah Nimr Darvish, and his pupil, the Israeli Arab political leader Mansur Abbas, were and are working towards accepting foreign, i.e., Israeli,

---

[40] Eliezer Berkovits, "On Jewish Sovereignty," in David Hazony (ed.), "Essential Essays on Judaism," Shalem Press, Jerusalem 2002, pp. 179.

[41] Eliezer Berkovits, "On the Return to Jewish National Life," in Hazony, "Essential Essays on Judaism," pp. 170–171.

sovereignty and creating a supportive political environment. While there is still much work to be done, an important beginning had been made.

The Threat: Inflaming Religious Militant Fanaticism Through Political Rhetoric

The incoming Israeli government is largely dominated by Bezalel Smotrich's racist ideology and Itamar Ben Gvir's terrorist Kahanist ideology. This has intensified conflicts within Israeli society, creating a threatening environment for the Israeli Arab community and the Israeli Left. The potential for a vicious cycle of violence and the dangerous power of these ideologies to change realities on the ground pose unpredictable consequences. The mutual provocations of religious militancy lead to repeated cycles of violence and war, as well as to a process of creeping annexation. The tragedy is that hate-mongering and incitement is a most effective political tactics. It largely determines public opinion and undermines the political maneuvering space of the leadership and its legitimacy to achieve progress in any peace-making effort.

Addressing Joshua A. Cohen's "Misconclusion"

Joshua Cohen's conclusion that Netanyahu's reign represents the ultimate triumph of occupation:

> Netanyahu became the longest-serving head of state in Israel's history. His supporters call him "Bibi, King of Israel." His reign, marked by the building of walls, the construction of settlements, and the normalization of occupation and state violence against the Palestinians, represents the ultimate triumph of the formerly disgraced Revisionist vision promulgated by his father.[42]

This view reflects a growing tendency among American progressive Jews to dismiss Israel in order to align with their non-Jewish liberal friends.[43] They overlook the complexities of the Israeli reality and fail to consider the threats faced by Israel, such as the thousands of rockets and missiles provided by the

---

[42] Cohen, *The Netanyahus*, pp. 237.

[43] Leading American Jews did often in the past write off the Zionist cause. The historian Sir Lewis Namier denounced Edward Warburg, Arthur Krock and Walter Lippmann "as trembling amateur gentiles." Michael Ignatieff, *A Life—Isaiah Berlin*, Chatto and Windus, London 1998, pp. 105.

Ayatollah regime to Hezbollah. Cohen also ignored Iran's support of Palestinian Jihad and Hamas terrorism, along with their propaganda to destroy Israel. And he left no place for the powerful political revival of Israel's liberal and democratic forces.

Furthermore, Cohen overlooked the fact that President Abbas has rejected peace proposals and frameworks, including the 2014 framework agreement supported by Netanyahu. Instead of asserting pressure on President Abbas to support the negotiated framework agreement, Obama and the world accused Netanyahu and Israel for the renewed deadlock.

Suggested Reading

Understanding the US Middle East Policy Under Obama

Richard Haass and Martin Indyk (eds.) *Restoring the Balance—A Middle East Strategy for the Next President;* Brookings Institution Press, Washington D.C. November 2008; most important are three contributions: Stephen Biddle, Michael O'Hannon and Kenneth Pollak "The Evolution of Iraq Strategy" pp. 27–58; Suzanne Maloney and Ray Takeyh "Pathway to Co-existence: A New US policy toward Iran; pp. 59–92; and Stephen Cook and Shibley Telhami "Addressing the Arab–Israeli Conflict" pp. 121–158. These articles suggested a simple US strategy: In order to get out of Iraq, the US had to befriend Iran and make an effort to impose an agreement on Israel. It most clearly put the US and any Israeli government on a confrontational path.

William J. Burns *The Back Channel—American Diplomacy in a Disordered World*; Hurst and Co. London 2019; particularly Chaps. 7, 8, 9 and 10. Chapter 9 entitled "Iran and the Bomb: The Secret Talks" is fascinating to read, although from an Israeli point of view not encouraging.

Barack Obama *A Promised Land*, Crown, New York 2020. President Obama is a most brilliant speaker and writer. Sharing by and large his Weltanschauung, and admiring his domestic policies, has made it for me even more difficult to grasp the tremendous gap of understanding reality as seen from Washington, and living it in Israel.

Making an Effort to Understand the Policies of President Abu Mazen (Mahmoud Abbas)

Grant Rumley and Amir Tibon *The Last Palestinian—The Rise and Reign of Mahmoud Abbas*, Prometheus Books, New York 2017; this is a political biography of Mahmoud Abbas. Chapters 6–12 cover the period of Abbas' presidency.

Sari Nusseibeh *What is a Palestinian State Worth?*, Harvard U.P. Cambridge 2011. The chapters have the following titles: 1. How Did We Come to This? 2. What Makes Life Worth Living? 3. What Are States For? 4. Can Values

Bring Us Together? 5. What Does the Future Have in Store? 6. Who Runs the World, "US" or "Thugs"? 7. How Can we Move the World? Epilogue: What Should we Educate For? Nusseibeh does not advocate either for a one- or a two-state solution. Instead he writes: "*The vision of the peaceful and prosperous future may take any of several forms: one state, two states, confederation, federation involving one country, or two, or three, and so on. But whatever form it takes, it has to be a moral political order, and its foundation must be the two elements of freedom and equality.*" (p. 193).

Negotiating Non-negotiables

Ofer Zalzberg *Non-Negotiability and Conflict: Religious Zionist Attachment to Land and Temple in the Israeli-Palestinian Conflict*—Ph.D. confirmed 2022 by: The School of Religion, Theology and Peace and Conflict Studies; Trinity College Dublin, 2022.

Zalzberg describes and analyzes the limits of diplomatic peacemaking and he discusses ways and means to overcome value-based tradeoff resistance, by reframing sacred values and promoting conflict transformation, coupling Hermeneutics and Diplomatic Peacemaking.

10

Seeking a Way Forward: Brainstorming in Norway, and the Abraham Accords (2017–2021)

Against all odds, in October 2015, Jon-Hanssen Bauer, the newly appointed Norwegian ambassador to Israel, took the initiative to overcome past failures and break the conceptual, political, and diplomatic deadlock. I had the opportunity to meet Jon shortly after his arrival in Israel in the early autumn of 2015. To my surprise, he remembered the detailed content of the policy paper I had written for the European Union in 1991–1992[1] and inquired about reactivating some of the ideas developed there. This not only flattered me but also gave me the impression that Jon was determined to explore ways to revive the peace process.

What was equally important was his, and his senior colleague Tor Wennesland's, expressed desire to depart from long-standing dogmatic thinking and chart a new path forward. Jon, responsible for overseeing and managing donor support for the Palestinian Authority, was concerned that regional and international donor attention was focused on Syria, Lebanon, and Iraq, leaving the Palestinian Authority struggling to manage a growing deficit.

Jon was aware that President Abbas's pursuit of international unilateral recognition of Palestine had created a vicious cycle of punitive measures between Israelis and Palestinians. He also raised concerns about settlement expansion and how to prevent radicalized young settlers from engaging in criminal violence against Palestinian villagers, as well as minimizing house

---

[1] Yair Hirschfeld, "Israel, the Palestinians and the Middle East: From Dependency to Interdependence," *Hirschfeld Khoury-DeConcini Papers*, *Substack*, forthcoming (originally written in September 1992), https://hkdpapers.substack.com/p/israel-the-palestinians-and-the-middle-east.

demolitions. Jon and Tor sought not to engage in a confrontational discussion with mutual accusations but rather to explore ideas for breaking free from the prevailing quagmire.

Consequently, starting from early autumn 2015, I had an open door at the Norwegian Embassy in Tel Aviv, located on the 9th floor of the Ramat Aviv Mall. I facilitated meetings, with or without my physical presence, between Jon and Othniel Schneller, an Israeli counterpart, as well as Palestinian counterparts. The emerging common ground encouraged them to test understandings based on the concept of "what shall be agreed will be implemented," focusing on an incremental process of agreement.

This time, the impetus to move forward came from the Palestinian side. Whether they were reacting to our discussions or motivated by other considerations remains unknown. Nonetheless, they presented their paper to me and subsequently to the Norwegians. We were aware that the paper had been authorized without obligating Abu Mazen in any way. The aim was to test ideas while maintaining complete deniability, following what we referred to as the "waste-paper principle." The ideas put forth could not only be denied but also discarded at any moment. The paper became known as the "Ten Point (Non)-Paper," and it was presented on March 6, 2016, with the following points:

The Ten Point (Non)-Paper

1. Israeli-Palestinian negotiations should be resumed with the goal of concluding a permanent status agreement within two years.

2. Israel shall recognize the state of Palestine and not oppose its full membership in the UN.

3. The negotiations, conducted by the governments of both states, will establish agreed borders based on the 1967 lines with reciprocal and agreed-upon swaps. They will also entail mutual recognition of Palestine as the homeland of the Palestinian people and of Israel as the homeland of the Jewish people, without prejudicing the rights of all citizens in both states. The negotiations will mark the end of the conflict and the finality of mutual claims.

4. The negotiations will address all other core issues, including security arrangements, refugees, Jerusalem, and water.

5. The negotiations will also address the nature of the relationship between the two states and establish appropriate frameworks to ensure the sustainability of the agreement.

6. Whenever possible, the implementation of each agreement on any single issue shall commence immediately, without waiting for the conclusion of all other issues.

7. The governments of Israel and Palestine shall take immediate action to prevent all forms of violence, including by civilians from both sides. They shall refrain from any act or declaration hostile to each other and actively take measures to prevent incitement. The trilateral joint committee against incitement will resume its work in this context.

8. International and regional actors, including but not limited to the Quartet members, the permanent members of the Security Council, and the members of the Arab Peace Initiative follow-up committee, will be invited to participate in the launching event of the direct negotiations. These actors will also be welcome to discuss their active role in monitoring, verifying, and implementing the agreed-upon issues during the negotiations.

9. Parallel to the bilateral talks, multilateral talks on various regional topics will be conducted with the participation of Israel, Palestine, regional countries, and other interested states.

10. The Israeli-Palestinian agreement shall lead to full and normal relations between Israel and all Arab states, as envisioned by the Arab Peace Initiative.[2]

The Very Real Reactions to the Non-paper

On top of the agenda was the demand for Israel to recognize Palestine upfront. In return, there was a promise to recognize Israel as the homeland of the Jewish people. The commitment was to engage in a phased process, implementing what had been agreed upon while dealing with all outstanding core issues and state-to-state matters by creating agreed frameworks for stability. There was also a commitment to fight violence and incitement, seek regional support, and achieve full normalization with Israel as envisaged by the Arab Peace Initiative.

The Norwegians were equally impressed and immediately took action to test whether we could move forward from friendly discussions to a well-organized "academic exercise." To do so, they needed to determine whether the innovative approaches from the Palestinian side had a chance of reaching a possible consensus on the Israeli side. Within a week, they organized a workshop at the Dead Sea with the Israeli team led by Othniel Schneller and me.

---

[2] Yair Hirschfeld, "Ten Point Paper," March 6, 2016, ארכיונים ואוספים אישיים/אוסף יאיר הירשפלד (trans. Archives and personal collections/Yair Hirschfeld collection), ישראל גינוך המדינה (trans. Israel State Archives), Jerusalem.

While we discussed all the issues raised by the Palestinian Non-Paper, the focus was on the future of the settlements. Othniel presented two seemingly contradictory messages: that a fair give and take was possible and a plan for establishing Special Status Areas in both Israel and Palestine. This included providing important extra-territorial Palestinian rights on Israeli sovereign territory to serve the Palestinian economy. Israeli extra-territorial rights in Palestine would allow settlers to remain in their present residences, while evacuation of settlers had to be kept to a minimum.

To emphasize the last point, Othniel took Jon and me on a tour through the West Bank to understand the depth of the settlement issue. We visited Har Bracha, on top of Nablus (the biblical Shchem), the settlement blocs of Tapuach, Ariel, and Karne Shomron, and even entered an illegal outpost (according to Israeli law). It became clear that neither Israel's right wing nor Israel's left wing offered a practical solution.

During the trip to Har Bracha, moving in and out of Area C, passing through Palestinian villages one after the other, it became evident that Naftali Bennett's plan to annex Area C and establish a "minus State entity" in areas A and B was a dangerous farce. The Palestinians would be trapped in fragmented areas, while Israeli settlers in Area C would have to pass through their villages, likely with armored cars. This reminded me of a visit I made to Kosovo years ago, where Serbian houses near Muslim villages had to be surrounded by NATO tanks day and night, and movement was restricted for both sides.

We discussed Bennett's plan on the way to Har Bracha. I believe his plan expressed a genuine concern for the future of the settlers, who form his electoral constituency, but it demonstrated ignorance of the situation and a lack of innovative thinking. In contrast, Othniel's approach, unlike Bennett's, addressed the needs of the settlers and proposed a fair quid pro quo for the Palestinians. If managed cleverly, it could be politically sustainable.

We also discussed the unrealistic claim of Israel's peace camp that a center-left government would have the power to evacuate around 150,000 settlers. The dangerous populism of Israel's right wing and the detachment from reality of Israel's peace camp tempted our Norwegian friends to explore Othniel's ideas. Othniel's openness about the settlement issue, his initiative to confront the Norwegians with the depth of the problem from the start, and his willingness to test any possible idea to offer the Palestinians a fair quid pro quo impressed Jon-Hanssen Bauer and Tor Wennesland. They made the decision to proceed with the "academic exercise."

To be successful, Othniel and I knew we had three important challenges: forming a small but effective team, conducting research to address upcoming issues, and understanding that our own opinions were not relevant. The only relevant understandings were those acceptable to the Prime Minister of Israel (at that time, Benjamin Netanyahu) and Palestine's President Abbas or his successor.

Assembling a New Israeli Working Group

In forming our team, we needed to cover four issues. For the legal aspects, we asked Yehoshua Gurtler from the top law firm Herzog Fox Neeman to join us. He had previously worked in the international legal department of the IDF. Brig. General Baruch Spiegel was asked to oversee the economic and state-building issues, providing an Israeli perspective. Colonel Ron Shatzberg would handle the maps and discuss the implications in every inch of the West Bank. I would be responsible for negotiation tactics, and Othniel and I would share the overall responsibility.

The division of work between Othniel and me was unusual. We would discuss every move and detail, and in case of a difference of opinion, Othniel's view would be deemed right and mine wrong. Othniel's pragmatic right-wing thinking and his consideration of the concerns of the settler community had a better chance of being accepted in the present Israeli political climate. My task was to anticipate the possible reactions of the Palestinians and the Norwegians and ask questions. Together, we would find the best way to address the concerns of all parties involved.

We recognized that the issue of up-front Israeli recognition of the State of Palestine was at the top of the Palestinian agenda. Previously, I had requested Pnina Baruch Sharvit and Ruth Lapidoth, both experts in international law, to write separate papers on the pros and cons of recognition. Pnina Baruch Sharvit, who had led the International Law Department of the IDF, and Prof. Ruth Lapidoth, Israel's distinguished professor of international law and recipient of the Israel Prize, provided legal assessments that highlighted the serious pitfalls and dangers involved in recognition. A couple of years earlier Pnina Baruch Sharvit had published a paper on the issue.[3]

According to their assessments, recognizing Palestine upfront would have irreversible consequences. It would grant the Palestinian leadership access to international institutions such as the International Criminal Court, which could impose sanctions or take anti-Israel actions. Furthermore, it unilaterally defined the cease-fire line of June 1967 as the border between the two states,

---

[3] Pnina Sharvit Baruch, "A Palestinian State: Legal Implications and Significance for Israel," *Strategic Assessment*, vol. 15, no. 4, January 2013, pp. 54–65.

effectively abrogating the Israel-PLO understandings of the Oslo Accords, which had legalized Israeli military presence, installations, and settlements. This upfront recognition would create a situation where the newly recognized State of Palestine could, with legal justification, call for terror or military action against any Israeli presence in the West Bank.

To gain another perspective, we sought the expert opinion of Ambassador Alan Baker, an internationally highly esteemed legal expert who often was being consulted by Netanyahu and enjoyed his full confidence. His review offered a more positive outlook and suggested a process of mutual recognition. He prepared the following paper:

"Joint Declaration on Mutual Recognition and Agreed Arrangements for a Return to Negotiations

Acknowledging the importance of achieving a two-state solution, in line with the vision of President G.W. Bush, of two states living side by side in peace and security;

Concerned that the continued lack of progress in realizing that vision enhances tension, mistrust, and extremism between our peoples, and serves to undermine our common interests;

With a view to restoring a common basis of mutual respect and trust, and to jointly creating an appropriate and respectful ambiance for realizing the two-state solution, we mutually declare the following:

1. Israel expresses its intention to recognize in principle the State of Palestine as the state of the Palestinian People, and Palestine expresses its intention to recognize in principle Israel as the State of the Jewish people.
2. This mutual recognition in principle will allow both sides to renew direct bilateral negotiations on all outstanding bilateral issues, including Jerusalem and refugees, in accordance with the terms of this declaration and on the basis of state-to-state negotiations.
3. The negotiation will at first cover the following basic bilateral issues:
    a. Security
    b. Borders
    c. Political and legal issues and relations
    d. Economic and commercial issues
    e. Culture of peace

And will last for two years. Annex One describes a detailed and agreed upon negotiating plan, which has been designed in such a way, as to achieve as quick as possible the necessary change on the ground, as well as mutual security, confidence, trust, and the legitimacy of the people in support of the peace-finding process.

4. With a view to encouraging a positive negotiating ambiance between the two sides and among their respective publics, the resumption of negotiations will be based upon the following principles of mutual conduct:

   a. All previous agreements between the PLO and Israel, will remain valid pending agreement on each outstanding issue.
   b. The negotiations will be conducted continuously and in a confidential manner at locations to be agreed upon.
   c. Both sides will refrain from unilateral actions that might affect the issues to be negotiated and agreed.
   d. All petitions, complaints, and initiatives addressed to international organizations, international and national tribunals and courts, directed against the other and its leadership will be revoked.
   e. The parties will work together in order to permit Palestine to join various UN organizations, as well as international conventions. All actions involving boycott, divestment and sanctions, whether in the economic or cultural spheres, intended to prejudice the rights, integrity, interests, and legitimacy of the other side, will be revoked.
   f. Seeking to replace the "logic of war" by a common commitment to the "logic of peace" both sides will refrain from adverse public statements relating to the negotiations and to the leadership and negotiators of the other side. In order to do so a joint committee will take action to prevent adverse statements and cooperate in creating a constructive and supportive atmosphere for the negotiations.
   g. The negotiations will be based on the principle of "what has been agreed upon shall be implemented," without losing sight of the commitment to reach a final agreement that will bring about end of conflict and finality of claims to both parties;
   h. Neither party shall be deemed by virtue of having entered into this Agreement to have renounced or waved any of its existing rights, claims or positions.

5. Principles (parameters) for negotiations on the issue of territory, security, economy, and the culture of peace have been laid out in the Quartet statement of....both parties have responded to the proposed principles in separate letters and have committed with reservations described there,

to engage in direct bilateral negotiations, as well as being committed to pursue the jointly accepted Action and Negotiating Plan.

6. Upon the successful outcome of the above negotiations, mutual recognition in principle will become full recognition."[4]

In order to confirm the suggested move, we suggested to add to the document a letter to the Quartet powers (US, Russia, EU, and UN)

"Letter to the Quartet

Israel is willing to recognize a State of Palestine.

This recognition will be in principle, and subject to a bilateral final agreement regarding the joint borders, security issues, political and legal issues, economic and commercial issues and the establishment of a culture of peace between the two states.

Upon completing negotiation on these issues, full recognition will be reciprocally granted."[5]

Regarding Palestinian state-building and economic development, each member of the Israeli team had acquired extensive knowledge and experience over the past twenty years. We had relevant papers from the Palestinian side on various aspects such as transport infrastructure, energy, water, and trade.

From Working Group to Workshops

The Norwegians organized a first workshop only with the Israeli team, at the Dead Sea. In a way it was like an exam, testing whether our ideas were innovative and dynamic enough to convince the Norwegian government to get involved. After the successful outcome, Tor and Jon organized three more trilateral workshops, two in Norway and one in Athens. In March 2016, the Israeli and Palestinian teams met at Losby Gods, located near Oslo. The surroundings were covered in deep snow, and during breaks in our discussions, we had the opportunity to take walks in the Norwegian woods and appreciate the beauty of the winter landscape. In mid-April, we gathered at

---

[4] Alan Baker, "Joint Declaration on Mutual Recognition and Agreed Arrangements for a Return to Negotiations," May 15, 2016, *Hirschfeld Khoury-DeConcini Papers, Substack*, forthcoming (originally written May 15, 2016), https://hkdpapers.substack.com/p/mutual-recognition-and-agreed-arrangements (hereafter cited as Hirschfeld, "Joint Declaration on Mutual Recognition," *Hirschfeld Khoury-DeConcini Papers*).

[5] Hirschfeld, "Joint Declaration on Mutual Recognition," *Hirschfeld Khoury-DeConcini Papers,* pp.2.

Lysebue, a lovely inn in the hills above Oslo, close to where international ski-jumping competitions were held. The view over Oslo Bay and the hilly forest landscape was breathtaking. The third meeting took place in June at the residence of the Norwegian Ambassador in Athens.

During these meetings, we focused on two major activities: seeking common ground in a general paper and delving into the details of state-building and economic issues. In Athens, the Palestinian team presented insightful ideas regarding state-building and economic measures they wanted to promote. Their suggestions highlighted the need for territorial control or, in the absence of a final agreement on borders, comprehensive state-building actions that would restrict settlement expansion while considering legitimate requests from settlers.

The Israeli team argued that a prosperous State of Palestine could be achieved without reverting to the cease-fire lines of June 1967, while still referring to them. The Palestinian team emphasized the importance of optimal territorial control for economic development. However, we found common ground in recognizing the significance of creating Special Status Areas. We also acknowledged that no Israeli Prime Minister would make concessions on the territorial issue without addressing the interests of the settler community, and President Abbas or his successor could not make concessions on settlements without a clear understanding of territory.

Shortly after the meeting in Athens, in July 2016, the Middle East Quartet (US, EU, Russia, and the UN) published a report and recommendations that marked a conceptual shift. Instead of focusing on the core issues of the conflict, the Quartet proposed an incremental approach, highlighting four areas: ending violence and incitement, halting Israeli settlement construction and expansion, supporting Palestinian state-building, and promoting Israeli-Palestinian cooperation.[6]

The Palestinian leadership criticized the report as it contradicted their strategy of seeking unilateral recognition and international pressure on Israel. The Quartet Report demanded that the Palestinian leadership take proactive action against violence, incitement, and anti-normalization policies, and address the situation in Gaza. This shift unsettled our Palestinian team and likely influenced their reluctance to discuss an incremental strategy during our fourth meeting in August 2016 in Stavanger, Norway.

---

[6] "Report of the Middle East Quartet, July 1, 2016," Middle East Quartet, July 1, 2016, https://reliefweb.int/report/occupied-palestinian-territory/report-middle-east-quartet-july-1-2016-enarhe (accessed July 12, 2023) (Text in Arabic and Hebrew, English summary), archived at https://web.archive.org/web/20230712114907/https://reliefweb.int/report/occupied-palestinian-territory/report-middle-east-quartet-july-1-2016-enarhe.

Unfortunately, the Stavanger meeting ended in a deadlock when the Palestinian team rejected ideas they had previously proposed themselves. Our Norwegian friends announced the end of the exercise, expressing gratitude for our efforts but leaving the door open for future continuation.

From the end of August to November, all attention was focused on the upcoming US presidential election. Othniel was invited to present his ideas at the Washington Institute in front of former Middle East advisers, including Dennis Ross, Aaron Miller, David Makovsky, and others. However, his suggestions were politely rebuffed, with no willingness to explore new approaches.

Many in Israel, including Othniel, celebrated the electoral victory of Donald Trump. Our Norwegian friends decided to revive the "academic exercise," and we reconvened in Sarpsborg in February and in Moss in March 2017. These locations held historical significance, as the Oslo negotiations began in Sarpsborg 24 years earlier, and Moss was where the Moss Convention, allowing for the personal union of the King of Sweden over Norway, was signed in 1814. The choice of these locations seemed to convey a message: "nations can work together, even if they resent each other."

Various Leadership Shows Interest in an "Academic Exercise"

Over the course of a year, we (Othniel Schneller, the Palestinian team, and I) had collaborated with the Norwegians. We were aware that April 2, 2017, was a crucial date. It was when the Norwegian Minister of Foreign Affairs would discuss the "academic concept" with Prime Minister Netanyahu and, separately, with President Abbas.

After these meetings with the leaders on both sides, we gathered at the King David Hotel, in order to be briefed. Tor and Jon, the Norwegian facilitators, were pleased and optimistic.

Tor reported that the "*meeting, yesterday, Sunday was in the morning before the government session; it took three quarter of an hour beyond the allocated time, and all the cabinet ministers were waiting outside, seeing the Norwegian delegation coming out of the meeting.*" And he continued: "*The decisive moment with the PM came when we discussed how to continue. We got the green light, to do so. Later in the day, Abu Mazen also offered the necessary support.*"

The next step for the Norwegians was to involve the US peace team at an Ad Hoc Liaison Committee (AHLC) meeting in Brussels on May 11, 2017. Following the Brussels meeting, Jason Greenblatt, a prominent member of the US peace team, didn't have a direct flight home. The Norwegian Minister of Foreign Affairs invited him to fly via Oslo on a private governmental plane. During the flight, they discussed various issues, including the Norwegian role in assisting the Americans in the negotiations, but not wanting an initiative of their own. They also explored topics such as minimizing Iranian influence in the Middle East and US–Norwegian cooperation regarding Russia on the Norwegian-Russian border.

To follow up on these talks, Jon traveled to the United States and had in-depth meetings with Jason Greenblatt and Jared Kushner. When finalizing his report, Jon told me, "*Yair, we are in the kitchen.*" Our Norwegian friends believed that we had achieved a significant historical breakthrough. Unfortunately, this turned out not to be the case at all.

Specific Reactions from the Israeli and Palestinian Leadership

Netanyahu engaged and provided very critical remarks on what would be unacceptable and needed changes. He suggested that we obtain additional advice from Daniel Reisner, a lawyer he and the Palestinians trusted. As a result, Reisner prepared for us a paper, which most likely was in line with what Netanyahu was willing to support, although the substance of the paper remained fully deniable. In order to stress the deniability, the paper was defined as an "academic understanding." It read:

> ### *Academic Understanding on Renewing Israeli-Palestinian Negotiations*
>
> Both Parties are committed to a mutually recognized two-homeland state solution ("TSS") to their conflict.
>
> Both Parties recognize that past negotiations based upon the methodology of "all or nothing" have so far failed in advancing this goal.
>
> The Parties acknowledge that an active Israeli-Palestinian peace process will significantly contribute to regional stability and strategic change and that, conversely, new regional realities can significantly contribute to the viability of the Israeli-Palestinian negotiations.
>
> The Parties recognize the importance of the Arab Peace Initiative, as an indication of the willingness of the Arab States to play an active role in promoting and supporting Israeli-Palestinian peace.
>
> The Parties both share an interest in effectively combating radicalism and terrorism, one of the purposes of which is to prevent the success of the TSS.

The Parties recognize that the active assistance of the United States, and of both neighboring states—the Hashemite Kingdom of Jordan and the Arab republic of Egypt—will be essential for the purpose of advancing toward the TSS.

The parties further recognize the special role of the Quartet and the AHLC as conduits for, and facilitators of, wider international support for their bilateral negotiations.

Principles

The bilateral negotiations will focus on 4 separate substantive "layers" with supporting "packages," the primary components of which are outlined below.

The Parties will jointly agree on the sequencing of the negotiation on the various layers and packages, throughout a mutually defined 24 month negotiating period, to be extended by mutual agreement if required.

With the purpose of generating observable on-the-ground achievements and mutual trust, the Parties can agree that implementation of agreed packages and other, including partial, substantive arrangements within the layers, can commence immediately, where practicable.

During the negotiations, the parties will not take unilateral steps which will change the legal status of any areas under discussion between them.

Parallel to the bilateral negotiations, multilateral talks will commence with the goal of advancing regional cooperation and promoting additional bilateral peace negotiations between Israel and other Arab states.

Layers of Negotiations:

Layer 1—Borders, Security, and Settlements

- *The border between Israel and Palestine will be based on the 1967 lines with agreed swaps and other complementary arrangements.*
- *Multi-layered security arrangements will ensure the security of Israel, whilst enabling the demilitarized Palestine to effectively protect itself against domestic and mutually agreed external threats.*
- *Maximum contiguity for Palestine.*
- *Minimum disruption of existing life for both Parties.*

Layer 2—Recognition, Refugees, Jerusalem, and other Holy Sites

- *Phased mutual recognition of both States as the respective homelands of the two peoples.*
- *A just solution to the Palestinian Refugees issue, including end of Palestinian Refugees claims.*
- *A fair arrangement for those Jews who were displaced from Arab countries.*
- *A multi-faceted (territorial, security, administrative, economic, and religious) solution for Jerusalem and its inhabitants.*

- *Mutual arrangements for the protection and preservation of, and secure access to, Holy Sites for all religions.*

…*(Additional packages to be developed)*[7]

Our reading at the time was that Netanyahu was most seriously interested to follow up and allow the track-two exercise to pave the way to negotiations, while accepting the 1967 lines with agreed swaps and other complementary arrangements as the basis for negotiating the border, and offering two supportive packages regarding planning and zoning, and economic state-building.

Not so Abbas. He offered a friendly nod. It was later revealed that Abbas planned a very different approach from what we were discussing. He had been in discussions with Egyptian, Jordanian, and Saudi leadership to suggest a US-Palestinian-Jordanian-Egyptian-Saudi-Israeli forum, where the Palestinians would dictate the negotiation strategy. I knew Netanyahu and most likely any Israeli government would not accept this. I was uncertain, however, whether President Trump and his team might be tempted to follow a fully coordinated Saudi-Egyptian-Jordanian-Palestinian lead. Thus, Abbas nodded to the Norwegians in a friendly manner as he awaited the American response to his proposed strategy.

In December 2017, President Trump's decision to move the US embassy from Tel Aviv to Jerusalem caused international protests. It ended the ongoing dialogue between the American peace team and the Palestinian leadership. President Abbas hardened his position and obstructed any dialogue with the Americans. In response, the US implemented punitive measures against the Palestinians, only causing further embitterment. The US-Norwegian dialogue also went sour. The Americans ceased support to the Palestinian Authority. The US maintained contact with the Norwegians, by continuing to participate in AHLC meetings, but they disregarded any Norwegian political ideas. Tor and Jon feared that the Americans were raisin-picking some of the ideas we had developed, potentially distorting the basic concept.

Our trilateral Norwegian-Israeli-Palestinian deliberations went from on to off. The "academic exercise" had ended for most of 2018, but I continued to brief Jon on discussions Othniel and I had with our Palestinian counterparts. Eventually, early in 2019 our meetings resumed, and we began working on a common concept again. These efforts bore fruit. In early May, the Norwegians organized a finalizing workshop at Brussels. Our three teams agreed

---

[7] Daniel Reisner, "Academic Understanding on Renewing Israeli-Palestinian Negotiations," *Hirschfeld Khoury-DeConcini Papers*, *Substack*, forthcoming (originally written April 17, 2017), https://hkdpapers.substack.com/p/academic-understanding-on-renewing-negotiations.

on a Nine-Point paper. This agreement aimed to commit both parties to the two-state solution. It also offered a formula for territorial issues and mutual recognition. We hoped this would pave the way for the official parties to return to negotiations.

The Nine-Point Paper

Brussels, May 1 and 2, 2019:

1. *Both parties commit to a two-state solution.*
2. *Negotiations on territory shall be based on the June 4, 1967 lines. Modifications to the border must be agreed and will include land swaps and other arrangements in line with national interests.*
3. *Mutual recognition will be three-phased:*

   - *In the first phase Israel will announce its principled commitment to recognizing the State of Palestine.*
   - *In the second phase, when concluding an agreement on territory, both parties will recognize the territory and the borders of both sides.*
   - *In the third phase, when reaching understanding on Jerusalem, refugees, and agreement on mechanisms to handle outstanding claims, Palestine recognizes Israel as the nation-state of the Jewish people with full civilian and political rights for its other citizens, and Israel recognizes Palestine as the nation-state of the Palestinian people, with full civilian and political rights for its other citizens.*

4. *The parties will ask the regional powers and the international community for support, including to:*

   - *Palestinian state-building and economic development;*
   - *Provide incentives to both sides during the process and according to their achievements;*

5. *The viability and prosperity of the Palestinian national economy shall be obtained in cooperation with the international community and the neighboring Arab states, including by:*

   - *An update and improvement of arrangements for economic cooperation and trade relations between Israel and Palestine;*
   - *Improved access to and trade with international markets, as well as promoting private sector investments;*

– Increased support to Palestinian institution- and state-building, as well as to infrastructure for the state;

6. The parties will engage to create a culture of understanding and peace between the Israeli and the Palestinian peoples, inter alia by:

   – Ending mutual accusations and defamation by the Israeli and Palestinian leaderships;
   – Supporting and coordinating education for peace;
   – Engaging in a religious dialogue, including on the Holy Places; and
   – Promoting cross-border cooperation.

7. The principle "what will be agreed upon shall be implemented" will be pursued, without prejudice to the claims of both sides.
8. In order to underpin the peace-finding process, international support will be granted, including with a coordinating entity monitoring progress against agreed milestones.
9. Both parties are obliged to refrain from unilateral action in contradiction to the promotion of the agreed peace-building process.[8]

Abu Ala' Takes Over

We soon discovered that the Palestinian side wanted to delve deeper into each of the nine points.

A few weeks later, I visited Abu Ala' at his office in Abu Dis. The welcome was warm, and despite his age of 82, he looked youthful in an elegant black jalabiya. We discussed politics and found common ground in our belief in a gradual process leading to a two-state solution. He expressed interest in promoting the peace process and mentioned the possibility of convincing President Abu Mazen to join if everything aligned.

I read the Nine-Point Paper to him. His initial reaction was to inquire about its confidentiality. He regarded the paper as an excellent basis for serious discussions but stressed the importance of keeping the talks secret for the time being, even from the Norwegians. It took another three weeks before meetings with Othniel Schneller commenced at his brother's home in Jerusalem. Abu Ala' emphasized the need to address all core issues of

---

[8] Yair Hirschfeld, "Nine Point Paper," May 2, 2019, הירשפלד יאיר אוסף/אישיים ואוספים ארכיונים (trans. Archives and personal collections/Yair Hirschfeld collection), המדינה גינזך ישראל (trans. Israel State Archives), Jerusalem.

the conflict and make the paper the Terms of Reference for restarting negotiations.

The second task would be to determine how to strengthen the PA politically. After that, we would resolve economic issues. Abu Ala' would need a "full package" to take to Abu Mazen. The diplomatic sequence would involve first reaching an Israeli-Palestinian agreement, then involving the Americans, and only thereafter including the Arab states. I prepared a draft entitled "Principles for an Israel-PLO Agreement on Palestinian State-building, Economic Development, and Good Neighborly Relations."[9]

Othniel added four points: committing to an incremental approach, addressing all core issues of conflict, allowing each side to maintain its desired final vision of the outcome, and ensuring stability of implementation while still guaranteeing controlled passage over each other's sovereign territory.

While Othniel Schneller and Abu Ala' continued their meetings, I was excluded. I am not sure why I was excluded. However, my educated guess was that Netanyahu, knowing that Abu Ala' was now the negotiating partner on the Palestinian side, would refer to this track-two exercise more seriously, and thus wanted me out. Schneller and Abu Ala' concluded and signed a detailed document in June 2020, covering topics such as borders, Jerusalem, security, water, prisoners, economic relations, collaborative relations, dispute resolution, mutual recognition, and refugees.

Although I was not directly involved, Othniel asked me to confirm with Abu Ala' if the agreed document would be accepted as the basis for official negotiations. On June 15, 2020, Abu Ala' asked his confidante Maher el-Kurd (who was a member of the original Palestinian team in Oslo) to send me the following response:

Dear Yair,

Regarding the draft of the "Palestinian/Israeli Joint Thinking Team," I have been given to understand that this draft, in its present form, if presented to us by a third party, would constitute an acceptable basis for joint talks on which to build and expand, provided that a third party is incorporated to carry out concrete monitoring, follow-up, and verification role.

With Regards
Maher el-Kurd[10]

---

[9] ECF, "Principles for an Israel-PLO/PA Agreement on Palestinian State-Building, Economic Development and Good Neighborly Relations," *Hirschfeld Khoury-DeConcini Papers, Substack*, forthcoming (originally written September 2, 2019), https://hkdpapers.substack.com/p/principles-for-an-israel-plo-pa-agreement.

[10] Maher el-Kurd, "Correspondence with Maher el-Kurd," *Hirschfeld Khoury-DeConcini Papers, Substack*, forthcoming (originally written 10:03 PM, June 15, 2020), https://hkdpapers.substack.com/p/correspondence-with-maher-el-kurd.

Both of these drafts (the Nine Points concluded in Brussels in May 2019 and the longer text from June 2020) as well as the draft paper prepared by me, regarding State-building, Economic Development, and Good Neighborly relations, could potentially serve as a starting point for future dialogue on renewing negotiations. These three texts offered possible approaches to reach the necessary "Take Off Point," allowing each side to move forward while maintaining their reservations. I recognized at the time that the relations had become too antagonistic to immediately move toward these envisioned understandings. It instead required a preparatory period to build trust and goodwill on both sides.

The Abraham Accords Are Signed: Abu Dhabi, Bahrain, and Casablanca Begin the Waltz

Israel had maintained secret contacts and relations with Arab Gulf states and others for many years. In August 2020, these contacts were brought into the limelight and normalized. Israel signed a peace agreement with the UAE, marking a significant milestone. This was followed by a similar peace agreement with Bahrain in September 2020, and with Sudan in October. Morocco also established diplomatic ties with Israel. Since then, relations have been sustained with strong support from the incoming Biden administration, as well as various European states and the EU.

The signing of the Abraham Accords, which established peaceful relations between Israel, the United Arab Emirates, Bahrain, Sudan, and Morocco, was a groundbreaking event. It showcased the potential for cooperation between Israel and Arab states and created an opportunity to support an Israeli-Palestinian peace-finding strategy through cooperation, rather than boycotts.

However, as expected, the Palestinian reaction to the Abraham Accords was mostly negative. For decades, Palestinians had viewed the normalization of relations between Israel and the Arab world as a bargaining chip that should only be granted after reaching a Permanent Status Agreement. Palestinian leaders vehemently attacked the UAE and Bahrain, resulting in significant pushback. In Israel, this led to the dangerous conviction among the pragmatic right that peace with the UAE, Bahrain, Sudan, Morocco, and even Saudi Arabia could be possible without making concessions on the Palestinian front. There were even suggestions that it could potentially create conditions supportive of territorial annexation at a later stage.

The sustainability of the Abraham Accords is being most seriously tested by the horror of October 7, 2023 and the presently ongoing war. At the time of writing we are witnessing an uphill battle against the powerful forces of militant Islamic radicalism and the repeated genocidal threats against Israel and the Jewish people of Iran, Hamas, and Hisbollah, which are being reinforced by the suffering of the Palestinian people.[11,12]

Conversely, a strong and decisive stand of the US-Europe-Saudi Arabia-the UAE and Egypt against Hamas and its allies Iran, Hisbollah, the Houtis, reassuring Israel and offering the Palestinian people humanitarian relief and hope for a better future to end their present nightmare, may be the only way out. As difficult as it may be, the cost of appeasing Iran, Hamas, Hisbollah, the Houtis will be more dangerous, and open the way for Islamic militancy addressed at the liberal values cherished particularly in Europe. Internal unrest, combined with Russian aggression against Ukraine and beyond adds most substantially to these threats. After October 7, 2023, a Middle East Security Process, rather than a peace process is needed. The individual and collective Israeli and Palestinian lack of security must be addressed and the safety of all guaranteed, against all odds.

Suggested Reading

Understanding US Policy Under President Trump

Jason Greenblatt, *In the Path of Abraham—How Donald Trump Made Peace in the Middle East and How to Stop Joe Biden from Unmaking it*, Pro-Book, Tel Aviv 2022.

Jared Kushner, *Breaking History—A White House Memoir*, Harper Collins, New York 2022.

Both Greenblatt and Kushner wanted to broker an agreement with the Palestinians but failed to address Palestinian sensitivities and wider opposition to some of their proposed policies. Preparing the Trump Plan "*Peace to Prosperity: A Vision to Improve the Lives of the Palestinian and Israeli People*," suggested an Israel-Palestine two-state agreement, at conditions no Palestinian leader could accept. The hope of the American policy makers was that the Palestinian leadership might say "No, but…" accepting the offered advantages and declining everything else.

---

[11] Arnon Regular, "Roadmap-Risk Assessment, No. 853," November 5, 2022 (Hebrew) (offers a detailed report about the Arab Summit Meeting in Algiers in response to the Israeli election results) (confidential and unpublished).

[12] Meir Ben Shabat, *The Abraham Accords at Year Two: A Work Plan for Strengthening and Expansion*, November 2022.

A Palestinian Reaction: Two Interviews

Hussein Agha, "'We Must Liberate Our Thinking from the Oslo Straitjacket,' An Interview with Hussein Agha" (interviewed by Alan Johnson), Fathom Journal, August 2018, https://fathomjournal.org/oslo25-we-must-liberate-our-thinking-from-the-oslo-straitjacket-an-interview-with-hussein-agha/ (accessed July 12, 2023), archived at https://web.archive.org/web/20230619162151/https://fathomjournal.org/oslo25-we-must-liberate-our-thinking-from-the-oslo-straitjacket-an-interview-with-hussein-agha/.

Hussein Agha and Ahmed Samih Khalidi, "A Palestinian Reckoning—Time for a New Beginning," *Foreign Affairs*, https://www.foreignaffairs.com/articles/middle-east/2021-02-16/palestinian-reckoning (accessed July 12, 2023), archived at https://web.archive.org/web/20230712120420/https://www.foreignaffairs.com/articles/middle-east/2021-02-16/palestinian-reckoning.

Agha and Khalidi similar to Nusseibeh and other Palestinian intellectuals are looking for a way forward.

Understanding Israel's Strategic Imperative

Asher Susser, *Israel, Jordan, & Palestine: The Two-State Imperative*, Brandeis U.P., Waltham 2012 (describes the re-occurring necessity to seek in form or the other a two-state reality).

Developing Tools for Reaching an Agreement on Border and Territory

Michael J. Strauss, *Territorial Leasing in Diplomacy and International Law*, Brill, Leiden, 2015.

11

Netanyahu's Uphill and Downhill Road to Disaster

The Folly and the Seeming Success of Netanyahu's Conflict Management Strategy

Seen from retrospect, Abu Mazen's rejection of the 2014 Framework Agreement became a first fault-line. The conclusion of the Joint Comprehensive Plan of Action (JCPOA) between Iran and the "Five Plus-One" Members of the Security Council (USA, Russia, China, United Kingdom and France) and Germany regarding the Iranian nuclear build-up became the second fault-line.

Netanyahu perceived the agreement with Iran as a Damocles Sword hanging over Israel. Deadly confrontation had been postponed but had become a certainty. However, fear of Iranian aggression was shared with Saudi Arabia, most of the other Arab Gulf states, Jordan and Egypt. This fear opened the way to intensify and possibly upgrade relations between Israel and these countries. Thus, responding to repeated Palestinian rejections of all former and recent Israeli, as well as US peace proposals, a policy of Conflict Management seemed to make sense.

Opposing the US effort to reach an understanding with Iran, Netanyahu's march of folly began: March 2015, still before the JCPOA Agreement was concluded, Netanyahu addressed both Houses of Congress, in order to oppose President Obama's policy. It was a flagrant insult of the President of the United States and Obama paid him back: December 2016, while still in office, before having to allow president-elect Trump to take over,

Obama refrained to veto Security Council Resolution 2334.[1] The resolution ignored and overruled the Israel-PLO Agreement of September 1995, when the PLO granted Israel full jurisdiction over the settlements, and agreed that the future of the settlements would have to be negotiated in permanent status negotiations.[2] Instead, the new resolution proclaimed that all Israeli settlements including East Jerusalem constitute a flagrant violation of International Law. This Resolution followed President Abbas' rejection of the negotiated 2014 framework, and as such offered encouragement for a further Palestinian rejectionist strategy.

A year earlier, in October 2015, I edited a study entitled "Promoting a Coordinated Strategy for the Reconstruction of Gaza",[3] which included several policy papers, offering a proposed coherent strategy: Celine Touboul's contribution was entitled: "Promoting Humanitarian Relief for Gaza Rehabilitation and Stabilization: Obstacles and Challenges"; she suggested an action plan, on how to improve living conditions in Gaza; Ephraim Sneh's (a former Minister of Health; Minister of Transport and Deputy Minister of Defense) contribution asked "How to Develop Gaza's Economy", hoping to create stability and sustainable economic growth; an unnamed Israeli writer spoke of the need to seek ways and means to allow the Palestinian Authority to take over the government of Gaza; and I wrote a concluding paper "Developing a Coherent Strategy for Gaza". We were agreed that the main obstacle was not Israel's policy, but rather the determination of the military wing of Hamas to maintain the capability to attack Israel at any given moment. Hamas's ongoing threat to prepare for the next round of war turned our hope and effort to stabilize the situation in Gaza, into a fata morgana. It questioned the rationality and profitability of private and public investment in necessary development projects. And without prior action, it made the Palestinian Authority's ability to take control over the Gaza Strip implausible. Thus, I spelt out four conditions in October 2015, necessary to stabilize Gaza and allow the Palestinian Authority to unite both Palestinian regions under one government and pursue reconstruction and economic growth:

---

[1] 7853rd Meeting SC/12657, December 23, 2016 Israel's Settlements including East Jerusalem Have no Legal Validity, constitute flagrant violation of International Law, Security Council Reaffirms; press.un.org/en/2016/sc 12,657.

[2] See chapters 4 and 5 above.

[3] Yair Hirschfeld (ed.) Promoting a Coordinated Strategy for the Reconstruction of Gaza; S.Daniel Abraham Center for Strategic Dialogue, Netanya Academic College and Friedrich Ebert Stiftung, Herzliya, October 2015.

- The smuggling of arms and arms production had to be effectively stopped;
- The internal military build-up had to be limited and a gradual process of arms control had to be introduced;
- A wide and coordinated regional coalition necessary to counter Hamas' and Jihad/s military had to be formed; and
- Lastly, it was essential that the international community would recognize Israel's right to defend itself against Hamas attacks directed at Israel's civilians, and take action against Hamas' war crimes, including their tendency to build military installations and rocket-launchers, hiding behind their own civilian population.[4]

At the same time I naively asked AIPAC (the US pro-Israel Lobby) to launch an international campaign against Qatar, and I wrote a detailed policy paper, documenting Qatari financing of arms and modern military equipment to Hamas and other terror groups; financing militant Imams in mosques and madrassas everywhere, allowing them to propagate jihadist ideas; and inciting the Arab public globally, by extreme and one-sided Al-Jazeera Arabic broadcasting. The James Baker III Institute for Public Policy not only refused to publish the policy paper, but ended my well-paid fellowship. Qatari donations were more important. AIPAC also refrained from taking any meaningful action.

Several years later, in 2019 the Commanders for Israel's Security, published a similar paper "Gaza—An Alternative Security for Israel", demanding once more, to pave the way for the Palestinian Authority to take control over the Gaza Strip and promote reconstruction and economic growth in all parts of the Palestinian territory.[5]

Netanyahu knew better. He hoped to turn the internal division between the PA control on the West Bank and Hamas control of Gaza to Israel's advantage. Weakening the PA and maintaining Hamas control over Gaza, would allow Israel, so Netanyahu hoped, to manage the conflict, while relations with most Arab states could be improved. He asked Qatar to support the Hamas regime in Gaza, by delivering monthly cash payments of millions of dollars. Altogether, the Israeli government controlled 90% of Hamas' revenues, and Netanyahu allowed annually over $2 billion to sustain the

---

[4] Ibid. p. 29.
[5] Commanders for Israel's Security Gaza an Alternative Strategy for Israel; en.cis.org.il The study reached the same conclusions I had drawn four years earlier and demanded a three component strategy: a. Ceasefire consolidation and stabilization; b. Restoring the PA management of the Gaza Strip; and c. Large-scale reconstruction of the Gaza Strip.

Hamas control over Gaza. We know today, that much of these monies was invested in preparing the attack of October 7, and the still lasting barrage of rockets directed at Israel's civilian population.

Hoping for a US-Saudi Arabia-Israel-(Palestinian) Peace Initiative

Netanyahu's Strategy

The conclusion of the Abraham Accords achieving peaceful relations with the United Arab Emirates, Bahrein, Morocco and Sudan (described in the former chapter) was undoubtedly an impressive achievement of Netanyahu's strategy. Yet, it blinded him. He undoubtedly believed, he could advance and with the support of the United States reach a peace agreement with Saudi Arabia, normalizing Israel's relations with most of the Arab and Muslim states, allowing to keep Hamas financially afloat; while weakening the Palestinian Authority, with the intent to eliminate the Palestinian capability to veto any agreement between Israel and Arab states, eventually allowing for the creation of a Palestinian national entity.

Still, this hope was not irrational. Netanyahu in his speech on December 29, 2022, presenting his newly formed government to the Knesset, committed to "*dramatically expand the circle of peace.*"[6]. The basic concept was: peace with most Arab states first, to be followed thereafter, by peace negotiations with the Palestinians. Reflecting upon earlier experiences, Palestinian friends, who had been pro-actively involved in negotiations (rather than Israeli sources), assured me of Netanyahu's intention to seek a two-state solution, while it was Abbas who consistently would say "No."

The experience gained during the Norwegian track-two effort (2016–2020) seemed to confirm this. The paper we received from Ambassador Alan Baker regarding conditions for the recognition of the State of Palestine (see above), offered a first positive indication. Netanyahu's suggestion to consult Daniel Reisner and ask him to prepare for our team a paper suggesting an "Academic Understanding" (see above) offered for me another indication at the time that Netanyahu was willing to pursue a positively game changing

---

[6] "PM Netanyahu's Remarks at the Start of the First Cabinet Meeting of the 37th Government," December 29, 2022, Israeli Ministry of Foreign Affairs, https://www.gov.il/en/departments/news/pm-netanyahu-s-remarks-at-the-start-of-the-cabinet-meeting-29-dec-2022 (accessed July 12, 2023), archived at https://web.archive.org/web/20230712121742/, https://www.gov.il/en/departments/news/pm-netanyahu-s-remarks-at-the-start-of-the-cabinet-meeting-29-dec-2022.

development on the basis of conditions, I thought were fair and created a win–win–win situation. I was also encouraged by the fact that the paper we received referred specifically to the "Arab Peace Initiative."[7] I hoped that Netanyahu's strategy complemented by US, EU and Saudi action could and woud lead the way to the creation of a prosperous Palestinian State. Moreover, Netanyahu was quoted by the Saudi controlled *al-arabiyya* network, of saying that *"peace with Saudi Arabia is the key for ending the Arab–Israeli conflict."*[8]

The Strategy of the EU Peace Envoy

Hence, the EU Peace Envoy to the Middle East and his team worked on a supplementary strategy. In cooperation with Saudi Arabia, the Arab League Secretariat, Egypt and Jordan with the support of the UAE planned a "Peace Supporting Package" that would maximize peace dividends for Palestinians and Israelis. Activities were to be carried out in three working groups:

- A **Political and Security Working Group**, focusing on developing an outline of potential post-peace regional, political and security cooperation mechanisms;
- an **Economic and Environmental Working Group,** focusing on developing proposals for economic cooperation, including in the areas of trade, investment, innovation, transport infrastructure, natural resources, as well as climate change and the environment; and
- a **Human Dimension Working Group**, focusing on developing proposals for cooperation in humanitarian, inter-cultural, and human security issues, as stipulated by UNGA Resolution 66/290.

Following the example of the multilateral working groups that followed the Madrid Conference of 1991, interested governments were invited to participate in these working groups.[9] The participants in the "Peace Day

---

[7] The Initiative stated: "Parties recognize the importance of the Arab Peace Initiative, as an indication of the willingness of the Arab States to play an active role in promoting and supporting Israeli-Palestinian peace." Daniel Reisner, "Academic Understanding on Renewing Israeli-Palestinian Negotiations," *Hirschfeld Khoury-DeConcini Papers, Substack*, forthcoming (originally written April 17, 2017), pp. 1, https://hkdpapers.substack.com/p/academic-understanding-on-renewing-negotiations.

[8] Tuqa Khalid, "Netanyahu Says Peace with Saudi Arabia is Key to Ending Arab–Israeli Conflict," *al-arabiya*, April 17, 2023, https://english.alarabiya.net/News/middle-east/2023/04/17/Netanyahu-says-peace-with-Saudi-Arabia-is-key-to-ending-Arab-Israeli-conflict (accessed July 12, 2023), archived at https://web.archive.org/web/20230712122008/, https://english.alarabiya.net/News/middle-east/2023/04/17/Netanyahu-says-peace-with-Saudi-Arabia-is-key-to-ending-Arab-Israeli-conflict.

[9] "MEPP: The European Union, Saudi Arabia, the Arab League in cooperation with Egypt and Jordan launch the Peace Day Effort for the Middle East and invite the world to join"; September

Effort" would determine when the work of the Working Groups would have progressed sufficiently to combine the various contributions into the "Peace Supporting Package" on the way to an Israel-Palestine two state agreement.

In mid-July the EU envoy Sven Koopmans asked the Israeli team I was coordinating to prepare suggested inputs to support his effort.[10] In response we prepared a five chapter paper (in progress), which we discussed with all interested parties. The paper was entitled "The War in Ukraine and its Strategic Repercussions". The first chapter addressed the global confrontation between the West, Russia, China and Iran and warned of upcoming dangers:

"Vital interests of the United States, Europe, the Arab Sunni states and Israel are increasingly threatened from a Shiite militant radical coalition in the region. To counter-act a three layered regional security structure has to be formed: Layer One will include a Security Pact. Layer Two, will guarantee on a bottom-up approach the free flow of people, goods and services, by establishing a joint Control and Command Structure, while securing the flow of trade from outside the region to the region, within the region, and from the region to the East, as well as to the West.[11] Layer Three, shall allow for dialogue and cooperation structures: creating ideological incentives for mosques, madrassas, synagogues and rabbinical centers, to contribute to the struggle against militant extremism[12]; fiscal coordination aimed at halting the flow of funds to terror groups; and coordination between think tanks seeking innovative ways in the common struggle against unemployment, as well as rising environmental threats to the region".[13,14]

We proposed a detailed plan for upgrading the Palestinian economy in such a way as to reach over the coming decade a more than 10% annual growth rate; we discussed constraints and opportunities and referred to major lead projects for regional cooperation, and we discussed 'suggested action', hoping to create a Israeli-Palestinian-Egyptian-Saudi working group to promote economic development in the Red Sea area, Egypt, particularly the Sinai Peninsula, Gaza and Southern Israel; a parallel, Saudi-UAE-Jordanian-Palestinian-Israeli working group to develop the East–West

---

[18], 2023, New York; eeas.europe.eu/eea/mepp-european-union-saudi-arabia-arab-league-cooperation-egypt-and-jordan-launch-peace-day effort/en.

[10] Meeting with Sven Koopmans, Bjoern Kuehne and Michel Rentenaar, July 18, 2023—stack.

[11] Under the leadership of Brigadier General Baruch Spiegel a detailed concept how to achieve this has become available.

[12] Under the leadership of Ofer Zalzberg and his team ongoing work is being carried out.

[13] On all these issues much operational work has been done.

[14] Policy Paper "The War in Ukraine and its Strategic Repercussions for the Middle East", September 6, 2023.

axis between the Arab Gulf and the Eastern Mediterranean; and a third Israeli-Palestinian working group to allow the emerging State of Palestine to decrease its economic dependency on Israel, and instead create a healthier inter-dependent relationship,.[15]

In separate deliberations we discussed with European counterparts the possibility to establish Saudi and UAE Special Economic Zones in Israel's South that would support Palestinian economic development, allow for intense Saudi and UAE-Israeli-Palestinian cooperation, and prepare the way for an Israeli-Palestinian territorial grand swap, when the parties would be ready to engage in such negotiations.[16]

Netanyahu's March of Downhill Folly

After the Palestinian rejection of the 2014 Framework Agreement, Netanyahu, instead of seeking support from centrist parties, turned to the Right. And in July 2014 the Knesset legislated the "Jewish National State Bill". It differentiated between its Jewish and non-Jewish citizens, in contradiction to Israel's Declaration of Independence which committed to:

> foster the development of the country for the benefit of all its inhabitants; it will be based on freedom, justice and peace as envisaged by the prophets of Israel; **it will ensure complete equality of social and political rights to all its inhabitants irrespective of religion, race or sex; it will guarantee freedom of religion, conscience, language, education and culture; it will safeguard the Holy Places of all religions; and it will be faithful to the principles of the Charter of the United Nations.**

Shimon Peres commented that the "Jewish Nation State Bill" will destroy Israel's democratic status at home and abroad.[17] What followed was legislative action to drastically limit the High Court of Justice's power of judicial

---

[15] Ibid.
[16] Meeting Othniel Schneller, Yair Hirschfeld, and Michel Rentenaar, August 30, 2023. The proposal suggested a territorial swap and lease arrangements. Israeli presence in the West Bank would be in Special Zones, emphasizing Palestinian sovereignty; while reciprocally maintaining Israeli sovereignty in areas where Palestine would have rights on Israeli territory.
[17] Quoted from jewishvirtuallibrary.org./2015-elections.

legislative review. It allowed the Knesset to re-legislate laws, give the government control over judicial appointments, turn the Ministry's legal advisers into political appointees, and make their counsel non-binding.[18]

More so, what followed was Netanyahu's support for the rise of Bezalel Smotrich and Itamar Ben Gvir. Still, in March 2020, Naftali Bennett, the former leader of the religious-nationalist Jewish Nation Party, remarked that vetoing Ben Gvir and keeping him out of the Knesset (as was done to Rabbi Kahane years earlier) was so self-evident, it amazed him, it had to be explained.[19]

Taking the Path to Disaster

The actions of the government Netanyahu formed end of December 2022 caused internal rift; alienated Israel's important allies, the United States and European friendly nations; damaged relations with the Kingdom of Jordan; provoked Muslim religious sensitivities globally by provocations on the compound of Haram ash-Sharif/Temple Mount, all while creating a confrontation between the government and the Israeli army.

These were all the result of the power Smotrich and Ben Gvir gained under Netanyahu's leadership. The threat of mutual incitement and hate-mongering felt the worst to me. Internal rift was created by hate-mongering in the social media. Observing these trends I had written several months before October 7:

> The tendency of mutual escalating hate-mongering can all too easily get out control, and lead to another round of war. And nobody can predict what the costs and the outcome will be. The only fact that is certain, in case a conflagration will not be prevented, it will cause more and more human tragedies.

The October 7 attack against Israel and the Jewish people was caused by many other events. Nevertheless, Netanyahu has eased rather than prevented the path to disaster.

Suggested Reading

---

[18] "The Daily Edition," *Times of Israel*, January 19, 2023, https://www.timesofisrael.com/the-daily-edition/2023-01-19/ (accessed July 12, 2023), archived at https://web.archive.org/web/20230128093925/, https://www.timesofisrael.com/the-daily-edition/2023-01-19/.

[19] Calev Ben Dor "the Rise Itamar Ben Gvir" Fathom Journal, September 2022; fatomjournal.org/the-rise-of-itamar-ben-gvir.

Regarding Netanyahu's World View:

Benjamin Netanyahu, *A Place Among Nations—Israel and the World*; Bantam Books, New York 1993; of particular relevance are chapter 3 "The Theory of Palestinian Centrality"; chapter 4 "The Reversal of Causality"; chapter 5 "The Troyan Horse" and chapter 6 "Two Kinds of Peace".

Regarding Global Dangers and the Struggle Against Terrorism:

It is dangerous to recommend literature written before the events described. Even analytical pieces need updating, adaptation and re-thinking. Nevertheless, several articles published the United States Institute of Peace Press publication under the title "*Leashing the Dogs of War—Conflict Management in a Divided World*; 2007, remain of some interest: For instance:

Michael E. Brown "New Global Dangers"; pp. 39–52; Geoffrey Kamp "Arms Acquisition and Violence: Are Weapons or People the Cause of Conflict?" pp. 53–66; Martha Crenshaw "Terrorism and Global Security" pp.6782; Mohammed Ayoub "State-Making, State-Breaking and State Failure"; pp. 95–114; all in: Chester A. Crocker et.al (eds). *Leashing the Dogs of War—Conflict Management in a Divided World*; United States Institute of Peace Press—Washington D.C. 2007.

On Iran and its Danger to the Region

Dore Gold *The Rise of Nuclear Iran—How Tehran Defies the West*; Regnery Publishing, Inc. Washington D.C. 2009; and

Alireza Jafarzadeh *The Iran Threat—President Ahmadinejad and the Coming Nuclear Crisis*; Palgrave Macmillan, London 2001.

12

My Suggested Conclusions for Future Peace Work

As I reflect on over forty years of political activism, I feel it is now time to pass on the knowledge and experience I have gained to the younger generation. It will be their task to accept my conclusions or possibly reject them. Meeting young activists I was asked conceptual questions: How has the horrendous attack of October 7 2023 changed reality as well as my own views; how does it impact or change the work of civil society and peace activism; how to deal with Palestinian rejections of Israeli peace proposals; how to approach the many political and security challenges, and how to expand people-to-people activities. And what to do, in case our effort fails.

My Take on the Iran-Hamas-Hisbollah-Jihadist-Houti—Genocidal Challenge Against Israel and the Jewish People

How has the Hamas attack of October 7 and the war changed reality as well as your views?

The very existence of the State of Israel and the well-being of the Jewish people, wherever they live has been mortally endangered, now and for many years to come.

Why? Israel is far more powerful than Hamas?

This is not a bilateral confrontation. Israel has been attacked from Hamas in the South, it is being threatened from Hisbollah in the North; from the Houti rebels in the far away South, all being supported from Iran, supplying them with missiles, rockets, armed equipment and military training and calling "Death to Israel" with unhidden genocidal intentions. These threats are being backed by Russia, and partly also by China. All too many in the Western world have either ignored or minimized these threats. Worse, their propaganda machine financed mainly by Qatar, has infiltrated and bought Western academic think tanks, who are joining in the choir of shouting "Palestine from the River to the Sea", which—if turned into action—means to eliminate Israel, by a repetition of the crimes of Hamas committed on and since October 7, (of attacking, murdering, torturing and raping civilians, burning babies alive, and more).[1] These crimes are either ignored or even legitimized, while at the same time, Jews living outside Israel are being attacked, molested and sporadically killed.[2] In addition Iran is making a major effort to develop a nuclear bomb and missile heads that can carry these bombs.

Under such threats, how does this impact personally on you, as well as on the entire community of the Israeli peace-seeking civil society?

We all are going through an emotional, ideological, political and moral rollercoaster; back and forth, back and forth. The first reaction is anger, the second understanding the need to adapt to changing circumstances.

How?

I personally have reached several important insights: Our peace effort has to move from the practical-political-secular approach to a wider Jewish-Muslim commitment for peace, based on the conviction that religious commandments of each side are needed, to stabilize and cement any future peace-building effort.

---

[1] See for instance the remark of Ghazi Hamas in *Ghazi Hamad the spokesperson told CBS he can provide proof that Shiri Bibas and her two little boys, 4 year-old Ariel and 10 months old Kfir were killed*; he remarked "it does not matter how many hostages are still alive." Hamad added, "the babies were kidnapped in order to pressure the Israeli government to end the occupation." See: msn.com/en-gb/news/other/hamas-it-doesn't-matter-how-many-hostages-are-still-alive/amAA1kPBXg. December 1, 2023. The murder of other hostages is now gradually becoming known: …

[2] See: Chuck Schumer "What American Jews fear most" New York Times, December 1, 2023.

12 My Suggested Conclusions for Future Peace Work

Does this mean that you now oppose an Israeli-Palestinian two state solution?

No. But it means that the present call "Palestine from the river to the sea" and Ghazi Hamad's "commitment" to attack Israel again and again, makes a simple bilateral agreement on a two state solution impossible, knowing that strong forces among the Palestinians, in the region, and in the world, will take action to renew terror and war.[3]

Why, then, do you still believe a two-state agreement may be achievable?

The threat of Islamic radical militancy, of terror, rocket and missile attacks, and nuclear warfare, is directed seemingly only at Israel. In reality the aim is to overthrow pro-Western Arab regimes in the Middle East and reach Europe and the entire Western world.[4] Hence, a bilateral Israeli-Palestinian effort, combined with a wider regional and comprehensive global struggle against the threat of Islamic aggressive militancy is needed. It means that an Israeli-Palestinian two state solution has to be embedded in a wider regional context, concluding peace between Israel and most—if not all—Arab states. And it has to be accepted and ratified by religious-based conviction, by economic and social cooperation and interdependence, and by supportive security agreements.

Why do you believe regional and global actors, like Saudi Arabia, Egypt, Morocco and the United States will be willing to get involved in the Israeli-Palestinian quagmire and help to lead the way out?

All parties have a vested interest to stabilize the entire Middle East. Even the Israeli Prime Minister Netanyahu and the head of the Palestinian Authority President Abbas agree, that neither one can stabilize Gaza; they disagree on the substance and details but support the idea of creating a Transitional Interim Body for a given period of time. It means that a wider global-regional effort to pacify the situation in Gaza and beyond is essential. We have already started in talks with foreign diplomats to brainstorm, what might be possible, and how.

---

[3] See also: Bret Stephens "Dooming any hope for a Palestinian state"; New York Times, December 1, 2023.

[4] After the Israel-PLO Declaration was signed in September 1993 a Dutch journalist, Dorethea Forma prepared a documentary on my role in the peace talks. She then told me that having been romantically engaged with a Muslim from Turkey, he and his friends spoke of the intention to "reconquer" Europe for Islam. See also: James Cory *Turkish Influence and Intelligence Operations in Germany* Institute of World Politics; January 6, 2021; and Bulent Usta "Erdogan tells Turks in Germany to vote against Merkel" reuters.com/article/us-germany-turkey-idUSKCN1AY17Z; The article says that Erdogan asked also not to vote for the SPD and the Green Party.

Why do you believe a local Israeli-Palestinian, combined with a wider regional and global effort to fight Islamic aggressive militancy by a moderate peace-loving Islam is realistically achievable?

For several simple reasons: it is a world-wide problem and the liberal democratic West has to engage; the United Arab Emirates is leading an effort to promote a moderate Islam and a religious interfaith dialogue and is being supported—still passively—by Saudi Arabia, Jordan and Egypt; and most important Muslim intellectuals are engaged in leading the struggle against militant Islamic Fundamentalism.[5]

And what about Jewish aggressive militant Fundamentalism?

This is doubly dangerous. Within Israel these forces represented in the Israeli Government by Smotrich and Ben Gvir cause tremendous internal rift; and on the regional and global front their hate-mongering provocative action all too easily creates an escalating vicious circle of extremism. The Israeli army and security authorities are taking some action against them, but need to do far more. Civil society has to marginalize them. Recently the United States is also taking action to sanction militants by blocking their visa applications. Stronger action will be necessary.

Under the present conditions of war, can civil society and the peace movement play any constructive role?

Astonishingly enough, the answer is "yes". In Israel, civil society played a decisive role in changing the priorities of the government and take every possible action to bring the hostages back home: in return for release of Palestinian prisoners, and temporary humanitarian cease-fires.

Okay, this is Israeli civil society and the tremendous emotional impact, the families and friends of the victims have on the entire Israeli society; but can peace activism achieve anything when the troops are still fighting?

---

[5] See: Bassam Tibi *The Challenge of Fundamentalism—Political Islam and the New World Disorder;* Berkeley, California U.P. 1998;Ahmad Mansour *Generation Allah—Warum wir im Kampf gegen relgioesen Extremismus umdenken muessen; Berlin,* Fischer 2015; Souad Mekkehnet *I was told to come alone—My journey behind the lines of jihad;* Varuga Press, London 2017,Seyran Ates Der Islam braucht eine sexuelle Revolution—Eine Streitschrift; Ullstein, Berlin, 2017; Margaretha A van Es; Nina ter Laan and Erik Meenema (eds.) *Beyond 'radical' versus 'moderate'? New perspectives on the politics of moderation in Muslim majority and Muslim minority settings;* Published on line, April 5, 2021.

Paradoxically enough, the answer is: we had even more impact, as in normal times and this on four fronts: Internally, the IDF established at the beginning of the war several brainstorming groups to plan for the Day After. Members of the peace camp were mobilized for this purpose, and others outside, enjoyed full access, allowing us to present our ideas in an ongoing back-and-forth dialogue. The practical outcome is the emerging gap between the endgame envisaged by Israel's security authorities, and the policies of the present Israeli government, which is still dominated by right-wing extremists.

We also enjoyed full access to American and European diplomats. The fact that the group I coordinate had before October 7, prepared much work on how to promote the Israeli-Palestinian peace process embedded in a regional structure, allowed us to develop with the help of European diplomats a (loosely) shared concept for the Day After and disseminate these ideas reaching the White House and other power centers elsewhere.

The most difficult, and probably most important task during the war, was to stay in touch with our Palestinian counterparts. Sustain existing personal relations and networks, listen to each other, and where possible offer help.

On the forth front, cooperation between different peace activist groups became far more effective. In normal times, different groupings tend to defend their own turf and often pursue different political or ideological concepts. Not that this has stopped completely. Nevertheless, the conclusions drawn from the horror of October 7, and what has happened afterwards, are by and large shared by the great majority of the Israeli peace camp, demonstrating the need to bridge between security-, economy-, culture-, and religious-oriented peace activism.

Addressing Past and Future Conceptual Issues

Should Israel and the Palestinians seek a Comprehensive Permanent Status Agreement in one go?

No, it was not realistic before October 7, and it became even less realistic since then. Nevertheless, the milestones we have to achieve on the way to concluding peace, have become more evident. As a first step: Israel cum regional security cooperation with the support of the US and Europe has to create conditions for humanitarian relief and reconstruction on both sides of the Israeli-Gaza border; an effective security structure can pave the way for economic growth and interdependence; while religious moderation and commitment to peaceful relations will have to defeat Islamic terror on the ideological front.

Is the proposed Gradual Approach not all-too Dangerous and didn't it fail in the past?

True, the gradual approach that we pursued has failed. It ignored the dangers of the combination of the powerful Iran-Hisbollah-Jihad-Houti = Hamas threat against Israel and unduly compartmentalized the different conflicts. The gradual approach we are pursuing now, is to allow Israel to destroy the military capacities of Hamas and create a strong US-European-Israeli-Regional security structure to prevent a revival of Hamas military capabilities, contain Hisbollah, the Houtis and Iran, as a basic precondition, to allow for economic reconstruction and growth; get the Israeli-Palestinian peace process underway, and reach not only a political, but also an ideological religiously-based commitment for peace.

In essence you are speaking of a long process of Conflict Transformation. However, judging from past experience Conflict Transformation has also not worked so far?

It is true. The second intifada, of 2000–2005, eliminated many of the conflict transformation measures we had developed. We actually did develop in the late 1990ies a four component parcel, essential to sustain a policy of continuing Conflict Transformation. It included a code of conduct, obliging the parties to move from the logic of war to the logic of peace; a state-building parcel which we called Economic Permanent Status; a security-building parcel, which we called Security Permanent Status, and a great variety of People-to-People action. As a matter of fact we also developed detailed concepts for conflict transformation on the Jerusalem issue, as well as in regard to moving forward in regard to the Palestinian refugee problem.

We have to adapt these four components to present conditions: Obliging the parties to move from the logic of war to the logic of peace, will have to address the traumatization of both the Jewish and the Palestinian people and make it evident that neither the Holocaust nor the Naqba will ever occur again, while also involving religious obligations. The Economic Permanent Status understandings will have to include a far wider regional economic growth concept; Security Permanent Status also will have to build a functioning regional security structure. People to People activities, work we did in regard to Jerusalem and refugees has not lost its relevance and needs to be renewed.

12 My Suggested Conclusions for Future Peace Work

My Take on Palestinian Rejectionism

Knowing that Abbas retracted from his commitment to the "Beilin-Abu Mazen Understanding", Arafat said in fact "no" to the Clinton Parameters, and Abbas said "no" to Olmert's peace proposal, as well as to the 2014 "framework agreement", as well as to later attempts, how has the Israeli peace camp in your opinion to respond?

We underestimated the strategic threat inherent in Palestinian rejectionism to the many Israeli peace offers. We did not understand that it paved the way to the mortal attack of October 7, 2023. I believe this is also true for many Palestinians. They tended to think that rejecting Israeli peace offers was a valid and justified tactics to obtain even a better agreement. Others viewed it as a path to renewed militant confrontation.

Is it not unfair to accuse only the Palestinian side of 'rejectionism'?

Yes, Israeli governments, even those with the best intentions, tended to offer "too little, too late", mainly on two accounts: No prior commitment for the creation of the State of Palestine was given, at times, when it mattered; and no effective control mechanisms to prevent further settlement expansion was granted. Under the governments of Barak and Olmert "too much, too early" was being offered; not understanding the constraints the Palestinian leadership needed to address.

In case an agreement may not be possible, would unilateral Israeli or Palestinian moves be recommendable?

My short answer is "no" in both cases. Unilateral Israeli withdrawal that is not fully coordinated with the Palestinian Authority is perceived as a victory of Palestinian steadfastness and terror and accordingly makes matters worse, not better. The case of unilateral withdrawal from Lebanon and Gaza has illustrated this simple truth. Unilateral Palestinian moves tend only to create a dangerous confrontation.

Olmert coined the phrase of "Coordinated multilateral Unilateralism"; do you support this?

My short answer is "Yes". It means that the Government of Israel in cooperation with the Palestinian Authority and with the full support of Arab governments and the international community, change realities on the ground, paving the way for Israeli-Palestinian negotiations to follow. It offers the Palestinians the advantage that they are not asked to give up any of their demands; it offers Israel the opportunity to reinforce its relations with regional powers and the international community, and creates essential safety networks for future negotiations, while creating hope, and decreasing the motivation to return to violence.

What you are describing contradicts the Palestinian and a wider Arab demand to oppose any normalization with Israel ?

True. The Palestinian and Arab anti-normalization campaign is irrational and self-defeating. Historically, the Arab boycott provided most essential impulses to the Israeli economy, obliging Israel to become fully competitive on European and American markets. Moreover, Palestinian dependency on the Israeli economy makes it necessary to devise a strategy to move from complete dependence to interdependence. This can only be done on a kind of a sliding scale, when Palestinian infrastructure and economic capacities are developed in coordination with Israel. Our macro-economic study will show that the Palestinian economy can gain by upgrading its financial, economic and other cooperation with the Arab world, while maintaining Israel as an essential market for Palestinian goods, for outsourcing, high-tech development and more.

Politically, don't you think that a process of internal PLO-Hamas Reconciliation would serve the peace process?

No, by no means. Hamas has committed to attack Israel again and again and their spokesperson Ghazi Hamed justifies the most horrendous crimes, which were capitating people, burning baby's alive and torturing children in front of their parents before killing them all. It is essential to outlaw Hamas, wherever they are, delegitimize them and apply for them Article One of what was UN Security Resolution 1368.[6] In effect it is a precondition to make it possible for the Palestinian Authority and the PLO, who are ideologically

---

[6] Article One: The Security Council unequivocally condemns in the strongest terms the horrifying terrorist attacks which took place on (September 11, 2000) October 7, 2023 against (American) Israeli civilians and regards such acts, like any act of international terrorism, as a threat to international peace and security; expresses its deepest sympathy and condolences to all victims and their families and to the people and Government of Israel; calls on all States to work together urgently to bring to justice the perpetrators, organizers and sponsors of these terrorist attack and stresses that those responsible for aiding, supporting or harboring the perpetrators, organizers and sponsors of these acts will be held accountable; calls also on the international community to redouble their efforts to prevent and suppress terrorist acts including by increased cooperation and full implementation of the relevant international anti-terrorist conventions and Security Council resolutions and to combat all forms of terrorism, in accordance with its responsibilities under the Charter of the UN.

and by agreement committed to non-violence, to cooperate with Israel. It is difficult enough to reach the "Zone of Achievable Agreement" between Israel and the PLO, only a fully delegitimized Hamas will make it possible for the Palestinian peace-supporting leadership to move forward.

Do you support the policy of the Netanyahu Government to sustain the division between the West Bank and Gaza, and refer to a "three state solution"?

Absolutely, no. This policy only strengthened Hamas. More so, allowing annually over $2 billion to reach Hamas, gave them the means to arm and prepare for war. In Oslo we committed to the unity of the West Bank and Gaza. Ever since 2007, ECF prepared policy papers to improve the social and economic situation of Gaza. And we repeatedly discussed with counterparts in Egypt, Jordan and also Saudi Arabia, essential measures to stabilize the situation in Gaza as a preliminary move to reunite the two areas under the control of the Palestinian Authority.

You seem to suggest solely a "top-down" approach for reaching an agreed path forward?

If you, the younger generation create a "bottom up" movement, achieving full coordination between Israelis and Palestinians, I would applaud you from the bottom of my heart. The difficulties are immense: hate, ignorance and indolence about the fate of the other is all powerful and reinforced by institutional interests and the activism of those groups on both sides of the divide who oppose peace and think in absolute zero-sum game terms. What you will need is a well thought out strategic plan, defining step-by-step action, based on the logic of "minimal demands and optimal pressure". Some of the steps will have to be militant, in order to succeed, and at the same time will need to reconcile with opponents.

Do you think the BDS movement could play a supportive role?

Absolutely, No. The existing tendency within the BDS movement is to question altogether Israel's right to existence. Many of their supporters tend to legitimize most destructive action and a war-mongering state of mind. They are now showing their real face, demanding "Palestine from the River to the Sea". It is a demand for genocide; and they incite also violent Anti-Semitic action in the United States, Europe and elsewhere.

My Take on Israel's Strategy and Policies Towards Regional Powers

What Role does Egypt Play in Your Strategic Thinking?

Egypt was and remains a central pillar in any Israeli strategic thinking. Shared interests are manifold: Stability in Gaza necessitates Egyptian support; the struggle against criminal and terror groups in the Sinai Peninsula at times needed Israeli backing of Egyptian military action; security in the Red Sea is by all means a shared interest. This is even more so in the Eastern Mediterranean, there cooperation with the Palestinians, Jordan, Cyprus, Greece and others in the Eastern Mediterranean Gas Forum is of major economic and political importance. Saudi and UAE investment in Egypt, and Gaza, in the coming years, based on effective Saudi-UAE-Egyptian-Israeli-Palestinian cooperation, has the potential of becoming an important political and economic game changer.

During the entire history of the peace process, every Israeli government, as well as the Palestinian leadership have steadily coordinated moves with Egypt. There is all reason to continue this.

What Role does Jordan Play in Your Strategic Thinking?

Jordan is a second central pillar in Israel's strategic thinking. Peace with Jordan only became possible after the conclusion of the first Oslo Agreement in September 1993. The good news are that Israeli-Jordanian security cooperation serves on a daily basis the interests of both countries and the stability in the region. Cooperation on water and energy fulfill vital needs of both sides (see also the forthcoming report of the Dutch project). At the same time the relationship is potentially very vulnerable. Palestinian refugees of 1948 and those of 1967, living in Jordan often tend to be very critical of ongoing Israeli-Jordanian cooperation and challenge the policies of King Abdallah II and his government. Even more sensitive are developments in Jerusalem and particularly on Haram ash-Sharif/the Temple Mount. The Jordanian waqf is responsible for whatever happens there. Provocations of Israeli militant politicians, like Itamar Ben Gvir and parallel provocations of the Northern Israeli-Palestinian Muslim movement, headed by sheikh Rayyad Salah, repeatedly cause unrest. The good news are that long-lasting friendships between Israeli and Jordanian generals and diplomats have served so far relatively successfully as an effective safety network.

More important, present economic developments of the Arab Gulf States, and their interest to develop trade routes by land and sea from the Indian

Ocean to the Mediterranean offer an opportunity to allow Jordan to become the regional central hub of trade. Constructing an efficient railway and road network in Jordan connecting the Arab Gulf with Palestine and Israel could and should be accompanied by the creation of industrial parks, Logistic Centers, High-Tech Research, and Environmental Protection activities in Jordan and offer economic growth and stability to the Jordanian people and the region.

Still, the October 7 events and the Israel-Hamas war is creating deep wounds on both sides, of the Israeli-Jordanian relationship. We will need to take sufficient time and action, to heal these wounds.

What Role does Saudi Arabia Play in Your Strategic Thinking?

Under present conditions, Saudi Arabia has the potential to become the decisive game-changer along the lines of the Saudi Peace Initiative, allowing Israel and the Palestinians to negotiate peace with the clear agreed aim, of seeking an agreed Two State Solution, allowing Israel to conclude peace with most if not all Arab and Sunni Muslim nations, while allowing the Palestinian nation to establish a State of its own, living in good neighborly relations with Israel and all its other neighbors. This dovetails with Saudi security, political and economic interests, all at a minimal financial cost. It will need a determined US policy to offer Saudi Arabia additional incentives and guide the Saudi leadership in paving the way to peace along agreed milestones.

What Role does the UAE and Bahrein Play?

The Abraham Accords became possible due to the courage and leadership of the UAE and the willingness of Bahrein to follow. Since then, relations have shown to be sustainable. In discussions some of my friends had with UAE leading strategists, we were told that the UAE would not support the Palestinian Authority, as long as no leadership being determined to reach peace, is in charge there. Their argument is very simple. As long as terror would be all dominant, any investment in infrastructure might rather sooner than later be destroyed. Moreover, without a functioning independent legal system, no investment will be secure. I do not think that this can be a "sit and wait" approach. Rather, related brainstorming and coordinated action of UAE strategic thinkers, the Palestinian private sector, Israelis and the Americans have to prepare the necessary dynamics, to allow the UAE, to offer their full political, financial and business support for Palestinian state-building.

Presently, the UAE in cooperation with Jordan, Egypt and Israel provide massive humanitarian assistance to displaced Palestinians in Gaza. Part of their assistance strengthens the prestige and standing of the former Palestinian minister, Muhammad Dahlan and his supporters in the Gaza Strip. The recent formation of a new Palestinian government headed by Dr. Mohammad Mustafa is very good news. Its program of "Building Palestine" promises to pursue a very constructive way forward.

What Role has Qatar played in the past, and what role can Qatar play in the present and future?

During the last two decades Qatar supported Hamas' militancy and helped to build up its military capacities; moreover support for imams all over the world has reinforced the dangerous radicalism of many Muslim communities abroad. Demands to the United States to curb this kind of Qatari action were ignored, mainly due to massive financial donations to a great number of American academic and other institutions. When President Biden started to work with Israel and Saudi Arabia, and the Europeans with the Arab League Secretariat, Egypt and Jordan on a global-regional peace effort, the Qataris started to go along with the emerging diplomatic process and started to decrease support for Hamas. This was not only one of the reasons for the timing of the Hamas attack against Israel, it also allowed Qatar to play a pivotal role in mediating temporary ceasefires and helping to find a way out of the quagmire.

In the forthcoming effort to pacify the situation in Gaza, Qatar's role will be in many ways critical. It will have to help to contain Hamas controlled pockets that will remain, and it has to include the expulsion of Hamas leaders from Qatar. The US administration has shown that Washington possesses all the necessary means to convince Qatar to do so.

My Take on the Role of the USA, European Powers and Russia

Do you think the United States have still a decisive role to play in the Middle East?

Absolutely, yes. President Biden and Secretary of State Blinken have fully understood what is at stake in the war against Hamas, is not only the existence of the State of Israel, but the capability of the free and democratic world to stand up and defeat the axis of evil, Russia, China, Iran and all its proxies in Iraq, Yemen, Lebanon and Palestine. Israel cannot and will not move forward along a peace path, without the United States. Understandings between Jerusalem and Washington are essential to prevent any political or diplomatic initiative that would be perceived as hostile to Israel. Intelligence and military cooperation is similarly vital. Any assumption that the EU, or China, or Russia can replace the United States as the chief mediator is—seen from Israel's vantage point—unrealistic and untenable.

Should the United States make an effort to impose an agreement?

NO, but forcefully lead the way, yes. Presently, President Biden is phoning Prime Minister Netanyahu often twice a day. The pattern was that Netanyahu at first publicly rejected Biden's demands speaking to his base and after some days, responding to pressure from the IDF, allowed Israel to comply. As we go along this pattern will have to change. And Netanyahu will have to go. The post-Netanyahu incoming leadership will have to work very closely together with the United States leadership, whoever this will be.

You said before that Europe cannot replace the US mediating role, is there anything constructive European governments or the EU could do?

Sure. For Europe the Israel-Hamas war is existential. If Israel should lose and the Iranian coalition with all its proxies, Russia and China should prevail and Turkey will compete with them in offering support to militant Islamist movements, as Erdogan presently does, Europe is next in line. The danger is of course that European politicians will try to appease radical militant Muslim groups and their state supporters. Another danger is the virulent rise of Anti-Semitism. The present German, French, British and EU leadership is aware of the rising threats and challenges and accordingly determined to offer their full support.

The most urgent task is to strengthen the Palestinian Authority on the West Bank and contribute to a wide effort of preparing decent temporary housing and services for over one million civilian Palestinians who have fled to the South of Gaza, and prevent there Hamas or various criminal gangs to take control. The second task will be to participate in developing action plans for Reconstruction.

In the past European powers, the EU, and various European governments have played a most important role in supporting and sustaining workable Israeli-Palestinian Authority relations; offering most generous funding to the Palestinian government, as well as to Israeli and Palestinian civil society, allowing to pursue People-to-People activities; European funds have assisted in encouraging Palestinian trade and the movement and access of people, goods and services; as well as security assistance on borders. All these programs will have to be revisited and decisions taken how most effectively to invest European tax monies.

Altogether, during the coming weeks and months US-European leadership in assisting the pro-Western Arab Sunni states, Israel and the Palestinian Authority to move forward on a peace-finding and –building path will be essential. And senior European diplomats will have to participate in a collective brainstorming effort, necessary to deal with the many challenges ahead.

What about Russia? Particularly, now at times of the War against Ukraine, how to evaluate the Russian Role?

Before October 7, I wrote that Russia had become the most dangerous spoiler. And I then explained: "Even if we imagine a good case scenario, when the United States, Israel and Saudi Arabia are moving forward to achieve a necessary breakthrough, Russia has the capacity and possibly also the interest and determination to undermine such a move, in coordination with Iran, Hesbollah, Hamas and maybe also with Assad's Syria, it being unclear, what Turkey's position will be under such a constellation. Such a powerful spoiler coalition will be a tremendous threat to Israel and Jordan." And I added: "If such a possible scenario is not being deterred by the United States, NATO forces and Israel, it will spell major trouble to the entire region."

Now, after this threat scenario has become reality, the USA and NATO are creating the necessary deterrence capacity. As a next step, the US and Europe will have to make an effort to isolate Iran and its proxies and seek a process of confrontation and dialogue with Russia and China, in order to break up the axis of evil. The idea that is presently being tested, is to suggest to Russia and China simultaneously to seek understandings to secure stable trade routes to and in the Eastern Mediterranean, where Russia and China have legitimate trade interests. This then should include, recognizing Russian legitimate interests in the Eastern Mediterranean.

My Take on Forthcoming Security Challenges

You are speaking of "forthcoming" security challenges. Don't you think that moving ahead on the peace-front, will put an end to terror and other security threats against Israel ?

Terror, as a wide-spread phenomena is not so much a result of the Israeli-Palestinian conflict, but the result of the breakdown of illegitimate regimes, failing states, deeper socio-economic, socio-cultural, processes and the confrontation between Western liberal-democratic values, with militant radical anti-liberal regimes.

If this is the case, what could and should be done?

What we need is a closely knit US-Israeli-Middle Eastern Security structure, most likely under the roof of CENTO, the US lead NATO command overseeing security from Afghanistan to Egypt. Forceful US military presence in the Mediterranean, the Red Sea, the Horn of Africa, the Arab Gulf and the Indian Ocean, will be one essential component of a new security structure. A second component will be the formation of a restructured and enlarged Israeli army working in close cooperation with the NATO forces, as well as with the Egyptian, Jordanian, Saudi and other Arab armies in the region, under a joint Command and Control structure. Another component should be to adapt the recommendations of a study written by Ami Ayalon, Idit Shafran Gittleman and Zvi Lanir on "Democracy's struggle against Terror". In order to deter terror adapting "Smart Power", i.e. a combination of hard and soft power is being proposed. The aim has to be to fight the strategy of the terrorists, on the basis of six fundamental principles.[7] In ECF we prepared

---

[7] Amichay Ayalon, Idit Shafran Gittleman, and Zvi Lanir, *"Democracy's Struggle Against Terror,"* Israel Democracy Institute, Jerusalem 2018. "The following are several fundamental principles that underpin the shift to inclusive democracy: 1. Recognizing the right of each community to maintain its uniqueness, identity, culture, and customs on a collective basis, and examining how this can be expressed in the public sphere. 2. Maintaining a common civil baseline without erasing or blurring each group's distinct narrative. In an inclusive democracy it is not revoking minority rights for an extended period of time damages social resilience and deepens divisions until they turn violent. The goal of inclusive democracy is to allow for co-existence between free and equal citizens who may have differences and conflict. The essence of democracy is not to hide the conflicts, but rather to manage them. Thus, there is no aspiration to enforce one unitary culture. 3. Holding continued conversations with and among communities regarding core values, coalescing around agreed "rules of the game." The acceptance of such rules is a basic condition for life in a divided society without the resort to violence. One of the challenges of inclusive democracy is determining where the lines are for both containment and inclusion, and finding ways to handle illiberal groups and those that seek to undermine democratic principles. 4. Creating an array of social conventions through various mechanisms to address areas of difference between communities. Clarifying common fundamental principles can serve as a basis for mobilizing legislation, determining practical ways to implement both equal rights and the distribution of resources. To be clear, these are bottom-up processes—not top-down—that are driven by civil organizations rather than official decision-makers. 5. Maintaining a robust democracy that places limits on majority rule. In a divided society with a solid ethnic majority and a large permanent minority, the principle of majority rule is problematic. Thus, there is a need to anchor minority rights in law and practice. In order to ensure social resilience, a state has to care for the welfare of all its citizens. 6. Decentralizing political power through the separation of powers and the devolution of political authority. This is critically important in a divided society in which there is a dominant group that may arrogate to itself absolute power based on its democratic majority. What is required is a balance between the various branches of government, in order to moderate the majority's power and mitigate the threat of authoritarianism.".

two additional policy papers. The one paper was written by a former member of the Shabak, suggesting legal action, and administrative coordination of the work of the police, the IDF and the Shabak aiming to deter Jewish terror.[8] The second policy paper, suggested a system of releasing Palestinian prisoners on an ongoing basis, while halting any release, in case of a terror act.[9]

Another team prepared what may be called "bottom-up", or "trade security". This would comprise eight complementary elements.[10]

All this sounds impressive. However, most of Israeli military action is perceived internationally as not being proportionate, and in contradiction to international law?

The international community tends to ignore the basic facts of Hamas aggression. Hamas invasion of Israeli territory has caused 180,000 Israeli civilians to take refuge and leave their homes; 1200 innocent civilians were murdered; babies burned to death, children tortured in front of their parents. 240 hostages taken; raping some of them publicly before letting them die; torturing them in captivity and murdering them; attacking with rockets civilian targets all over Israel; hiding behind civilian Palestinians and keeping them as human shields, and announcing the intention of Genocide, to wipe Israel off the map, justifying any means whatsoever and committing to attack again and again. We are still waiting for a UN Security Council Resolution to condemn all these crimes.[11]

To understand the horror and its proportionality its numerical dimensions must be understood. A comparison with the tragedies of the 9/11 ISIS attack on the United States may illustrate this. Israel with its close to 10,000,000

---

[8] ECF, "Recommendations for Enhanced Enforcement against Jewish Nationalist-Motivated Crime in the Palestinian Territories," *Hirschfeld Khoury-DeConcini Papers, Substack*, forthcoming (originally written July 2012), pp. 1–24, https://hkdpapers.substack.com/p/enhanced-enforcement-against-jewish-crime.

[9] A former Palestinian Minister for Prisoner Affairs worked with us in preparing the paper. We submitted our suggestions to the Olmert-Livni Government. Their response was that they feared strong opposition of Israeli terror victims to the plan, and accordingly did not follow up. ECF, "A Joint Israeli-Palestinian Work Plan for the Release of Palestinian Prisoners as an Incentive for Maintaining a Stable Ceasefire (July 2007)," *Hirschfeld Khoury-DeConcini Papers, Substack*, forthcoming (originally written July 2007), pp. 1–22, https://hkdpapers.substack.com/p/plan-release-of-prisoners-for-stable-ceasefire.

[10] Israeli-Palestinian Chambers of Commerce and Industry, "Promoting Economic Growth and Development for Palestine Within a Wider Regional Setting—An Israeli Perspective," *Hirschfeld Khoury-DeConcini Papers, Substack*, forthcoming (originally written 2021), pp. 38-65 (the provisions for security are pp. 60-62), https://hkdpapers.substack.com/p/economic-growth-and-development-for-palestine.

[11] See Douglas Murray remarks on the issue of "proportionality", saying "there is a deep perversion in Britain, whenever Israel is involved". Douglas Murray "Proportionality in Conflict is a joke"; talk.tv/news/31465/douglas-murray-proportionality-in-conflict-is-a-joke; October 13, 2023.

inhabitants is about 1/30 of the 330,000,000 Americans. It means that the death of 1200 murdered victims of October 7, would mean over 36,000 victims in America. Another 8000 heavily injured would amount to 240,000 wounded Americans; and over 180,000 Israelis evacuated would be equal to 5400.000 Americans having to leave their home.

Israel has a moral, political and diplomatic interest to keep Palestinian casualties as low as possible, whereas Hamas terrorists are hiding behind civilian targets and exposing them to the threats of war.

Still Israel for its own interest, should respect the Laws of War?[12]

Definitely. There are three basic legal principles Israel is definitely determined to observe: First, the principle not to attack civilians. Israel is attacking civilian buildings, undoubtedly causing tremendous damage. Yet, if civilian buildings are hiding military installations, the buildings become a lawful military target. Yet, undoubtedly too many Palestinian civilians have been killed, particularly during the first two months of the war. And too many Palestinian civilians are still dying. The second principle demands to take *feasible* precaution to defend civilians from being hurt. Here the discussion is about the question what is "feasible". The challenge is to prevent famine and diseases of the Palestinian civilian population. Following the recent tragic death of seven relief workers more effective action is being taken. The third principle, is the principle of proportionality, i.e. the need to balance between the collateral damage to citizens and assure that it should not become excessive.

The Israeli army is making an effort to respect the Laws of War, but as long as the military capacities of Hamas are not most substantially destroyed, this is a very complicated challenge and far too often civilian targets are being hit. The most important challenge now is to provide massive humanitarian assistance to the civilian population.

What do you suggest? What can be done?

Israeli civil society activism to agree for a temporary ceasefire in order to free hostages allowed most substantial humanitarian aid to enter Gaza and provide a first relief. During renewed fighting, the major problem is the delivery system. Recently, UN Envoy Sigird Kaag has established "the United Nations 2720 Mechanism for Gaza" (see Concept Note of March 15, 2024), which hopefully will allow to deliver aid effectively to civilians without Hamas interference and abuse. When a longer ceasefire will be concluded, learning from American experience in Iraq an initial checklist includes the following points:

---

[12] Compare with INSS Podcast, October 24, 2023 "Israel at War: Laws of Armed Conflict".

- Under international oversight decent housing and services will have to be established for about one million Palestinian temporarily replaced persons. A first task will be to provide movable housing, and restore sewer, water, electricity and trash removal.
- Prevent looting, and particularly create a policing structure that will prevent Hamas militants and/or criminal gangs to control temporary living areas.
- Establish field hospitals and necessary medical provisions.
- Israel will have to establish detention facilities for captured Hamas militants.
- For the Palestinian civilian population it will be essential to identify and renew Gazan businesses needed for ordinary live and provide them with the ability to re-open quickly.

We also have to take immediate action in the West Bank: ease access and movement, allow Palestinian workers to return to their work in Israel, allow Israeli Palestinians to reenter West Bank cities for purchasing goods; and transfer tax monies to the Palestinian Authority.

Don't you think preparations for a "Truth and Reconciliation Committee" to address Palestinian and Israeli war crimes should be undertaken?

You know, Ben Gurion at the end of Israel's War of Independence ordered to research and document Israeli, Palestinian and other Arab war crimes. These files are still being kept secret, although a film discussing the entire issue is being presently in preparation. Calling upon international legitimacy and respecting UN Resolutions cannot be a one-sided affair. One day after the UN General Assembly voted by a great majority for the partition of Mandatory Palestine to a Jewish and Arab state, the Palestinians started the war, and one day after the Israeli proclamation of State, on May 14, 1948, the Arab armies invaded Israel, in absolute disregard of the UN General Assembly Resolution 181. Today, and already for some years, bereaved Israeli and Palestinian parents meet together in a shared effort to overcome the wounds of the past. Now these wounds have been deepened. The fear of a new Holocaust and of a new Naqba have to be addressed.

The Palestinians would argue that Israel was and is the aggressor?

If there is a commitment to reach a two state solution, we Israelis can argue and document that they are the aggressor, having rejected every offered peace solution; not forgetting that Haj Amin el-Husseini, the Mufti of Jerusalem, mobilized Muslim troops in the Balkans in support of the Nazi regime with the aim to round-up Jews; not forgetting that the Palestinians and the Arab armies started the war of 1947–1949 and so on. If we do not understand that both people, Israelis and Palestinians, are here to stay, we will never be able to reach a peaceful way out and to a better future for all.

The better option is to recognize the legitimate rights of the Palestinian and the Jewish people, each to its homeland in former British Mandatory Palestine. I am convinced the way out is to pursue a peace-building process leading to a two state agreement. Or, as Nusseibeh has pointed out, a vision of a peaceful and prosperous future in any one of several forms: one state, two states, confederation, federation involving one country, or two, or three, and so on. But whatever form it takes, it has to be a moral political order, protecting the national aspirations of each side, based on security, freedom and equality.

My Take on People-To-People Activities

Do you think that people-to-people action can contribute to security?

Absolutely yes, in case people-to-people action is carried out within both societies. We have seen (above) that "Talking Peace" work with the rabbinical leadership has helped to commit their supporters to non-violence. Further work is necessary and ongoing to take authoritative rabbinical action against the policy of "price tag", which has aimed to take aggressive action against Palestinians, in order to prevent Israeli governmental policies of seeking to evacuate or relocate illegal or legal settlements.

Parallel work is carried out on the Palestinian side. Mansur Abbas, the leader of Israel's Islamic Party, is taking anti-violence even further, by accepting Israel as the state of the Jewish people, demanding full civilian rights for its Arab citizens.

What other tasks should be pursued by People-to-People activists?

Basically building as many as possible human relations. One task is to provide essential services to people in need. Physicians for Human Rights for instance have provided medical services to Palestinians in Gaza and the West Bank. A major task is to create shared interests and activities, over one hundred Israeli-Palestinian civil society groups belong the ALLMEP (Alliance for Middle East Peace) engage in a great variety of joint or coordinated action. Of great importance is cross-border cooperation between municipalities on both sides of the divide. Joint action of bereaved parents expresses shared emotional longing for peace. The activities of Eco-peace Middle East, combining Israeli-Palestinian-Jordanian activists allows to work together for a better future, by acting against the many dangers of climate change and recreating water and energy resources in and for the entire region. Other NGO's pursue policy planning activities that if fully coordinated with government authorities, may pave the way (as happened in the past) forward on the way to bilateral and regional cooperation. Most—but not all—of these activities have been stopped as a result of Hamas attack. These activities have to be revived.

My Take on What Happens if All This Does not Succeed

In the event that all these activities will not bear fruit and the "common knowledge bad-case scenario" unfolds, where a two-state solution becomes less probable, what would you advise us the young generation to do?

I believe, life in Israel and the occupied territories will continue. Israelis and Palestinians may endure hardships, but they will persist. Polarization in Israeli society will deepen, leading to increased animosity and resentment among militant radicals on both sides. However, it may also foster more cooperation and joint action among those who understand the necessity of finding a way to coexist.

The fear of a one-state solution, the erosion of Israel's democracy and its potential transformation into a semi-theocratic state, as well as the apprehension of regional and international isolation, remains a driving force in Israel's deeply polarized society. These fears fuel the motivation, capabilities, and political power of Israeli civil society. You, the younger generation will have to create a forceful leadership and to achieve what my generation has failed to do: to deal with the "elephant in the room" and take a clear decision, either the one way, or the other.

I tend not to give up the quest for searching a peace process leading the way to a two state solution.

Do you want to add a final comment?

Why not. The future remains uncertain, whether it entails war, repeated failures, or successful outcomes. In any situation, we can draw guidance from Winston Churchill's words: "In war, resolution; in defeat, defiance; in victory, magnanimity; and in peace, good will." For peace activism, this advice can be adapted: we must display resolution in fighting militant radicalism on both sides of the divide; in the face of defeat and failure, we must persist in the struggle, always seeking new approaches; once success is achieved, we must engage in outreach activities aimed at those who remain opponents.

It is important to recognize that after every step forward and success, new challenges and problems will emerge. To the next generation of peace activists, I can assure you that there will always be much work to be done, as peace work never truly ends.

Timeline of the Israeli-Palestinian Conflict and Peace-Seeking Process

The Historical Development

1892 Muslim and Christian Palestinian Notables ask Sultan Abdul Hamid II to prohibit Jewish immigration to Palestine, as well as land sales to Jews.

1917 The British Balfour Declaration promises Haim Weitzman, head of the World Zionist Organization to establish a Jewish Homeland in Palestine;

1919 The Faisal-Weitzman Agreement is signed, endorsing the Balfour Declaration and providing for Jewish–Arab cooperation, conditional on French acceptance of King Faisal's rule over Syria;

1922 The League of Nations endorses the Balfour Declaration and proclaims the British Mandate over Palestine;

1936 After the outbreak of the Arab Revolt, the Mufti of Jerusalem, Haj Amin el-Husseini asks the leaders of all Arab states to join the Palestinians in the struggle against the Yishuv, (the Jewish community living in Palestine). The conflict between the Palestinian and Jewish communities in Palestine turns hereby into a wider regional conflict.

1937 The British Peel Commission proposes the partition of Palestine into a Jewish and Arab State. The Zionist leadership accepts the proposal, the Palestinian leadership rejects it.

1939 Great Britain publishes the White Book, limiting Jewish immigration to Palestine and completely ending it after five years. The Jewish and Palestinian leadership reject the White Paper.

1947 The United Nations Resolution 181, provides for the Partition of Palestine into a Jewish and Arab State, the establishment of a *corpus separatum*, for Jerusalem, to be administered by the United Nations, and an economic union between the Jewish and the Arab State. The Zionist leadership accepted the resolution. The Palestinian leadership rejects it and on the next day started war.

1948 Ben Gurion proclaims the State of Israel. The next day, Egypt, Transjordan, Syria, Lebanon and Iraq enter the war against Israel.

1964 The PLO (Palestinian Liberation Organization) is founded as a roof organization uniting different Palestinian groups under Arab tutelage. The PLO and most Arab nations oppose the very existence of the State of Israel and take political, diplomatic, and military action against the State of Israel.

1967 Israel occupies in the Six Day War the Egyptian Sinai Peninsula, the West Bank and Gaza, and the Golan Heights.

1967 The Security Council of the United Negotiations accepts Resolution 242, calling for Israeli-Arab negotiations on the basis of the "territory for peace" formula.

1968–1970 Egypt with Soviet political and military support start the "War of Attrition"

1970 The United States mediates successfully an Israeli-Egyptian ceasefire agreement.

1971 Egypt's President Sadat submits a peace offer to the United Nations, suggesting complete Israeli withdrawal from all territories against an agreement of non-belligerency, and an alternative offer to the United States, to engage in a step-by-step approach, allowing Egypt to regain control of the Suez Canal and the Western part of the Sinai Peninsula until the Mitla pass. Israel rejects the first proposal. Negotiations on the second proposal reach no agreement.

1973 Egypt starts the Yom Kippur War (October War).

1974 The United States successfully mediates an Israel-Egyptian and later an Israeli-Syrian Disengagement Agreement.

1975 The United States successfully mediates an Israeli-Egyptian Interim-Agreement.

1977 President Sadat visits Jerusalem and addresses the Knesset, followed by negotiations for a comprehensive Framework for Peace in the Middle East.

1978 The Camp David Accords are signed, comprising four parts: 1. a definition of conditions for peace and security; 2. a two-phase path to solve the Palestinian issue, by establishing at first Palestinian self-government to be followed after five years by a Permanent Status Agreement, to solve all outstanding core issues of conflict, territory and borders, Jerusalem, refugees, settlements, water, reaching end of conflict; 3.principles for a peace agreement between Israel and Egypt, and 4. principles for peace between Israel and its other neighbors (Jordan, Syria and Lebanon).

1979 Israel and Egypt conclude a Peace Treaty.

The Unfolding of Israeli-Palestinian Negotiations 1979–2000

1979 The PLO, Jordan, Iraq, Saudi Arabia, Syria and Lebanon reject the Camp David Accords. In Iran the Islamic Revolution puts an end to the rule of the pro-Western, pro-Egyptian, and pro-Israeli regime of the Shah. The regional coalition against the proposed agreement between Israel and the Palestinians becomes all powerful.

1980 In an effort to promote a peace-building bottom-up process, Chancellor Kreisky (following a suggestion of Yair Hirschfeld) meets a Palestinian delegation from the West Bank and offers economic assistance. And then visits King Hussein of Jordan and makes an effort to obtain further support from member parties of the Socialist International.

1981–1990 Based on this initiative the leader of the Israeli Labor Party Shimon Peres, and his deputy Yossi Beilin asked Hirschfeld to organize for them confidential meetings with Palestinian dignitaries from the West Bank and Gaza. The aim was to gain Palestinian support for an Israeli-Jordanian Peace-Initiative.

1987 The first Intifada starts and very quickly diminishes Jordanian influence in the occupied territories.

1988 King Hussein of Jordan withdraws any former claims over the West Bank and Gaza. At the end of the year the US start a dialogue with the PLO in Tunis.

1989 (February) An Israeli team led by Yossi Beilin and a Palestinian team led by Faisal Husseini meet at the Notre Dame Hotel and start seeking a formula to allow the official beginning of negotiations.

1989 (April) Prime Minister Shamir and Yizchak Rabin announce a Four Point Israeli Peace Plan.

1989 (July) Faisal Husseini (Yossi Beilin and Yair Hirschfeld) announce a first formula to allow a Palestinian delegation to attend negotiations.

1989 (September) In order to bridge the still prevailing gap President Mubarak announces a 10 Point Plan, and Secretary of State James Baker III a 5 Point Plan. Negotiations lead to a first formula agreed by the US, Egypt, the Government of Israel, and the PLO.

1990 (February) The Likud Central Committee rejects the peace formula accepted by the Government of Israel.

1990 The Economic Cooperation Foundation (ECF) is founded obliging Hirschfeld to prepare a study "Israel, the Palestinians and the Middle East from Dependency to Interdependence," which becomes the blue-print for negotiations in Norway.

1990 (July) Sadam Hussein invades Kuwait.

1991 (January–March) The first Persian Gulf War leads to the defeat of Saddam Hussein.

1991 (October) The Madrid Conference provides for the beginning of bilateral Israeli-Jordanian-Palestinian, Israeli-Syrian and Israeli-Lebanese negotiations; as well as five groups for multilateral negotiations on arms control; economic cooperation; water; environment and refugees.

1992 (June) Rabin is elected Prime Minister of Israel.

1992 (December) Two meetings between Abu Ala' and Hirschfeld are held in London, deciding to engage in follow up meetings in Norway.

1993 (January–May) Hirschfeld and Pundak engage in back-channel negotiations with a PLO team led by Abu Ala'.

1993 (May–September) Secret official negotiations in Norway lead to the conclusion of the Oslo Accords; which are signed September 13, on the White House Lawn.

1995 (September) The Oslo II Agreement is signed.

1995 (October) The Beilin-Abu Mazen Understanding is concluded;

1995 (November) Prime Minister Rabin is assassinated by a Jewish religious militant extremist.

1996 (May) Benjamin Netanyahu is elected Prime Minister of Israel.

1996 (September) The opening of the Hasmonean Tunnel is followed by violence between Palestinian and Israeli forces, killing 15 Israelis and 50 Palestinians, causing each side to draw conclusions that will lead to the Second Intifada.

1997 (January) Netanyahu and Arafat sign the Hebron Agreement and the "Note for the Record".

1998 (October) Netanyahu and Arafat sign the Wye River Memorandum.

1999 (May) Ehud Barak wins elections in a landslide and becomes Prime Minister of Israel.

1999 (September) the Sharm el-Sheikh Agreement is signed. (The eleventh agreement of the Oslo process).

2000 (July) Under US auspices Israeli and Palestinian negotiating teams meet at Camp David and fail to reach agreement.

2000 (September) The Second Intifada starts and will last until 2005.

2000 (December) President Clinton submits his proposal to the Israeli and Palestinian negotiating teams. The Israeli government accepts, whereas the PLO de facto rejects.

Reassessment: Seeking a Peace-Building Formula in a Complex World

2001 (September 11) Al Qaeda attack on the USA kills over 3000 Americans.

2003 The Quartet Powers (USA, Russia, EU, and UN) publish the "*Benchmarked Roadmap to Peace in the Middle East*" designing a three-phased process to an Israel-Palestine Peace Agreement.

2004–5 Prime Minister Sharon initiates Unilateral Israeli Disengagement from the Gaza Strip evacuating all settlements there, as well as 5 settlements from the Northern West Bank;

2006–2007 The Brodet/Hirschfeld-Hussein Agha/Ahmed Khalidi backchannel prepares for the Annapolis process.

2008 Prime Minister Olmert submits his peace proposals to President Abbas, which are rejected.

2014 Under the auspices of Secretary of State Kerry a Israel-Palestine Framework Agreement is being concluded and again rejected by President Abbas.

2016–2020 A Norwegian track-two exercise produces new understandings but fails to achieve a renewal of the Israeli-Palestinian peace process.

2021 The Abraham Accords are signed at the White House, between Israel, the United Arab Emirates, and Bahrein; follow-up agreements are signed with Morocco and Sudan.

Glossary

- **100 Day Program**: Planning for the first 100 days of an incoming government.
- **1936–1939 Arab Revolt in Palestine**: also known as the "Great Palestinian Revolt," it was a series of protests, strikes, and acts of resistance by Palestinians against British Mandatory rule in Palestine during the period of 1936–1939.
- **1974 Arab Summit**: a meeting of Arab leaders in Rabat, Morocco, in which the Arab states recognized the Palestine Liberation Organization (PLO) as the sole legitimate representative of the Palestinian people.

A

- **African National Congress (ANC)**: a political party in South Africa that played a significant role in the fight against apartheid.
- ***Ahdut Avoda***: "*Ahdut haAvoda*" is a political party in Israel that emerged in the early 1930s. It was aligned with the Labor Zionist movement and played a role in the pre-state and early post-independence period (English name: "Labor Unity")
- ***Aliya***: a Hebrew term referring to the immigration of Jewish people to Israel, typically with the intent of permanent settlement. Jewish immigration to Israel has been a significant aspect of the country's history and identity (English: "rising").

- *Ashkenazi*: the Jewish people who migrated from Eretz Yisrael and the Mediterranean countries to Central and Eastern Europe .
- *Arbeiter-Zeitung*: The daily newspaper of the Austrian Social Democratic Party.
- **Austro-Marxism**: a Marxist political current within the Social Democratic Party of Austria, associated with the ideas of Otto Bauer and others.

B

- **Back-Channel**: the diplomatic or unofficial channel of communication used for confidential discussions and negotiations between parties, often outside the public eye.
- **Balfour Declaration (1917)**: a public statement issued by the British government in 1917 expressing support for the establishment of a "national home for the Jewish people" in Palestine.
- **Bar Kochba Revolt (132–136)**: the Jewish rebellion against the Roman Empire in the second century CE.
- *Brit Shalom*: an organization founded in the 1920s by Jewish intellectuals in Palestine advocating for peaceful coexistence between Jews and Arabs and suggesting the creation of a bi-national Jewish-Palestinian State.
- **Brookdale Institute**: Israeli research organization known for its work in the field of healthcare and social policy.

C

- **Camp David Accords (1978)**: a series of agreements signed in 1978 between Egypt and Israel, mediated by the United States at Camp David, leading to the normalization of diplomatic relations between the two countries.
- **Clash in Gaza (1994)**:
- **Copt**: a member of the Coptic Christian community in Egypt.
- **Cossacks**: historically a group of predominantly East Slavic people who lived in the borderlands of Eastern Europe.

D

- *Das rote Wien*: a German term that refers to the period in Vienna's history when it was governed by a socialist administration, known for its progressive policies and social reforms (English: "the red Vienna ").

- **Demandeur**: a term used in negotiations to describe the party or entity seeking specific concessions or outcomes from the other side.
- **Deputy Chief of Mission (DCM)**: a senior diplomatic position within an embassy or consulate, typically responsible for assisting the ambassador or chief of mission in various diplomatic duties.
- **Diktat**: an order or decree imposed by one party upon another without negotiation.

E

- **Ebert Foundation**: "*Friedrich-Ebert-Stiftung e.V.*" is a German political foundation associated with the Social Democratic Party of Germany (SPD). It promotes democracy, social justice, and political education (English name: "Friedrich Ebert Foundation").
- **Economic Cooperation Foundation (ECF)**: an Israeli think tank and research organization focused on policy issues in the Middle East, particularly concerning Israeli-Palestinian relations and regional political, security and economic cooperation.
- *Eretz Yisrael*: a Hebrew term referring to the historical and biblical land of the Jewish people (English: "Land of Israel").

F

- *Fafo*: "*Forskningsstiftelsen Fafo*" is a Norwegian organization that conducts research on labor and employment-related issues (English name: "The Fafo Institute for Labor and Social Research").
- *Fatah*: "*Harakat al-Tahrir al-Filistiniya*" (whose reverse acronym is *Fatah*) is a Palestinian political party and the dominant faction within the PLO, founded by Yasser Arafat. It advocates for Palestinian nationalism and self-determination (English name: "The Palestinian National Liberation Movement").
- *Fellahin*: an Arabic term used to describe rural agricultural peasants or farmers in the Middle East, particularly in countries like Egypt, Palestine, and Syria (English: "peasant").
- **First Gulf War (1990–1991)**: also known as the "Persian Gulf War," it occurred in 1990–1991 and was a conflict between Iraq, led by Saddam Hussein, and a coalition of countries led by the United States, following Iraq's invasion of Kuwait.
- **First Intifada (1987–1993)**: the Palestinian uprising that began in December 1987 in the occupied territories, primarily the West Bank and

Gaza Strip. It was a series of protests, strikes, and acts of civil disobedience against Israeli rule and occupation, lasting until 1993 when the Oslo Accords were signed.
- *Frisch-Misch*: a Yiddish term for the "reshuffling of the cards."
- **Front for the Liberation of Occupied South Yemen (FLOSY)**: Marxist-Leninist political and military organization that operated in South Yemen during the 1960s and 1970s, seeking to end British colonial rule.

G

- **Gaza First Proposal (1992)**: an early phase of the Oslo Accords that involved Israeli withdrawal from parts of the Gaza Strip and Jericho area, allowing for limited Palestinian self-rule in those regions.
- **Gentile**: a term used to describe someone who is not Jewish.
- **German Socialist Party**: "*Sozialdemokratische Partei Deutschlands*" (SPD) is a major political party in Germany with a social-democratic ideology. It has played a significant role in German politics and governance.
- *Gestapo*: the "*Geheime Staatspolizei*" (abbreviated as *Gestapo*) were the secret police of Nazi Germany (English: "State Secret Police").
- **Golan Heights**: Region in southwestern Syria that Israel captured during the Six Day War in 1967 and later annexed, a source of ongoing dispute between Israel and Syria.
- **Gordian Knot**: Legendary knot from ancient Phrygia (modern-day Turkey) associated with a dilemma that appears unsolvable. Alexander the Great famously "cut the Gordian Knot" with his sword, symbolizing a bold and unconventional solution to a seemingly insurmountable challenge.

H

- *Hamas*: "*Harakat al-Muqawamah al-Islamiyya*" (abbreviated as *Hamas*) is a Palestinian militant organization ideologically committed to Islamic fundamentalism and organisationally connected to the Muslim Brethren movement. It has been in control of the Gaza Strip since 2007 and repeatedly launched terror attacks from there against Israel. (English: "Islamic Resistance Movement").
- *Histadrut*: "*HaHistadrut HaKlalit shel HaOvdim B'Eretz Yisrael*" is a prominent Israeli labor organization founded in 1920 during the British Mandate period (English name: "The General Federation of Laborers in the Land of Israel").

I

- **Ibrahimi Mosque/Tomb of the Patriarchs**: a religious site in Hebron, West Bank, significant to both Muslims and Jews. It is believed to be the burial place of biblical figures such as Abraham and Sarah.
- *Infitah*: an Arabic term referring to a policy of economic liberalization and openness pursued in Egypt under President Anwar Sadat in the 1970s. It involved market-oriented reforms and a shift away from socialist economic policies (English: "opening").
- **Israeli Civil Administration**: a branch of the Israeli government responsible for civilian and administrative matters in the West Bank. It operates in areas of the West Bank under Israeli control as a result of the Oslo Accords.
- **Israeli Defense Forces (IDF)**: the army of the State of Israel which plays a crucial role in the country's defense and security.
- **Israel-PLO Declaration of Principles (DoP)**: Also known as the Oslo Accords, this is a historic agreement signed in 1993 between Israel and the Palestine Liberation Organization (PLO). It marked the beginning of the Israeli-Palestinian peace process and outlined a framework for the resolution of the Israeli-Palestinian conflict.

J

- **Jewish Enlightenment**: also known as *Haskalah*, it was a cultural and intellectual movement among Europeans Jews in the late eighteenth and nineteenth centuries that sought to modernize Jewish life, integrate into European society, and promote secular education.
- *Jihad*: "*Harakat al-Jihad al-Islami fi Filastin*" is an extremist Palestinian militant organization that is ideologically aligned with Islamic fundamentalism. It has been involved in armed conflicts and acts of terrorism against Israeli targets (English names: Islamic Jihad Movement in Palestine or Palestinian Islamic Jihad (PIJ)).
- **Joint Economic Committee (JEC)**: the committee formed to facilitate economic cooperation and address economic issues between Israel and the Palestinian Authority.
- **Joint National Platform**: An understanding reached between the Israeli peace camp and right wing Israeli parties with the aim to pursue a coordinated peace policy.
- **Jordan-Palestine Confederation**: the proposed political arrangement that would involve closer cooperation or union between the Hashemite Kingdom of Jordan and the State of Palestine.

- *Judea* and *Samaria*: the biblical names for the West Bank, historically associated with two Jewish kingdoms that ruled in this area.

K

- **Khartoum Resolution (1967)**: the declaration issued by Arab leaders in Khartoum, Sudan, in September 1967, following the Six Day War between Israel and Arab states, rejecting to recognize Israel, to negotiate with Israel and to sign a peace agreement with Israel.
- *Kibbutz*: a unique form of collective community in Israel and historically in other parts of the world, characterized by shared ownership of property, resources, and a commitment to cooperative living. *Kibbutzim* (plural) originated in the early twentieth century as part of the Zionist movement, with the goal of creating self-sustaining agricultural communities (English: "gathering").
- **Kishinev pogrom (1903)**: a violent anti-Jewish riot that took place in Kishinev (now Chisinau, Moldova) in 1903.
- *Knesset*: Israel's 120 member parliament.
- **Koor Industries**: a prominent Israeli conglomerate and holding company with diverse business interests in various sectors, including industrial manufacturing, defense, and telecommunications.
- *Kristallnacht (1938)*: also known as the Night of Broken Glass, it was a pogrom against Jews in Nazi Germany in 1938, during which synagogues were burned, Jewish-owned businesses were vandalized, and Jews were arrested and killed (English: "Crystal Night").

L

- **Labor Zionist Movement**: a political and ideological movement within Zionism that emerged in the late 19th and early twentieth centuries. It advocated for the establishment of a Jewish homeland in Palestine and emphasized socialist principles and cooperative labor as integral components of nation-building.
- **Lebanon War of 1982**: the Israeli invasion of Lebanon in 1982, in which Israel pushed back Palestinian and Lebanese forces.
- *Likud*: "*Likud-Liberalim Leumi*" is a conservative and right-wing political party in Israel. It was formed in 1973 through the merger of several right-wing and liberal parties, with the goal of representing a broad spectrum of Israeli conservatives (English name: "Likud—Union").

M

- **Maccabean Revolt (167–160 BCE)**: Also known as the Maccabean Uprising, it was a Jewish rebellion led by the Maccabees against the Seleucid Empire in the second century BCE.
- **Madrid Conference (1991)**: the international conference held in Madrid, Spain, in 1991, where Israeli and Palestinian representatives met face-to-face for the first time to discuss the Middle East peace process.
- *Mapai*: "*Mifleget Poalei Eretz Yisrael*" (abbreviated as *Mapai*) was a prominent political party in Israel during the early years of its existence. Founded in 1930, Mapai played a significant role in the pre-state Zionist movement and later in the establishment and governance of the State of Israel (English name: "Workers' Party of the Land of Israel").
- *Mapam*: "*Mifleget HaPoalim HaMeuhedet*" (abbreviated as *Mapam*) was a left-wing political party in Israel. It played a role in the early years of the state and was known for its socialist and Marxist-Zionist principles (English name: "United Workers Party").
- **Marshall Plan**: a reference to the proposed economic aid and development plan for the West Bank, Gaza Strip, and the wider region, inspired by the post-World War II Marshall Plan that helped rebuild Europe.
- *Mashov*: a Hebrew term that translates to "feedback". Here it refers to Yossi Beilin's political group within the Labor Party.
- **Messianic**: the belief or anticipation of the arrival of the Messias, often associated with religious or eschatological expectations.
- **Middle East Contemporary Survey**: an annual publication documenting developments and events in the Middle East, including Arab and Islamic political thought, regional and international relations, and economic developments.
- **Middle Eastern Community of Water, Energy, and Tourism (MECWET)**: an envisioned regional cooperation initiative encompassing water resource management, energy production, and tourism development in the Middle East.
- **Middle Eastern Security Organization (MESO)**: a proposed regional security organization that aimed to enhance security and cooperation among Middle Eastern countries, including Israel and its Arab neighbors.
- **Moshe Dayan Center**: the "Moshe Dayan Center for Middle Eastern and African Studies," originally known as the "Reuven Shiloah Center for Middle Eastern and African Studies," is an academic research institution located in Tel Aviv, Israel. It specializes in the study of intelligence

and security-related issues, with a particular focus on the Middle East and Israel's national security concerns.
- **Mossad**: "*ha-Mossad le-Modiin ule-Tafkidim Meyuhadim*" is the national intelligence agency of Israel. It is responsible for intelligence gathering, covert operations, and national security (English name: Institute for Intelligence and Special Operations).
- **Mufti of Jerusalem**: the religious leader in charge of Islamic religious affairs in Jerusalem, including oversight of religious sites and services.

O

- **Oslo Accords (1993–2000)**: the series of eleven agreements signed between Israel and the PLO between September 1993, and September 1999, aimed at establishing a framework for Palestinian self-rule and a path to a permanent peace agreement.
- **Oslo II Agreement (1995)**: it is an interim agreement between Israel and the Palestine Liberation Organization (PLO) that established the Palestinian National Authority in parts of the West Bank and Gaza Strip.

P

- **Palestine Liberation Organization (PLO)**: "*munazzamat at-Tahrir al-Filastiniyyah*" is a political and paramilitary organization founded in 1964, representing the Palestinian people in their struggle for self-determination and a Palestinian state. Led by figures like Yasser Arafat.
- **Palestinian National Authority (PNA or PA)**: "*as-Sulta al-Wataniya al-Filastiniyyah*" is the governing body of the Palestinian territories, including parts of the West Bank and the Gaza Strip. It was established as part of the Oslo Accords in preparation of an Israel-Palestinian Permanent Status Agreement.
- **Palestinian Legislative Council (PLC)**: "*al-Majlis al-Tashriiyy al-Filastiniyyah*" is the legislative body of the Palestinian Authority responsible for making laws and regulations in Palestinian territories.
- **Palestinian Liberation Army (PLA)**: "*jaysh at-Tahrir al-Filastini*" is a military organization formed in the mid-1960s to support the Palestinian national liberation movement. It was established as a branch of the Palestine Liberation Organization (PLO).
- **Peace Now**: an Israeli grassroots movement advocating for peace, particularly in relation to the Israeli-Palestinian conflict.

- **Peace Propaganda Plan**: A plan suggested by Abu Ala' to allow to prepare the Israeli and Palestinian public for planned peace negotiations and create the supportive public legitimacy for necessary concessions of each side.
- **Peres–Hussein London Agreement (1987)**: also known as the "London Agreement," it was an agreement signed in April 1987 by Israeli Foreign Minister Shimon Peres and King Hussein of Jordan and later rejected by Israel's Prime Minister Yizchak Shamir.

Q

- **Quality of Life policy (1983)**: the policy announced by U.S. Secretary of State George Shultz in 1983, which related to economic empowerment and development in the Palestinian territories.

R

- **Rabbinical Ruling**: a legal decision or interpretation of Jewish religious law (*halakha*) made by a rabbi or a group of rabbis. These rulings can cover a wide range of religious, ethical, and legal issues.
- **Ringstraße**: the famous circular boulevard or ring road located in the historic center of Vienna, Austria (English name: "Ring Road").

S

- **Sarpsborg Document**: A first document concluded in March 1993 in Sarpsborg, Norway between the PLO negotiating team and an unofficial Israeli team. It became a first blue print for the Israel-PLO Declaration of Principles signed in Washington, September 13, 1993,
- **Seleucid Empire**: Hellenistic dynasty that ruled over parts of the Eastern Mediterranean and the Middle East, during the Hellenistic period.
- *Sephardim*: The Jewish people who lived in Spain and Portugal, North Africa and most of the Middle East and their descendatns. The term is derived from Sepharad, the Hebrew word for Spanish and Hispanic.
- *Shabak*: "*Sherut haBitahon haKlali*" (abbreviated as *Shabak* or *Shin Bet*) is Israel's internal security agency responsible for counter-terrorism, counter-espionage, and domestic intelligence (English name: "Israeli Security Service").

- **Shah Regime (1941–1979)**: the rule of the Pahlavi dynasty in Iran, under Mohammad Reza Shah Pahlavi. His rule, characterized by authoritarianism and close ties to Western powers, came to an end with the Iranian Revolution in 1979.
- *Shoah* **(1941–1945)**: also known as "the Holocaust," it was the systematic genocide of approximately six million Jews and millions of others (including Romani people, disabled individuals, and political dissidents) by Nazi Germany and its collaborators during World War II (English: "calamity").
- *Shomer*: "*haShomer haTzair*" is an international socialist Zionist youth organization that played a role in Jewish youth education and activism (English name: "The Young Guard").
- **Shuttle Diplomacy**: is a diplomatic negotiation technique where a mediator or diplomat travels back and forth between parties involved in a conflict or dispute to facilitate communication, build trust, and work toward a resolution.
- **Simulation Game**: different strategy planners imagine various scenarios and try to anticipate possible reactions of adversaries.
- **Six Day War (1967)**: a war in June 1967 between Israel and its neighboring Arab states in which Israel emerged victorious and gained control of territories including the West Bank, Gaza Strip, Sinai Peninsula, and Golan Heights.
- **Socialist International**: the worldwide organization of political parties, most of which adhere to socialist, social democratic, or labor-oriented ideologies. It aims to facilitate cooperation and dialogue among socialist and labor parties globally.
- **Stockholm Document**: October 31, 1995, Israeli and Palestinian track-two negotiators presented a detailed concept for an Israel-Palestine Permanent Status Agreement to Yossi Beilin and Abu Mazen (Mahmoud Abbas). the document is publicly known as the Beilin-Abu Mazen Understanding.
- **Syrian Ba'ath Regime**: "*hizb al-Ba'th al-'Arabi al-Ishtiraki–qutr Suuriyai*" is a political party that espouses pan-Arab nationalism and socialism and the government of Syria after it took control through a coup in 1963 (English name: "Arab Socialist Ba'ath Party—Syria Region").

T

- **Taba Negotiations (2001)**: also known as the Taba Summit, it was a series of intensive negotiations that took place in January 2001 between Israeli and Palestinian representatives in Taba, Egypt.

- **Temple Mount:** the religious site in Jerusalem that is sacred to both Muslims and Jews. It is commonly believed to be where the past Jewish temples stood. *al-Aqsa* mosque is located on the mount, within the *al-Haram ash-Sharif* complex.
- **Temporary International Presence in Hebron (TIPH):** the international monitoring mission established to observe and report on the situation in the city of Hebron, West Bank.
- **Track-Two Diplomacy:** the unofficial, informal diplomatic efforts involving non-governmental actors to address conflicts and promote peace.
- **Tunis Leadership:** the leadership of the Palestine Liberation Organization (PLO), which was based in Tunis, Tunisia, after 1982 and until 1994.

U

- **UN Security Council Resolution 242 (1967):** a crucial diplomatic document adopted in 1967 that called for the withdrawal of Israeli armed forces from territories occupied during the Six Day War, for peace and the recognition of the sovereignty, territorial integrity, and political independence of all states in the region.
- **UN Security Council Resolution 338 (1973):** a United Nations Security Council resolution adopted in 1973 that called for a ceasefire in the Yom Kippur War and urged negotiations between the parties to achieve a just and lasting peace in the Middle East.
- **United States Agency for International Development (USAID):** agency of the U.S. government responsible for providing humanitarian and development assistance to countries around the world.

W

- **War of Attrition (1968–1970):** a war President Nasser of Egypt launched with Soviet support against Israel's occupation of the Sinai Peninsula, aiming to return these territories to Egyptian sovereignty, either by war, or by an imposed action of the two superpowers, the United States and the Soviet Union.
- **Warsaw Ghetto (1940–1943):** the confined area in Warsaw, Poland, during World War II, where Jewish residents were forcibly relocated by the Nazis. The Warsaw Ghetto Uprising in 1943 was a significant act of Jewish resistance against Nazi oppression.

- **Washington Talks (1991–1993)**: the negotiations and discussions held in Washington, D.C., as part of the Israeli-Palestinian peace process, particularly during the lead-up to the signing of the Oslo Accords.
- **Wastepaper Principle**: the concept in negotiations indicating that each side could raise ideas and proposals they might withdraw later on, and then throw into the waste-paper basket.
- *Wien*: the capital city of Austria, where Dr. Yair Hirschfeld grew up (English: "Vienna").
- **World Zionist Leadership**: the collective leadership and organizations within the Zionist movement that have worked to promote Jewish immigration to Israel and the establishment and development of the State of Israel.

Y

- *Yiddish*: a High German-derived language historically spoken by Ashkenazi Jews. It developed as a fusion of Middle High German with elements of Hebrew, Aramaic, Slavic languages, and Romance languages.
- *Yishuv*: the organized Jewish community in British Mandatory Palestine, which between 1920 and 1948 established the pre-state governmental institutions of the State of Israel.
- **Yitzhak Rabin's Assassination (1995)**: the assassination of Israeli Prime Minister Yitzhak Rabin in 1995 by a Jewish extremist opposed to the Oslo Accords, which had been intended to promote peace between Israelis and Palestinians.
- **Yom Kippur War (1973)**: the conflict between Israel and a coalition of Arab states, including Egypt and Syria that began on the Jewish holy day of Yom Kippur in 1973.

Z

- **Zion Square Demonstrations (1995)**: Israeli religious-nationalists demonstrated against the Oslo Accords and portrayed Prime Minister Rabin as a SS officer, creating the atmosphere which a month later led to his assassination.
- **Zionism**: the national movement of the Jewish people, seeking to return to Zion, the historic homeland of the Jewish people.

Index

A
Adler, Viktor 24, 29
Al-Jabari, Mohammad Ali 38
Anilewicz, Mordekhai 31
Anti-Semitism 25–27, 29, 29–31, 33, 34
  Holocaust 28
Anwar as-Sadat 41, 43, 44, 46, 48, 66, 100, 270
Apartheid 30, 155, 157, 158, 167
Arab
  Arabs 36, 40, 63, 98, 123, 143, 164, 189, 190, 201, 205
  leadership 40, 164
  military 40
  nations 30, 210, 270
  states 39, 171, 204, 206, 208, 219, 230, 232, 233, 259, 269
  territories 36
  world 45, 202, 205, 233, 254
Ausch, Karl 28
Austria 27, 29, 37, 46, 47, 49, 51, 52, 63, 112, 146, 150, 172
  Hof Gastein 29
  Schoenbrunn 25
  Vienna 23–29, 33–35, 45, 46, 50, 52, 134, 146, 155
Austria, see Austria1 and Austria2 24
Austro-Hungarian Empire 26, 27, 35, 36
  Habsburg monarchy 33, 36

B
Baer, Gabriel 37
Balfour Declaration 32, 269
Baron Reitzes 29
Bauer, Otto 24, 24
Beilin, Yossi 42, 53–55, 58, 65, 67, 72, 74, 82, 88, 92, 94, 98, 105, 106, 111–113, 150, 167, 203, 271
Bonaparte, Napoleon 36, 150
Borchert, Wolfgang 32
Brecht, Bertolt 32
Breitner, Hugo 24
Brit Shalom 27
Broda, Christian 28
Buber, Martin 27

C

Camp David
   Accords (1978) 42–46, 51,
     55–57, 69, 70, 270, 271
   Agreement, *see* Accords (1978)
   Framework for Peace in the
     Middle East, *see* Accords
     (1978)
Chamberlain, Neville 32
Churchill, Winston 31, 267
Communism 28

D

Dayan, Moshe 38

E

Egypt
   Cairo 45, 47, 100, 102, 195,
     202, 203
   economy 38, 48
   military 38, 40, 41
   presidency 38, 40–42, 46, 48
   Sinai 39, 256, 270
   Suez Canal 41, 270
Egypt-Israel
   agreements 42, 43
   economic relations 46, 47
   peace 38, 39–41, 43, 44, 47, 57
Egypt-Jordan 38
Egypt-Palestine 44, 45
Egypt-Syria
   Ba'ath 50
Eisenhower, Dwight 40
El-Husseini, Faisal 39, 57–60, 62,
   74, 81, 114, 115
Eretz Yisrael 156, 210, 212
   Judea 31, 44, 107, 212
   Samaria 44, 107, 169, 212
Eshkol, Levy 38, 39

F

Farhi, David 38
Fascism 27, 29, 30, 211
Fatah 35, 101, 111, 121, 166, 208
Fawzi, Mahmoud 40
Feldmann, Nira 36

G

Germany 26, 33, 34, 36, 37, 49, 52,
   142, 150, 165, 169, 174, 194,
   210
   Crystal Night (1938) 25
   German Socialist Party (SPD) 49,
     53
   Gestapo 28
   Ministry of Foreign Affairs 165
   Nazi Party 24–26, 29
   Reich 30, 35
   Warsaw Ghetto uprising 31

H

Hammer (family)
   Hammer, Milan 25, 26
   Hammer, Rachel 25, 25
Herbert, Herr 28
Hersey, John 31
Hirschfeld (family)
   (author's father) 26, 26–32, 36,
     46, 47, 155
   Hirschfeld, David 43
   Hirschfeld, Jakob 26
   Hirschfeld, Keile 26
   Hirschfeld, Lola 23, 24, 24–26,
     28, 29, 31, 35, 36, 63, 148
   Hirschfeld, Max 27
   Hirschfeld, Miriam 23, 24, 24,
     25, 27, 28, 30–32, 36, 59,
     138, 159, 175, 194
   Hirschfeld, Ruth (author's sister)
     24, 25
   Hirschfeld, Ruth (author's wife)
     43

Hirschfeld, Sigi 27, 31
Michal (nee Hirschfeld) 43
Naomi (nee Hirshfeld) 43, 147
Hitler, Adolf 23, 27, 36
Holaubek, Josef 28
Holocaust 32, 107, 155, 212
Hubalek, Felix 27, 28, 32, 33
Human rights 30, 259
Hungary 26, 28
Hussein bin Talal 38–40, 42, 46, 50–52, 56, 62, 97, 111, 135, 146, 170, 207, 235, 271–273

I

Iran 45, 111, 170, 171, 198, 199, 209, 227
  Shah 45, 101, 271
Israel
  Haifa 36, 99, 118, 129–131
  Herut Party 36
  Israeli Defense Forces (IDF) 42, 76, 104, 108, 118, 120, 132, 141–143, 164, 165, 168, 173–175, 187, 197, 221, 262
  Kibbutz 107, 142
  Kibbutz Ein Gev 37
  Kibbutz Gadot 37
  Lake Tiberias 37, 193
  Mapam party 39
  Ministry of Defense 38, 57, 64, 204
  Netanya 38, 106, 165
  peace camp 27, 157–159, 194, 206, 209, 220, 253
  Peace Now 43
  Prime Ministry 38, 39, 41, 43, 44, 46
  Tel Aviv 25, 45, 55, 69, 97, 104, 107, 112, 117, 122, 157, 164, 171, 173, 185, 190, 191, 200, 218, 229, 234
Israel-Syria

Israeli-Syrian Disengagement Agreement (1975) 43
Italy 29, 196, 199, 201

J

James "Jimmy" Carter 43, 46, 150
Jarring, Gunnar 41
Jaures, Jean 32
Jerusalem
  Hebrew University 26, 27, 37, 48, 68, 112
  National Library 37
  Old City 36, 37
Jordan 36–40, 42, 43, 46, 50–56, 60, 61, 70, 84, 87, 88, 92, 108–110, 113, 117, 118, 123, 128, 130, 131, 139, 156, 158, 174, 178, 190, 196, 201, 212, 229, 234, 235, 255–257, 260, 266, 270–272
Jordan River 36–38, 174
Joseph, Franz 25, 26
Judaism 26, 30, 37
  Jewish Enlightenment 26, 33
  Orthodox 26
  Torah 25, 211

K

Karni, Boaz 42, 54, 64, 139, 152, 154, 165, 170, 173, 177
Kästner, Erich 32
Khomeini, Ruhollah 45
Kissinger, Henry 39, 40, 43, 65, 149, 209
Kreisky, Bruno 45–47, 49–55, 62, 63, 67, 112, 201, 271

L

Land for peace 39
Lebanon 43, 54, 76, 82, 84, 117, 121, 137, 156, 170, 180, 190, 217, 253, 270, 271

Beirut 37, 84, 111
Lueger, Karl 25

M

Madrid Conference 35, 58, 60, 61, 64, 65, 67, 75, 166, 272
Marxism 24
Matteotti, Giacomo 29
Meir, Golda 39, 41, 49
Menachem Begin 43, 44, 46, 171, 233
Mendelsohn, Moses 26
Middle East 36, 40, 43–45, 47, 49, 63, 65–68, 73, 80, 84, 95, 97, 98, 109, 116, 118, 124, 127–129, 136, 137, 148–151, 162, 166, 167, 169, 171, 178, 188–190, 193, 195–197, 201, 204–206, 209, 214, 217, 225–227, 234, 258, 266, 270, 272, 273
  Middle Eastern 35, 38, 63, 65, 66, 69, 72, 149, 172, 191
Middle East Contemporary Survey 45
Mussolini, Benito 29

N

Nasser, Gamal Abdel 38, 40, 41, 48
Netherlands 27, 49, 59, 164, 172
New Zealand 29
Nixon, Richard 40
Novik, Nimrod 42, 59, 60, 64, 83, 111, 115, 116, 121, 135, 137, 138, 169, 178, 202, 203
Nusseibeh, Sari 39, 60, 73, 74, 84, 102, 103, 113, 115, 146, 150, 154, 214

O

Oslo Accords 35, 65, 95, 104, 106, 107, 150, 222, 272

Ottoman Empire 38, 57, 63

P

Palestine
  East Jerusalem 42
  Gaza 42, 44, 46, 50–56, 58, 59, 70, 76, 77, 80, 81, 83–87, 89–94, 100–102, 104–110, 113, 114, 119, 123, 136, 140, 164, 168, 171–173, 175, 177, 178, 180, 185, 190, 194, 196, 200–204, 225, 253–256, 266, 270, 271, 273
  Hebron 38, 52, 103, 104, 114, 115, 123, 187, 272
  Jericho 37, 87, 187
  Ramallah 37, 38, 107, 147
  Tulqarem 38
  West Bank 39, 42, 44, 46, 50–56, 58, 59, 70, 76, 80, 81, 85, 87, 91, 93, 94, 101, 104, 105, 107–110, 113, 114, 119, 131, 134, 136, 140, 142, 164, 165, 168, 171, 172, 174, 177, 179, 180, 184, 185, 190, 220–222, 255, 266, 270, 271, 273
Palestinian Liberation Organization (PLO) 35, 38, 39, 45, 46, 50–52, 55, 57, 58, 61, 62, 67, 68, 72, 74, 75, 80, 86, 89, 90, 94, 95, 97, 99, 101, 102, 107–109, 116, 120, 123–126, 166, 178, 222, 223, 232, 254, 255, 270–273
Pittermann, Liesl 28
Pogrom 25, 25
Poland 27

R

Racism 30, 213
Remarque, Erich Maria 32
Rogers, William 40

Roman Empire 32
   Bar Kochba Revolt 31
   Maccabean Revolt 31
Russia 37, 84, 85, 105, 162, 227, 260
Russian Empire 26, 36

S

Salinger, Liesl 29
Scheu, Friedrich 28
Scheu, Herta 28
Seleucid Empire 32
Sinai War of 1956 39
Six Day War 35, 38, 49, 149, 151, 270
Slovakia 26
Socialism 26, 26, 27, 27–29, 49
   Austria 24, 26, 27, 28, 29
   Italy 29
South Africa 30, 155, 157, 158, 165, 167
   African National Congress (ANC) 30, 31, 155, 157, 158, 167
   Johannesburg 30, 31, 167
   secret police 30
Soviet Union (USSR) 23, 28, 39, 40, 49, 84, 151, 193, 270
Step-by-step 41–43, 255, 270
Sudan
   Khartoum 39
Suleiman I 36
Syria 37–39, 43, 50, 60, 61, 83, 84, 101, 110, 117, 123, 128, 132, 133, 156, 170, 190, 217, 260, 269–272
   Ba'ath 38
   Golan Heights 39, 83, 270

T

Tandler, Julius 24
Tell, Wilhelm 32
Theresa, Maria 26, 27

Tucholsky, Kurt 32

U

Ukraine 25, 26, 162, 260
United Arab Republic 50
United Kingdom (UK) 35, 38, 39, 49, 69, 100, 101, 108, 113, 161, 197, 265, 269
   London 23, 32, 33, 40, 49, 56, 57, 60, 63–65, 74, 96, 101, 102, 111, 122, 127, 129, 135, 146, 150, 160, 162, 193, 195, 211, 213, 214, 272
United Nations (UN) 39, 41, 43, 70, 71, 81, 92, 99, 188, 197, 204, 218, 223–225, 264, 273
   Peace envoy 41, 166, 197, 204
   Security Council Resolution 242 39, 43, 70
United States
presidency 39
United States of America (USA) 39–42, 49–51, 55–58, 60, 62, 64, 65, 67, 69, 75, 80–88, 90, 92, 95, 98, 100, 105, 114, 115, 117, 121, 123, 124, 126, 133–139, 142, 145–151, 154, 162, 164, 166–171, 173, 174, 177, 182, 184, 189–191, 193–195, 197–199, 202–209, 211, 213, 213–215, 224–227, 229, 232, 234, 254, 257–260, 270–273
   National Security Advisor (NSA) 40, 135, 196
   presidency 40, 46
   Secretary of State 40, 55, 57, 59, 60, 81, 83, 86, 168, 181, 187, 188, 191, 196, 204, 214, 271, 273

V

Von Suttner, Berta 32

W

Walden, Harry 28
War of Attrition 39, 40, 151, 270
Werfel, Franz 32
Wilhelm, Friedrich 36
World War I (WWI) 27, 32, 63
World War II (WWII) 29, 32, 33, 63, 87

Y

Yasser, Arafat 35, 61, 84, 116, 125
Yiddish 25, 28
Yom Kippur War of 1973 41, 42, 100, 151, 270

Z

Zionism 24, 27, 30, 31, 36, 59, 63, 73, 156, 157, 210, 213, 215, 269, 270
   Hashomer Hatzair 30, 34, 156
   Labor 37
Zweig, Stefan 32

GPSR Compliance

The European Union's (EU) General Product Safety Regulation (GPSR) is a set of rules that requires consumer products to be safe and our obligations to ensure this.

If you have any concerns about our products, you can contact us on

ProductSafety@springernature.com

In case Publisher is established outside the EU, the EU authorized representative is:

Springer Nature Customer Service Center GmbH
Europaplatz 3
69115 Heidelberg, Germany

www.ingramcontent.com/pod-product-compliance
Lightning Source LLC
LaVergne TN
LVHW010336260326
834688LV00036B/737